A GAELIC EXPERIMENT

The Preparatory System
1926 – 1961
and Coláiste Moibhí

Valerie Jones

With a Foreword by
SUSAN PARKES

The Woodfield Press

This book was typeset in 11 on 12.5 Bembo
by Datapage Private Limited for
THE WOODFIELD PRESS
17 Jamestown Square, Dublin 8
www.woodfield-press.com
e-mail: terri.mcdonnell@ireland.com

Publishing Editor
Helen Harnett

Publisher
Terri McDonnell

House Editor
Aidan Culhane

Indexer
Gloria Greenwood

A catalogue record for this title
is available from the British Library.

ISBN 1-905094-01-9 (10 digit)
ISBN 978-1-905094-01-1 (13 digit)

SPECIAL ACKNOWLEDGMENT
The publication of this book has been supported by
The Church of Ireland College of Education.

Le cuidiú Choláiste Oideachais Eaglais na hÉireann

Printed in Ireland
by Colour Books, Dublin

For Stuart, Heather and Mark

CONTENTS

LIST OF ABBREVIATIONS

'A' school	A school where the teaching is through Irish
ASTI	Association of Secondary Teachers of Ireland
BA	Bachelor in Arts
BCG	Bacillus Calmette-Guerin vaccination which provides protection against tuberculosis
BMus	Bachelor in Music
Br	Brother
BSc	Bachelor in Science
Capt.	Captain
CEC	Central Executive Committee
CEO	Chief Executive Officer
CICE	Church of Ireland College of Education
CITC	Church of Ireland Training College
DE Papers	Department of Education Papers
Department	unless otherwise stated refers to the Department of Education
DF Papers	Department of Finance Papers
DSMA	Dublin School Managers' Association
DT Papers	Department of the Taoiseach Papers
GAA	Gaelic Athletic Association
IDTA	Irish Dance Teachers' Association
INTO	Irish National Teachers' Organisation
IQ	Intelligence Quotient
IRA	Irish Republican Army
IRB	Irish Republican Brotherhood
JAMS	Junior Assistant Mistresses
JGS	Journal of the General Synod
MA	Master in Arts
MEd	Master in Education
MLitt	Master in Letters
MP	Member of Parliament
NCCA	National Council for Curriculum and Assessment
NS	National School
PhD	Doctor of Philosophy

PNTU	Protestant National Teachers' Union
PP	Parish Priest
PPA	Past Pupils' Association
PSA	Past Students' Association
RE	Religious Education
RHMS	Royal Hibernian Military School
RI	Religious Instruction
RTE	Raidió Teilifís Éireann
Sr	Sister
TB	Tuberculosis
TCD	Trinity College Dublin
TD	Member of Dáil Éireann (the lower house of the Irish Legislature)
UCC	University College Cork
UCD	University College Dublin
UCG	University College Galway
VEC	Vocational Education Committee
YMCA	Young Men's Christian Association

GLOSSARY OF IRISH TERMS

Aireacht na Gaeilge	The Ministry for Irish
An Gúm	Section of the Department of Education responsible for publishing material in Irish
An tOireachtas	The Irish Legislature
An t-Oirmh.	The Reverend
An Seabhac	The hawk
Árd Teastas	Higher Certificate
Áras an Uachtaráin	Residence of the President of Ireland
Ard-Thimthire Tighis	Chief domestic science organiser
Breac-Ghaeltacht	Partially Irish-speaking district.
Bun rang	A junior class
Bunreacht na hÉireann	The Irish Constitution
Céimseata	Geometry
Coimisiún na Gaeltachta	The Gaeltacht Commission
Coláiste ullmhúcháin	A preparatory college
Coláiste na Mumhan	The Munster college
Craobh na gCúig gCúigí	The Branch of the Five Provinces
Criosanna	Girdles or belts
Cumann Gaelach na hEaglaise	The Irish Guild of the Church
Cumann na mBan	The women's branch of the Irish Volunteers
Dáil or Dáil Éireann	The Lower House of the Irish Parliament
Feiseanna	Irish language festivals with competitions
Fianna Fáil	A political party founded in 1926
Fíor Ghaeltacht	District where everyone speaks Irish
Gaeilgeoirí	Irish speakers
Gaeltacht(aí)	Irish-speaking area(s)
Gaelscoileanna	Primary schools where only Irish is used
Galltacht	English-speaking area
Garda Síochána	The Irish police force
Grá	Love
Leas phríomh-oide	Vice-principal
Múinteoir	Teacher

Naíonraí	Pre-school where Irish is spoken
Oireachtas na Gaeilge	Gaelic League annual cultural festival
Príomh ullamh or oide	Principal teacher
Rang D	First year in a preparatory college
Rang C	Second year
Rang B	Third year
Rang A	Fourth or final year
Saorstát Éireann	The Irish Free State
Sceilg	A rock or crag
Scoil Ullmhuighthe	A preparatory school organised by the Gaelic League in 1920/21
Sinn Féin	A political party founded in 1905
Seanchaíthe	Story tellers
Seomra bia	Dining room
Tánaiste	The Irish deputy prime minister
Taoiseach	The Irish prime minister
Trí Gaeilge	In Irish

Cad é an Ghaeilge a chuirfidh tú ar sin?	How would you say that in Irish?
Caidé chuirfidh ar seo?	How would you say this?
Lasair Ghaedhealachais i scoileanna na tíre	Becons for Irishness in the country's schools

LIST OF ILLUSTRATIONS

ACKNOWLEDGEMENTS

This book has been a long time in gestation and many people helped me to bring it to completion. I owe a deep debt of gratitude to all those, who over the years, have assisted me in many different ways with this project. I must begin by thanking the many former students and teachers of the different colleges who assisted me, and particularly those who shared their experiences with me through questionnaires, 'phone conversations, and interviews, or who put me in touch with other former students. I am especially grateful to Breandán Ó Croinín, Liam Ó Mainnín, and Diarmaid Ó Seadaigh, former members of the inspectorate, who supplied me with very useful material at crucial stages of the project.

During the research I visited various religious houses and I thank them for their warm welcome and hospitality, particularly the De La Salle Order at Castleton, the Mercy Order in Tuam and the Loreto Order in Rathfarnham. I am also greatly indebted to the following: Mr David Sheedy, Dublin Diocesan Archives, Drumcondra; Mr Tom Maye, Galway Diocesan Archives; Róisín Purcell, St Patrick's College, Drumcondra; Sr Fionbarra, The Mercy Order, Tuam; Karen Johnston, Christian Brothers' St Mary's Provincialate; Michelle Cooney, Christian Brothers' St Helen's Provincialate; Marianne Cosgrave, Mercy Congregational Archives, and Dr Kenneth Milne, the Church of Ireland historiographer.

I must also express my appreciation of the archivists and staff of a number of institutions, including the National Library, UCD Archives, TCD Library, the National Archives, and the RCB Library.

My special thanks goes to Prof. Áine Hyland, Professor of Education and vice-president of UCC, Dr John Coolahan, Emeritus Professor of Education, NUI, Maynooth, and to Dr Susan Hood, RCB Library, who read the earlier drafts and to the Rev. Patrick Comerford and Florence Armstrong, who read the draft material on Coláiste Moibhí. I thank them for their perceptive comments and stimulating remarks.

I am greatly indebted to the following: *The Limerick Leader* for supplying the photo of Frances Condell with President J.F. Kennedy; *The Irish Times* for permission to use photos of the official opening of Coláiste Moibhí and other photos of the college; Lt.-Col. Dan Murphy of the Department of Defence for permission to use material relating to Coláiste Chaoimhín;

Sr Mary Theodora of the Holy Faith Convent, Glasnevin, for assistance
with material regarding Glasnevin House; Miss Siobhán Quinn, principal of
Coláiste Éinde, Galway, and Séamus Ó Ceallaigh for permission to use mate-
rial from the college archives and from *Coláiste Éinde 1928–2003 Seachtó
Cúig Bliain Faoi Bhláth;* Séamus Ó Conghaile chairperson of the Board of
Management of Coláiste Mhuire, for permission to use an aerial photo of
Coláiste Mhuire; John Knightly and Valerie Bary for permission to use pho-
tos of the Ruths' wedding and John Knightly for information regarding the
Ruths; Moya Nolan for permission to use her photo of Sally Sheils, presi-
dent of the INTO, 1994/95; Pam Shorten for material regarding her aunt,
Gladys Allen; Oireachtas na Gaeilge for permission to use a photo of Miss
Allen. I must also thank Alice Carr and Dr Seosamh Kelly from Cumann
Staire is Seanchais Chloich Cheann Fhaola, for their assistance with material
relating to Coláiste Bhríde, and Dáithí Ó Maolchoille of Cumann Gaelach
na hEaglaise for supplying me with copies of *The Gaelic Churchman.* The
Presbyterian Historical Society, Tom Kenny of Kenny's Book Shop, High
Street, Galway, and Sr Deborah Lynch, of the Mercy Order also deserve my
gratitude for their help so readily given.

I thank the Archbishop of Dublin, the Most Revd Dr John Neill, chairperson, and the Board of Governors of the Church of Ireland College of
Education, for permission to examine the Minutes of the Board of Governors
and for their support for this project.

Throughout the different stages of the research the principal of CICE,
Sydney Blain, has been unfailingly encouraging and I thank him for this and
for supplying material from *The Ardara View* regarding Coláiste Moibhí and
Douglas Hyde. I thank all my former colleagues at CICE for their support,
particularly Valerie Coghlan, the librarian, Tim Keatinge, the bursar, and
the secretary, Sandra Woods. Special thanks goes to Risteárd Giltrap, former
principal of Coláiste Moibhí, for information regarding the final years of the
college and for supplying photos of George and May Ruth, and of Lil Nic
Dhonnchadha.

Over the years Susan Parkes played many roles in this study, as supervisor
of both my MLitt and PhD research on which this book is based, and also
as archivist and Governor of CICE. I am very grateful to her for writing the
preface and for all her advice and assistance so graciously given.

I must also express my gratitude to the publisher, Terri McDonnell of The
Woodfield Press and her associates, Helen Harnett, Aidan Culhane, Gloria
Greenwood and Richard Cox, for their expertise and professionalism in see-
ing the material through the publishing process.

Finally, I thank my husband, Stuart, and our children, Heather and Mark,
for reading the manuscript at various stages and for their acute observations.
As committed history researchers themselves their help has been invaluable.

I alone am responsible for any errors.

FOREWORD

The Preparatory Colleges (Na Coláistí Ullmhúcháin) which were founded in 1926, were a major initiative of the Cumann na nGael government to educate primary school teachers who would be fluent in the Irish language. In the days before free secondary education, the Preparatory Colleges provided a 'bridge' for senior pupils from the national schools to enter the teacher training colleges. There were seven such colleges, three for boys (Coláiste Chaoimhín, Glasnevin, Coláiste Éinde, Galway, Coláiste na Mumhan, Mallow); three for girls (Coláiste Íde, Dingle, Coláiste Bhríde, Falcarragh, Coláiste Mhuire, Tourmakeady) and one mixed college (Coláiste Moibhí) for Protestant students. In accepting the offer of a distinct preparatory college for Church of Ireland students, Archbishop J.A.F. Gregg of Dublin gave formal recognition to the new compulsory Irish language policy of the Irish Free State and thus encouraged the Protestant community to accept it. In the years that followed Coláiste Moibhí made an important contribution to Protestant education by providing fluent Irish-speaking teachers for Protestant primary schools and the language policy ceased to be an issue for Protestant young people.

However, by the 1960s, the Preparatory Colleges were seen as expensive to run and were deemed to be no longer necessary as the standard of honours Irish had been raised in secondary schools. Moreover, the teaching profession criticized the early separation of young people who were destined to be teachers into specialist institutions. Five of the colleges were closed in 1961. Coláiste Moibhí was allowed to continue as the standard of honours Irish in Protestant secondary schools was not considered high enough, and it was agreed that there was still a need for a specialist all-Irish institution for Protestant student-teachers. In 1968, when the Church of Ireland College of Education moved to its new site in Rathmines, Coláiste Moibhí was integrated into the College, and the students undertook a two-year Leaving Certificate course. The preparatory college was finally closed in 1995.

Valerie Jones' study of the Preparatory Colleges, and in particular of Coláiste Moibhí, shows the remarkable contribution that these colleges made to Irish education. They provided an access route to second-level education for able pupils who might otherwise not have had such an opportunity, and they provided well-educated and committed Irish-speaking recruits for the primary teaching profession. Valerie herself having been a student at Coláiste Moibhí has insight into and understanding of the life of the student-teachers. Her meticulous research into the history of the foundation of the colleges in 1926 and the difficulties faced by the government in maintaining the institutions, reveals the earnest effort made to implement the Irish language policy in the twentieth century.

Valerie's particular study of Coláiste Moibhí shows how fortunate the college was to have a succession of excellent principals who established the high reputation of the college, and who gave strong leadership to the Irish language cause among the Protestant community. The book is a tribute to them, and to the staff and students of all the Preparatory Colleges who led the way in Irish education.

Léiríonn an leabhar seo an áit speisialta a bhí ag na Coláistí Ullmhúcháin i stair oideachas na hÉireann. Bhí thart ar 4,500 macléinn sna coláistí idir 1926 agus 1961 agus bhí ról an tábhachtach acu ag cothú na teanga sa stát nua. Tugann an leabhar seo omós dóibh agus dona múinteoirí go léir a bhí sna Coláistí Ullmhúcháin. I ndáirire is féidir a rá go raibh siad mar 'lasair ghaedhealachais i scoileanna na tíre.'

Susan M.Parkes, M.A., M.Litt., FTCD,
Former Senior Lecturer in Education, Trinity College, Dublin,
Governor of the Church of Ireland College of Education
September 2006

INTRODUCTION

In 1959 I unwittingly became part of a great Irish educational experiment when I entered Coláiste Moibhí in Shankill, Co. Dublin. Coláiste Moibhí was one of seven preparatory colleges which were established by the state in the 1920s as all-Irish boarding schools for student teachers. At the time this history escaped me as I focused on coming to terms with living my daily life through Irish. I knew that Coláiste Moibhí was a *coláiste ullmhúcháin* (a preparatory college) because that was printed on all our stationery, but apart from that the college seemed just like any other secondary school. It wasn't until the 1980s, when I became interested in studying the contribution of members of the Church of Ireland to the development and preservation of the Irish language, that I realised the importance of Coláiste Moibhí as a preparatory college and the significant role it played as the only Protestant 'A' school (all-Irish school) in the history of the state.

Earlier that year I had passed the Intermediate Certificate Examination with honours at the Diocesan School for Girls, Adelaide Road, Dublin. From an early age, I wanted to be a primary teacher, and as 'Dios' was only an Intermediate School in those days I had to go somewhere else to complete the Leaving Certificate course before entering a teacher-training college. I can well remember the first days in class at Coláiste Moibhí when I had to rely on Neans Hic, a native speaker from Co. Kerry, to help me out when I had difficulty understanding the lessons. Everything was in Irish and there were no concessions for those who had only arrived. That year four students were admitted after the Intermediate Certificate Examination and we joined twelve others for the Leaving Certificate course.

We quickly adapted to the all-Irish atmosphere and were soon chatting away just as fluently as the others, though I do recall being reprimanded by a teacher for using too many gesticulations when talking! The teachers were very little different to those I had been accustomed to in 'Dios'. I greatly enjoyed the sports, with hockey most afternoons and we took great pleasure in showing off our Irish when we played hockey matches against other schools! I found the Irish dancing much easier than in 'Dios' where the PE teacher had placed great emphasis on the steps – in Coláiste Moibhí we did Irish dancing every Thursday evening. It was great fun – the only difficulty was the names of the dances. Mr Willis would call out 'Ionsaí na hInse' or

'Fallaí Luimnigh' and everybody changed into the correct formation for the dance while the newcomers were left standing bewildered until someone showed us where to go. In due course I went on to the Church of Ireland Training College and qualified as a primary teacher.

Eventually my study of Protestants and the Irish language developed into a thesis, 'Recruitment and formation of students into the Church of Ireland Training College 1922–1961,' for which I was awarded an MLitt degree by the University of Dublin in 1989. By that time, however, I had become interested in the development of the other six preparatory colleges and their contribution to Irish education. Once started, the research gained a momentum and life of its own which resulted in another thesis entitled 'The Preparatory Colleges 1926–1961, an experiment in Irish education', and a PhD degree from the University of Dublin in 1999. The material gathered for the two theses forms the basis for this book.

★ ★ ★ ★

Before the establishment of the Irish Free State, the leaders of the movement for Irish independence were greatly influenced by the ideology of cultural nationalism and there was considerable public support for the idea that the new Ireland should not only be free, but Gaelic as well. In the early 1920s it was envisaged that the education system would play a major role in effecting the gaelicisation of the new state. The teaching of the Irish language in primary schools was crucial to this plan.

The majority of primary teachers, however, knew very little Irish. The preparatory system was established in 1926 to ensure a supply of Irish-speaking recruits to primary teaching. It consisted of seven residential colleges, mainly in the Gaeltacht: three for Catholic boys, Coláiste Chaoimhín, Coláiste Éinde and Coláiste na Mumhan; three for Catholic girls, Coláiste Mhuire, Coláiste Bhríde and Coláiste Íde; and Coláiste Moibhí, for Protestant boys and girls. All the students received a secondary education through Irish. Furthermore, the language of the classroom, extra-curricular activities and all other personal intercourse was Irish. In effect each college was a 'mini-Gaeltacht'. On the successful completion of the Leaving Certificate course, preparatory students were assured of places in the training colleges, which were seen as the key to gaelicising the primary teaching profession.

The establishment of the preparatory system was one of the few serious initiatives undertaken by the state in keeping with its ideology of cultural nationalism, and it was to make a significant contribution to the gaelicisation policy during the first four decades of the state's existence. The preparatory system was also to provide student-teachers with access to second-level education at a time when it was becoming increasingly apparent that only students who had passed the Leaving Certificate Examination would be able to complete the training college course successfully. The setting up of the preparatory system as a new basis of recruitment to primary teaching was particularly important, as existing recruitment sources, the monitorial system and the old pupil-teacher scheme, were failing to provide sufficient numbers of well-educated students for the training colleges.

In the early twentieth century the Irish language was in a state of continuous decline despite efforts to revive the language in the late nineteenth century. In addition, the Gaeltacht was contracting and the quality of life for native speakers was shown by the Gaeltacht Commission to be dismal and depressing with a dearth of modern facilities. In 1926, the commission drew up a series of proposals to improve the lot of the native speaker and to gaelicise the public service. It endorsed the establishment of the preparatory colleges.

The preparatory system was one of the few successes in the state's efforts to gaelicise the nation. Overall attempts at gaelicisation failed because the policy was over-ambitious, ill-thought out and over-dependent on the schools and the civil service. In addition, the poor state of the country's finances resulting from the civil war made governments unwilling to allocate scarce resources to the Irish language, though large sums were spent on the preparatory colleges in their early days. Furthermore, the gaelicisation policy failed because it had no support outside the school environment, while the failure of politicians to set an example by speaking the language led to the policy being regarded with increased cynicism by the public.

★ ★ ★ ★

From its foundation the preparatory system was controversial. In the 1920s there was much resistance to its establishment, particularly in the Irish National Teachers' Organisation. It was also opposed by Department of Education inspectors because in their view it would not be possible to find sufficient numbers of Irish-speaking teachers with an ability to impart knowledge through the language. Other educationalists believed that Leaving Certificate courses could not be taught through Irish – such was the weak state of the language. Such beliefs were to be proved unfounded, and by the beginning of the 1930s the colleges were obtaining excellent results at the Intermediate and the Leaving Certificate Examinations. The inspectors soon changed their minds as the personnel retired and were replaced by others with a greater enthusiasm for the policy. However, the hostility of the INTO did not change and the preparatory system was dogged by its antagonism throughout its existence.

The preparatory system also had certain fundamental flaws. The founders' view that large numbers of native speakers were necessary for its success was a mistake, as was the belief that the preparatory colleges had to be in the Gaeltacht. It was also very costly to maintain. There has been much speculation as to why the system was allowed to continue for so long without radical alteration, for failure to reform the system eventually led to its demise. This book will analyse why the system was problematic and how it continued to operate for so long without major reform. An opportunity for change was presented by a confidential inquiry into the system in 1938, but while this led to some modifications they were not sufficient to deal with the major deficiencies of the preparatory system. The following year, the system was further undermined by the sudden closure of Coláiste Chaoimhín, one of the most successful colleges. The system's survival in the 1940s owed much to Derrig, who was Minister for Education for most of the period, and it was largely through his efforts that the temporary take-over of two of the colleges – Coláiste Éinde and Coláiste Moibhí – by the Defence Forces during the Emergency did not lead to their permanent closure.

Certain themes appear throughout the book. A key factor which bedev-illed the preparatory system throughout the 35 years of its history was the continuous dissension between the Departments of Education and Finance. Much of this was due to the failure of the new state to reform the civil ser-vice in 1922. As the majority of civil servants stayed *in situ* after indepen-dence, there were many in the Department of Finance who had little sympathy for the gaelicisation policy. This explains the sceptical view which that department had of the preparatory system from the very beginning. This attitude contrasted strongly with that of the Department of Education, where ardent Gaeilgeoirí, fervent exponents of the gaelicisation policy, were promoted to the highest posts as soon as the Free State Government was established. These officials lacked experience in school management, and the early days of the preparatory system were marred by incompetent planning and a disregard for timetables.

Relationships between officials in the two departments were further compounded by the Department of Education's inability to accurately fore-cast the number of teachers required to staff the nation's primary schools. In the 1930s there were too many trained teachers, while the late 1940s and early 1950s were characterised by a shortage. The attitude of the two depart-ments to expenditure varied greatly, particularly regarding the costs of the preparatory colleges. In the Department of Education there was a cavalier attitude towards the high costs of the preparatory system, while in the Department of Finance even the smallest outlay was queried. These factors contributed to a deterioration in the relationships between the two depart-ments. Dissensions between the Departments of Education and Finance were of major importance in allowing the system to continue unchanged for so long, as the former feared that even the smallest change would be per-ceived as a victory for the latter.

Throughout the period 1926–61, the role of the Catholic hierarchy, the most powerful body in Irish society at that time, was of crucial importance. The history of the era clearly demonstrates the submissive attitude of suc-cessive governments to the church. The least hint of the hierarchy's disap-proval was sufficient for the government of the day to timidly abandon any proposed educational reform. The bishops had a considerable role in the management of the preparatory colleges and fear of upsetting the hierarchy was an important factor in successive governments allowing the system to continue for as long as it did. Certain aspects of the system more than fulfilled the bishops' requirements for student-teachers. There was an emphasis on the religious formation of students, and each Catholic college was run by religious personnel chosen by the bishop of the diocese. As the colleges were totally financed by the state, the church had control of six well-run, well-maintained colleges at no expense to itself and it was more than happy to maintain the *status quo*. It was not until a scandal at Coláiste Éinde in 1956 showed the weaknesses of the system that the hierarchy turned against it, and this was a significant factor in the decision to end the system in 1959. The ending of the system coincided with wide-ranging changes taking place in the country generally, and particularly in education, in the late 1950s and early 1960s. These included the introduction of an oral test in Irish at the Leaving Certificate Examination and of suitability interviews for all candidates for training colleges. This meant that students from the preparatory colleges would no longer proceed automatically to the training colleges but would have to compete for places with candidates from ordinary second-level schools.

★ ★ ★ ★

The first five chapters of this book deal with the history of the preparatory system in chronological order from its origins until it ended in 1961. Chapter Six examines the experiences of former students and teachers. Much of the information regarding the colleges was received from those who worked or studied in them through the use of questionnaires. By writing to the heads of those colleges, still in existence as educational establishments in the early 1990s, the names and addresses of former students and teachers were obtained. Questionnaires were sent to them and, in some cases, these were followed up with personal interviews or telephone conversations. Of approximately 100 questionnaires distributed, 70 were returned and some 25 former students and teachers gave more detailed accounts of their experiences at the colleges. As all the information supplied was given in confidence, their comments quoted here are anonymous.

Part II is devoted to a case study of Coláiste Moibhí, the sole Protestant preparatory college. The part played by Coláiste Moibhí in providing the Church of Ireland Training College with well-educated students, fluent in Irish, in the opening decades of the new state was noteworthy, for it ensured the survival of primary schools under Protestant management in the new Ireland. The attitudes of the Protestant minority to the Irish language varied considerably. There were those Protestants who were enthusiastic Gaeilgeoirí and who were members of the Gaelic League and of Cumann Gaelach na hEaglaise (The Irish Guild of the Church), while there were others, particularly the heads of Protestant secondary schools, who were very opposed to the gaelicisation policy.

During its existence from 1927–95, Coláiste Moibhí had five principals. George Ruth was responsible for getting the college off the ground in its early days. John Kyle, who was seconded from his post as an inspector in the Department of Education, saw to it that the college's emphasis was on academic success. He also oversaw the move of the college to spacious premises in the Phoenix Park. After six years he was succeeded by the Gaelic scholar Lil Duncan. During her 17 years as principal the college moved four times. The building in the Phoenix Park was taken over by the Defence Forces in 1941 and the college was temporarily accommodated in the Church of Ireland Training College at Kildare Street. From there it moved again to cramped accommodation in Merrion Street, where it stayed until 1946 when it returned to the Phoenix Park. It was not long there, however, before it moved in 1948 to Shankill, Co. Dublin. After all the upheavals Lil Duncan retired in 1951 and the college settled down to a relatively tranquil existence under the fourth principal, former pupil Gladys Allen.

Despite the outward appearance of serenity, however, there were times when the college's future was uncertain The first major threat was in 1961 when the preparatory system came to an end. Unlike the other preparatory colleges, Coláiste Moibhí was not closed, because it was felt that the standard of Irish teaching at Protestant secondary schools was too weak to provide sufficient entrants for teacher training. Towards the end of the 1960s the college's future again appeared uncertain. But the Department was persuaded to keep the college open and in 1968 it moved to Rathmines Castle where it became the juniorate of the Church of Ireland Training College (later known as the Church of Ireland College of Education). In the early 1980s, as Miss Allen's retirement approached, Coláiste Moibhí's existence was again in doubt as the Board of Governors of the Church of Ireland College of Education considered it no longer had a role to play in supplying students for training. This view was not shared by officials in the Department of Education and so Coláiste Moibhí gained a further reprieve. The fifth principal, Risteárd Giltrap, was appointed in 1984. Despite the high academic achievements of the students, the Department decided in the early 1990s to close the college on the grounds that it was too costly to maintain. So closure finally came in 1995.

This book contends that the preparatory system was a successful educational experiment, for it achieved the primary aim of those who founded it: the provision of the training colleges with well-educated students, fluent in Irish, and able to teach through Irish. This was due to the system's reliance on the 'total immersion method' of learning a language. The colleges also inculcated in the students other cherished objectives of the founders, such as a *grá* (love) for Irish, a respect for their country, and a commitment to their religion, much prized characteristics of the period. Whether the preparatory system could have survived in a different form is a matter for speculation. The way in which Coláiste Moibhí continued from 1969–95 offered one possible model, though it was not without drawbacks. Furthermore, due to reforms in recruitment introduced in the late 1950s, the preparatory system became unnecessary, while extensive changes in Irish society in the 1960s, plus the introduction of free second-level education for all, meant that the Irish language was no longer the dominant focus of the education system.

PART I

CHAPTER ONE

The origins of the gaelicisation policy: 1800–1926

'If this generation does not save Irish,
it will be dead in 20 or 30 years'

The late nineteenth and early twentieth centuries were characterised by efforts to restore the Irish language. These were to gain considerable public support, particularly during the struggle for Irish freedom. This had two fundamental aims: to win independence from Britain, and to develop a new state with its own separate Irish identity. Everything English was to be discarded as alien and replaced by a form of cultural nationalism, which emphasised the language, history and distinctive Irish culture of the new state. The vision of a new Ireland, symbolised by the Irish language, inspired the struggle for independence, and the phrases 'Ireland free' and 'Ireland Gaelic' became synonymous.[1] The first piece of legislation passed by the new parliament, an act to establish a constitution, embodied this dream; Article 4 declared the national language of the new Free State (Saorstát Éireann) to be the Irish language. During the early years of the twentieth century the language had come to symbolise Irish nationalism to such an extent that, in the final years of British rule, the language and the struggle for independence became intertwined.

In the early 1920s, there was widespread support for the aspirations expressed in the new constitution, with all political parties in agreement. Enthusiasm for the language was widespread. Many county councils levied a penny rate for language promotions and the public flocked to language classes. Indeed, so keen were politicians that the new state should be Gaelic-speaking that the meeting of the first Dáil, in January 1919, was conducted largely in Irish, and a Minister for the Irish Language was appointed before

---

1. Akenson, *A mirror to Kathleen's face*: education in independent Ireland 1922–60, p. 36.

a Minister for Education. By June 1920, the Ministry for Irish had reported on the position of the language and produced a scheme for its preservation. The influence of the Gaelic League, an organisation founded in 1893 to restore the language as a living tongue, was at its strongest, and there were few dissenting voices from the new education policy, summarised as:

> The strengthening of the national fibre by giving the language, history, music, and tradition of Ireland their natural place in the life of the school.[2]

However, much of the public support evaporated following the civil war which greatly weakened the country's economy and threatened the stability of the new state. Despite efforts to revive it, the Irish language continued to decline and the Gaeltacht continued to decrease. This was not surprising as the findings of *Coimisiún na Gaeltachta* in 1926 showed the quality of life there to be dismal and depressing.

Nevertheless, the dream of restoring the language was to become a major aim of government policy for several decades. There was a naïve belief that with independence the Irish public would support efforts to gaelicise the new state. Restoration plans took little account of certain realities, such as the costs involved, the poor economic condition of the country or the difficulties in learning the language. Furthermore, growing disenchantment among the public with the politicians following the civil war led to public dissatisfaction with the language policy. The fact that the policy began at a time when the nation was recovering from the trauma of a post-colonial mentality meant that it could never be rationally or dispassionately examined. Those who criticised the policy risked being branded enemies of the state by defenders of the language, who became more and more fanatical in their zeal to revive it.

The major thrust of the gaelicisation policy soon devolved on the schools and the civil service. Once the Free State was established, the primary school system became the main thrust of the government's education policy, and primary teachers the immediate focus for action. To ensure a supply of Irish-speaking students to the training colleges, the preparatory system was established. This was an important educational initiative, both in terms of the gaelicisation policy and of teacher recruitment, where existing recruitment schemes were failing to produce sufficient numbers of qualified candidates for primary teaching.

DECLINE OF THE IRISH LANGUAGE

The Irish language, however, had declined steadily in the nineteenth century. During the 50-year period between 1861 and 1911, the number of

---

2. Pádraic Ó Brolcháin, (Patrick Bradley) chief executive officer, Department of Education, quoted in *Report of the Department of Education*, 1924/25, p. 22.

native speakers decreased from about a quarter of the population, approximately one million people, to half a million.[3] This decline has been attributed to the establishment of the national school system in 1831 and its failure to include Irish in the curriculum. There were, however, other significant factors which contributed to the language's decline. By the beginning of the nineteenth century the use of English was widespread and Irish was spoken mainly in the poorer and more inaccessible parts of the country. The desire to acquire English was given further impetus by the famine and emigration which characterised the first half of the century. In addition, English was perceived as necessary for advancement at home and as the language of necessity for life abroad, while Irish was regarded as the badge of social inferiority at home and of economic disadvantage abroad. A further significant factor was the role of one of the most influential bodies in the country, the Catholic Church, which did little to halt the language's decline. Moreover, by speaking English, Irish Catholic missionaries were able to make a greater contribution to that church's development as a world faith.

One of the greatest difficulties faced in the early 1920s by those who set about restoring Irish was its structure. There was no standardised spelling, vocabulary or grammar. Irish was spoken in a number of areas, each with its own dialect: Connemara, Cork, Kerry, Donegal, Waterford, Clare and Mayo being the most prominent among them. The lack of literature in Irish – classical, fictional or functional – was a further difficulty. In the nineteenth century, an awareness of the literary value of the language had developed in certain strands of society, and a number of societies were founded to preserve the language. The most significant was the Gaelic League, founded in 1893, which provided an intellectual rationale for a separate Irish identity. Its vision for the language permeated the struggle for independence. Unlike the earlier societies, it concentrated on the spoken language, and focused on the formal educational system as a means of extending the use of Irish. Founded by Fr Eugene O'Growney, Eoin MacNeill, and Douglas Hyde,[4] its objectives were: the preservation of Irish as the national language of Ireland; the extension of its use as a spoken tongue; the study and publication of existing Gaelic literature; and the cultivation of a modern literature in Irish.

The League played an important role in providing a cultural platform for the development of a separate Irish identity and succeeded in altering the public's attitude to the language. Furthermore, many of those involved in the 1916 Rising and the War of Independence were members of the League. Other organisations which contributed to the movement for an Irish Ireland were the Gaelic Athletic Association, founded in 1884, and Sinn Féin, started by Arthur Griffith in 1905.

The League's educational policy was significant because it focused not just on achieving a place for Irish in the curriculum, but also on teaching

---

3. Akenson, *A mirror to Kathleen's face*, p. 36. See also Foster, *Modern Ireland 1600–1972*, p. 517.
4. Biographical details of people named on pages 5 and 6 are included in the Appendix.

methods and teacher training, and by degrees its objectives were achieved. Much of the League's success was due to the skilful use of propaganda, chiefly devised by Pádraig Pearse. A man of many talents, he had a profound influence on the League and on the gaelicisation policy of the new state. A stern critic of the education system and its emphasis on examinations (which he condemned in the pamphlet, *The Murder Machine),* he was one of the few revivalists to study education systems in other countries. He was also a strong advocate of the Direct Method of teaching languages, where only the language being learned is used, as well as of the use of modern teaching aids. Much of the inspiration for the new state's language policy came from Pearse, and because of the heroic status conferred on him following his execution for his part in the 1916 Rising, it was accepted without question.

THE FIRST DÁIL AND THE MINISTRY FOR IRISH 1919

The Rising and its aftermath gave a considerable impetus to the development of cultural nationalism and injected a new enthusiasm into the campaign for the incorporation of the language and other aspects of Irish culture, such as history, literature and music, into the school curriculum. In keeping with this ideology, one of the earliest actions of the first Dáil in October 1919 was the establishment of a Ministry for Irish (Aireacht na Gaeilge). The influence of the Gaelic League was probably at its strongest during this period. The appointment of the president of the League, Seán Ó Ceallaigh, known as 'Sceilg', as Minister for Irish and, subsequently, as Minister for Education, reinforced the League's influence, as did the incorporation of the League's educational programme into the work of the ministry. In addition, the establishment of a Ministry for Irish was a clear indication that the Provisional Government was in earnest in its endeavours to gaelicise the new state. Furthermore, in the financial estimates for the first half of 1921, the Dáil voted £5,000 to the Ministry for Irish, much more than was allowed for agriculture or labour.

'Sceilg' was aware that the majority of Gaeltacht people did not esteem the language very highly. So he initiated a public relations campaign to raise its standing and developed a system of organisers to oversee language development in the Gaeltacht. He also established a committee to investigate the condition of the language and to produce plans for its revival. Its members included Cathal Brugha, Minister for Defence; Ernest Blythe, Minister for Trade; Piaras Beaslaoi; and Pádraig Ó Caoimh. Indeed, the holding of weekly meetings, at such a critical time, showed the importance the fledgling state attached to the language. This committee drew up the *Report of the Ministry for Irish*[5] *(Aireacht na Gaeilge)* which was presented to the first Dáil

---

5. *Report of the Ministry for Irish*, National Archives, DE2/54.

REPORT OF AIREACHT NA GAEDHILGE.

Owing to the arrest of the Secretary to the Ministry some days after the last session of the Dail and his imprisonment for three months, the Ministry of Irish, though decided upon at that session, came officially into existence only a couple of months ago. About that time the Governing Body of the Gaelic League appointed a sub-committee to co-operate with Aire na Gaedhilge; and from that body and from Irish-speaking representatives of the various national organisations a Committee, which meets weekly, has been formed to investigate the position of the language and recommend a scheme for its preservation. The Aire Cosanta and Aire Trachtala, Cathal Brugha and Earnan de Blaghd, kindly consented to act on the Committee of which Piaras Beaslai and Padraig O'Cauimh are also members. Care has been taken to make it, as far as feasible, representative of the whole country.

So far, the possible avenues for the spread of the language which have been surveyed in detail are:-

(1) The primary schools, especially in the Gaedhealtacht;
(2) Parish Committees to promote among other things rivalry in the use of the language between Irish-speaking families.

(3) Irish-speaking co-operative Societies; and
(4) The Public Boards and National Institutions generally.

In the matter of the primary schools in the Gaedhealtacht, the Committee adopted with slight modifications the "Gaelic League Educational Programme," as follows:-

IN PURELY GAELIC DISTRICTS

(1) All school subjects to be taught through the medium of Irish.

(2) Irish History to be taught to all pupils.

(3) Irish music to be taught in all music classes; the words of the old songs to be taught as poetry, and the music to which they are set to be taught in the music class.

(4) Irish dances to be taught as well as the ordinary drill exercises and teachers to be urged to encourage them.

IN SEMI-GAELIC DISTRICTS

(1) Irish to be the official school language, i.e. Irish to be used for roll-call, orders, prayers, and so on.

(2) A bilingual programme to be in use wherever possible.

(3) Irish history, Irish music and Irish dancing to be taught as in the purely Gaelic districts (above).

IN PURELY ENGLISH-SPEAKING DISTRICTS

(1) Irish to be the official school language as in the semi-Gaelic districts.

(2) Irish to be taught for vernacular use to each child for at least one hour per day, in every school having a competent Irish teacher, and in such other schools as can be provided with travelling teachers.

2 Report of Aireacht na Gaeilge – The Ministry for Irish 1920. *National Archives DE2/54.*

in 1920, and it laid the foundations of much of what was to be the gaelicisation policy of the Irish Free State.

The level of public support for the language policy was at its highest at this time, and 'Sceilg' reported addressing large gatherings, mainly under the auspices of the Gaelic League, throughout the country. Such audiences may have led to the unfortunate conclusion that public support for the language revival could be easily sustained. A detailed estimate of the costs of the programme, totalling £10,000, was also included. This was less than the amount spent by the British administration to support the teaching of Irish and showed the failure of the ministry to comprehend the magnitude of the task required to restore the language. The report ended with a strong recommendation that the publication of standard works in Irish, and of popular reading matter, should not be subsidised by the Dáil. This recommendation was accepted, with disastrous consequences. There was no popular reading matter in the language, and without large subsidies it could not be produced; what money was available was used to produce textbooks, which were in very short supply.[6]

Central to 'Sceilg's' policy was the primacy of the Irish language in both the primary and secondary school programmes. The report included a programme for schools based with slight modifications on the Gaelic League Educational Programme. This prescribed teaching for three kinds of districts: purely Gaelic, semi-Gaelic, and purely English-speaking. In purely Gaelic districts, Irish was to be the medium of instruction for all subjects, with Irish history, music and dancing featuring prominently. In semi-Gaelic districts, a bilingual programme was to be followed, where possible, with Irish as the official school language for roll-call and orders. In purely English-speaking districts, Irish was to be the official school language, as in the semi-Gaelic districts, and to be taught for vernacular use to each child, for at least one hour per day, in every school which had a competent Irish teacher. In schools where teachers were unable to teach Irish, travelling teachers were to be provided, and a scheme to increase the number of travelling teachers by offering scholarships was devised. Eight scholarships to the total cost of £100 to the Irish College in Dublin for the month of August were offered annually by the Gaelic League, and the ministry recommended that the Dáil should sponsor a similar scheme. In addition it recommended that a further eight scholarships, to the value of £50 each, to a preparatory training college be awarded to eight Gaeltacht residents, 'as an encouragement to young Irish speakers and as a practical step towards the Irishising of Primary Education'.[7] The ministry envisaged that arrangements could be made with a teaching order to provide instruction through Irish.

Many of these ideas were to form the basis for an experimental system of preparatory colleges, set up by the Ministry for Irish in the early 1920s.

---

6. Memo on the Preservation of the Irish Language (UCD Archives, Blythe Papers P24/15).
7. *Report of the Ministry for Irish*, p. 1.

Indeed, so strong was the influence of the League at this time that serious consideration was given to its being formally recognised as a department of the Dáil. It was decided, however, that 'the time was not quite ripe for such a step', as this would prevent the League from legitimately engaging in agitation for the better treatment of Irish by the existing educational boards, something a Dáil department could not do. A further consideration was finance where large sums of money had been provided for the teaching of Irish by the British administration. These included the payment of more than £14,000 in fees alone by the National Board for the teaching of Irish during 1917 and 1918. A further source of finance was the Department of Agriculture, whose grants to the Irish Colleges 'assisted very materially' in maintaining the colleges.

However, the ministry did propose, with the approval of the Gaelic League, taking over the direction and financing of the language revival in the Gaeltacht. It also envisaged involving public boards in the task of restoring Irish, and 'lines of activity' were submitted to the Ministry of Local Government. Furthermore, its recommendation that the language issue be borne in mind by these boards foreshadowed what later became government policy in the new state: only those able to pass an examination in Irish would be employed in the public service. Surprisingly, the report contained only a brief reference to the Catholic Church: 'Its (the language's) position in relation to the church and other institutions is having consideration'.[8]

REPORT OF THE MINISTRY OF THE NATIONAL LANGUAGE 1921

In August 1921, the Ministry for Irish produced another report, *The Report of the Ministry of the National Language*. Though this was longer, much of it was devoted to aspirational material, rather than detailed planning, a weakness which was to characterise the gaelicisation policy. But its greatest significance lay in the lack of realism displayed in two important areas: its dealings with the Catholic Church and the financial implications involved in any potential language revival. The report began by outlining how consultations with the church, hinted at in the earlier report, were progressing: 'Bishops in Irish-speaking areas where the hierarchy wield most influence in educational matters, with two exceptions, have promised active co-operation in the revival of Irish'. In addition it noted that in the dioceses of Tuam, Kerry and Waterford, only teachers with satisfactory certificates for teaching Irish would be appointed.

While the writers appeared satisfied with this progress regarding the church's involvement in educational matters, no reference was made to the church's power in ecclesiastical issues, such as the appointment of priests.

---

8. *Ibid.*

Neither does any effort seem to have been made to persuade the bishops that only Irish-speaking priests be appointed in the Gaeltacht. As priests were the leaders of the community their ability to speak Irish was of great importance. There is, however, this muted criticism: 'Moreover, the church alone could restore and perpetuate the national language, if only it so willed.' While there were many bishops who gave tacit support to the language's revival, and certain religious orders were noted for the zeal with which they taught the language, overall, the church's role was passive, and while it did not oppose the government's policy, it did not greatly assist it either.

The report contained no mention of how the plans outlined for the language's development in the earlier *Report of the Ministry for Irish to the First Dáil* in 1920 had progressed, and references to education were confined to reporting the results of school competitions and the lack of textbooks. Concern was also expressed about the status of Irish in the National University, and county councils were urged to use their scholarships to further the language policy and 'the nationalising of the university'. That Irish would become essential in the public service was again signalled, and the need to convince Gaeltacht people that Irish speakers would obtain posts in the public service once the new state was established, was reiterated.

The report noted with satisfaction that the campaign to make the country bilingual was progressing. Irish speakers were being chosen to chair public meetings, official documents were printed in Irish, and many people had gaelicised their names to indicate support for the language policy. The tone of the report was noticeably optimistic: 'In spite of the disturbed state of recent times the use of Irish in all these spheres is extending visibly.' However, even at this early stage of the revival campaign there were signs of a lack of enthusiasm. Furthermore, small successes were magnified; the Gaelic League was commended for co-operating actively in the work despite its grievous suffering 'through the attention of the army of occupation', while 'the public's interest in the language had not lessened', and the report again recorded that since the establishment of the Ministry for Irish, the minister had addressed 'great hostings' around the country.

In the midst of such romantic idealism, however, one paragraph stood out with its reference to the cost of primary education, 'Alien Estimate for primary education in Ireland over £5,000,000.' Again, the failure to evaluate the implications of the cost of the language revival was clearly demonstrated. The report concluded sanguinely: 'When we are again free to urge and address our people to do their duty by their mother tongue, prompt and satisfactory results may be safely anticipated'.

These two documents: *The Report of the Ministry for Irish to the First Dáil* and the *Report of the Ministry of the National Language,* laid the foundation for the new state's gaelicisation policy. Furthermore, the new state's education policy owed much to the work undertaken by the Ministry for Irish, and the establishment of the preparatory college scheme was based on the earlier experience of the ministry.

The period 1919–22 was crucial in the development of the gaelicisation policy. There has been much speculation as to why de Valera[9] did not continue the Ministry for Irish after 1921. As President of the Executive Council, he had a decisive say as to which ministries were set up. It has generally been assumed that de Valera created a Ministry for Irish in 1919, instead of a Ministry for Education, as a means of avoiding difficulties with the Catholic Church at that time.

DIFFERING VIEWS OF THE GAELICISATION POLICY

Indeed, the disappearance of the Ministry for Irish and the absorption of its role into the Department of Education was an indication that the education system was expected to bear the brunt of efforts to revive the language. A further reason for the disappearance of the Ministry for Irish may have been that divisions over the aims of the language policy were becoming apparent. While there was general agreement amongst the leaders of the new state that the language should be the main focus in the drive for cultural nationalism, and that its revival was necessary to emphasise the separation from Britain, there were those who wanted an Irish-speaking state, while others favoured an emphasis on bilingualism. That radical action was needed to save the language was accepted by Eoin MacNeill, who became the Free State's first Minister for Education in December 1922. He forecast that 'if this generation does not save Irish, it will be dead in 20 or 30 years,'[10] but he did not believe that the school system could revive the language. As early as 1893, he wrote: 'No language has ever been kept alive by mere book-teaching,[11] and from this view he never deviated, later saying: 'You might as well be putting wooden legs on hens as trying to restore Irish through the schools' system'.[12]

MacNeill was more realistic about the prospects of reviving the language than some of his colleagues in the first Free State Government. Many of them held a rather sentimental view of the language, naively believing that the general public would support any government efforts to save it. Typical of their views were those expressed by W.T. Cosgrave, President of the Executive Council, in March 1925:

> The Irish people as a body recognise it to be a national duty, incumbent on their representatives and their government as on themselves to uphold and foster the Irish language, the central and most distinctive factor of the tradition which is

---

9. For biographical details of people named on this page see the Appendix.
10. Memo on the Teaching of Irish in Primary and Secondary Schools, UCD Archives MacNeill Papers, LAI/E/25–7.
11. MacNeill, 'A plea and a plan,' *The Gaelic Journal,* 4 March 1893.
12. Ó Broin, *Just like yesterday: an autobiography,* p. 66.

Irish nationality and that everything that can be rightly and effectively done to
that end will be in accordance with the will of the Irish people.[13]

He described the language as having been

> waylaid, beaten, robbed and left for dead by the wayside and we have to ask our-
> selves if it is to be allowed to lie there, or if we are to heal its wounds, place it
> in safety and under proper care, and have it restored to health and vigour.[14]

The new state's civil servants, however, were not so sanguine about the
prospects of reviving the language. As early as 1915, P.S. O'Hegarty,[15] a
member of the IRB who became secretary of the Department of Posts and
Telegraphs in 1922, commented:

> We are constantly told that as Irish was threshed out of Irish children by the cane
> so it can be threshed into them. But it was not the cane, nor any sort of direct
> compulsion, that lost Irish. It was the fact that English had more to offer. The
> Irish boy in the 1840s was offered official life, the churches, the professions, the
> British Empire and America as his scope. He was offered with them one of
> the greatest of literatures and the key to modern civilisation and development.
> Irish offered him none of those things. It has practically no modern literature, its
> vocabulary is centuries out of date, it is not habitually used anywhere in Ireland
> for official, church, business or professional purposes nor is it possible so to use
> it. It has no international value outside philology.[16]

The early leaders were agreed, however, upon one measure which the
government could take to increase the prestige of the language:

> Irish is dying because the people of the Gaeltacht think that Irish and poverty
> and social inferiority are inextricably connected. The government must show by
> acts, appointments, and salaries, the use of Irish as a real language; that Irish is a
> superior language, socially and economically, in other words that Irish pays.[17]

Those with this view believed that the gaelicisation of the public services
would make a significant contribution to the language revival, and proposed
that Irish be made essential for all public services, central or local. They also
believed that where there was not a sufficient supply of candidates, those
with a knowledge of Irish should be placed in a preferential position.[18] The
lack of realism of those who favoured the language revival was nowhere
more clearly demonstrated than in this policy. In attempting to gaelicise the

---

13. Letter from Cosgrave, President of the Executive Council, to Mulcahy, chairman of *Coimisiún na
    Gaeltachta,* 4 March 1925, *Report of Coimisiún na Gaeltachta,* p. 3.
14. *Ibid.*
15. For biographical details see the Appendix.
16. Ó Broin, *Just like yesterday....* p. 66.
17. *Report of the Ministry of the National Language.*
18. The Gaelicising of Ireland, UCD Archives, Mulcahy Papers, P7/C/71.

public service, they overlooked the fact that, at the establishment of the Free State, over 21,000 civil servants transferred from the old regime to the new state, and many of them regarded the language policy with scepticism.

One of the prime exponents of the language revival was Ernest Blythe,[19] who played a significant role in the development of the gaelicisation policy, and it was due to him that the preparatory system developed in the way that it did. The main features of his policy were: the use of propaganda to improve the status of the language among native speakers and among the public generally; the improvement of conditions in the Gaeltacht; and the promotion of the language by gaelicising the public service. He greatly favoured the preparatory college system. He was particularly attached to the Connemara Gaeltacht, and devised special regulations to assist students from that Gaeltacht to gain entry to the preparatory colleges.

THE FIRST NATIONAL PROGRAMME CONFERENCE 1920

The new emphasis on the language in the schools created difficulties for the INTO. In 1920 it convened the First National Programme Conference which was to have far-reaching consequences, as its decisions were to affect primary education for decades. The conference drew up a programme for schools with a heavy emphasis on Irish. Its main features were a concentration on a comparatively small number of key subjects, and an insistence on the Irish language and the history and geography of Ireland as essential parts of this programme.[20] The conference recommended that the programme's obligatory subjects should be Irish, English, mathematics, history and geography, needlework for girls (in third and higher standards), singing and drill. This meant the elimination of drawing, elementary science, cookery and laundry, needlework (in lower standards), hygiene and nature study as formal obligatory subjects, and the modification of the programme in history and geography (which became one subject), singing and drill. Teachers, generally, were pleased with these changes as they had long complained that the programme contained too many obligatory subjects.

Teachers gained further freedom under the new programme with regard to the grouping of classes and the allotment of time. The only subject with a time restriction was Irish, where it was laid down that each pupil should receive instruction for 'at least one hour per day as an ordinary school subject'. The changes which aroused the most controversy were the proposals that Irish should be used as a teaching medium and that the work of the infant classes was to be entirely through Irish, with no teaching of English. For senior standards it recommended that geography, history, singing and

---

19. For biographical details see the Appendix.
20. *The National Programme of Primary Instruction,* The National Programme Conference, p. 4.

———

Programme for Infants

JUNIOR INFANTS.

LANGUAGE.

To be taught to speak audibly and distinctly by means of conversation, object and picture lessons, story-telling and recitation.

DRAWING.

Drawing in sand, and afterwards in mass with chalks on small blackboards, or on other suitable surfaces.

NUMBERS.

To count up to 9 by means of kindergarten gifts and occupations.

KINDERGARTEN GIFTS AND OCCUPATIONS.

Colour sorting, building with bricks, threading large beads, arranging shells or tablets, &c. in twos, threes and higher numbers, fraying, stick-laying. Gifts I., II., III.

SONGS AND GAMES.

Nursery rhymes and simple songs connected with child's surroundings. Finger-plays. Colour and movement games with Gift I. Ring games with music and free play.

3 A page from the First National Programme 1920.

drill should be taught through Irish. This was going further than the Gaelic League had proposed.

CORCORAN'S INFLUENCE

While teachers generally accepted that Irish should be an obligatory subject, there was much debate about its use as a teaching medium. Many teachers and educationalists believed that this would be psychologically damaging to young children. The INTO delegates were doubtful as to the practicability of this recommendation and thought it premature. However, the conference was influenced by the Rev. Dr Timothy Corcoran,[21] who believed that at the infant stage, children's minds were especially receptive and that this was the surest way of laying the foundation of an oral knowledge of the language. Corcoran, a Jesuit, became the first professor of education at UCD in 1909, a position he held until shortly before his death in 1943. During that period he had a major influence on many aspects of Irish education. Amongst his first students was Éamon de Valera, who shared Corcoran's vision of a Catholic, Gaelic Ireland. Subsequently, Corcoran canvassed successfully for de Valera's appointment as chancellor of the National University in 1921.

Corcoran wrote extensively on education. In much of his writing, he tried to direct attention towards the European mainland, and away from British educational methods and outlook. Corcoran's impact on Irish education was most marked after the establishment of the Irish Free State. Of his influence during that period, Joseph O'Neill, secretary of the Department of Education, wrote:

> In the reconstruction of the Irish State he was from the beginning the master-builder in education. The commissions on education, set up in 1921, were guided so largely by him that it may be said that the curricula, aims and methods in primary and secondary education which emerged from them were, in the main, the works of his hands.[22]

A staunch advocate of the gaelicisation policy, Corcoran blamed the national school system for the widespread decay of Irish between 1830 and 1850, and believed rather simplistically that the system which crippled the language could just as easily revive it, blithely disregarding other factors, such as the Great Famine and emigration, which also contributed to the language's decline. Corcoran maintained that the language could be revived successfully by the education system if two conditions were fulfilled: first, that only Irish was used in infant classes and secondly, that native speakers were recruited as teachers for pre-primary language work. Corcoran maintained

---

21. For biographical details of people named on this page see the Appendix.
22. O'Neill, Joseph, *Studies* xxxii.

that 'Irish-speaking districts of first quality could provide hundreds of such adolescent teachers-to-be every year,' and claimed that 'with few exceptions, girls who have had a full primary education in Irish are natural teachers'.[23] Such was Corcoran's influence, that though he himself neither spoke Irish nor took steps to learn it, his view prevailed and his assertions were accepted without any evidence that they were realistic. In their enthusiasm for the language his hearers believed what they wanted to hear.

The conference's report was quickly accepted by the government, and the new programme came into operation for all national schools on 1 April 1922. Such, however, was the zeal of the Provisional Government to begin the gaelicisation policy that on 1 February 1922, the day on which the Irish Free State Government took over responsibility for national education, the Minister for Education issued Public Notice No. 4, in which he ordered that, from the following St Patrick's Day, Irish was to be taught or used as a medium of instruction for not less than one hour each day in all schools where there was a teacher competent to teach it.[24]

The programme's significance cannot be overestimated for it was to remain virtually unchanged for almost 40 years. Under it, the main thrust of primary education became the promotion of the Irish language, and Irish not only assumed a new and dominant role in the curriculum, it was also to be used as far as possible as the medium of teaching.

But those who called the First Programme Conference in 1920 had not foreseen that the War of Independence, which ended with the Truce on 11 July 1921 and the subsequent signing of the Treaty on 6 December 1921, would be followed by a bitter civil war from 28 June 1922 until 24 May 1923. The effects of the civil war, in which 665 were killed and 3,000 wounded, following so soon after the War of Independence, gravely damaged the new state economically, and resulted in large numbers being unemployed. But of far greater consequence were its psychological effects. The deaths of Brugha, Griffith and Collins were major blows. In addition, some of the strongest supporters of the language movement, such as MacNeill, Beaslai,[25] 'Sceilg,' and Ó Caoimh did not remain long in politics.

Disillusionment among the public with the politicians, and with the difficulties of learning Irish, soon led to public disenchantment with the revival policy. This was well expressed in the following letter from a Tyrone priest in 1923:

> Teaching through Irish is premature. The teachers are not competent and some of them will never be. It is quite impossible for youngsters, who have learned English as their native language, to learn Irish and to master other subjects through Irish at the same time. It is only feasible in Irish-speaking districts. I do not

23. Corcoran, 'The Native Speaker as Teacher,' in *The Irish Monthly*, April 1923, p. 188.
24. Public Notice No. 4, *Concerning the Teaching of the Irish Language in the National Schools,* Ministry of Education, Irish Provisional Government, I February 1922.
25. For biographical details of people named on this page see the Appendix.

RIALTAS SEALADACH NA hEIREANN.
(Irish Provisional Government.)
MINISTRY OF EDUCATION.

Concerning the Teaching of Irish Language in the National Schools.

PUBLIC NOTICE, No. 4.

THE MINISTER FOR EDUCATION by virtue of the powers vested in him HEREBY ORDERS that the following regulations concerning the teaching of the Irish Language in all national schools shall come into force on St. Patrick's Day, the Seventeenth day of March, 1922, and shall remain in force until further notice :—

(1) The Irish Language shall be taught, or used as a medium of instruction, for not less than one full hour each day in all national schools where there is a Teacher competent to teach it ;

(2) The hour for the aforesaid instruction shall be divided in the following manner :—

   (*a*) One half-hour not earlier than 10 o'clock in the forenoon ; and

   (*b*) the remaining half-hour not later than 2.30 o'clock in the afternoon.

(3) That should it happen in any schools with more than one Teacher that all the Teachers of the school are not competent to give instruction in the Irish Language, then the division of the work in such school must be so readjusted as to enable such Teacher or Teachers in the school as are competent to give instruction in Irish to comply with the terms of this order ; provided, however, that in the carrying out of such readjustment, due regard shall be had to the amount of work which can reasonably be allocated to any teacher ;

(4) That in a school where the Teacher of a standard, though not certificated, is regarded by the principal teacher of the school and by the National School Inspector in charge of the school, as reasonably competent to give instruction in Irish in that standard, then the Principal Teacher will arrange for such teacher to give the instruction in Irish in that standard ;

(5) That all time-tables affected by the provisions of this Order should be revised and altered accordingly, and a copy of each time-table so revised and altered should be submitted without delay to the Inspector in charge of the school ;

(6) That in cases where there are any difficulties whatsoever in carrying out the regulations herein set forth, statements should be submitted as soon as possible to the Inspector of Irish Instruction, National Education Office, Dublin.

Given this 1st day of February, 1922.

DIARMUID Ó hÉIGCEARTUIGH,
Secretary to the Provisional Government.

4 Public Notice No. 4 concerning the Teaching of the Irish Language in National Schools 1922 *National Archives* ED8830.

believe in bilingualism though Pearse led us to believe the Belgians were bilingual. Experience of the Great War convinced me that the bilinguals of Belgium were not a conspicuous number. I met hundreds of Walloons and Flemings, who couldn't understand one another. It was the same with the Welsh.[26]

Typical of how things had changed in a short period is this description by writer León Ó Broin:

> I had seen in the Central Branch of the Gaelic League and in the Leinster College of Irish the crowds of teachers, civil servants and others that flocked to learn the language in 1922, but the beginnings of a decline of interest had set in as a result of the civil war and through the discovery that Irish was a difficult language to learn.[27]

Other factors which affected the learning of the language were a shortage of textbooks and of teachers competent to teach the language. These factors were of particular importance for those charged with the implementation of the new National Programme. An added difficulty was the need to reform the system of recruitment to primary teaching. This was not just because of the government's Irish language policy, but also because of the failure of existing recruitment methods. Of immediate concern was the need to ensure that all students entering training had received secondary education and were sufficiently well educated to derive full benefit from a third-level course. A further significant factor was the proposed introduction of a School Attendance Act. These were to be important considerations in the establishment of the preparatory colleges.

EDUCATIONAL BACKGROUND TO THE ESTABLISHMENT OF THE PREPARATORY SYSTEM

In addition to the problems created by curricular change, the political changes resulted in a significant reorganisation of the structure and administration of education. On the formation of the Provisional Government, the Minister for Education took over from the Commissioners of Education the supervision of primary and intermediate education and responsibility for the endowed schools. These functions became the nucleus of the Department of Education. A chief executive officer, Pádraic Ó Brolcháin,[28] was given responsibility for the conduct of primary education and in June 1923

---

26. Letter from Fr. T. Bradley, Plumbridge, Co Tyrone, to Patrick McGilligan, 13 December, 1923, UCD Archives, McGilligan Papers, P35d/105.
27. Ó Broin, p. 67.
28. For biographical details of people named on this page see the Appendix.

Joseph O'Neill, secretary of the Department, was one of two new commissioners given responsibility for intermediate education.

Pádraic Ó Brolcháin has acquired a place in the history of education as the official who dismissed the Commissioners of National Education. A career civil servant, he worked with the Health Insurance Commission before being appointed CEO in 1922. An ardent Gaeilgeoir, he was responsible for National Education from February 1922 until his sudden death in 1934, and played a major role in the implementation of the new state's gaelicisation policy. As CEO, he had a pivotal function in the establishment of the preparatory colleges, working closely with the Minister for Finance, Ernest Blythe, who had been involved with similar schemes, run by the Ministry for Irish. A major feature of Ó Brolcháin's policy was a close involvement with the Catholic Church. He was a friend of the archbishop of Dublin, Dr Edward Byrne, with whom he kept in close contact.

Ó Brolcháin's brief included the oversight of 13,000 primary teachers in 5,636 primary schools, with an enrolment of approximately half a million pupils and a budget of over £3 million. Most of the schools were small with only one or two teachers. The dominant influence in primary education was the Catholic Church which, through the management of all but one of the country's training colleges and of all except about 900 of the country's primary schools, controlled the training and appointment of teachers. The church's powerful role in education was accepted by the general public, and the new government, whose ethos was devoutly Catholic, made it clear from its earliest days that it had no intention of changing the *status quo*. Indeed, one of the government's first actions was the closure of the state's only non-denominational training college at Marlborough Street. In addition, it became part of government policy to consult members of the hierarchy, either individually or as a body, before possible changes were mooted in public.

An immediate difficulty for Ó Brolcháin was school attendance, where the average daily attendance was only 70 per cent. A further difficulty was the school-leaving age. Most pupils left school at 11 with only a small proportion going on to second-level education. The provision of second-level education was of significance for the recruitment of primary teachers, because by the 1920s it was obvious that candidates entering training colleges needed not only to have received a secondary education but also to have passed the Leaving Certificate Examination.

A major difficulty for the Department was the large number of untrained teachers. Of the 13,043 primary teachers, a high proportion (2,957) were untrained, while a further 2,000 were members of religious orders. The Department made the reduction of the number of untrained teachers a priority. In the Department's view, the success of the new programme depended on three factors: ensuring that pupils attended school regularly; an adequate and competent body of teachers; and proper school accommodation. Of these, the most immediate was ensuring that there were sufficient teachers competent to teach the new programme. To achieve this the Department had to devise two strategies: to enable the current body of teachers to become proficient at Irish[29], and to devise a means of ensuring that all future teachers would be fluent in Irish.

To overcome the deficiency of teachers in Irish, the Department organised a series of compulsory summer courses for all teachers under 45 years of age, in Gaelic League Colleges in the Gaeltacht during 1922–25. Many people complained that the courses were too short. More cynical critics questioned the value of such courses, where 'teachers got a cheap holiday at some seaside resort and did not over exert themselves at study'.[30] The high costs were another factor.

COST OF SUMMER COURSES

1922 = £75,668
1923 = £65,945
1924 = £42,770
1925 = £43,034
£227,417

Source: *Report of the Department of Education, 1924/25, p. 31*

The Department defended such expenditure on the grounds that it was 'an indication of the whole-hearted manner in which the problem of the language was being approached by the government'. The summer courses, however, were only a short-term measure to improve the teachers' fluency in the language. The Department's long-term policy was to concentrate on the training colleges, which it saw as a key factor in its plan for the gaelicisation of education. Its aim was to gaelicise the training colleges: 'to substitute Irish for English as the language of instruction, recreation and of life generally in them.' It envisaged that when 'the training colleges were completely gaelicised, the primary schools would gradually pass from their almost uni-lingual English stage, through bilingualism, to a uni-lingual Irish stage in which Irish will be the normal speech of pupils and teachers in classes, playgrounds, etc'.[31]

THE TRAINING COLLEGES

To consider how this could be achieved, the Department set up an internal committee in December 1924 to examine recruitment to primary teaching. During the days immediately preceding the establishment of the Free State, there were seven training colleges. St Patrick's College, Drumcondra, and De La Salle College, Waterford, were for Catholic male students. Our Lady

---

29. Of the 12,000 lay teachers in the Free State in 1922, only 1,107 had bilingual certificates, though a further 2,845 had ordinary certificates.
30. Letter from Fr T. Bradley to Patrick McGilligan, 13 December 1923, UCD Archives, McGilligan Papers, P35d/105.
31. Memo on The Gaelicising of Ireland, UCD Archives, MacNeill Papers, P24/303.

of Mercy College, Carysfort; St. Mary's College, Belfast; and Mary Immaculate College, Limerick, were for Catholic female students. There were also two co-educational colleges: the Church of Ireland Training College, Kildare Street for Protestant students, and Marlborough Street Training College, a non-denominational college run by the state.

The establishment of the Irish Free State brought significant changes for the colleges: St Mary's became part of the educational system in Northern Ireland, while numbers in the Church of Ireland Training College reduced considerably, as the majority of its students came from Northern Ireland. Once the island was partitioned, northern students went to Stranmillis College.[32] In addition Marlborough Street Training College was closed and the students transferred to other colleges.

There were two major causes for concern regarding the training colleges: the lack of sufficient students and the poor academic quality of the entrants. As the Department was planning to introduce compulsory school attendance, the need to ensure that the training colleges had sufficient numbers of students able to complete the training college course was a matter of some importance. It also realised that only students who had received secondary education would be able to complete the training college course satisfactorily. This had become the norm in other countries. In the Irish system, the main emphasis in the 1920s was on teacher training, rather than teacher education. The out-dated idea that teachers could be recruited from primary school pupils with an aptitude for teaching, dominated the two major recruitment systems: the monitorial system and the pupil-teacher scheme. These were supplemented by graduates, untrained teachers known as JAMS, and private students. In 1924, the monitorial system supplied less than 14 per cent of those gaining places in training colleges at the Easter examination.[33]

The other major source of supply, the pupil-teacher scheme, supplied 40 per cent of candidates for women's colleges, though the number recruited for men's colleges had fallen to one or two per cent a year. So there was a danger of a grave shortage of male teachers. An advantage of both the monitorial and pupil-teacher systems was that candidates recruited through these systems had gained some supervised teaching experience as part of their courses. This emphasis on teaching practice was not totally discarded, but was retained in a modified form in the preparatory system, where an attempt at giving students some teaching experience was built into the system.

THE COMMITTEE ON RECRUITMENT 1924

These were some of the factors to be considered by the Committee on Recruitment, established by the Department in 1924 to determine how the

---

32. Parkes *Kildare Place: The history of the Church of Ireland Training College*, 1811–1969, p. 142.
33. *Report of the Department of Education, 1924/25*, p. 41.

training colleges could be gaelicised, and to examine how they could be supplied with native speakers from the Gaeltacht. Amongst those who made submissions to the committee was Professor Corcoran of UCD, the *éminence grise* of the Free State's education policy, who was a strong advocate of the recruitment of native speakers.[34] Corcoran advised reserving half the entrance scholarships each year for native speakers, and encouraging them to compete for the rest. Here again, Corcoran's view prevailed and in March 1925, the committee recommended, in an interim report, the abolition of the monitorial system, a revision of the pupil-teacher scheme and the establishment of preparatory colleges.

The establishment of preparatory colleges to recruit native speakers to primary teaching was not a new idea. Such recruitment had been tried before by the Ministry for Irish in 1920[35] when a small scheme was devised, offering eight scholarships, one for each county in the Gaeltacht. This did not work out very satisfactorily, however, as it had to be confined to boys when the organisers were unable to come to an arrangement with the management of a girls' school. Nevertheless, the scheme was considered worthy of development and was tried again in 1921–22. This time the arrangements were better, with 50 scholarships on offer, 24 for boys and 16 for girls from the Gaeltacht, six for boys and four for girls from the Galltacht, valued at £30 each. They were to be awarded according to the results of a competitive examination held on 16 August 1921. The successful candidates were to attend a *Scoil Ullmhuighthe* for one year, for which the Ministry for Irish would pay £30 to each candidate. From there, they were to enter training college for two years, at their own expense, though later the Ministry decided to pay £10 to each candidate on entry to training.

To be eligible for a scholarship, candidates had to fulfil certain conditions regarding age and health. They were also to be recommended by the organiser from the Ministry for Irish and by their school manager or teacher, and to pass an academic examination. A further condition for an award was that they would undertake to become primary teachers. Otherwise, the students or their parents would repay the cost of the scholarship. Any student who did not do well at the final examination at the *Scoil Ullmhuighthe,* would have his scholarship taken from him. The scholarship examination had three subjects: Irish, English and mathematics, and in keeping with the policy of promoting Irish, there were twice as many marks for Irish as for English.

The advertisement for the scholarships left no doubt as to the organisers' intentions:

> The education system of the country must be gaelicised and this will do it. The new primary programme is almost ready, a programme that will give equality of treatment to Irish. Are there suitable teachers to put the programme into effect?

---

34. Corcoran, 'The native speaker as teacher,' in *The Irish Monthly,* April 1923, p. 188.
35. *Misneach,* 19 March 1921.

Indeed not. We must remedy this. It will not be long before we have native speakers from the Gaeltacht as teachers. The training colleges will have to do their part also. If they do not do it willingly we will have to make them.[36]

In 1921, the numbers competing increased. To ensure the candidates' attendance, they were given their train fares to attend the nearest centre. Though 50 scholarships were on offer, the examiners recommended that only 44 should be awarded. While the second scheme was more successful than the first, it had some unsatisfactory aspects. The scheme, however, was repeated in 1922 when 50 scholarships were once more offered. Again the full number of scholarships was not awarded; only 25 girls and 10 boys received scholarships. Furthermore, as none of the winners for 1921–22 gained a place in a training college, the scheme was considered a failure. It served, however, as a useful experiment for the establishment of the preparatory colleges, which was announced on 11 June 1925.

Behind the announcement lay many different ideas as to how the colleges should be established and it was at this point that three important decisions had to be made. The location and management of the colleges had to be decided, and whether the colleges would be for student-teachers only. In the Department of Education, the system had the full support of Ó Brolcháin, while at Cabinet it was strongly supported by Blythe, and his view prevailed in all three decisions despite the fact that MacNeill, the Minister for Education, had other ideas. Correspondence between the two departments, from early 1923, shows how the scheme evolved. The early proposals were for six schools for 12-year-olds who had completed sixth class in a national school in the Donegal, Mayo, Galway, Kerry, Cork and Waterford areas of the Gaeltacht. The Department of Education proposed calling them higher grade schools and estimated their costs at £21,000.[37]

In June 1924, departmental secretary O'Neill, aware that both the monitorial system and the pupil-teacher scheme had failed as recruiting methods, proposed four preparatory colleges, run by religious orders, one each in Donegal and Connacht, and two in Munster; two for boys and two for girls, with 100–150 students. Native speakers only were to be admitted and all training was to be through Irish. O'Neill believed that 'all candidates for training colleges needed to have attended a special type of secondary school or preparatory college', and as Irish-speaking districts were 'almost entirely lacking in the type of large school to give monitorial training', and as the supply of pupils from the Gaeltacht to training colleges was inadequate, he proposed that the first preparatory colleges should be in the Gaeltacht. By November 1924, O'Neill was successful in persuading the Department of Finance of the need to provide schools in the Gaeltacht to bridge the gap between primary education and the training colleges.

---

36. *Ibid.*, 4 June 1921.
37. Letter from Ó Brolcháin to secretary, Department of Finance, 1 March 1923, DF Papers, National Archives, S20/9/25.

A further significant factor in the decision to locate the colleges in the Gaeltacht was the requirement that the Irish language should have a prominent place in the primary school curriculum. Ó Brolcháin believed that to be successful the system should be based on 'the total immersion method' of language learning:

> The difficulty is the present condition of the country, and the view of those framing the programme and of the present Minister for Education and of the government generally, is to look to the continuity of the historic Irish nation based on Irish and in order to bring that back through the teaching profession it is necessary to have intensive centres to train our future teachers on an Irish basis, rather than to have them scattered with other students.[38]

The reference to 'intensive centres' was an indication that the Department's policy was to be based on the earlier experiments run by the Ministry for Irish. By locating the colleges in the Gaeltacht, it was believed that students would absorb aspects of Gaelic culture and be in touch with Irish as it was spoken, and that general intercourse with native speakers, such as storytellers, would be good for the students. Blythe believed that the establishment of the colleges in large mansions associated with the Ascendancy would raise esteem for the language among native speakers. Furthermore, it was envisaged that the colleges would provide economic relief for the Gaeltacht, and by helping to keep emigration down would preserve the Irish-speaking areas. It could be claimed also that the schools would provide second-level education in the Gaeltacht, which had few such schools, a defect pointed out by the Report of *Coimisiún na Gaeltachta*.

Originally, MacNeill had proposed that eight experimental schools should be established. In his plan, the schools were not to be confined to the Gaeltacht, but were to be established in the Model School buildings in English-speaking areas. This raised interesting questions about management, but in view of the absence of any definite indication of MacNeill's intentions, one can only speculate on what he had in mind. As MacNeill was a devout Catholic, he is unlikely to have considered anything which would have diluted the power of the Catholic Church in school management.

MANAGEMENT OF THE PREPARATORY COLLEGES

Originally, it was proposed that the preparatory colleges would be under the patronage of the bishop of the diocese in which they were located and that the patron would nominate the local manager of the college, subject to ratification by the Department, but this was changed following negotiations

---

38. *Report of Coimisiún na Gaeltachta*, p. 5.

with the hierarchy.[39] In June 1925, Ó Brolcháin informed the Council of Catholic Bishops that the monitorial system was to end and that six preparatory colleges, five in the Gaeltacht and one in Dublin, were to be established. Apart from the Munster boys' college in Co Waterford and the 'house of residence for Protestant girls', the houses would be run by religious orders, though the teachers could be religious or lay, provided they were persons with high qualifications. Following discussions with representatives of the hierarchy, it was agreed that the bishop in whose diocese a college was located would be appointed manager, and that he could invite whichever order he favoured to take over the running of the college in his diocese. One can only speculate as to why this change was made. It is likely that as the preparatory students were going to become teachers, the bishops felt that the system of management should be similar to that for the training colleges.

Throughout 1925, details of the curriculum, entrance examinations and administration were worked out, and interested bodies, such as the INTO, the managerial and ecclesiastical associations and the Gaelic League, were informed. By February 1926, it was envisaged that when the colleges were in full working order, they would provide for 650 students, 300 boys and 350 girls, and that allowing for a 'possible small wastage' they would supply the training colleges with about 150 of the 300–350 students required annually.[40]

UNWISE DECISIONS

Despite MacNeill's wish that the colleges should be co-educational with a wide range of students, including those intended for careers in the civil service and commercial life, they were confined to student-teachers. Both MacNeill's and Blythe's views were summarised by Ó Brolcháin, in evidence to *Coimisiún na Gaeltachta,* in April 1925. The decision to confine the preparatory colleges to student-teachers was unfortunate for it was to be a weakness of the system throughout its history and one of the main reasons for the INTO's opposition.

Despite Blythe's enthusiasm for the new system, the officials of his department were never convinced of its worth and, at their insistence, the preparatory course was reduced from five to four years. Finance's great fear at this time was that the establishment of second-level schools in Irish-speaking districts would lead to calls for similar schools in English-speaking areas.[41] The reduction of the course to four years was an unwise decision for it meant that the Intermediate Certificate course had to be completed in two years, and this had the effect of narrowing the curriculum and preventing the teaching of Latin or a modern language for examination

---

39. Letter from Ó Brolcháin to Department of Finance, 20 June 1924, DF Papers, S20/9/25.
40. 'Scheme for Preparatory Colleges,' 22 February 1926, UCD Archives, Mulcahy Papers, P7/C/70.
41. DF Papers, S20/9/25.

purposes. The failure to include Latin as a Leaving Certificate subject was to be the cause of much resentment among preparatory students over the years.

Officials in Finance disliked the system and when the costs of acquiring suitable premises, originally estimated at £150,000,[42] had by 1927 swollen to £340,000, they queried the necessity of having the colleges in the Gaeltacht. When one considers that £1,000 in the 1920s equalled £34,000 in 2000, the alarm expressed by Finance was not surprising. Indeed, such had been the financial squeeze after the civil war that Blythe, as Minister for Finance, had made some drastic cutbacks in public expenditure, including cutting teachers' salaries and reducing the old age pension.

An important factor which allowed the government's high expenditure on the preparatory colleges to go unchallenged was the fact that legislation establishing the system was enacted by ministerial order, and was not brought in by way of a Bill and debated in the Dáil. Once a ministerial order was published, it was up to any deputy to put down a motion on the agenda of the Dáil. This could be accepted or rejected by the government. The fact that there were no requests from deputies for the matter to be debated was an indication that they agreed with the decision, though it must be remembered that, throughout this period, there was no opposition party in Dáil Éireann, as Fianna Fáil did not enter the Dáil until 1927. The fact that the system was established by ministerial order was important, for it allowed the government to end the system in similar fashion in 1959.

Another unwise decision, made in response to Finance's criticism about costs, was the introduction of a regulation that all preparatory students had to give a signed undertaking of their intention to become primary teachers and to repay the costs of their education if they did not. The student's parent or guardian had to give a similar undertaking. Originally, Education proposed that the undertaking should be signed after the Intermediate Examination, but this was changed and students had to give the undertaking at the beginning of their course. This regulation was to be one of the major criticisms of the system. An alternative proposal by *Coimisiún na Gaeltachta*, that students who had obtained the Intermediate Certificate and 'who have the necessary competency in Irish' be admitted to a two-year course, was largely ignored, though this would have reduced costs considerably. In the early years, a small number of students were admitted in this way, but it was customary for the Department to insist on students who had already done the Intermediate Certificate Examination through English, doing it again through Irish. Indeed, this was a feature of the Munster boys' college, where it was quite common.[43]

---

42. *Dáil Reports,* 3 June 1926.
43. See Jones, V.A., 'The Preparatory Colleges 1926–1961, an experiment in Irish education', unpublished PhD thesis, Dublin University, 1999, p. 236.

OPPOSITION TO THE SYSTEM

The establishment of the preparatory system was viewed with concern by some educationalists, including a senior adviser to Dr Edward Byrne, who held the pivotal post of Catholic archbishop of Dublin in the early decades of the new state's existence. As archbishop, he enjoyed good relationships with the governments of both W.T. Cosgrave and de Valera. The adviser submitted a memorandum[44] in which he described the preparatory system as sound in educational principle, but false in the method of application, and costly at £45,000 per annum. The six colleges would require 40 professors, and he doubted if 12 with the required standard of Irish speech and cultural development could be found. The result, he believed, would be six inefficient organisations in Irish education, which 'will command the very heart of the educational sphere'. He went on:

> The establishment of six colleges, in several districts, would tend to stereotype a variety of dialects, while one of the purposes of such colleges should be the gradual development of a unified cultivated speech.

This was a significant criticism of the language revival policy, as the failure to devise a standardised form of speech and spelling added greatly to the difficulties of learning the language. It was also a difficulty for those who were trying to produce reading material in Irish. Indeed, the need for reading material had been noted by Blythe, and he was instrumental in establishing An Gúm, a special section in the Department to oversee the publication of such material.

The adviser also criticised the gaelicisation policy, which had been in operation for three and a half years, as an 'experiment upon an entire population, at a cost of £253,000, and an imponderable sum in accumulated illiteracy, educational inefficiency and stunted mental deficiency'. In his opinion, the government's method of reviving Irish had produced a reaction against the language itself, which might easily overflow in the region of government. However, he was quick to excuse the government, saying that it had shown 'great fortitude in trying times'. With so many demands, it had little time for the language issue, and had to accept the advice offered. He expressed disapproval of the government's language policy on the following grounds:

> Irish was untouched by the Renaissance, the language has not been used for the teaching of secondary or primary subjects in any real sense for a century and a half, and its greatest defect is that it is not a fit medium for the expression of higher educational thought or of the activities of modern life.

---

44. Confidential memo, 'Examination of educational sphere,' unnamed document, Byrne Papers, Dublin Diocesan Archives.

He accepted that Gaeltacht children should be educated through Irish but believed that they should also learn English. He denounced the First National Programme Conference as 'mirth-provoking if not so tragic in its projections' and went on:

> It is the intention of the 'Programmists' that the whole programme will be taught in a short time through Irish, ignoring the conditions of the children and teachers and incidentally proving that they had never read Davis or Pearse or if they had, that they were unable to understand them. Yet on a recommendation of the famous conference for the past four summers national teachers had been compelled to attend the courses to learn Irish from the lips of professors, five-sixths of whom do not know the language or even if they know it, have not the cultural nor the scientific method of teaching to produce results.

Despite the adviser's strong reservations, he failed to make any impression on Archbishop Byrne, who did not oppose the system at any point. The reason for the Catholic Church's lack of opposition may have been due to the way the colleges were to be managed; six of the seven colleges were to be under the direct control of the Catholic bishop in whose diocese they were situated, and staffed by a religious order of his choice, yet completely financed by the state (Coláiste Éinde was staffed by diocesan priests).

There was considerable opposition to the scheme in the civil service, particularly among the inspectorate. An inspector of the period recalled:

> The best of inspectors and many others were against the establishment of preparatory colleges, but Mr Bradley carried through his pet scheme, what he used to call his "pet lamb". Mr O'Neill acted as usual – backed up the winning side.[45]

Their opposition, however, like that of the archbishop's adviser, was based on the difficulty of obtaining competent teaching staff for the colleges:

> We all opposed the founding of the six (sic) preparatory colleges, pointing out the difficulty of procuring professors and the unfeasibility of speech intercourse between the native speakers and the students as claimed by their promoters.[46]

He had a very different view to that of Corcoran about the value of native speakers as teachers:

> In choosing teachers for the many Irish classes established after the Treaty it was common to meet men with a good knowledge of the language, quite incapable of imparting it. However, the clerical officers convinced the authorities of the soundness of the bizarre preparatory college scheme.[47]

---

45. Letter from former inspector, Séamus Fenton to Bishop Browne of Galway, 1 September 1944, Galway Diocesan Archives, Browne Papers.
46. Fenton, *It all happened: reminiscences of Séamus Fenton*, p. 268.
47. *Ibid.*, p. 269.

In October 1925, the INTO was sent details of the scheme. This influential body was opposed to the scheme from the very beginning on the grounds that student-teachers were segregated from other students and that they entered the colleges at too early an age. An editorial in the INTO's magazine, *The Irish School Weekly,* in March 1926 gave the union's views:

> No matter how liberal the curriculum in the colleges, the fact that all students are intended to be teachers will have a detrimental effect. The teacher of all others should be given the very broadest outlook on life. He has to guide and direct the citizens of the future and if he associates in his student career, only with young people without any diversity of outlook from his own, the effect on him must necessarily be narrowing.

T.J. O'Connell,[48] general secretary of the INTO, expressed the union's position on the age of selection. He believed that it was better to leave the choice of a career until the students were about 17 or 18 and to devise a system of bursaries and maintenance allowances, so that student-teachers could attend Intermediate Schools with candidates for other professions.[49] While O'Connell's views contained much wisdom, the context of the times has to be remembered. It was a period when large numbers of young people left school at 14 to start their working life, while others began apprenticeships at that age. In addition many young people were recruited to religious orders at the age of 12; Ernest Blythe himself started his working life at 15.

Whilst the inspectors' opposition to the preparatory system quickly changed as the personnel retired and were replaced by Irish-language enthusiasts,[50] the INTO neither changed nor modified its views. Indeed, its opposition grew stronger when changes in the selection procedure in the 1930s made it more and more difficult for teachers' children to obtain places in training colleges.

The public at large was sceptical about the scheme. An editorial in the *Irish Independent* of 26 February 1926 reflected their views:

> Official documents are now in two languages even though legislators themselves scarcely ever use a word of Irish. Irish is no value to those who have to emigrate to seek employment. People should be free to choose whether or not their children will learn Irish.

It expressed concern that students as young as 13 were choosing teaching as a career and prophesied that the location of five out of seven colleges in the Gaeltacht 'would entail a maximum of inconvenience and cost'.

Despite such public scepticism and the opposition of the inspectorate and the INTO, the preparatory system was seen by the Department as solving

---

48. For biographical details see the Appendix.
49. *The Irish School Weekly*, 6 March 1926, LXXVII, 10, p. 298.
50. Memo from the chief inspector regarding proposed changes in the inspection staff, UCD Archives, MacNeill Papers, LAI/H/134.

one of the most important problems facing the educational authorities in the newly established Irish Free State: the recruitment of primary teachers. The attitude of the inspectorate changed as the personnel changed, but opposition from the INTO and the Department of Finance was to dog the system throughout the 35 years of its existence. This was the difficult context in which the preparatory colleges were established.

CHAPTER TWO

Greening the public service while getting the colleges up and running: 1926–32

'We are going to drive the English language out of Ireland'

The period 1926–32 was of major significance for the government's gaelicisation policy. Irish was 'expressly recognised as the national language' in the Constitution, and with the announcement of the establishment of preparatory colleges its place in the educational policy of the new state was secured. Whilst leaving the Department to oversee the detailed decisions necessary for setting up the colleges, the government turned its attention to other ways of implementing the policy and to other areas of Irish life, particularly those areas of the country where the language was still spoken. The establishment of *Coimisiún na Gaeltachta* (The Gaeltacht Commission) to inquire into the preservation of the Gaeltacht was a logical sequel to measures already in place.

In the *Report of Coimisiún na Gaeltachta*, presented to the government in 1926, the commission produced a comprehensive series of recommendations for improving life in the Gaeltacht generally, and made a number of wide-ranging recommendations which, had they been put into effect, would have raised the standing of the language throughout the country. They included making Irish essential for entry to, and promotion in, the civil service, the Garda Síochána and the Defence Forces. In addition, the Commission endorsed the government's plans to gaelicise the education system and gave its approval to measures designed to ensure that all the country's teachers were fluent in Irish. In particular, it supported the government's plans to gaelicise the training colleges and to establish preparatory colleges to assist this process.

The First National Programme had been in operation since 1922. The majority of teachers, however, were still struggling to learn the language and they were not helped by the zeal of the inspectors, whose increased pressure led to the holding of the Second National Programme Conference in 1926. This resulted in a number of modifications to the programme, which made life a little easier for the teachers, though the submissions of various inspectors to the conference portrayed an almost Dickensian picture of the average school. They also clearly demonstrated the folly of the Department in squandering scarce resources on an unrealistic and over-ambitious gaelicisation policy. The submissions clearly reveal the strained relations between managers and inspectors, and between inspectors and teachers, which existed in the second half of the 1920s. In addition they show the context in which the preparatory students were to work as teachers and clearly demonstrated the need for teachers to be fluent Irish speakers, which was one of the primary reasons for establishing the preparatory colleges.

Much of the work of *Coimisiún na Gaeltachta* was influenced by Ernest Blythe, the most dedicated Gaeilgeoir in the government, and its report resonated with many of his ideas. While it had little effect in preventing the Gaeltacht from declining further, its recommendations regarding the gaelicisation of the public service made sufficient impact to give the required appearance of a new and culturally different state. This satisfied the aspirations of the most ardent members of the Gaelic League. It also effected sufficient change to assuage those, who suffering from a post-colonial mentality, needed to assert a new cultural identity.

The Commission's findings about the Gaeltacht were alarming. The report found that the total loss of Irish speakers over seven counties during 1911–25 was 137,509 or almost 32 per cent.[1] Furthermore, the picture of life portrayed in the Gaeltacht was dismal – not only was the number of native speakers declining, but the quality of life was depressing and without hope. Native speakers lived, mainly, in remote parts of the country with no infrastructure and few employment opportunities. There was little chance of education and such primary teaching as they received was inadequate. In addition, the school itself was likely to be in a remote area, small, unsanitary, badly heated and poorly equipped. Even this poor education did not continue beyond the age of 12, when Gaeltacht children had to work on the family holding. For the native speaker there were few prospects other than a life of drudgery unless he learned English and emigrated. The commission was quite clear that if social conditions did not improve the language would die.

A further cause for concern was the low esteem which native speakers had for the language itself. Indeed, the perception that positions of influence were held by those who spoke English encouraged the learning of English by the more ambitious. To combat this perception, the Commission made a series of wide-ranging recommendations to improve the standing of the language in the Gaeltacht generally. Many of them dealt with education, particularly the provision of facilities at primary level. They also stipulated

---

1. *Report of Coimisiún na Gaeltachta*, p. 10.

that only Irish-speaking teachers were to teach in Gaeltacht schools, and that free secondary education should be provided by establishing schools of continuation education. To ensure that Gaeltacht students could pursue third-level courses, it proposed that UCG be gaelicised. Finally, it gave effect to Blythe's doctrine that native speakers must be shown that Irish pays,[2] by approving a series of grants and loans to improve living conditions in the Gaeltacht.

EVIDENCE GIVEN TO THE COMMISSION

The commission produced its report in July 1926. Subsequently, a major policy document, *Statement of Government Policy on the Recommendations of Coimisiún na Gaeltachta presented to both Houses of the Oireachtas by Order of the Executive Council,* was published. Amongst those who gave evidence to the commission was Ó Brolcháin, who made a submission to the Commission on 17 April 1925. He was questioned about the progress of the government's plan to gaelicise primary education. He illustrated the Department's difficulties in trying to gaelicise the training colleges, which were seen as having a key role in supplying Irish-speaking teachers. Much of the teaching in the training colleges was through English and staff could not be changed at short notice. It was to overcome these difficulties that the preparatory colleges, where the curriculum was to be entirely in Irish, were to be set up.

Furthermore, Ó Brolcháin revealed that the state's control of the training colleges was limited because of the way in which the system operated and the power of the Catholic Church. Although state-financed and subject to government regulations regarding the prescribed programmes for entrants and the course of teaching, the training colleges were essentially 'private institutions'. All but one of them, the Church of Ireland Training College in Kildare Place (see chapter 7) were owned by the Catholic Church. This reflected the conservative nature of the government whose ministers appear to have readily accepted the church's claim that it had the primary responsibility for overseeing the training of teachers:

> We wish to assert the great fundamental principle that the only satisfactory system of education for Catholics is one, wherein Catholic children are taught in Catholic schools, by Catholic teachers, under Catholic control.[3]

With regard to financing the preparatory colleges, Ó Brolcháin revealed that it was hoped that the local authorities would assist the central authority by financing scholarships for needy pupils. Why this did not happen is not clear, for the method eventually devised to finance the system was to be

---

2. Jones, The Preparatory Colleges, p. 34.
3. Statement by the Central Council of the Catholic Primary Managers' Association in 1922, quoted in Ó Buachalla, p. 211.

extremely costly. Ó Brolcháin also defended the expenditure on summer courses for teachers to learn Irish and informed the Commission that almost all primary schools in the state were teaching Irish.

The Department's Secondary Education Branch was represented by Seóirse Mac Niocaill,[4] a zealous language enthusiast and a Protestant. Remarks made by him at a public meeting shortly after the announcement of the establishment of the preparatory colleges caused a furore, and led to a public rebuke:

> We are going to drive the English language out of Ireland. Why should English be on an equal footing with Irish? Going to see that every child born in Ireland will speak its mother tongue. Every hog, dog and devil will have to learn it.[5]

His subsequent failure to be appointed secretary of the Department may have been due to this outburst, though it has been attributed to his religion.[6] Mac Niocaill told the commission:

> Our policy is to encourage education entirely through Irish ultimately. Bilingualism we only regard as a step to that method of instruction …. We do not recognise bilingual schools as a permanent institution.[7]

He informed the Commission that the Department had considered introducing oral examinations but had decided these were not necessary as 'you couldn't teach a subject without it being done orally in Irish'. It was unfortunate that his views were accepted. Had an oral examination been instituted, it would have helped to focus attention on speaking the language.

RECOMMENDATIONS AND GOVERNMENT RESPONSE

To speed up the process of producing fluent Irish-speaking teachers, the Commission proposed that Gaeltacht boys and girls of 16 years of age, and upwards, be recruited for a short preparatory course at some of the training colleges before entering training. It also proposed the provision of a two-year course at preparatory colleges for students who had completed the Intermediate Certificate Examination and who were competent in Irish. These proposals would have ensured that students entered training colleges with sufficient spoken Irish to enable the work of the training colleges to be through Irish. Although they were worthy of implementation, the government's response was half-hearted. Had they been implemented, the costs of the preparatory system would have been considerably reduced.

---

4. For biographical details see the Appendix.
5. *The Irish School Weekly*, 6 March 1926, p. 300.
6. Ó Broin, *Just like yesterday*, p. 69.
7. *Report of Coimisiún na Gaeltachta*, p. 9.

To improve the standard of education in the Gaeltacht, the Commission recommended that only teachers with fluent knowledge of Irish be employed in Gaeltacht schools and demanded the removal of teachers who were unable to speak Irish after specified periods. The government's response, however, was fearful that such actions would 'arouse very serious opposition from teachers'. The offer of worthwhile compensation would have helped to solve this problem. The government also showed its fear of the Catholic Church. The removal of teachers, it said, might 'easily give rise to grave questions about the powers and rights of managers'.[8] These responses showed a lack of determination on the government's part to take worthwhile action to improve education in the Gaeltacht.

To overcome the lack of suitable textbooks for Gaeltacht schools, a standard set of cost-price readers, in English, was recommended. This, in the government's view, was 'acceptable in principle, but not feasible at present, due to serious practical difficulties', which in reality meant that it would not provide the necessary finance.

To remedy the lack of secondary education in the Gaeltacht, the Commission proposed that a number of free secondary day schools be established in Irish-speaking districts and in partly Irish-speaking districts, but the government's response was negative, with no reference to plans to introduce its long-awaited school attendance legislation:

> Owing to the poverty of the vast majority of people in the Gaeltacht it is very difficult in the present circumstances to induce parents in those districts to send their children to secondary schools. It is necessary for the children to earn their livelihood and to supplement the family income from the age of 12 onwards. One of the difficulties to be surmounted is compelling them to send their children to primary school up to the age of 14. Where parents show desire the government is prepared to consider providing in the Gaeltacht, as done elsewhere, finance for secondary education in the advanced classes of the larger existing primary schools in each of the Commission's recommendations in paragraph 68.

A proposal that a system of scholarships be established met a similar response. The likely explanation for this reaction was the government's fear that the provision of free secondary education in the Gaeltacht would lead to similar claims from the Galltacht. As one historian commented, 'An approach towards equality of educational opportunity was too high a price to pay for the gaelicisation of Ireland.'[9] The government may have also feared that had free secondary education been provided, Gaeltacht students would have availed of it rather than entering the preparatory colleges. The Commission also proposed that schools of rural continuation education[10] be established and that financial inducements be provided to encourage prestigious secondary schools, such as

8. Statement of Government Policy, p. 5.
9. Lee, *Ireland 1912-1985: Politics and Society*, p. 135.
10. Statement of Government Policy, pp. 10 and 11.

Clongowes Wood College and Castleknock College, to become 'A' schools (all-Irish schools). The latter recommendation reflected Blythe's determination to raise the standing of the Irish language.

To ensure that Gaeltacht students received third-level education, it was proposed that UCG become an Irish-speaking university. The government's response was that it had no control over the university, though it was expected 'UCG would try'.[11] The Commission also proposed that all officials in Irish-speaking areas, such as policemen and postal workers, should be Irish speakers, and where people knew Irish the language should be used in administration. Other areas of the public service were considered, including the Defence Forces, where it was proposed that one brigade of the army should be Irish-speaking and that all future officers should know Irish for promotion.[12] Many of the Commission's proposals showed a lack of realism and a failure to understand certain realities of Gaeltacht life. The proposal that places be reserved for policemen from the Gaeltacht was met with disdain by the secretary of the Department of Justice:

> During the civil war the western seaboard was controlled by the Irregular side and while a native speaker might not be an Irregular or a supporter of them, he was overawed by them. The time will come when they will get sense but, at the moment, we would not take a man, who had been blowing up our barracks the day before.[13]

It was also shown to have been unrealistic, as comments by Éamonn Coogan,[14] deputy commissioner of the Garda Síochána, show:

> We wanted 500 native speakers but there are only 195 in the Garda Síochána. To help with Irish we have four primary teachers who have been doing nothing but teaching men things they should have learned at school. We are spending four-and-a-half million pounds on education in the Saorstát and we cannot justify teaching men in the depot, things they should have got out of the four-and-a-half million.[15]

A major part of the gaelicisation policy focused on the civil service. As early as May 1922, the Provisional Government had ordered that the civil service should use Irish where possible,[16] and the Commission made a number of significant recommendations in this regard, including that all entrants to the civil service must possess a qualification in Irish for promotion and that a quarter of vacancies be reserved for native speakers. The Commission also

---

11. *Ibid.*, par. 29, p. 11.
12. *Ibid.*, No. 48.
13. *Report of Coimisiún na Gaeltachta,* Appendix p. 1.
14. For biographical details see the Appendix.
15. *Ibid.,* p. 2.
16. Memo on Irish in the Civil Service, National Archives, Provisional Government Minutes, S9604.

recommended that a special committee be established to see that all departments carried out government policy with regard to the language.[17]

In an attempt to promote the gaelicisation policy among the public generally, it was proposed that people be encouraged to use the Irish form of personal names. The importance of Gaeltacht culture was stressed in this somewhat exaggerated claim:

> The commission realises that in the memories, stories, folklore, songs and traditions of the Gaeltacht, there is preserved an uninterrupted Gaelic culture which constitutes the very soul of the Irish language. The native Irish speaker has a command of language, which is inculcated amongst English speakers only by the laboured teaching of the classics. There is no parallel in English for the refined popular culture which is the highly wrought product of generations of Gaelic civilisation.[18]

The anti-English sentiment in this statement encapsulated the thinking of many of the new state's leaders, and was typical of the manner in which newly emergent post-colonial nations bolster their own self-image as part of building up the ideology of a newly independent state. Yet for all their claims the Commission did not call for the re-establishment of a Ministry for Irish, or the establishment of a Department of the Gaeltacht. Their failure to do so would indicate that their hopes for the revival of the language were pinned on the government supporting their proposals for the gaelicisation of the education system and the civil service.

Though the report touched almost every area of life in the country, there was only a brief reference to one of the most powerful institutions in the state, the Catholic Church. Paragraph 79 recommended that the Executive Council draw the attention of the ecclesiastical authorities to the gaelicisation policy, and 'invite their co-operation'. This attitude was similar to that displayed by the Ministry for Irish in the 1920s.[19] It illustrated once again the timidity of the new state's leaders, who were afraid to suggest that the most powerful person in an Irish-speaking area, the parish priest, should be an Irish speaker. One can only speculate as to what would have happened had the Catholic Church vigorously opposed the government's gaelicisation policy, or how successful it would have been, if the church had endorsed it wholeheartedly.

One of the church's over-riding concerns at that time was the production of English-speaking personnel for its missionary endeavours, and this contributed to its lack of interest in the revival. Though there always were some priests who were ardent Gaeilgeoirí, the attitude of individual members of the hierarchy varied. Unfortunately, few bishops were concerned to send Irish-speaking priests to Gaeltacht parishes, while others made promises and

17. Statement of Government Policy, No. 82, p. 25.
18. *Report of Coimisiún na Gaeltachta*, p. 23, No. 79.
19. See Part I, chapter 1.

failed to keep them. Another response to requests that only Irish-speaking priests be appointed in the Gaeltacht was that it was the prerogative of the bishop to make such decisions and his business only.[20] A further concern about the church's role in Irish-speaking areas was that all priests, including native speakers, were educated in St Patrick's College, Maynooth, an English-speaking institution which showed little regard for the church's mission in the Gaeltacht.

ASSESSING THE EFFECTS OF *COIMISIÚN NA GAELTACHTA*

What effect did the Commission's proposals have? The government's response was significant for the number of times it undertook to accept or to consider a recommendation. Such acceptance, however, was often just a means of delaying decision-making. Certain recommendations were, indeed, put into effect, but often only in a minimal way. For example, regarding scholarships to secondary schools, a scheme of scholarships for Fíor-Ghaeltacht pupils[21] was devised, but this was limited to 15 students in total. To receive a scholarship a student had to satisfy certain conditions and to pass an examination, similar to the annual entrance examination for preparatory colleges. This limited its impact and appeal amongst the majority of students.

The scheme was reviewed in 1931 by the noted Irish scholar, Seoirse Mac Tomáis,[22] who identified 'the apathy of the native speaker' as its greatest weakness.[23] A response to his memo was drawn up by Professor Liam Ó Briain of UCG, who stressed that it was not sufficient to save the language in the Gaeltacht; consideration had also to be given to the Galltacht, and particularly to ensuring that a wide range of reading material in Irish was available cheaply.[24] The failure to provide reading material in Irish was one of the major failings of the gaelicisation policy and stemmed originally from 'Sceilg's' decision in 1919.[25] Furthermore, it was compounded by the failure to provide adequate finance to implement the policy. The shortage of reading material affected the preparatory colleges, where, due to the lack of textbooks, students depended on notes translated by teachers from English textbooks.

The Commission's proposals regarding the recruitment of 16-year-old Gaeltacht students for special two-year courses before entering the training colleges, were later shown to have been unrealistic, as there were few suitable candidates:

---

20. MacAonghusa, 'Mar a chuaigh an Conradh i bhfeidhm ar an nGaeltacht,' in *The Gaelic League Idea,* ed. Ó Tuama, p. 79.
21. Memo on 'A scheme of scholarships in secondary schools for pupils from the Fíor-Ghaeltacht,' UCD Archives, Blythe Papers, P24/303.
22. For biographical details of people named on this page see the Appendix.
23. Memo by Seoirse Mac Tomáis, (George Thomson). UCD Archives Blythe Papers, P24/303.
24. Response by Ó Briain to the memo by MacTomáis, UCD Archives, Blythe Papers, P24/303.
25. See chapter I.

Probably about 25 such students for each of the next two years would exhaust the number of Gaeltacht pupils who might have applied to become monitors but for the abolition of the monitorial scheme.[26]

This was an important admission for it clearly contradicted Corcoran's view, expressed at the First National Programme Conference, and on which much of the policy for the gaelicisation of education was based.

In all the efforts to restore the language a leading role was played by Blythe. He was mainly responsible for the establishment of the preparatory colleges and he monitored their development with great care. He also took great interest in seeing how the recommendations of *Coimisiún na Gaeltachta* were implemented and kept a careful watch on other departments. Blythe strongly believed that that the standing of the language could be improved through showing that fluency in Irish led to financial rewards. Yet paradoxically he rejected many of the Commission's proposals that involved financial expenditure. The government's refusal to invest sufficient finance in the gaelicisation policy, however, was probably due more to the state's poor economic condition than to Blythe's attitude to government spending. He was unfortunate in being in charge of finance during this difficult period. Indeed, some of his decisions as Minister for Finance were disastrous, and his decision to reduce primary teachers' salaries by 10 per cent in 1923 contributed significantly to teacher discontent in the early years of the state.

USE OF THE IRISH LANGUAGE IN THE CIVIL SERVICE

The Report of the Inter-Departmental Committee on Irish in the Civil Service published in 1934, revealed the ineffectiveness of the Commission's recommendation to gaelicise the civil service. Despite the introduction in 1925 of an Irish test at all open competition examinations for civil service appointments (certain minor grades, such as clerks and messengers, did not have an Irish examination), the committee reported:

> The majority of civil servants find little occasion to use Irish. Occasional letters in Irish from the public. Translated into English. Decisions in English and answers translated into Irish.[27]

No more than 20 school managers wrote to the Department in Irish, while only 11 officials in the primary branch were 'thoroughly Irish-using'. As results on the ground did not match ideology in government circles, the language policy became the subject of growing public scepticism. Indeed, as one writer put it: 'Time was to prove that the public service, like the letter

---

26. DE, 20302, Box 438, NA.
27. *Report of Inter-Departmental Committee on Irish in the Civil Service,* UCD Archives, Blythe Papers, P/24/927.

boxes, had merely been painted green.'[28] The Commission's proposals that native speakers should receive grants and loans were not satisfactory either, for they led to the development of a hand-out mentality and cultivated a dependency culture in the Gaeltacht. An aspect of the situation which caused resentment among the general public was the fact that in the years following the implementation of the Commission's recommendations, promotion in the civil service was often bestowed for proficiency in Irish, rather than on merit, a fact acknowledged by Blythe in 1931:

> For other public services, central or local, for which there was not a sufficient supply of such candidates those with a knowledge of Irish were placed in a <u>pref-erential position</u>.[29]

Efforts to gaelicise the civil service were unsuccessful, but it was many years before this was acknowledged publicly. Indeed, it was not until 1963 that the *Report of the Commission for the Restoration of the Irish Language* admitted that the requirement for civil servants to have Irish on entry to the public service, and the subsequent failure to use the language, was a mistake. In addition it censured the state and the Catholic Church for not giving 'an unequivocal lead' in the use of Irish in the Gaeltacht.

Even the inspectors who were to implement the government's language policy were limited in their knowledge of the language. Most of them had been inherited from the previous regime when Irish was not part of the political agenda. With the introduction of the gaelicisation policy, many inspectors left for Northern Ireland. A memo on the inspectorate from Ó Brolcháin to the Minister for Education in 1923 reported:

> Of the 11 senior inspectors two are competent with bilingual schools, one is competent to deal with Irish in ordinary schools and is learning Irish. One has quite a good reading knowledge and understands spoken Irish. Two are learning Irish and will soon be fit to inspect Irish classes. In a year's time we will be able to count on nine or perhaps ten or eleven of the seniors to be able to deal with Irish classes and six or seven (including three new appointments) to deal with bilingual schools.[30]

Relationships between inspectors and teachers tended to be uneasy and they became further strained by efforts to ensure the implementation of the gaelicisation policy in the schools. Ó Brolcháin's replacements were language enthusiasts who, because of their own quick progress in the language, had little sympathy for teachers struggling with Irish. There were growing numbers of complaints from teachers regarding inspectors' demands. This was despite the INTO's understanding that teachers' difficulties would be taken into consideration in the implementation of the new programme. It was also

---

28. Coogan, *Ireland since the Rising*, p. 189.
29. Letter from Blythe to O'Neill, UCD Archives, Blythe Papers P24/442.
30. Memo regarding proposed changes in Inspection Staff, UCD Archives, MacNeill Papers, LAI/H/134.

understood that it would be a decade or more before the full operation of the programme could be expected.

THE SECOND NATIONAL PROGRAMME CONFERENCE 1926

Teachers became increasingly unhappy with the zeal of the inspectors in implementing the National Programme, particularly with regard to Irish. It was obvious to them that its expectations were unrealistic and there were many calls for its review. This increased dissatisfaction forced the INTO to organise another programme conference. Its terms of reference were to report to the Minister of Education on the suitability of the National Programme of Primary Instruction and to recommend those changes considered necessary.

The Second National Programme Conference commended the National Programme, though it made some significant modifications to it, including 'higher' and 'lower' courses in Irish and English. It made little criticism of the Department, though it did point out that a more gradual approach to the implementation of the programme should be adopted.

Submissions from a number of inspectors clearly demonstrated the unrealistic approach of those who put the gaelicisation policy into operation. Furthermore, they agreed that certain factors made the teaching of Irish difficult. These included irregular attendance of pupils, teachers' lack of knowledge of the language, poor teaching methods and the lack of interest in the language shown by parents, managers, and even some inspectors, who continuously asked: 'What use is Irish?' The inspectors also portrayed a grim picture of the schools attended by the vast majority of the country's children and showed the need for a large amount of money to be spent in this area. Yet such was the government's desire to gaelicise education that it was quite happy to spend scarce resources on summer courses for teachers to learn Irish and on establishing the preparatory colleges.

While some inspectors were loath to admit that the level of general proficiency in all subjects had declined, others claimed that there had been no deterioration in the teaching of English, and that proficiency in oral English was no worse than it had been before the introduction of Irish. With regard to teaching other subjects through Irish, there was general agreement that the teaching of history and geography had not been successful, as neither the teachers nor the pupils had sufficient command of the language. The reports showed that due to the emphasis on Irish, the curriculum was restricted to the basic subjects; drawing had disappeared almost entirely, while vocal music was confined to the singing of songs, which were almost universally in Irish.

The list of experts selected for oral examination of their views was headed by Corcoran, so it was not surprising that *The Report and Programme of the Second National Programme Conference*, signed on 5 March 1926, commended the national programme and affirmed the ideal which it set before schools. The report acknowledged that the teachers' apprehensions about the programme had not been 'unintelligent', and accepted that its working was beset 'with difficulties involving an undue strain on teachers'. It refused, however, to admit that the reason for this lay in the programme, and in particular with its insistence on teaching through Irish. Instead, it endorsed this policy saying:

> The members of the conference agreed on the supreme importance of giving effect as far as possible to this principle; and in confirmation of this belief they received authoritative evidence. It was argued with much weight that a 'direct' method of Irish teaching continued during the length of an ordinary school day for a few years between the ages of four and eight would be quite sufficient – given trained and fluent teachers – to impart to children a vernacular power over the language. While in the case of older children it was shown that such a result would be more difficult of attainment.[31]

The 'authoritative evidence', which was not included in the report, most likely refers to Corcoran, who was a staunch advocate of teaching infants through Irish only. Evidently, he spoke convincingly on the topic, for the report went on:

> Members of the conference were at onc in holding that the true and only method of establishing Irish as a vernacular is the effective teaching of it to the infants.

Nevertheless, the 1926 Second National Programme Conference modified the policy of teaching infants through Irish only by allowing English to be taught before 10.30 am and after 2.00 pm, and proposed the introduction of higher and lower courses in both Irish and English in older classes during the transition period. It also acknowledged that efforts to teach history, geography or mathematics through Irish had resulted in an indifferent teaching of these subjects and 'adverse criticism of the general teaching standard of our schools'. To allow for the demands of teaching through Irish, courses in these subjects were reduced.

The report defended the reduced curriculum on the grounds that account had to be taken of the difficulties entailed by efforts to restore Irish as a vernacular and it expressed confidence that 'these temporary difficulties will be more than counterbalanced by the better mental development which a command of two languages confers upon young children'. The lack of realism here contrasted with the descriptions of the conditions of the schools, which it said 'were often such as gravely to impair the quality of the work done in them', with faulty sanitary arrangements, poor provision for heating and cleaning and often no proper playgrounds.

---

31. *Report and Programme of the Second National Programme*, p. 7.

INFANTS' SCHOOLS AND INFANTS' DEPARTMENTS OF SCHOOLS.

JUNIOR INFANTS.

LANGUAGE.

Conversation, object and picture lessons, story-telling, and recitation, all used for the purpose of training the children to understand Irish and to speak it distinctly and correctly as their natural language.

(The following details are merely suggested as a guide to teachers when drawing up their own plans. It is to be clearly understood that all the details below need not necessarily be included in each plan).

A. *Where all work between* 10.30 *and* 2 *is done in Irish* :—

1. Simple lessons identifying objects, and the asking and answering of simple questions as to their colour, location, etc. This to be alternated with the memorising of about half a dozen rhymes, dialogues, or short stories, such as can be wholly or very largely illustrated by actions or pictures, with a general (not word-for-word) understanding of their meaning, and ability to answer simple questions on them.

2. Pupils to know their Christian names, be able to ask and answer questions as to the location, colours, and other common properties of objects within view ; to use and answer common salutations or to ask and answer questions about the weather, their health, their clothes, and the principal parts of the body. While no grammatical form required by the correct idiom of the expressions occurring in

5 *Second National Programme Conference Report*, 1926 p. 22.

★ ★ ★

Once the Second National Programme was accepted by the Minister for Education, John Marcus O'Sullivan,[32] as the official programme for use in all schools in May 1926, many of the teachers' grievances were removed. The production of a new series of *Notes for Teachers* in the school year 1932–33 was a further help in reducing friction over the teaching of Irish. The notes were used, not only in the schools, but also in the training colleges, and they continued to be used until the 1960s when new methods were introduced.

KEY DECISIONS REGARDING THE PREPARATORY COLLEGES

After the official announcement on 11 June 1925 that the preparatory colleges were to be established, many decisions had to be taken regarding the

32. For biographical details see the Appendix.

premises in which the individual colleges were to be housed and the criteria for staffing and student selection. The most urgent task for the Department was finding suitable premises so that the colleges could be established as soon as possible. Three conditions were laid down for selecting premises: they were to be in the Gaeltacht, large enough for a school of about 100 pupils, and available for immediate use, as the Department wanted the colleges to open at the beginning of the 1926 school year. This meant establishing some of the colleges in temporary premises. The Department's long-term intention was that they would be show-pieces for Irish education and no expense was to be spared to fulfil this aim.

A number of state agencies owned large houses and the Board of Works was entrusted with the task of examining them and other potential choices. These included Ring College, Co. Waterford; Ballinskelligs Cable Station and Burnham House, Co. Kerry; Furbough House, Galway; Ballyconnell House, Co. Donegal; Swastika House, a former orphanage at Spiddal, Co. Galway; Ebor House, near Cong; and St Mary's Monastery, Tourmakeady, Co. Mayo. Most of them, however, failed to fulfil the three conditions, and eventually the list of likely premises was reduced to Ballyconnell House, Ring College, Furbough House, Ballinskelligs Cable Station and Burnham House.

Burnham House, an imposing mansion at Ventry, near Dingle in the Kerry Gaeltacht, was quickly chosen to house Coláiste Íde. The former home of the De Moleyn family, Barons of Ventry, the house was sold to the Land Commission in 1922. As early as May 1924, the bishop of Kerry had approached the Sisters of Mercy in Tralee with a proposal that the order establish the Munster girls' college.[33] For the nuns, the choice lay between Burnham House and the abandoned Cable Station at Ballinskelligs. The former was chosen as it was in a good state of repair with 45 rooms. As it was owned by the Land Commission, it could be used immediately.

The former premises of Marlborough Street Training College, Marlborough House and Marlborough Hall, at Glasnevin in Dublin were chosen in

Preparatory College, Dingle. 1924→27

On the 23ʳᵈ May, 1924, his Lordship, most Reverend Doctor O'Sullivan, paid a short, but momentous visit to St. John's. It was for no other purpose, than to acquaint Reverend mother mary Elizabeth Moynihan, that the minister of Education proposed establishing Preparatory

6 A page from the *Annals of Coláiste Íde. Courtesy The Mercy Order.*

---

33. *Annals of the Sisters of Mercy*, St John's Convent, Tralee.

7 Burnham House, Ventry, Co. Kerry.

March 1925.[34] Though not in the Gaeltacht, they were owned by the Department of Defence and were considered very suitable as they would require little expenditure. As they were unoccupied, they could be used almost immediately. A letter from Ó Brolcháin to Archbishop Byrne shows that it was envisaged that Marlborough Hall would be for Catholic girls, while Marlborough House would be for Protestant girls with classes for all in Marlborough Hall. When this was not possible, MacNeill proposed setting up a separate college for Protestants. As Marlborough House could accommodate only 50 students and it was envisaged that 75 places would be necessary, it was decided that the Protestant college would occupy the premises temporarily, while a new college was built. Meanwhile, it was decided to establish Coláiste Chaoimhín, a college for Catholic boys, in Marlborough Hall. This was to open in September 1926, but it was not ready until 1 March 1927.[35]

Marlborough Hall had a chequered history. An imposing Gothic structure, from 1908–1917 it was a residence for male students of the non-denominational Marlborough Street Training College. From April 1917 to 1922 it was used by the British Army as a convalescent home for wounded British soldiers. In March 1922 the building transferred to the newly-formed Irish Free State Army Medical Service, who used it as a convalescent home

---

34. DF Papers, S20/9/25.
35. *Análacha Choláiste Chaoimhín*, St, Helen's Christian Brothers' Provincialate, York Road, Dun Laoghaire.

for soldiers wounded in the civil war. Later that year it was used to house refugees from the pogroms in Belfast. In 1924 the Irish Army left Marlborough Hall and it remained unoccupied until Coláiste Chaoimhín opened there.

In its haste to get the other four colleges started in the Gaeltacht, the Department made some strange decisions with little regard for cost, convenience or the students' welfare. It was not unusual for students to start in one college and later to be transferred to another. Often students from Co. Kerry were sent to the Donegal college, because of a shortage of places in Coláiste Íde, while some of the early classes in Coláiste na Mumhan had students from the Donegal Gaeltacht. This led to requests from parents to the principals of the colleges to keep the students over the holidays as they could not afford the fares home and overnight accommodation in Dublin. It also led to a complaint from a teacher in Co. Kerry that parents could not allow their children to sit the entrance examination because of the cost of travel to Donegal. Furthermore, the inaccessibility of the colleges created difficulties for students requiring hospital treatment and led to a dispute between the Departments of Education and Finance as to who should pay for the treatment.[36]

Despite the support of Blythe, the Department of Finance continuously questioned Ó Brolcháin's decisions, resulting in endless bureaucracy and delay. Five of the seven colleges opened in temporary premises. Only Coláiste Chaoimhín and Coláiste Íde started in their permanent locations.

An t-Óglách"]   *[Exclusive Photo.*
Marlborough Hall, Glasnevin, which is being utilised as a Convalescent Home for sick and wounded soldiers.

8 Marlborough Hall in the 1920s. *Courtesy Department of Defence.*

36. DF Papers, S25/11/28.

Dates of Opening of the seven Preparatory Colleges

COLLEGE	LOCATION	DATE	FIRST CLASS	RUN BY
C. Chaoimhín	Glasnevin	1 March 1927	63 students	Christian Brothers
C Íde	Ventry	1 March 1927	47 students	Mercy Sisters
C. Moibhí	Glasnevin	25 April, 1927	20 students	Lay Staff
C. Bhríde	Letterkenny	23 May 1927	24 students	Loreto Sisters
C. Mhuire	Letterkenny	24 October 1927	49 students	Mercy Sisters
C. Éinde	Furbough	23 October 1928	29 students	Diocesan priests
C. na Mumhan	Mallow	24 October 1928	34 students	De La Salle Brothers

Source: *Department of Finance Papers, S20/3/27*

POOR ORGANISATION

The establishment of the colleges was characterised by poor organisation and a failure to realise that temporary short-term arrangements would last longer than anticipated. The remoteness of the Gaeltacht was a further delaying factor. An example of this was the decision to locate Coláiste Bhríde at Ballyconnell House at Falcarragh in the Donegal Gaeltacht. Built around 1763 in the heart of a magnificently wooded park of 500 acres, it was the former residence of the Olphert family. During the War of Independence they left the area and the house was unoccupied for some time. In 1921 it was taken over by the Irish Republican Brotherhood. The following year the Free State Army commandeered the house for use as a barracks.[37] The house and lands were bought by the Commissioners of Public Works in 1926. The Department planned to extend the house by adding three large wings, a chapel, a large study and a science room. As it could not be got ready for some time, temporary accommodation had to be found. Coláiste Bhríde opened in May 1927 with 24 students in temporary accommodation in Rockhill House (home of Sir Charles Stewart) in Letterkenny. The following October it moved to Ballyconnell House.

Rita Nic Chába, one of the first students at Coláiste Bhríde, recalled her time there:

I well remember the first day I came to C. Bhríde, then located at Rockhill House outside Letterkenny. My mother and I travelled by train from Drogheda on a bright May morning. When we reached Letterkenny a taxi quickly brought us to the college where we were graciously received by Mother de Lourdes and Mother Melissa. Mother Melissa had a loud speaking voice and I was rather in

---

37. I am indebted to Dr Seosamh Kelly for this information.

9 Ballyconnell House, Falcarragh, Co Donegal.

awe of her. I remember thinking to myself. She's very nice today but what will she be like tomorrow. I need not have worried. She was always lovely. I was not the first arrival. Bridie Hanmore from Roscommon was already there. She had come, by mistake a week too soon but the good nuns looked after her until the opening day.

Even when renovated, Ballyconnell House had neither gas nor electricity and was lit by paraffin lamps. As it could accommodate only 47 students and five teachers, a second branch of Coláiste Bhríde was established temporarily in Talbot House in Dublin. The role of Talbot House was crucial in getting the system started, and between 1928 and 1933, three preparatory colleges in succession were temporarily housed there. It was not until August 1930, later than anticipated, that Ballyconnell House was ready for more students, and the students at Talbot House were distributed between Coláiste Íde and Coláiste Bhríde.

St Mary's Monastery, Tourmakeady, Co. Mayo, was chosen as the location for Coláiste Mhuire. Situated on the shores of Lough Mask in the shadow of the Partry mountains it was in one of the most picturesque parts of the country. During the Famine the Franciscans came to work in the area and built a monastery and two schools there. As these buildings were unsuitable, the Department planned a purpose-built school for Coláiste Mhuire. Since this would take some time, the Department started Coláiste Mhuire in Rockhill House in Co. Donegal in October 1927, as soon as Coláiste Bhríde had moved to its permanent premises in Falcarragh. Dates for the completion for Coláiste Mhuire were again wrong, and in September 1930 it moved temporarily to Talbot House, where it remained, until its new building in remote Tourmakeady was finally completed in February 1931.

10 Coláiste Mhuire, Tourmakeady, Co Mayo.

In October 1928, the Connacht boys' college, Coláiste Éinde, opened in Furbough House, Galway. Four years later, difficulties arose over the title to the house, and the Department decided to relocate the college to Salthill. As this building was not ready until 1937, the college had to find a new home and it moved to Talbot House following Coláiste Mhuire's vacating of the premises there. There it stayed until 1934 when it moved to Coláiste Moibhí's old premises at Marlborough House and Glasnevin House. Three years later it finally moved to its new premises at Salthill.

Originally, the Department planned to locate the Munster boys' college, Coláiste na Mumhan, at Ring College in the Waterford Gaeltacht. But this decision was changed in 1927,[38] when it was decided that it would be housed in a purpose-built school in Ballyvourney in the West Cork Gaeltacht. Meanwhile, temporary accommodation had to be found for the college. The choice of Avondhu House, Mallow, was due to an initiative taken by the provincial of the De La Salle Order, Br Joseph Hannigan, who offered the order's premises on a temporary basis until the Ballyvourney college was built.[39] To ensure a good supply of candidates for its training college in Waterford the order had bought Avondhu House in 1920 to use as a private preparatory college. The government responded coolly to Hannigan's offer, informing him that the order would have to obtain the approval of the bishop of Cloyne before a new preparatory college could be located in his diocese. It was some time before the bishop's approval could be obtained as relations between the order and the bishop had been strained due to complaints about the students. Eventually, arrangements were made by the Commissioners of Public Works to rent Avondhu House from the order and in October 1928, Coláiste na Mumhan opened there. This temporary arrangement lasted until 1940.

The Department's lack of experience in school management showed in the failure to consider the needs of students when making decisions. Nowhere

---

38. Ó Domhnaill, *Iolscoil na Mumhan Coláiste na Rinne Geárr-stair*, p. 79.
39. *De La Salle Records of all the Communities in Ireland*, De La Salle Archives.

11 (a) The entrance to Avondhu House, Mallow, home to Coláiste na Mumhan. (b) All that remains of Coláiste na Mumhan following a fire in the 1970s.

was consideration given to the difficulties involved in moving a school from campus to campus, or as in the case of Coláiste Bhríde, in running a school on two campuses such a distance apart; rather *ad hoc* decisions were made as problems occurred. As Talbot House had no playing fields, the Department rented grounds from Loreto College in North Great George's Street for the girls' colleges. These, however, were not suitable for the students from Coláiste Éinde, who used the Phoenix Park for recreation. The cost of bringing the boys to the park three times a week was of some significance, as many of them were from the Gaeltacht, and 'in very poor circumstances'. When the matter was brought to Ó Brolcháin's [40] attention, he proposed a grant of £20 to cover their costs. A further request from the principal of Coláiste Éinde that fares should be paid for all the students resulted in the grant being increased to £75. This was a typical example of the generous manner in which Ó Brolcháin responded to requests from the preparatory colleges.

THE ROLE OF THE CHURCH

Throughout the history of the preparatory system the role of the hierarchy was important, particularly those bishops who were managers of the colleges. Arrangements at Talbot House were a cause of concern to the Catholic archbishop of Dublin, Dr Byrne. He supported the state's Irish language policy and could speak some Irish. Yet despite his support for the gaelicisation policy, disagreements arose between him and the Department over some of the temporary arrangements regarding the colleges in Dublin. Byrne was quick to express concern over the appointment of a chaplain to the Loreto Order while Coláiste Bhríde was in Talbot House:

> It is not the business of the education authorities to give directions to priests re duties – privilege of the archbishop. It is for the education authorities to put their requirements before the archbishop who will look into the matter and give directions to his priests as he thinks proper.[41]

Byrne showed his annoyance again when Ó Brolcháin requested permission for Coláiste Mhuire to move to Talbot House as the lease had expired on Rockhill House in 1930. A letter from Byrne stated: 'The archbishop does not approve of the transfer of C. Mhuire from Letterkenny to Talbot Street. These temporary arrangements appear to him to have a way of becoming permanent.' While he accepted that it was quite within the rights of the Department to place a college there without his approval, he did not want a religious community from outside the diocese to take charge of the college. Byrne was

---

40. DF Papers, S18/34/31.
41. Dublin Diocesan Archives, Byrne Papers.

further displeased when Coláiste Éinde moved to Talbot House in 1931. A memo to Ó Brolcháin stressed that the arrangement was not to last longer than two years and six months and went on:

> This scheme sets down an ecclesiastical state of things in Dublin, which is thoroughly undesirable and I see no reason why I should assent to it anytime. It was a cause of embarrassment to me when extern nuns were introduced. It is a far greater embarrassment to introduce secular priests, who are not my subjects.[42]

A further example of the archbishop's influence in education was clearly shown in his refusal to allow teachers trained in colleges outside his diocese to be appointed to posts in Dublin. This matter had been taken up by the INTO, without success. In 1932 the Minister for Education, John Marcus O'Sullivan, took it up with Byrne. He pointed out that at entry to training college preference was given to preparatory college students. This meant that Dublin students who had not been to preparatory college had to go to training colleges elsewhere. In 1933, Byrne agreed to accept candidates trained in Waterford and Limerick.

A more complex matter, however, was that of Catholic teachers who had trained in the non-denominational Marlborough Street Training College. Byrne would not allow them to teach in schools in his diocese. As early as May 1922, Micheál Ó hAodha,[43] Minister for Education in the Provisional Government, had written 'unofficially' to Byrne to 'obtain his advice as to the possibility of such teachers being allowed to teach in Catholic schools'. In 1931, O'Sullivan again asked for the policy to be modified.

THE DEPARTMENT'S STRATEGY

The Department under-estimated the costs of turning the colleges into educational show pieces, with first-class accommodation and facilities for extra-curricular activities. New buildings were planned for Coláiste Mhuire, Coláiste Moibhí and Coláiste na Mumhan, with large extensions for Coláiste Íde, Coláiste Bhríde and Coláiste Éinde. Coláiste Chaoimhín in Marlborough Hall was the only college which did not require large expenditure. By 1934, Coláiste na Mumhan and Coláiste Éinde were still not in permanent accommodation and the costs of establishing the colleges had seriously overrun the Department's earlier estimates. These had been estimated in August 1927 as £339,900.

This was greatly in excess of the original estimate of £150,000 given in the Dáil on 4 June 1926, and, not unreasonably, led to protests from the Department of Finance. In its defence the Department emphasised the large amounts of farm land attached to most of the properties. That the government was

---

42. *Ibid.*
43. For biographical details of people named on this page see the Appendix.

Costs of Preparatory Colleges

Preparatory College	Estimated 1927 £	1934 £
Marlborough Hall	12,600	15,500
Marlborough House	500	—
Burnham	57,600	64,275
Ballyconnell	61,500	68,103
Furbough	56,900	124,957
Tourmakeady	51,200	72,359
Munster	53,700	86,037
Protestant College, Dublin	44,800	44,650
Rockhill	1,100	—
TOTAL	**339,900**	**475,881**

Source: *Department of Finance Papers, S20/9/25*

willing to invest such large amounts of money shows the seriousness which it attached to the system and the importance of Blythe's support as Minister for Finance. It also showed the government's naivety in expecting to gaelicise the education system through seven colleges, with little money or resources put into other efforts. Furthermore, it is ironic that while so much of the exchequer's resources were being spent on the preparatory system, reductions were taking place in teachers' salaries. Yet the government seemed oblivious to rising teacher discontent, and from 1934 until the outbreak of the Second World War, agitation for the restoration of earlier salary scales formed one of the main activities of the INTO.

Government efforts in the Gaeltacht continued to focus on the effective use of propaganda and the cultivation of self-interest. Locating the colleges in imposing buildings, such as Burnham House and Ballyconnell House, owed much to Blythe's desire to raise the standing of the language amongst native speakers. That some of the colleges were so far removed from the nearest village as to make intercourse with native speakers almost impossible was not considered. Discipline was a further factor. A former student at Coláiste Íde recalled that students were never allowed out of the grounds. This contrasted with the way boys at Coláiste Chaoimhín in Glasnevin were treated in the early years of the college. An enthusiastic supporter of Gaelic games, the first principal, Br Hurley, allowed the students to go into town on Saturday afternoons and to attend sporting fixtures at Croke Park on Sundays.

OFFICIAL OPENING OF COLÁISTE CHAOIMHÍN

The significance attached by the young state to the preparatory system was shown at Coláiste Chaoimhín's official opening ceremony on 19 March 1927.

12 Burnham House with the coat of arms of Lord Ventry.

Coláiste Chaoimhín appears to have been the only college to have an opening ceremony that year (Coláiste Moibhí had an official opening ceremony in May 1934). This was probably because it was one of the first colleges to open, and the government wanted to use the occasion for propaganda purposes. It was also the only college to open in its permanent location without requiring an extension or major alterations. A further factor may have been that it opened in a building of some splendour in Dublin.

Addressing the assembled representatives of church and state, including W.T. Cosgrave and Archbishop Byrne, the Minister for Education, John Marcus O'Sullivan, spoke of 'the revolution in education' and enunciated the ideology behind the system:

> The training of a strong national character amongst our people is one of the greatest services that a Department like mine can render to the nation. As well as the purely intellectual side, we can not forget that the religious and moral aspects are also to be looked after .... By these preparatory colleges we hope to get a large number of teachers to instill the Irish language into the very outlook of their pupils.[44]

He stressed that in order to foster the spirit of nationalism, the colleges would be thoroughly Gaelic from the very start, and all staff, not just teachers but domestics and farm labourers, had to be Irish speakers. O'Sullivan emphasised that the main focus of language learning was to be based on the 'total immersion' method:

---

44. *The Christian Brothers' Educational Record, 1927*, p. 285. See also *Irish Times,* 21 March 1927.

The whole attitude of these colleges will be thoroughly Gaelic from the very start. Not merely will Irish be the language of the class-room, but they will live in an Irish atmosphere. In that way we hope to foster a spirit of nationalism, which even from the material point of view, is very important.

In his address, Cosgrave drew on the history of the early nation and recalled the college's patron saint, Caoimhín (Kevin), who founded a school at Glendalough. Recalling that Caoimhín had pioneered a new era, he sentimentally likened the principal of Coláiste Chaoimhín and his assistants to him, saying:

We are founding these colleges on the same principles and we are looking forward to similar results. We are laying the foundations of these colleges, firm in the spiritual tradition of the historic Irish nation, believing with Thomas Davis that 'the language of a nation's youth is the only easy and full speech for its age' and that 'a people without a language of its own is only half a nation'.[45]

The ideals expressed by Cosgrave and the florid language he used were typical of the government's simplistic approach to the gaelicisation policy.

In addition to the emphasis on nationalism, the ethos of the colleges was profoundly religious. Before a college opened, the local bishop had to be satisfied with arrangements for a chapel and a full-time chaplain. Each day began with Mass and ended with prayers. Once a week, chaplains heard confession and gave an address. They also took some religion classes and organised an annual three-day retreat, paid for by the Department. Ó Brolcháin showed the same readiness to provide funding for minority denominations, though their attitude to the students' religious formation was much less rigorous.

There was also a strong concentration on sporting activities, particularly in the boys' colleges. Typical of their attitude to sport was this account concerning Coláiste Chaoimhín:

The brothers soon had several teams playing hurling and Gaelic football and the college developed a name at sport, winning many championships. In 1929 and in 1930 they won the Leinster Senior Championship at football and in hurling in 1934. That same year, 1934, they won the Football and Hurling Championship for Christian Brothers' Schools. They repeated this feat at hurling the following year. This was mainly due to the brothers' enthusiasm for the game for the annals record that, while many of the pupils were from the Fíor-Ghaeltacht, most of them had never seen a hurley until they came to the college. Many of the students were chosen for inter-provincial or county teams. The college also won the Handball Championships many times.[46]

---

45. *Ibid.*
46. Ó Flaitile, 'Coláiste Chaoimhín', *An Réiltín*, Fómhar 1956.

An Br. Oir. D. L. ó Muirthile.

13 Br. Dónall Hurley, first principal of Coláiste Chaoimhín. *Courtesy The Christian Brothers.*

STAFFING THE COLLEGES

Finding teachers to staff the colleges could be problematic. The teaching staff appointed to Coláiste Chaoimhín included a principal, vice-principal and four teachers. It also had a lay brother, a chaplain and a medical officer. Domestic staff included a matron, a cook, five maids, a porter/messenger, a boiler man, a gardener and a labourer. The college also had its own doctor who paid weekly visits to check on the students' health, in addition to attending when requested by the principal. The Christian Brothers would have liked a post of bursar to have been included but this was refused by the Department. This was one of the few occasions when Ó Brolcháin refused a request from a preparatory college. As in the other colleges, domestic staff were native speakers and the Department generously undertook to pay travel expenses for them to return home for holidays.

The appointments at Coláiste Chaoimhín formed a pattern for the other colleges. Although the bishop of the diocese was the manager, the day-to-day management of the colleges was undertaken by the principal who was responsible to the Department for all expenditure. Because of these administrative demands on principals, vice-principals were appointed. The main

Iml ....

OIFIG AN OIDEACHAIS NÁISIÚNTA

OFFICE OF NATIONAL EDUCATION,

BAILE ÁTHA CLIATH,

21st. August   19 26

Madam,

With reference to the visit of the Deputy Chief Inspector, Mr
Mangan, and General Inspector, Mr Nicholls to Tralee, relative to the
question of the members of your Community proposed for Principal and
Vice-Principal of the new Preparatory College at Ventry, I am to inform
you that it is understood that Sister Columbanus Horan is now proposed
for principal of the College and Sister Mary Borgia for the position of
Vice-principal.

I am to state that this Department will be prepared to favourably
consider the temporary appointment of these members of the Community to
these positions, subject to the discussion of the matter with the
Bishop at a later date.

I am, Madam,
Your obedient servant,

Pádraig Ó Brolcháin

The Mother Superioress,
Mercy Convent
Tralee.

14 Letter from Ó Brolcháin approving the appointments of a principal and vice-principal to
Coláiste Íde. *Courtesy The Mercy Order.*

---

terms of contracts for principals included provisions for accommodation and
salary, with three months' notice in writing by either side of the intention to
end the employment, or three months' salary in lieu of notice. A further condition was that the principal would ensure the college was kept in good
repair. In addition the contract stressed that the Minister for Education was
the employer and not the manager.[47] One of the great weaknesses of the
system was that principals did not have access to funds which they could use
at their discretion. They had to obtain approval of any expenditure which,
subsequently, had to be sanctioned by the Department of Finance. This led
to endless correspondence and bureaucratic delays, often worsened by wran-
gling between the two departments. In its efforts to support the colleges, the
Department's policy was to grant them almost any request, while the Department of Finance's attitude was coloured by its scepticism about the system.

---

47. DF Papers, S25/9/25.

Regulations for teaching staff emphasised that they were to be fluent Irish speakers with high qualifications and competent to teach through Irish the secondary school programme up to the Leaving Certificate Examination. As it was not possible to get sufficient secondary teachers to fulfil these conditions, nine primary teachers were among the early appointees. To give the colleges a higher status than other second-level schools and to entice teachers to this pioneering work, the Department called the teachers 'professors'. It wanted them paid a higher salary scale, with residential 'perks', despite objections from the Department of Finance that they should be paid similar rates to secondary teachers and teachers in training colleges. Eventually, it was agreed that the basic salary for single men would be £260 per annum, with five increments of £10, and six of £15 up to £400; while for women the basic salary was to be £220, with increments of £10 up to £300. This was a lot less than the Department had suggested. Different salary scales for men and women were a feature of the period. In 1949 the INTO began demanding a common salary scale for all teachers and an end to discrimination on gender grounds.

In June 1929, it was reported that special agreements had been signed with the staffs of the preparatory colleges.[48] Over the years it became necessary to work out pension, holiday and sick leave arrangements. All appointments were on a probationary basis because, as revealed in a memo from Ó Brolcháin to Finance, of fears that those teachers who had been primary teachers might not be able to teach the Leaving Certificate course. In an effort to encourage teachers to improve their Irish, Ó Brolcháin generously arranged to back-date their salaries to include time spent in the Gaeltacht before their official appointments. Amongst those who benefited were three Loreto sisters who spent eight months in the Donegal Gaeltacht in 1926 and an appointee to Coláiste Moibhí, W.T.E. Condell.

THE ENTRANCE EXAMINATION

At the same time as officials were making staffing arrangements, they were also establishing criteria for student entry. Students were to be 'clever boys and girls from Irish-speaking districts who desire to become teachers, or from all parts of the country, who are highly qualified in Irish'. Students had to be clever, because they had to complete the Intermediate Certificate Examination, a three-year course, in two years, as well as adapting to teaching through Irish. To ensure that only clever students were admitted, a complex entrance examination was held annually in June. Strict regulations for entry and a complicated marking system characterised it. Candidates were to be between the ages of 14 and 16 years. They had to pass the entrance examination in five compulsory subjects: Irish, English, arithmetic,

---

48. Memo from Ó Brolcháin to the Department of Finance, NA S1730.

history and geography, plus needlework for girls. Optional subjects included algebra, geometry, drawing and nature study or rural science. The standard of the examination was that of seventh class in a national school, and it was conducted by inspectors and examiners appointed by the Department. In keeping with the emphasis on Irish, a high standard was demanded. Candidates had to gain at least 50 per cent in Irish, which had two sections, oral and written, with 200 marks for each. To pass, a student had to obtain at least 60 per cent in oral Irish. By contrast, the emphasis in English was on the written part of the examination for which 120 marks were awarded, with only 80 marks for the oral part. To pass, a candidate had to obtain only

1926.

ROINN AN OIDEACAIS.

DUL ISTEAC INS NA COLÁISTÍ ULLAMÚCÁIN.

GAEDILG.

Uain go leit do'n páipéar so.

1. Mór ceapadóineact (.i. ceist 8) do scríobad, agus ceitre ceisteanna eile do freagairt.

1. An giota so a leanas d'aitscríob san aimsir gnát-lá tríg. Tosuig le "Gac Satarn . . ." agus bain amac "noé."

Fuaramar roinnt aingid indé, agus cuamar síos an tsnáid go rabamar ag amarc isteac i ;uinneoga na siopaí bréagán. Connacamar rudaí deasa éigin ionnta, agus ceannuigeamar iad. Rugamar orca agus cugamar linn a baile iad. Annsan d'iceamar ár séire go sásta.

[16 marcaí.na].

2. Cuir isteac, ins an ngiota so a leanas, na focla atá ar iarraid ; focal amáin i ngac beárnain :—

"Abair . . . . an maigisteár nac racaid lóinin . . . . na scoile indiu mar go bfuil tinneas fiacal . . , . , agus iann . . . . tú féin do leigint a baile go luat. Innis . . . go mbéid tú ag teastáil . . . . d'atair sa tráthnóna.

Bí an doctúir ag cainnt leis indé, agus d'fiafruig sé . . . . anb' fada go mbéad a cuid féin baincte . . . . Níor cuir d'atair suim ar bit . . . . a cuid cainncte, ac ag cainnt leis féin . . . . n-a fiacla."

[20 marcanna].

15 1926 Entrance Examination Irish paper.

40 per cent in both sections. These regulations were a deliberate attempt to ensure the success of Gaeltacht students.[49]

The pass mark in both arithmetic and singing was 40 per cent, while in the other compulsory subjects, history and geography, no set mark had to be obtained but an overall mark of 50 per cent was required in the compulsory subjects. To these marks were added the marks in excess of 30 per cent obtained by candidates in three of the optional subjects. Gaeltacht candidates were further favoured by a rule that those who answered wholly in Irish were given a bonus of 10 per cent in each paper (except in arithmetic where five per cent was awarded). The selection procedure was also biased towards Gaeltacht students. Though candidates were to be selected according to merit, 50 per cent of available places in each college were reserved annually for those who obtained 85 per cent or over in oral Irish, provided they reached the qualifying marks in other subjects.

The fees for preparatory colleges, including board and tuition, were £40 per annum. Few students paid the full amount. Alarm at the high number of students paying no fees, or small amounts, was expressed by the Committee of Public Accounts in 1929. Ó Brolcháin tried hard to defend the Department's generosity regarding fees:

> Such students were Gaeltacht children, whose fathers had only five, six or ten acres of rocky land. Others were labourers, or fishermen, who find it very hard to clothe their children.[50]

In response to questioning, Ó Brolcháin used the Department's inexperience in running colleges as an excuse and this certainly was a contributory factor. However, there was no reason why the funding system should not have been changed when it became obvious that over-spending was occurring. The Department had a means test which was euphemistically described as a 'scholarship'. Ó Brolcháin explained how the system worked:

> First, we inquire from parents as to their income and what they are prepared to pay. This is referred to the inspector with instructions to consult local parties, especially the Garda Síochána.

The naivety of Ó Brolcháin's approach was clearly shown in his remarks about asking parents 'what they were prepared to pay'. This rather casual arrangement was soon replaced with a more rigorous investigation of parents' means:

> The Department and the Commissioners of Inland Revenue take very precise measures to ascertain the means of parents and to check their statement which they are requested to submit. The local school inspector, and the inspector of

---

49. Circular from J. O'Neill, secretary, Department of Education, 1927, CICE Archives.
50. DT Papers, S1730

taxes, collect and supply the relevant information to the Department, which then fixes the fee in accordance with a definite and official scale which has been drawn up by the Department of Finance.[51]

Furthermore, the Public Accounts Committee examination revealed a wide difference in attitude to expenditure between the Departments of Education and Finance. Ó Brolcháin's approach was to provide the colleges with the best educational facilities and resources available but this was not done in a methodical manner, as was clearly shown to the committee when Ó Brolcháin was asked to justify expenditure on musical instruments. While five colleges received a variety of musical instruments and two colleges had orchestras, Coláiste Moibhí had only one piano, and in May 1928 the Minister for Finance refused to sanction the provision of a piano for Coláiste na Mumhan.

A further example of the Department's generosity was the provision of stationery. All students, regardless of their means, were supplied with stationery at the nominal rate of 12s.–6d. per annum. Principals were to collect the money and the Department was to be informed of any cases of hardship. Preparatory students were also exempt from paying examination fees. In addition, a scheme was introduced in 1929 whereby training college fees were paid for those preparatory college students whose families could not afford to pay them. Under its terms, such students were to repay the money when earning. This was typical of Blythe's actions as Minister for Finance. In an endeavour to assist poor Gaeltacht students, he was willing to advance their fees but his generosity was always conditional. Furthermore, he gave

16 The orchestra at Coláiste Bhríde. *Courtesy Cumann Staire is Seanchais Chloich Cheann Fhaola.*

---

51. Letter from J.A. Kyle, principal of C. Moibhí, 1928–1934, Hodges Papers, CICE Archives.

little consideration to the effects on education of some of his proposals. As the costs of the colleges continued to rise, in 1930 the Department of Finance proposed reducing the preparatory course to three years as this would reduce the cost per head and also increase output.[52] How the course could have been undertaken in three years was not really considered. As it had already been reduced by a year with students undertaking the Intermediate Certificate course in two years, a further reduction was not possible. But the suggestion was a further indication of the Department of Finance's uncaring attitude to education.

THE AGREEMENT

From 1930, arrangements regarding the agreement preparatory students had to make became more stringent. Failure to teach for five years as a national teacher would result in having to repay the costs of their education. Another condition of the agreement was that the principal of the preparatory college, with the approval of the Department, might remove a student at any time. Furthermore, students who failed to perform satisfactorily at teaching practice would not be allowed to continue. To this agreement, a student's parents or guardians had to give written assent.[53]

The agreement was to be a source of contention throughout the history of the colleges. Critics claimed that due to it, students who were unsuited to the teaching profession went on to training because they were unable to repay their preparatory college fees. In the early years, a number of student-teachers left training and the Department was unable to reclaim the money spent on their education. They were not all past pupils of preparatory colleges. In 1934, there were four such cases. Of these, only one had been at a preparatory college. Her fees were not recoverable because of her parents' poverty. Of the others, two were entering the religious life. According to officials, the Department was precluded from taking legal action because there would be little public sympathy where a religious vocation was concerned.

A further factor inhibiting the Department from legal action was the age of the students when making the agreement. The Department was also careful not to seek reimbursement of fees from Gaeltacht students of low means, as it feared the response 'that free secondary education for general purposes should be provided throughout the Gaeltacht'. The fee system was problematic and many of the difficulties regarding the preparatory colleges might have been avoided had a proper system of scholarships been introduced at the start. The insistence that students must become primary teachers and the early age of recruitment were fundamental flaws in the system and were, eventually, to contribute to it being abolished.

---

52. DF Papers, S20/14/30.
53. *Ibid.,* S25/6/32.

Throughout the history of the colleges there were difficulties over text-books. It was the Department's intention that textbooks would be supplied to students for use during their time at the colleges. This was opposed by the Department of Finance. It also opposed providing library books on the grounds that there were few books in Irish, and the colleges should 'wait until more were available, otherwise they may countermand gaelicisation work', phrases that echo Blythe. To help the colleges build up their own libraries, it was eventually agreed that they should receive £50 per library and 30 shillings for each first-year student. This arrangement was fine until it was discovered that the colleges were receiving different rates per student. This meant that the contents of the libraries varied from college to college. Coláiste Bhríde had a good library which had cost £180, while the limited nature of the library at Coláiste Éinde was noted by the Bishop of Galway. That Ó Brolcháin had little understanding of suitable reading material for young people was shown by his proposal that each library should have all modern Irish texts published since 1898 and also a complete set of Cork Historical and Archaeological Journals.

Bun Sraith 1928

17 The first class at Coláiste Éinde 1928.
Seated (L-R) Feilim Mac Enrí, Micheál Mac Gabhna, Pádraig Mac Giolla Bhríde, Seán Mac Fhionghaile,
Second Row: Seán Ó Leadarain, Séamus Mac Enrí, Labhrás Mac Bradaigh, Feilim Mac Aoidh, Pádraig Mac Giolla Íosa, Maitias Ó hEidhin, Tomás Mac Suibhne, Tomás Midheach, Pádraig Mac Gongail, Máirtín MacGiobúin, Seán Ó Cléirigh,
Back row: Pádraig S. Mac an Ghoill, Cathal Ó Gallchobhair, Brian ua Gafacháin, Aodh Mac Giolla Bhríde, Aodh Ó Farraidhe, Éamonn Ó Gallchobhair, Seán Mac an Ghoill, Pádraig Ó Ceithearnaigh, Seosamh Ó Ceallacháin, Pádraig Ó Finneadha, Brian Mac Giolla Easbuig, Aodh Ó Duibhir, Eighneachán Ó Cléirigh, absent Seán de Crúis, *Archives of Coláiste Éinde.*

THE FIRST STUDENTS

From the earliest days there was keen competition for places in the colleges. The first entrance examinations were held in June 1926 when 1,946 students – 607 boys and 1,339 girls – competed for places. Though only 154 in all – 69 boys and 85 girls – were awarded places, reports of the Department of Education (1926–35) show that the trend established in the early years of well over 1,000 students competing for approximately 150 places was to continue. Generally, the number of girls entering the examination was twice the number of boys. Several factors may account for the gender imbalance. Many rural families needed their sons to work on the family farm. Primary teaching was perceived as a career for women. The fact that there was already a large gender imbalance meant that there were more female teachers to encourage girls to enter.

The first students came from all over the country and from varied social backgrounds. The college registers show that there was also considerable variation between colleges. As was to be expected, students from Cork and Kerry were very prominent in Coláiste Íde and Coláiste na Mumhan, though from time to time the latter had students from Donegal also. In the early days, Coláiste Mhuire's students also came from Cork and Kerry though later they were mainly from Galway and Mayo. The majority of students at Coláiste Bhríde came from Donegal, with a number from Cork, Kerry and Tipperary. From the beginning Coláiste Chaoimhín had many students of reduced means from Gaeltacht families, and from its early days the principal paid for repairs to pupils' clothes. The registers of Coláiste Moibhí show that the college always had a wide range of students with varying financial backgrounds, and most classes included students who paid full fees and those who paid none. The average age on entry of the early students was 15+, though it decreased as time went by.[54]

A typical day in a preparatory college began at 6.45 am and ended at 10.00 pm. Each day there was Mass at 7.00 am. Following breakfast at 8.00 am there was a short period of free time before classes began at 9.00 am. Classes continued throughout the day with a short break at 11.00 am and a longer break for lunch at 1.00 pm. After classes finished at 4.00 pm there was a period of free time for sporting activities and hobbies until the main evening meal at 6.00 pm. Evenings were spent in study followed by prayers at 9.30 pm. On Thursday evenings there was a free period for Irish dancing.

THE CURRICULUM

In the early years, the prescribed curriculum was limited to Irish, English, mathematics, history, geography and science. This was criticised as being too narrow for primary teachers, a claim that was refuted by Blythe in the Dáil in 1932:

---

54. Registers of the colleges.

18 The first class at Coláiste Bhríde 1927. *Courtesy Cumann Staire is Seanchais Chlóich Cheann Fhaola.*

The work of giving a full secondary course through Irish was an experimental matter when the preparatory colleges were set up. It was necessary to have a minimum curriculum in the beginning because of the difficulties involved.[55]

However, a study of the different colleges shows that while the basic curriculum was taught in all colleges, there were considerable variations as to which other subjects were taught (French was taught in two of the preparatory colleges). This was mainly due to the availability of staff competent to teach extra subjects. Once the colleges were established in permanent locations, the curriculum broadened, and rural science, drawing and music were included with domestic science for girls and manual instruction for boys. From 1933, courses in physical training were given by army instructors in some colleges. This wider curriculum was criticised for its failure to include Latin and a modern language. Most Catholic boys' secondary schools of that time taught Latin, while French was taught in the majority of girls' schools. Latin was later introduced in most preparatory colleges. The teaching of Latin was of importance to the INTO as it would facilitate future teachers in getting university degrees.[56]

The level at which a subject was taken at the Leaving Certificate Examination also varied from college to college. At Coláiste Chaoimhín, students studied all subjects, except English, at honours level while at Coláiste Mhuire some students studied mathematics at Leaving Certificate honours level, which was unusual in girls' schools of the period.

TEACHING PRACTICE

On successful completion of the preparatory course, students were assured of places in training colleges. In order to emphasise that they were to become primary teachers, teaching practice was introduced. This, the Department claimed in its 1932–33 Report, was to ascertain the student's personal suitability for the profession and whether he or she had an aptitude for teaching. It also claimed that it was to help students discern whether teaching appealed sufficiently to them to be their choice of career. Teaching practice varied from college to college and never really served any useful purpose.

As the colleges differed from ordinary secondary schools, it was decided in 1929 that the Secondary Branch of the Inspectorate should inspect examination classes to ensure that they were suitably taught, while the Primary Branch was to be responsible for the administration and the examination of non-examination subjects. It was also to supervise arrangements for recreation, concerts, *céilís* and what was euphemistically described as the 'organisation of opportunities for turning to advantage the Irish-speaking population and environment'.

---

55. *Dáil Reports,* 28 October, 1932.
56. Primary teachers with university degrees received an annual bonus. DF Papers, S25/11/34.

THE GAELTACHT LOCATION

The location of the colleges in the Gaeltacht had been a prime consideration from the beginning. It was also a matter that was raised occasionally in the Dáil. In 1930, a questioner asked:

> Why the students are brought from one end of the country to the other and the object is never realised, as the pupils are practically locked up and have no intercourse with the peasantry? Does the Minister think that there is something in the air that would give the pupils the *'blas'* (accent) and make them Irish speakers?[57]

From then on, each college had to make reports on interaction with native speakers. To improve 'an spriod Ghaedhealach' (the Irish ethos) of the colleges, principals were instructed to ensure that native speakers visited the colleges and met with students. A detailed report from the principal of Coláiste Íde, Sr Columban, described concerts, drama, story-telling and singing sessions with native speakers. She complained, however, of the cost of organising transport for such visits as the nearest village was seven miles away. Indeed, it was not long before the question of paying native speakers to visit the colleges arose, and a grant of £5 per year was allowed to each college.

In keeping with the emphasis on native culture, the Department insisted that Irish dancing was taught in each college, and this led to a complicated wrangle between the Departments of Finance and Education and *Coimisiún an Rince,* (The Irish Dance Teachers' Association). The latter insisted that only qualified dance teachers, paid the professional rate, should be employed. This, the Coimisiún argued, would ensure that future national teachers would be properly taught. This argument was firmly resisted by the Department of Finance which again showed its lack of commitment to the gaelicisation policy:

> It is one thing for the state to encourage and directly assist the revival of the Irish language, quite another to attempt to spread Irish step and jig dancing. We should not allow ourselves to be driven by the Department of Education which has been bullied by the IDTA, greedy dance teachers, intent on seeking to impose on the community as a whole, a self-constituted exclusive body of teachers, obviously out to establish a monopoly in their own financial interests.[58]

The Department of Education was not slow in declaring the preparatory system 'a complete success' as it achieved its main objective, securing a large number of boys and girls, highly qualified in Irish, and able to do their school work through Irish. But an analysis of those securing places showed that the early students came mainly from outside the Gaeltacht, a fact noted

---

57. *Dáil Reports*, 21 May 1930.
58. DF Papers S18/2/33.

19 An Irish dancing group at Coláiste Moibhí, Eibhlín Ní Cearra, Isbéal Nic Uilcín, Virginia Nic Ionmhain, Béibhinn Ní Bhriain, Beatrice Shuetnam, Bhealraí Ní Ghabhann, Péarla Nic Liam, Norma Veitch, Marta de Bréadún, *CICE Archives.*

with disappointment by the Department in 1930. Amongst those most concerned with the failure to attract Gaeltacht students was Blythe:

> I am afraid it shows clearly that the present system will not deliver the goods. The number of boys and girls from the Fíor-Ghaeltacht, half of whom are from West of Dingle, is much too few to enable the colleges to do their work with real efficiency …. I regard the results of the examination, as not only deplorable, but as tragic.[59]

Blythe had this explanation for the lack of interest in the Donegal and Connemara Fíor-Ghaeltacht:

> Probably a good proportion of children attend school hungry. Many of the teachers are not as efficient as they ought to be, but above all, parents have not the habit of making sacrifices to keep children at school in order to give them a chance of entering more lucrative employment.[60]

To encourage more Gaeltacht entrants, he proposed a system of 'exceptional entry', similar to the device whereby Protestant students who had not reached the required standard in Irish were admitted to Coláiste Moibhí.[61] A maximum of 12 places would be awarded in proportion to candidates from the different Irish-speaking areas not sufficiently represented among the successful candidates. He further proposed the establishment of special preparatory one-year courses for these candidates before they were admitted to the ordinary classes.

59. Letter from Blythe to O'Sullivan, Minister for Education, UCD Archives, Blythe Papers, P24/302.
60. *Ibid.,* P24/443.
61. Parkes, p. 166.

EFFORTS TO ATTRACT GAELTACHT STUDENTS

In July 1931, Ó Brolcháin responded to Blythe, adding these reasons for the lack of interest: poor economic conditions, 'bordering on semi-starvation in many areas', irregular school attendance owing to a lack of clothing, particularly boots, and the tradition of leaving school at 14. He believed the education system also contributed to the lack of interest. The programme was unsuitable for Gaeltacht children. The schools were small and lacking in textbooks in Irish. Ó Brolcháin concluded that the entrance examination requirements in English and mathematics were too high, while the age limit of 15 years and six months was too low. He believed that the length of time it took to qualify as a teacher also contributed to parent apathy. In addition Gaeltacht students were seen as 'unsophisticated and overawed by examinations and so unable to give of their best'. To improve matters, Ó Brolcháin suggested itinerant teachers on motorcycles or in cars to go round the Gaeltacht, giving special instruction. He also proposed the provision of central schools, with residential facilities, or 'secondary tops', for Fíor-Ghaeltacht schools.

To encourage more Gaeltacht students to enter the entrance examination, Ó Brolcháin initiated a special scheme. It included extending the upper age limit to 16 years and six months, providing a preparatory one-year course at the preparatory colleges, with grants to cover travel, outfits and the expenses of attending the examination. A scheme of bonuses for Gaeltacht teachers and pupils was also devised.

These measures were successful in increasing the number of candidates from the Fíor-Ghaeltacht who sat the entrance examination and the Department reported with satisfaction that the numbers had increased from 100 in 1931, to 329 in 1934. In addition the quality of the candidates improved, and in 1936 the Department decided that the one-year course was no longer necessary.

The entry of more Gaeltacht students to the colleges meant an increase in the number of those from low-income families. Blythe, who was ever happy to assist them, had to make provision in the Annual Estimates for 1931–32, for small grants for needy Gaeltacht students. A typical case was that of a student, from Co. Kerry, at Coláiste Éinde:

> Father, a casual labourer with 12 shillings a week income. Very poor, neighbours sent 'the hat round' to provide clothes. The morning going to college teachers and class made a collection for pocket money. They have three acres of cut away bog; the cabin was cold and empty. The family often go to bed hungry; all barefoot, ill-clad, and miserable, on the day of my visit which was very inclement.[62]

Details of other students in similar circumstances were included, and in 1932–33, a system of grants for Gaeltacht students came into operation. The Department's proposal to extend assistance to non-Gaeltacht students, by

---

62. DF Papers, S25/1/31.

giving each student £15, was refused by the Department of Finance. It emphasised that the state wanted national teachers who were 'bred in the bone' Irish speakers and to educate other native speakers to the stage where they could compete for university scholarships for Fíor-Ghaeltacht students. The Department of Finance dismissed the idea:

> Non Fíor-Ghaeltacht students are essentially a different matter. There is never any difficulty filling places in preparatory colleges. Therefore no new inducements are necessary. If poor students adopted any other calling in life, e.g. Christian Brothers, or emigrated to England, they would be obliged to find considerable amounts to buy clothes, fares etc.[63]

Not surprisingly, this system did not find favour with the INTO, which had opposed the preparatory colleges from the beginning. The new regulations, and particularly those allocating 40 per cent of reserved places to candidates from the Fíor-Ghaeltacht and a further 40 per cent to candidates from Breac Ghaeltacht areas, alarmed the organisation. In July 1933, the CEC passed the following resolution:

> While we have every sympathy with any reasonable efforts towards the revival of Irish and the fair treatment of the Gaeltacht, we consider the regulations for entrance to preparatory colleges as reactionary and unjust, and such as will ultimately injure Irish, in the non-Irish speaking districts, by excluding from these colleges practically all candidates from outside the Gaeltacht. That we suggest to the minister the advisability of allocating to Irish a certain substantial portion of the total marks given to all subjects and insisting on a high standard in Irish oral, as well as written, for successful candidates, entrance otherwise to be settled in strict order of merit. That we direct the attention of parents and all those interested in our language, and the Irish public generally, to the present unfair and invidious differentiation against the vast bulk of potential aspirants to the teaching profession.[64]

The INTO's criticism was significant, because it was made by a group which, up to then, had supported the language policy. Undoubtedly, one reason for the teachers' opposition was that the new regulations made it more difficult for their offspring to follow them into teaching. Discrimination in favour of Gaeltacht students reaffirmed the INTO opposition to the system and consolidated the view of many members of the profession that the gaelicisation policy was unrealistic.

Nevertheless, at the end of the first decade of the Irish Free State's existence, the government could claim that the country had not only gained its independence from Britain, but that the state had made considerable progress in effecting a cultural revolution by measures to ensure universal gaelicisation. Proposals for the gaelicisation of the public service and for

---

63. *Ibid.*
64. *The Irish School Weekly*, XXXV, 29, p. 687, 22 July 1933.

improving life in the Gaeltacht, recommended by *Coimisiún na Gaeltachta*, were being implemented. The government could further claim that the education system, which was seen as having a key role in reviving the language, had been almost completely transformed, and that considerable progress had been made in ensuring that all primary teachers were competent to teach Irish. It had initiated a series of summer courses for serving teachers, and the preparatory system had been established so that all future teachers would be fluent in the language. Furthermore, the system had been commended by *Coimisiún na Gaeltachta*. With the opening of the colleges, it had provided second-level education in the Gaeltacht and with the entry of preparatory students to training in 1931, the work of the training colleges was almost entirely through Irish.

Yet such success was not without cost. The programme in primary schools had been reduced. The Irish language had come to assume a new and dominating role in the education system, leading to the weakening in the teaching of English and other subjects. In a country where large numbers received only primary education, and where thousands had to emigrate annually to English-speaking countries, this should have been a major cause for concern.

CHAPTER THREE

Failure to get the numbers right leads to closure of Coláiste Chaoimhín: 1932–39

'The prime consideration is the saving of expenditure'

The period 1932–39 began well for the preparatory system. Large numbers continued to compete for places in the newly established colleges. Furthermore, students from the colleges successfully completed their courses and played a considerable role in transforming the training colleges into Irish-speaking institutions, thus fulfilling a key part of the government's strategy for producing teachers fully capable of implementing the language policy in the schools. But all was not as satisfactory as it seemed, and shortcomings in the preparatory system led to the appointment of a Committee of Inquiry into the Preparatory Colleges in 1938. The failure of the Department to regulate the numbers of student-teachers required was also problematic. Over-recruitment soon became the dominant feature of this period, and this was a factor in the closure of Coláiste Chaoimhín, one of the leading preparatory colleges. Rising costs at a time of economic stringency were a further factor, as was the continuing friction between the Departments of Education and Finance. This had been evident from the beginning of the system but was exacerbated by the personalities of the ministers involved: Thomas Derrig[1] in Education, a staunch supporter of the preparatory system, and Seán MacEntee in Finance, who wanted to abolish it.

From 1932–48, Thomas Derrig was Minister for Education (except for the period 8 September 1939 to 18 June 1940, when Seán T. Ó Ceallaigh was minister for 19 days and de Valera for the remaining time) and it was mainly due to Derrig's robust defence that the preparatory system lasted into the 1950s. Derrig was deeply committed to the language revival and made

---

1. For biographical details of people named on this page see the Appendix.

strenuous efforts in a number of areas to assist its progress. Within the Gaeltacht, he tried hard to improve educational facilities. He increased the numbers of university scholarships and drew up comprehensive plans for the provision of second-level education. At national level, he increased curricular emphasis on the language through the 1934 *Revised Programme of Primary Instruction,* while at second-level he made the award of the Leaving Certificate contingent on obtaining a pass in Irish.

During the period that the Cumann na nGaedheal Government had been in office, the preparatory system had been supported in cabinet by Blythe. It is possible that had Cumann na nGaedheal continued in government, modifications to the system could have occurred more easily. Fianna Fáil was keen to demonstrate its nationalist credentials, and being in government for the first time made it difficult for the party to modify the language policy.

At the beginning of the 1930s the preparatory colleges were busy overcoming teething difficulties which were to be expected in establishing any new system. There were also the added difficulties caused by the Department's lack of planning and undue haste in getting the system established. Nevertheless, by 1934 five of the colleges were located in their intended permanent accommodation. Coláiste Chaoimhín was at Glasnevin. Coláiste Íde at Ventry and Coláiste Bhríde at Falcarragh had both been extended. Coláiste Mhuire's purpose-built college had opened at Tourmakeady in February 1931, and in January 1934, Coláiste Moibhí had moved to new premises. The exceptions were Coláiste na Mumhan, which still awaited its promised new building at Ballyvourney, and Coláiste Éinde, which in 1931 had to move to Talbot House. Despite the difficulties of their early days, however, all the colleges continued to achieve high success rates at public examinations. Demand for places was keen with more than 10 students competing for each place in a preparatory college between 1932 and 1934. As the system was heavily subsidised, this was not surprising. Students were certain of secure, pensionable employment, provided they passed their examinations.

SOURCES OF RECRUITMENT FOR TRAINING COLLEGES

At the beginning of the decade, students entered training colleges from three sources: the preparatory colleges, the revised pupil-teacher system and open competition. Pupil-teachers were selected from students who had passed the Intermediate Certificate Examination with honours, including honours in Irish. Subsequently, they were admitted to a secondary 'A' school, where they undertook the Leaving Certificate course through Irish. This system worked well for girls, as there were a number of girls' 'A' schools. The Department was happy to declare in its 1932/33 Report that such students were 'little inferior' to preparatory college girls. It was more problematic for boys, however, as the only schools they could attend had English as the medium of instruction.

The third source by which students could enter training was open competition, which in 1931 replaced the Easter Scholarship Examination. Students entering training in this way had to be successful at oral tests in Irish and English, at a test in music, and in needlework (for girls). These preliminary tests were held annually at Easter. The results of the Leaving Certificate Examination, together with the results of the 'Easter orals', determined whether a student obtained a place in training. Open competition students had to obtain a pass in the Leaving Certificate Examination generally, with honours in Irish, and a pass in English, mathematics, history and geography.

The Department's preferred method of recruitment continued to be the preparatory system, despite the fact that its costs were significantly higher than the other systems. For the school-year 1932/33, the cost of maintaining 605 students in the preparatory colleges was £37,342–9s.–6d. compared with £3,299–8s.–9d. for the maintenance of 245 pupil-teachers. The cheapest method of entry by far was open competition, where the only cost incurred was the financial outlay on the holding of the 'Easter orals'.

By 1933 the three systems were working well and the Department was able to declare with some satisfaction that almost all students admitted to training had 'completed a course in secondary education' and obtained honours at the Leaving Certificate.[2] From 1934 on, the increased efforts by the Department to assist the recruitment of Gaeltacht students resulted in the numbers from preparatory colleges increasing considerably, while the number of pupil-teachers decreased. The Department's satisfaction at having solved the shortage of well-qualified students was to be short-lived, as already there were indications that the output of male teachers was somewhat in excess of requirements. By 1936 the Department's failure to estimate correctly the required number of primary teachers led to large numbers of fully-trained teachers being unemployed. As the number of unemployed teachers rose, many students abandoned the idea of teaching and, despite having to repay the cost of their training, entered the civil service, as the Department noted plaintively in 1934.[3]

The possibility that the preparatory system was being used as a means of securing cheap education by students with no intention of fulfilling their undertaking to become teachers was seriously examined. An analysis of the numbers involved showed that the annual leakage from the training colleges was as small as five per cent and the students involved were not all from preparatory colleges. The Department's policy in such cases was to recoup the money spent on their training, by instalments deducted from their salaries as civil servants.[4] Pupil-teachers and preparatory college students also had to repay the costs of their secondary education. Furthermore, in an effort to

2. *Report of the Department of Education*, 1932/33, p. 7.
3. *Ibid.*, 1933/34, p. 18.
4. DF Papers, S25/9/34.

discourage students from leaving teaching, consideration was given to ways of making it more difficult for them to repay their fees, by insisting on the repayment being in one large sum, instead of by instalments. Consideration was also given to barring preparatory college students from entering the civil service examination. When this proved impossible, the question of raising the fees in preparatory colleges to £50 per annum was considered.

EFFORTS TO REDUCE THE NUMBER OF TEACHERS

The Department's failure to review its recruitment policy sooner is difficult to understand, as its own statistics published in its annual reports showed that enrolments had fallen from 522,090 in 1926 to 495,829 in 1934 while the number of schools decreased from 5,648 in 1926 to 5,212 in 1936. Some of the decrease was brought about by the Department's policy, introduced in 1927, of amalgamating small schools. The lack of planning by the Department, which had a recruitment drive for the preparatory colleges and the new pupil-teacher scheme at the same time as it was reducing the number of teaching posts, led to a series of panic measures to absorb the surplus teachers. The marriage ban, whereby female teachers had to resign their posts on marriage, was announced in 1933. This was followed by the discontinuance of the pupil-teacher scheme in 1936. From 1938, entry by open competition ceased, and the subsequent curtailment of male admission to training resulted in the temporary closure of St Patrick's Training College. Finally, in 1939, when these and other measures proved inadequate, recruitment to the preparatory colleges was suspended.

Séamus Fenton, who was chief inspector at the time the preparatory colleges were established, had this explanation for the failure of the Department's recruitment policy:

> A good <u>National Board</u> would have checked many of the foolish innovations and would have forced the lazy officials to work. In the old days the '<u>secs</u>' worked till midnight before 'Board Day' preparing for such questions as the 'No. of trained teachers unemployed'. The number rarely exceeded 20. In our day the number once reached <u>800</u> and the official in special charge of <u>training 'cols.'</u> Mr. James Brennan (the famous footballer), was called to account by nobody. Neither was he punished. Instead he is in charge of broadcasting. 'A man who reads books,' said he one day to Mr. Henry Morris (a senior inspector) 'is a square peg in a round hole'.[5]

The Department's lack of planning was compounded by its relationship with the Catholic Church, which due to the managerial system wielded

---

5. Letter from Fenton to Bishop Browne of Galway, 1 September 1944, Galway Diocesan Archives, Browne Papers.

enormous power in education. An example of the power of the church to frustrate the Department's plans was the proposal to build a training college in Galway in the 1920s.

A TRAINING COLLEGE FOR GALWAY?

In July 1926 the authorities of UCG proposed setting up a training college for nuns in the Galway model school building. Both the Department and the hierarchy approved the proposal but it came to nothing. In 1928 a second proposal was made by the Department to establish a training college in Galway for 160 women students, including nuns. The Department was keen that the church or the order which was to run the college would make a financial contribution to the building costs. But none of the orders considered – the Loreto, the Dominicans, the St Louis, or the Mercy Order, Galway – was able to do so. Nevertheless, the minister decided that land adjoining the model school would be bought, a plan for the building prepared and the St Louis Order, from Monaghan, would be in charge.

From the beginning, the plan was opposed by the Department of Finance. It proposed that the new college should be located at the Royal Hibernian Military School in the Phoenix Park, on which over £100,000 had been spent on refurbishment. In response, the Department argued that Galway was a better choice than Dublin, as it offered more opportunities for speaking Irish and the model school could be used for teaching practice. These advantages did not satisfy the Department of Finance, where an official noted pragmatically:

> Two preparatory colleges in Dublin already. No detriment to gaelicising. Pool teaching staffs from St Patrick's and Carysfort. Health point very good in Phoenix Park. As near to university as All Hallows. Tramline passes door. Two schools, one in the Park and one in Chapelizod.[6]

In response, Ó Brolcháin reiterated the somewhat sanguine view that Galway held a 'pivotal position' for the gaelicisation of Ireland, and a training college there with 160 Irish speakers would strengthen Irish in the west. This comment provoked the following reply from an exasperated official in the Department of Finance:

> What contact do training colleges have with local areas? Have been passing through Blackrock for years past, never any visible evidence of the existence of the institution (Carysfort College).[7]

Despite its earlier objections, however, £160,000 was sanctioned by the Department of Finance for the college, and in 1930 a 17-acre site at Polnarooma,

---

6. DF Papers, S20/4/28. See also Ó Buachalla, p. 225.
7. *Ibid.*

Salthill, was purchased at a cost of £2,210 (not including the purchaser's legal costs). Shortly afterwards, an extra 14 acres, at £100 per acre, were purchased and building started following the signing of a £16,500 contract for steel. These were large sums of money at a time when the initial salary for a male teacher was £170 per annum. It was the Department's intention that the St Louis Order would run the college and it believed that the bishop had agreed to this, though it had no written agreement with him. It was not until the reverend mother wrote to the bishop that he realised that an order from outside his diocese would be involved. This he rejected totally, insisting that the Order of Mercy, Galway, should be in charge. It is likely that he would have got his way but for the inadequate education of his chosen personnel.

In 1932 Fianna Fáil formed the government and to avoid any disagreement with the hierarchy, it sanctioned a training college for nuns in Galway. Shortly afterwards, the bishop's nominees were interviewed.[8] The interview committee described the proposed principal, 33-year-old Sr Mary Alphonsus Coghlan, and vice-principal 28-year-old Sr Mary Anthony Boland, from the Order of Mercy, Galway, as having 'no knowledge of training colleges or their work; nor were they qualified for recognition as principal teacher of a national school'. The committee further noted that: 'Neither had the education, training, experience, outlook or personality for the posts', adding that Sr Mary Anthony, whose 'grasp of Irish was not very wide or very exact' would qualify only as an untrained assistant. With that, the whole project was stopped, as the bishop refused to consider any other order.

Despite this setback, there were further negotiations between the Department and the hierarchy. By this time, Derrig, the new Minister for Education, must have been well aware that there was an over-supply of teachers in training and that recruitment would have to be curtailed. Some time later, the hierarchy proposed that instead of a new training college, more nuns should be accepted into Carysfort Training College, in Dublin. Despite the fact that work on constructing the Galway college had begun and that an extension to Carysfort would be costly, the Department agreed to admit twice as many as planned into Carysfort. In its desire to please the bishops, the Department paid little heed to its own statistics. At the same time that it was increasing the number of nuns in training, its annual report (1934/35) noted that the number of unemployed male teachers was 'a matter of serious concern'. Of considerable concern too was its note that it was 'difficult to adjust the numbers entering training', because students from the preparatory colleges and the pupil-teacher scheme were starting their courses in the training colleges. This was a further indication of incompetent planning by the Department, which had little idea of the number of teachers required. Surprisingly, officials do not seem to have considered using the additional number of trained teachers to reduce the pupil-teacher

---

8. Dublin Diocesan Archives, Byrne Papers.

ratio or to eliminate the large number of untrained teachers, which in 1933 was almost 12 per cent.

Fortunately for the government, at the time it decided to abandon its plan for a training college in Galway, Coláiste Éinde was in temporary accommodation in Dublin. In 1934, it was decided to turn the half-built training college at Salthill into a preparatory college and to house Coláiste Éinde there. By this time, the building was derisively known to the Galway public as 'the hen-roost,' or 'the white elephant'.[9]

Throughout this whole episode, the Department of Education displayed a cavalier attitude to the large sums of money involved, and the ineptitude which characterised the establishment of the preparatory system was clearly to be seen. Indeed, it was little wonder that an official in the Department of Finance noted plaintively:

> Education not greatly concerned. Will use building as a preparatory college. Had Furbough House six miles from town. £50,000 sanctioned. £1,200 spent, satisfied title could not be established. Abandoned. Preparatory college only 90 pupils. Furbough and training college bad business for the taxpayer.[10]

A further area where the Department avoided a clash with the church was on the question of amalgamating preparatory colleges. As early as 1933, when difficulties arose over Coláiste Éinde's lease at Furbough, the Department of Finance sought to reduce costs by amalgamating that college with Coláiste na Mumhan and abandoning plans for a new building at Ballyvourney. But mindful of the power of individual bishops to determine which orders could operate within their dioceses, particularly following the débâcle over the Galway training college, the Department feared a refusal

20 An aerial photo of Coláiste Éinde. *Courtesy, S. Ó Ceallaigh, ed. Coláiste Éinde 1928–2003 Seachtó Cúig Bliain faoi Bhláth.*

9. Coláiste Éinde PPA, *Coláiste Éinde 1928–1978,* p. 15.
10. DF Papers, S20/4/28.

and the plan was dropped.[11] As all the costs connected with the colleges were borne by the state, including the costs of religious requirements, provision of chapels and chaplains' salaries, the Department's behaviour was somewhat subservient.

A further example of the Department's deference to the hierarchy arose in 1932, when Ó Brolcháin sought Archbishop Byrne's views on the proposal to introduce a ban on married women teachers. A letter from departmental secretary Joseph O'Neill to the hierarchy in March 1932 gives some insights into the conservative thinking on social issues prevalent at that time:

> Is the employment of married women desirable in mixed schools? Generally, it is satisfactory but there must be some loss in home or school; money saved in salaries by substitutes on the main scale could provide gratuities for retirement on marriage.[12]

Noting that the average age of teachers on marriage was approximately 31, with 10 years service, O'Neill blamed the employment of married women for limiting the number of jobs for young people. He also observed that there was local resentment at two-income houses, particularly where the husband had a shop or large farm. From this letter, it would appear that the marriage ban developed from a conservative social policy, as much as in reaction to the surplus of trained teachers. The idea that the place of married women should be in the home was later affirmed in the 1937 Constitution.

DERRIG'S EFFORTS TO PROVIDE SECOND-LEVEL SCHOOLS IN THE GAELTACHT

The hierarchy's powerful role in education was further demonstrated when it opposed Derrig's plans to provide second-level education in the Gaeltacht. Derrig wanted to improve second-level educational facilities in the Gaeltacht, a need highlighted by *Coimisiún na Gaeltachta*. In January 1934, the Department drew up detailed proposals for 21 higher primary schools in Irish-speaking districts, to be finalised after discussion with the hierarchy, the managers and the INTO.

A significant part of the plan was dependent on the provision of transport. Pupils living three miles or more from a school were to travel on bicycles supplied by the Department. The projected capital cost of the schools was £79,475, with annual running costs estimated at £29,000. As the money could not be raised locally, the full costs would be borne by the state and a system of joint management inaugurated.[13] This innovative scheme was ridiculed by the Department of Finance:

---

11. *Ibid.*, S22/5/44.
12. Letter to secretary of Catholic Bishops' Conference, Dublin Diocesan Archives, Byrne Papers.
13. DT Papers, S2512.

The proposal re: bicycles for pupils three miles from the new schools is 'fantastic'. Won't last long on mountain roads. Will 'disappear' frequently. Accident riding Department machine.[14]

As an alternative, the Department of Finance proposed that there should be a school managed by the local Vocational Education Committee in each Irish-speaking area: Donegal, Mayo, Galway, Kerry, and Cork. In February 1934, the Executive Council deferred making a decision on the matter until the hierarchy had been consulted.

The hierarchy viewed the scheme with alarm. Proposals for joint management would be a further extension of state control, an issue which greatly exercised the bishops at that time. They also feared the danger 'from the moral point of view' of boys and girls aged 12 to 16 years travelling long distances without supervision. Furthermore, they considered extra educational provision unnecessary in view of the existence of vocational schools.[15] Despite this setback, Derrig continued his efforts to extend educational provision in the Gaeltacht, and in 1938 he and de Valera were responsible for establishing vocational schools at Cnoc na hAille and Inis Mór Árann. Derrig's commitment to Gaeltacht education was clearly demonstrated the following year, when he strongly resisted the proposed closure of Coláiste Chaoimhín, arguing that it should become a college for Fíor-Ghaeltacht scholarship holders. Derrig summarised his view in this firm declaration of policy in 1939:

> The policy has been to monitor and extend Irish as a living speech in the Gaeltacht and to revive it in the Galltacht. Personally, I am strongly in favour of additional measures and I am sure the Taoiseach desires that much more should be done in each of the main Gaeltacht areas.[16]

Unfortunately for Derrig, it was a period of severe economic depression. Even if the economic climate had been more favourable, it is doubtful whether he would have succeeded, for there was little sympathy for Gaeltacht education in the Department of Finance.

There was also much criticism at this time that many Gaeltacht students were using the preparatory system to obtain free secondary education. As a result of this criticism, the Department undertook an analysis of fees paid by Gaeltacht and non-Gaeltacht students. The comparison showed that out of a total of 1,258 students entering between 1930 and 38, more than half, 648, were from the Gaeltacht, of whom 117 paid partial fees, while the remaining 531 paid no fees.[17] It also showed that from 1930–31 to 1937–38, only 16 per cent of all students paid full fees. The average fee for the period was

---

14. DF Papers, S20/1/34.
15. DT Papers S2512.
16. DF Papers, S25/2/39.
17. Jones, The Preparatory Colleges, p. 300.

only £10-10s-10d. Clearly, the Department of Finance's complaints that the preparatory system was too costly were justified.

DISAGREEMENTS BETWEEN DERRIG AND MacENTEE

While there were financial grants of different kinds for Gaeltacht students, they were not the only ones in poor circumstances. The question of equality of treatment of such students led to a serious clash between the Departments of Education and Finance, revealing fundamental ideological differences between them. In 1935, the Department of Education claimed that a number of Galltacht students were in circumstances worse than the poorest Fíor-Ghaeltacht student. It cited as an example a student whose mother asked the principal to keep the boy over Christmas, because she could not afford the fare for him to return home. A subsequent survey to establish the number of needy Galltacht students showed cases of considerable hardship in all colleges. Furthermore, the wide divergence in approach between Derrig and MacEntee (the Minister for Finance) was clearly illustrated in the following comment by MacEntee:

> On reading the enclosures from Education one gets the impression that there is a tendency to regard the preparatory colleges as charitable institutions or homes for orphans. Is neither category and was never intended to be. No case for extending grants to outside the Fíor-Ghaeltacht.[18]

In addition there was this revealing comment: 'If pupils can't afford travel and outfit, they shouldn't be in the preparatory colleges. Ample facilities elsewhere for post-primary education.' This showed how out of touch MacEntee was. Facilities for post-primary education were very limited. It also showed clearly his ambivalent attitude towards the gaelicisation policy. He opposed Derrig's attempts to provide higher primary schools in the Gaeltacht, and yet he used the gaelicisation policy, in this instance, as the reason for favouring Fíor-Ghaeltacht students in the preparatory colleges:

> For the first time in centuries there is a chance of better opportunities for the Fíor-Ghaeltacht. At the same time contributing an immeasurable 'something' to assist re-Gaelicisation of their contemporaries and of future generations. Others from homes with acute poverty and depressed social conditions must be subject of grave doubt if wise to seek, in such circumstances, material out of which to evolve inculcators of morals, manners and culture for future generations. Cases with trouble are pupils from undesirable home surroundings.[19]

---

18. DF Papers, S25/1/31.
19. *Ibid.*

In equating poverty with trouble and wrongdoing MacEntee's prejudice against impoverished students was clearly revealed, as was his double standard regarding poverty. He was willing to accept disadvantaged students from the Fíor-Ghaeltacht, but not students from deprived homes in the Galltacht:

> The theory of equal opportunity for all does not impose on the state the obligation to incur exceptional expenditure of a charitable nature with the object of facilitating entry of poor children from the Galltacht to those higher walks of life for which superior education is a necessary qualification.[20]

MacEntee also queried whether students, 'from homes so far below the economic line that adequate care and nourishment in childhood has been impracticable', could be physically fit for the teaching profession. Yet MacEntee had taken part in the 1916 Rising, which began with the proclamation that the new state would cherish all the children of the nation equally. Nowhere does it seem to have occurred to him that it was the state's responsibility to ensure that all homes provided adequate care and nourishment. The fundamental difference between the two men was further illustrated by Derrig's robust reply that 'great poverty should not be a bar to a talented boy or girl taking up teaching'.[21] He recalled that under the British system,

> which we have displaced, there was equality of opportunity at a great cost to the state. This undemocratic policy gives less chance to the poorest pupils, than under that of the former undemocratic regime.

Furthermore, Derrig easily refuted MacEntee's argument that students from poor backgrounds were trouble-makers, by enclosing an analysis of the home circumstances of students who had been expelled. Derrig concluded trenchantly: 'No particular class has a monopoly of "undesirables" and the very poor come well out of the total, as regards character and conduct.'

THE REVISED PROGRAMME OF PRIMARY INSTRUCTION

At national level, Derrig was responsible for increased emphasis on Irish in the schools. In 1934 he introduced the *Revised Programme of Primary Instruction*, which included a reversion to an all-Irish school day for infants, and the teaching in all other classes of the higher Irish course, as set out in the Second National Programme in 1926.[22] English was made optional for first class, and in other classes the lower course of the 1926 Programme was to

---

20. *Ibid.*
21. *Ibid.*
22. See Part I, chapter 2.

be taken. The mathematics programme was reduced and rural science was made optional. These changes resulted in a very narrow curriculum compared with that of 1926, or its predecessor of 1922.[23]

They also led to increased teacher dissatisfaction, and in 1936 the INTO decided to establish an inquiry into the use of Irish as a teaching medium. Teachers complained, with good reason, that the burden of reviving the language had fallen on them and the *Irish School Weekly* predicted:

> A sigh of relief from thousands of our immortal patriots if it were announced that the Department had decided to cut out the Irish language altogether from the list of obligatory subjects in the school programme.[24]

THE INQUIRY INTO THE PREPARATORY COLLEGES 1938

Derrig refused to consider the teachers' complaints. However, in October 1937, he set up an internal departmental committee of three divisional inspectors: Tomás P. Ó Conaill, MA, Séamus P. Ó Modhráin, MA, and Proinsias E. Ó Suilleabháin, PhD, to examine the workings of the preparatory system. It is not clear why he did this. It may be that he hoped its findings would refute the Department of Finance's criticisms of the system. Apart from examining the methods of selection of students and of examinations in the colleges, its terms of reference were mainly to do with the Gaeltacht. It was to examine the suitability of life in the colleges for Gaeltacht students, particularly the suitability of the school programme in English and mathematics. It was also to assess the influence of the colleges as Gaelic centres on the surrounding countryside. Finally, the inspectors were to bring to the minister's attention any other matter they thought necessary concerning Gaeltacht students intended for the teaching profession. It was envisaged that the work would be completed within seven weeks. But it was five months before the inspectors produced a comprehensive report (*Report of Committee of Inquiry into the Preparatory Colleges,* DF Papers S25/4/ 37). Furthermore, its findings were described as 'revolutionary' by the Department, which refused to give it to the Department of Finance, despite repeated requests. Indeed, the file was marked 'not to be released without the express permission of the secretary of the Department'.

The 28-page report, entirely in Irish, was significant because it was highly critical of the system and ambivalent about its future. On the one hand, the inspectors declared at the beginning of the report that they were satisfied that the colleges were still necessary, while on the other hand, at the end of the report, they suggested that falling enrolments would eventually bring about an end to the system. Apart from accepting that locating the colleges

---

23. See Part I, chapter 1.
24. *Irish School Weekly,* 29 July 1933, XXXV, 30, p. 722.

in the Gaeltacht had positive effects on these areas, the report had little that was constructive to say about the system. Three major aspects of the colleges, the teaching staff, student life and the way the colleges were run, were criticised. The greatest criticism related to the recruitment of Gaeltacht students, many of whom, it said, were unsuitable for the teaching profession. The report also emphasised, in several places, that candidates should be assessed for personal suitability before they were accepted.

At the beginning of their report, the inspectors outlined how they undertook their investigations, visiting each college, consulting with management and teaching staff, speaking to students and examining them 'as they felt necessary'. They also consulted people interested in the language revival. Somehow, the inspectors gave the impression to the staff of Coláiste Chaoimhín, that they were there to investigate complaints about girls from the Fíor-Ghaeltacht.[25]

On the sensitive issue of segregating student teachers in special colleges, the report acknowledged that this should occur only in exceptional circumstances. It said such segregation was necessary to give students a good grasp of the language, folklore and history of the country, at a time when there were no second-level 'A' schools. In addition the inspectors acknowledged that the students from the colleges were intended to be 'lasair Ghaedealachais i scoileanna na tíre' (beacons for Irishness in the country's schools).

SELECTION OF STUDENTS

In dealing with the selection of students and the special advantages given to Fíor-Ghaeltacht students, the inspectors concluded that the concession on age was not justified. They reported: 'Apart from Coláiste Moibhí, we were strongly told in all colleges, except Coláiste Chaoimhín, that the oldest students were the weakest and most difficult to mould'. They unanimously recommended a reduction in the age limit for Fíor-Ghaeltacht students.

In a review of the entrance examination programme, the inspectors recommended the abolition of the optional subjects, as with the exception of singing for boys, they were not taught in most primary schools. However, they showed some ambivalence in this area. On the one hand, they acknowledged that the teachers in the colleges would like students to have done some algebra and geometry before entry, while on the other hand, they claimed that the teachers were confident that with good students they could complete the mathematics course for the Intermediate Certificate Examination in two years. This was not an extravagant claim. It was borne out by the students' results, though one further unmentioned condition was necessary – the need for good teachers.

---

25. *Análacha Choláiste Chaoimhín*, 1938.

22 SCRÚDÚCHÁN I gCÓIR NA gCOLÁISTÍ ULLMHÚCHÁIN, 1930.— CAILÍNÍ.

Uimhir Scrúdúcháin	Adhbhair Riachtanacha									Adhbhair breise						Na Marcanna :—An t-Iomlán	Toradh an Scrúdúcháin
	Gaedhilg		Béarla		Uimhríocht	Stair	Tír-Eolas	Amhráchcht (Cailíní)	Adhbhair Riachtanacha An t-Iomlán	Gan thar trí cinn aca a ghlacadh. Ní h-áirmhtear acht na marcanna thar 30 per cent.						
	Tré Chainnt	Tré Scríbhinn	Tré Chainnt	Tré Scríbhinn						Algebar	Céimseata	Líníocht	Tuath-Eoluiocht nó Eolas ar Nádúir	Obair Shnáthaide		
Maxima	200	200	80	120	200	100	100	100	1100	100	100	100	100	100		
Marcan a Chu "Pa"	200 (120 aralaighead us chaint)		80		80			40	550		Féach an mi	níu th	uas			
5097	134	96	74	90	128B	54	40	52	668	18B	—	40	—	60B	708	D'éirigh
5098	130	76	74	37	127B	46	33B	78	601	28B	16B	—	—	28	601	D'éirigh
5092	150	58	64	50	113	36	23	52	546	24	4	—	—	52	—	Do theip
110?	—	—	—	—	—	—	—	—	—	—	—	—	—	—	—	As láthair
8146	88	54	60	75	178	28	59	45	587	56	48	—	—	42	643	•
8147	87	101	67	82	113	33	53	50	586	27	19	—	—	8	586	•

21 Preparatory College Entrance Examination results.

Reviewing the marking of the entrance examination, the inspectors showed some ambivalence in their attitude to English. At one stage, they pointed out that English was the language of the majority of the people of the country, though at another stage, they declared Irish to be more important than English. They recommended that marks for English be halved and only one paper set, with 100 marks for essay and grammar. This would give an advantage to Gaeltacht students whose English was generally weak. In keeping with the view that Irish was more important than English, they recommended that there should be two one-hour papers in Irish, each worth 100 marks. Gaeltacht students were further favoured by the recommendation that all examination papers should be in Irish and that the bonus for doing a paper through Irish should be abolished. Other changes recommended to the entrance examination were in arithmetic and penmanship. History, geography and needlework remained unchanged.

On the question of providing places for Gaeltacht students, the inspectors were again ambivalent. On the one hand, they accepted that some Gaeltacht students were necessary to assist the non–Gaeltacht students' progress, and to ensure that each college would be a small Gaeltacht. On the other hand, they were forthright in their declaration that the colleges 'were not a sop to the Gaeltacht but were founded to revive the language'. The report was also damning in its opinion of Gaeltacht students, totally refuting Corcoran's view[26] of Gaeltacht students as natural teachers:

> Native speakers are not always the most loyal to Irish. Some are cowardly and lazy and have a tendency towards decadence that goes with the Gaeltacht as long as there is a lack of understanding of the importance of Irish in national affairs.

26. See Part I, chapter 1.

They think they have done enough when they get a place, that the Department cannot do without them. So they take life easy. We saw students in some colleges and both for the country and for education it would be better if they didn't become teachers.[27]

The report examined the way places in the colleges were awarded and concluded that too many places were reserved for those with 85 per cent or more in oral Irish. This, they said, was the greatest complaint from college managers. From talking to students the inspectors formed the view that those who got 85 per cent in oral Irish did not deserve it. They were unanimous that half of the places should be awarded to those with 85 per cent in oral Irish, who achieved a pass in the examination. They disagreed, however, on how to ensure that candidates from each Gaeltacht obtained places. Nevertheless, they reiterated that they wanted to avoid taking students with little aptitude for teaching, as this was an injustice to the youth of the country.

The inspectors' final recommendation with regard to the selection of students was that 10 per cent of places should be reserved for students who had obtained an honours Intermediate Certificate Examination with honours in Irish and a pass in mathematics. They would also have to pass oral English and Irish tests plus a personal suitability assessment.[28] The inspectors also suggested abandoning entrance examinations and replacing them with IQ and personality tests, somewhat radical proposals for 1938, though they realistically admitted: 'we haven't the personnel in the country to do the tests'.

LIFE IN THE COLLEGES AND THEIR SUITABILITY FOR GAELTACHT STUDENTS

Examining the life of the colleges, the report found that students had not sufficient free time, though out-of-class activities were satisfactory. Sport was well catered for, with hurling and football for boys and camogie for girls. Extra-curricular activities included debates, drama, Irish dancing and addresses by visiting speakers. Food was declared to be excellent, and the pupils were taught good manners. Nevertheless, the inspectors felt that the routine life of the colleges was too restricted and recommended one half-day free per week and a free hour after dinner before study. They also recommended that students be allowed to study whatever subject they liked. This was not a very practical recommendation due to the shortage of textbooks and general reading material in Irish. The emphasis on personal development was further reiterated in the recommendation of more responsibility for prefects to help their personal development, particularly Gaeltacht students who were perceived as lacking in self-confidence.

---

27. *Report of Committee of Inquiry*, p. 7.
28. This recommendation was similar to one made by *Coimisiún na Gaeltachta* in 1926. See chapter 2.

The inspectors examined the role of Gaeltacht students in assisting the non-native students to become fluent in the language. While they acknowledged that there was a good spirit towards speaking and cultivating Irish in the colleges, they noted that Gaeltacht students stuck together and that little was done to use native speakers to help the others. Students from the Galltacht had a fluency in the language, but little else. They seldom had correct pronunciation, were unable to speak Irish naturally, and most damning of all, the Irish of Galltacht students 'was nothing but a translation of English phrases':

> There is not enough interest in Irish as a language and this must be improved. The time goes on memory work and assessment of prose and poetry. Often Galltacht students leave the colleges with nothing but a weak inaccurate mixture of dialects.[29]

This was an indictment of the whole *raison d'être* of the system, but the inspectors did not call for the colleges to be abolished. Instead they contented themselves with recommending that Galltacht students should be advised by the teaching staff to go to the Gaeltacht in the summer holidays. As four of the colleges had been specifically established in the Gaeltacht, and a fifth was waiting to move to the Ballyvourney Gaeltacht, this showed the ineffectiveness of the policy of locating the colleges in Irish-speaking areas. The inspectors concluded this section by saying that proficiency in Irish gained in a preparatory college should not be regarded as sufficient to enter training.

The teachers were also criticised: 'They do not all speak perfect Irish and some of them had unnatural pronunciations'. The inspectors called for only teachers with fluent Irish to be employed. They acknowledged, however, that many of the teachers were chosen for the posts as nobody else was available. They recommended that teachers whose Irish was poor should be encouraged to improve it. The teachers were further criticised for not requesting the Department to supply dictionaries and other reference books. The report recommended that students be allowed to keep their textbooks, whether they had paid for them or not, as this would encourage them to read and collect books and to use them as sources of information.

THE SCHOOL PROGRAMME FROM THE
GAELTACHT STUDENT'S VIEW

In this part of their remit, the inspectors examined the curriculum, particularly the teaching of English and mathematics. In both subjects they recommended that classes should be streamed, as there were wide variations of student knowledge and ability. This was particularly the case in mathematics, where not all students had studied algebra and geometry at primary school.

---

29. *Report of Committee of Inquiry*, p. 23.

They also criticised the teaching methods. Students were too dependent on the teachers' notes and rote-learning. While the inspectors' comments about learning by heart were sensible, they did not take into account the difficulties for the teachers in trying to teach without textbooks. The provision of textbooks in Irish was problematic throughout the history of the colleges. In the early years, the shortage was due to a lack of writers, but as time went by the failure to provide textbooks in Irish was due to their high costs. As the numbers required were small, their costs were much higher than textbooks in English.

There was little interest in Latin in most colleges apart from Coláiste Chaoimhín where Latin was taken in the Leaving Certificate Examination. The report accepted the teachers' claim that they had not sufficient time for Latin, with three years' study required for the Intermediate Certificate Examination. Nevertheless, it recommended that a modern language should be taught to the more able students.

ASSESSING STUDENTS' SUITABILITY FOR TEACHING

The report stressed that some teaching practice should be undertaken to assess the students' ability to express themselves clearly and to pick out unsuitable candidates. Each student should undertake a ten-minute informal lesson in mathematics, history or geography in the second term of each year. Only the student's name, lesson and date of lesson, should be recorded by the staff. Why they recommended such short lessons is difficult to understand, for little could have been discerned of a pupil's potential as a teacher in ten minutes. Furthermore, in discussing teaching practice, the inspectors again showed little respect for the teachers at the colleges, declaring that their explanation of insufficient time for teaching practice 'was only an excuse' because they could not be bothered. In the inspectors' opinion, the teachers wanted to give it up altogether.

The inspectors were emphatic that students should be reminded continuously of the vocational aspect of their chosen career. They further reiterated the need for certain personal qualities to be nurtured in student teachers. They also expressed criticism of the teachers, drawing attention to their poor teaching methods and the boredom of life in a preparatory college classroom:

> A teacher should be able to think clearly and to express his thoughts well. There is little done in this area, little interest in reading aloud, or in acting. Students are examined in writing only; therefore oral work is neglected. They are seldom asked a question in class or to come to the blackboard to do a sum. There is so much to do to get honours that their knowledge has gaps. It depends too much on memory.[30]

---

30. *Ibid*, p. 25.

TESTS AND EXAMINATIONS

In keeping with its emphasis on personal suitability, the report recommended oral tests in Irish and English and a test in singing at the end of the Intermediate and Leaving Certificate years. The Irish oral test should include reading, acting and explaining, and students should have to obtain 75 per cent to enter training college. In contrast to the high standard for oral Irish, only 40 per cent was required to pass in oral English. Again, the inspectors were ambivalent towards English. While they stoutly defended the introduction of an oral English test, they expressed the fear that, in view of the state's Irish policy, it would be regarded as a retrograde step:

> English is a modern language and spoken by the majority in the country. Therefore teachers should be able to teach it so long as it is a compulsory subject in the curriculum.[31]

A further example of the inspectors' ambivalence towards English was the recommendation that a pupil who failed English should be allowed into the training college, if he was usually 'very good'. There was nothing, however, to indicate who was to make this judgement or on what criterion it was to be based. As Gaeltacht students were more likely to fail English, this recommendation was an attempt to ensure that they went on to training. The report also noted that while teaching staff could send unsuitable students home anytime, seldom had anyone who passed the Leaving Certificate Examination not been admitted to training. In deciding if a student be allowed to continue, they recommended that performance at the oral tests, as well as the results at written examinations, be taken into consideration. To end competition between the colleges, the report recommended that examination results be published by numbers with a statement that the student was from an unnamed preparatory college.

THE ROLE OF THE COLLEGES AS GAELIC CENTRES

On the question of siting the colleges in the Gaeltacht, a key aspect of the system and something which Blythe had considered essential to its success, the report admitted that the expectations had been too high:

> We would not say the colleges could work every bit as 'Gaelach' and as well in every way if situated in the city. One advantage would be that the professors would be happier, it would be easier get lecturers for special occasions and to encourage students to be smarter in their outlook and behaviour.[32]

---

31. *Ibid*, p. 19.
32. *Ibid.*, p. 24.

The reference to location is noteworthy for its failure to compare Coláiste na Mumhan in temporary premises in Mallow, and the two Dublin colleges, Coláiste Chaoimhín and Coláiste Moibhí, with the colleges in the Gaeltacht. In the Gaeltacht, students could meet native speakers through concerts and drama. They could also encounter *seanchaíthe* (storytellers) on visits to the colleges or to Gaeltacht houses. The inspectors acknowledged that often the students did not receive a great welcome, because they called at 'inopportune times as they cannot be let out in winter, which is the best time for *seanchaíthe*'. The report noted that the colleges had a positive effect on the Gaeltacht. They were a clear sign that a new era in the nation's history had begun. They also demonstrated the state's commitment to the language.

In view of the criticisms of the teaching of Irish, the poor quality of the teachers' own Irish and teaching methods, and the lack of mixing between Gaeltacht and Galltacht students, it was surprising that the report did not recommend ending the system. It did, however, make this forecast:

> Falling enrolments in primary schools and the decrease in the number of teachers required, will lead to a decreasing number of students in preparatory colleges and, if this happens, then all the colleges will not be needed. So some of them could become ordinary secondary schools for Gaeltacht students, or vocational schools, or domestic science schools.[33]

The report ended with a list of recommendations with financial implications and was signed by Ó Conaill and Ó Modhráin. There was also a dissenting piece by Ó Súilleabháin, who promised to send his own report and recommendations.

CHANGES TO THE SYSTEM

As the report contained some harsh criticisms of the preparatory system, it was to be expected that many of its recommendations would have been speedily implemented. However, it was some time before changes were put into effect. One of the earliest to take effect was the Department's decision in 1939 that teaching practice should be undertaken annually, in the second term of the school year, when each student would teach his or her own class. The following year, the recommendation regarding oral and singing tests for preparatory students at the Intermediate and Leaving Certificate Examinations was implemented. This was an important change, for failure meant that a student would not be allowed to continue. Other recommendations took longer to put into practice and it was February 1942, before new Regulations for Preparatory Colleges were issued.[34] These included a reduction in the age limit for Fíor-Ghaeltacht candidates. From 1943, all candidates

---

33. *Ibid.,* p. 27.
34. Circular 2/42 New Regulations for Preparatory Colleges.

were to be between 13 and 15-and-a-half, while from 1944, they were to be between 13 and 15 on 1 August of the year of the examination. The decision that entrance examination papers would be in Irish only, with no bonuses for answering in Irish, was also announced. (An exception was made for Coláiste Moibhí whose examination papers continued to be set in English.)

Changes in the entrance examination requirements regarding arithmetic and the optional subjects were included. In addition it was also announced that singing would become obligatory for all in 1943, and that, from that year on, optional subjects would be abolished. Questioned in the Dáil as to why algebra and geometry were not on the entrance examination course,[35] the Minister for Education replied:

> The new regulations removed optional subjects, including algebra and geometry, to give '*comthrom céanna*' (equal opportunity) to pupils from small schools where such subjects were not taught.

This was a further attempt to ensure Gaeltacht students continued to be successful in gaining places in the colleges. By 1944, the entrance examination consisted of examinations in Irish, English, arithmetic, history, geography, penmanship, singing and needlework for girls. From 1945, all singing tests included tonic sol-fa and sight reading, but exceptions were allowed in certain cases. Candidates who got over 75 per cent in total, but failed singing, would be accepted.

The new regulations issued in 1942 also included the conditions whereby students who had completed the Intermediate Certificate Examination would be accepted into the preparatory colleges. Such candidates had to pass the Intermediate Certificate Examination with honours, including a pass in English, honours in Irish and satisfactory marks in mathematics, history and geography. However, the following year this form of entry was *curtha ar athló* (deferred) on the grounds that it was unfair to parents who could not afford secondary education to Intermediate level for their children. This was a mistake, because had that recommendation been implemented for all students, many of the weaknesses in the system would have been eradicated, particularly the age at which students entered the system. Furthermore, at 15 or 16 plus, students would have attended at least one other secondary school and have mixed with students going on to other careers. Of much more significance was the fact that the costs of running the system would have been greatly reduced and the fees to be reclaimed when a student did not continue would have been halved. It would have also made it much easier to match the number of students in training to the numbers required. In 1943, this form of entry was allowed for students to Coláiste Moibhí as a concession to the minority community, which was experiencing severe

---

35. DT Papers, S10999.

difficulties with recruitment. A further exemption for Coláiste Moibhí was that when the age limits for entry were reduced in 1946, to between 13 and 15, an upper age limit of 15-and-a-half was kept for its entrants.

THE *McDONNELL* COURT CASE 1939

The failure to make significant changes following the inspectors' report was compounded by a significant test case before the High Court. A teacher at Coláiste Mhuire, Mrs Margaret McDonnell, (née Gillan), a UCG graduate with a first-class honours BSc degree in mathematical science and the Higher Diploma in Education, claimed damages from the Minister for Education and the archbishop of Tuam for alleged wrongful dismissal from her position as 'professor of science'.

The case highlighted the casual way in which the Department treated preparatory college staff. In evidence, Mrs McDonnell claimed that on appointment in August 1929 she was told she would have to sign a formal agreement but was never asked to do so. Neither was she told that she would have to give up teaching on marriage. The case also clearly demonstrated the way in which the colleges were managed and the role played by the local bishop as manager. Evidence corroborated the view that ultimately the power to dismiss the teacher lay with the archbishop. Furthermore, in his summing up the judge declared:

> The position of managers of preparatory colleges was somewhat peculiar and, all the more so, by the fact that there were no statutory regulations governing these colleges. But as a matter of practical arrangements between the Department and the bishops, the manager was consulted with reference to appointments to, and control of these colleges. It was quite clear that the archbishop was consulted with reference to the dismissal.[36]

Nevertheless, the judge dismissed the action against the archbishop with costs, and directed the minister to pay to the plaintiff by way of compensation the costs of the archbishop and awarded £280, one year's salary, to Mrs McDonnell.

The *McDonnell* case, as it came to be known, was important because it established certain rights for preparatory staff, and resulted in changes to the way they were treated subsequently. The most significant change was that the verdict entitled redundant teachers to compensation, and this was a factor used by Derrig in his dealings with the Department of Finance. Furthermore, the case was notable, because facts given in evidence showed the casual way the Department had acted in the 1920s. In its haste, the preparatory colleges had been established without statutory provision or regulations,[37] factors which

---

36. *Irish Times*, 5 July 1939.
37. See Part I, chapter 1.

were to be of considerable significance when the Department decided to end the system in the late 1950s. In the Department's defence, its lawyers stated that they were established in 1926 by inclusion in the parliamentary vote, and while the teaching posts were pensionable and permanent, they pleaded that the colleges were 'in an experimental stage' and had never received legislative sanction.

Evidence in the case also showed that there was no longer a pressing need for the preparatory colleges, as there were 'A' schools (all Irish schools) in many places. The preparatory colleges, however, had a significant advantage in that each one was really a 'mini-Gaeltacht' where ideal conditions existed for the 'total immersion' method of language learning.

CLOSURE OF COLÁISTE CHAOIMHÍN 1939

The case was of some concern to the Department, as negotiations over the closure of Coláiste Chaoimhín were taking place at that time. Indeed, the sudden closure of the college dealt a hammer-blow to the language movement. For about 18 months before its closure, the Department fought strenuously to keep the college open. But with an enrolment of only 59 pupils for the school year 1939–40, the Department of Finance refused to keep it open any longer. Despite the fact that the college had more than fulfilled the government's aspirations for the preparatory system, and was a source of pride to the Department and the Christian Brothers and to its staff and students, the college was closed with very short notice in July 1939.

According to the Department, the reason for closure was an oversupply of student teachers, with sufficient material available for 10 years.[38] The primary reason given for closing Coláiste Chaoimhín was that it would be easier to dispose of the building or to find alternative uses for it, as it was in Dublin. But there were two other important factors. The Department could not close Coláiste na Mumhan as its new building, costing £100,000 in Ballyvourney, had not been used, and there would have been a public outcry about the large amount of money spent on its construction. The Department also wanted to avoid further upsetting the De La Salle Order, as it was in the process of withdrawing recognition from its training college in Waterford.[39] Negotiations concerning the Waterford college had involved the highest levels in both church and state and had led to strained relationships between the hierarchy and the de Valera Government, with the hierarchy strongly supporting the De La Salle Order in resisting the government's plan to close the training college. Eventually, the government climbed down and the disagreement ended on 25 November 1939. The De La Salle Order was allowed

---

38. Letter from Department to Archbishop Byrne, June 1939, Dublin Diocesan Archives, Byrne Papers.
39. Jones, *The Preparatory Colleges*, pp. 248–252.

Air Corps Photo - Sept. 1988

22 Aerial photo of Coláiste Chaoimhín. *Courtesy Department of Defence.*

to keep its training college open for religious students (the college was to cater for all religious orders except the Christian Brothers who had their own college at Marino).

The closure of Coláiste Chaoimhín exacerbated tensions between Derrig and MacEntee. Derrig tried hard to prevent the closure of the college which he told the cabinet was a model 'for the development of teaching through Irish' and for demonstrating 'the practicability of using the language as the sole medium of instruction' in a wide secondary school curriculum.[40] He emphasised the college's outstanding place in the educational and cultural life of the country and its valuable contribution to the advancement of Irish games in schools and colleges. These were not extravagant claims puffed up to overcome the Department of Finance's objections. The college had been outstanding as one of the first schools to show that the Leaving Certificate course could be taught through Irish with very successful results. But it was to no avail.

Earlier, in an effort to avert closure, Derrig suggested to MacEntee that savings made by closing the De La Salle Training College could be used to provide funds to keep Coláiste Chaoimhín open with scholarship pupils from the Gaeltacht. MacEntee, however, dismissed such suggestions, arguing that the whole population had fallen since 1926, and in greater proportion

40. DF Papers S20/26/27.

Irish Independent.

Luznay, 8ao la 1939. JH

CLOSING OF GAELIC COLLEGE

Dublin Surprise

Colaiste Caoimhin.

T HE closing of Coláiste Caoimhin, Glasnevin, Dublin, by the Department of Education has caused much surprise in education and Irish language circles.

It was established by the Cosgrave Government about twelve years ago as an Irish preparatory college for boys, and during its brief existence had established a fine record in education, hurling, and Gaelic football.

COLLEGE'S FINE WORK.

Its work for Gaelic and Gaelic culture will long be remembered.

A wonderful Irish spirit permeated the institution, and there is much heart-burning among teachers and pupils, to many of whom news of the closing has come as a "bombshell."

The College accommodated 120 pupils. In future pupils will probably be sent to Coláiste Einne, near Salthill, Co. Galway, a palatial building completed a few years ago.

When the Irish Preparatory College at Ballyvourney, Co. Cork, is ready for occupation, the Munster boys will likely be transferred there, while the Connacht and Ulster boys will remain in Coláiste Einne.

The future of the five lay teachers and four Christian Brothers who taught in the College has not been decided.

FOR ECONOMY.

Economy is said to be the reason for the closing of the College, which it is rumoured, may be turned into a museum. Recently it was visited by a prominent official of the National Museum.

Formerly the building was known as Marlboro' Hall, and was a training college for male teachers. During the Great War it was turned into a Red Cross hospital, and subsequently it was used as a hospital for National Army troops and as a training college for officers.

23 Report of the Closing of Coláiste Chaoimhín, *Irish Independent*, 8 August 1939.

in the Gaeltacht. He gave his opinion of preferential treatment of the Gaeltacht:

> Cannot agree (it) should be increased at the expense of the rest of the country. The number of preparatory college students from the Gaeltacht is excessive with regard to the number of vacancies in the teaching profession and the state cannot be expected to maintain a figure for scholarships and preparatory colleges based on what had been an error of judgement in the past as to requirements.[41]

He strongly opposed the use of scholarships to keep the college open:

> It is extremely undesirable that boys brought up in the same level of poverty should receive secondary education together. (They) Should come into contact as early as possible with boys of a different environment, outlook, etc.

In addition he had this to say regarding Coláiste Chaoimhín's educational record:

> Secondary scholarships were designed to combine with university scholarships for the Fíor-Ghaeltacht. The objective of the two schemes is the creation of a professional and academic class of person with his whole education received through Irish. If at Coláiste Chaoimhín grave danger main objectives of scholarships lost and Coláiste Chaoimhín merely a cramming institution for the civil service instead of a stepping stone to higher education for the professions.

While what MacEntee said about the students mixing with students from other backgrounds was reasonable, his remarks about students using Coláiste Chaoimhín as a cramming institution for the civil service did not stand up to scrutiny. In 1941, a further examination of numbers entering the civil service from the training colleges revealed that between 1939 and 1941 only eight students from training colleges were successful at the civil service examinations, and they were not all from the preparatory colleges.[42]

The Department of Finance used the poor condition of the country's economy to its political advantage, estimating that the closure would save the Exchequer £6,400 annually. Despite Derrig's best efforts, when the matter had to be decided de Valera concluded that 'the prime consideration was the saving of expenditure', and to the Department of Finance's delight the closure went ahead. The Department's lack of concern for the staff of Coláiste Chaoimhín was demonstrated by the short notice they were given of the closure. Lay teachers were told they would be offered posts in other preparatory colleges or, alternatively, they would receive three months' salary in lieu of notice. This was on the condition that the money was to be returned should they obtain posts within that period. In addition they were

---

41. *Ibid.*, S25/2/39.
42. *Ibid.*, S20/8/35.

OFFICE OF NATIONAL EDUCATION,
DUBLIN, C.8.
13th June, 1939.

Very Rev. Br. B. L. RYAN,
Provincial,
Irish Christian Brothers,
St. Helen's,
Booterstown, Dublin.

REV. SIR,

I am directed by the Minister for Education to inform you that the decline in the number of pupils enrolled in National Schools and the resultant decrease in the number of places available for National teachers in the Schools has rendered necessary a full examination of the position with regard to the future recruitment of candidates for the teaching profession.

In view of the total number of Catholic trained men unemployed together with the number of lay students at present in the Training Colleges for men and the 248 students in the Preparatory Colleges for boys, there is available material for a nine or ten years' supply of men teachers.

24 Letter from the Department of Education to the Christian Brothers informing the Order of the closure of Coláiste Chaoimhín. *The Christian Brothers' Educational Record, 1940, p. 300.*

to receive compensation according to their length of service. A further aspect of the closure was the poor treatment of the Christian Brothers, who received little reward for their dedicated service to the college. A letter from the departmental secretary to Br Ward, president of Coláiste Chaoimhín, on 20 July 1939, expressed in one sentence the minister's appreciation of his and the brothers' work since the foundation of the college.[43]

The brothers' reaction to the closure, however, was stoic: 'they had no option but to accept the decision'. One reason for their quiet acceptance may have been that they hoped to acquire the college's splendid building cheaply. It had been decided that the building was to be given to the Office of Public Works to be used by the National Museum. But shortly after the closure, the Christian Brothers' Provincial Council, with the approval of Archbishop Byrne, made a formal application to the government to let or sell the building to the order, as a house of studies for either postulants or scholastics. This might have happened but for the outbreak of the Second World War, when the building was taken over by the Department of Defence.

The Department showed scant concern for the students' welfare. Br Ward was instructed to inform them that they would not be returning to

43. Christian Brothers' Archives, Coláiste Chaoimhín Papers.

Coláiste Chaoimhín. They would receive word later from the Department as to where they were to go for the school year 1939–40.[44] Indeed, the Department's indifference to their welfare was further demonstrated when the 59 students were sent first to Coláiste Éinde, where 34 completed their course, and the remaining 25 were sent on to Coláiste Íosagáin after one year. The latter had the unusual distinction of having been students at the three boys' colleges.

OPPOSITION TO THE CLOSURE

The closure aroused some opposition, led mainly by the lay staff, though there was opposition from Irish language organisations also. The lay teachers appealed immediately to the manager, Archbishop Byrne, who showed little interest in their welfare. They appealed to the Taoiseach, de Valera, and in a lengthy memo pointed out that the preparatory colleges were the only effective way for Gaeltacht people to get higher education, and so be in a position to obtain professional posts. They further asserted that preparatory colleges were the only boarding schools where 'all teachers taught through Irish, and where Irish was the only language of the school'.

The staff made certain proposals to keep Coláiste Chaoimhín open. They proposed that it could continue as a secondary school for Gaeltacht boys with a mixture of fee-paying and scholarship pupils, or it could become a government-run secondary school giving 'Fíor-Ghaeltacht education' to boys from all over the country. This could be financed by students' fees of £35 per year and a similar amount in government subsidy. They believed:

> Such a college would give a lead to all the other colleges in the country and would help them to become gaelicised. There is no other way for the learned professions to become gaelicised because Irish will never ever be the usual language of young people of the Galltacht, particularly those who will be the country's leaders unless many of them spend some years in a school like that.[45]

This was a realistic proposal made by people who were deeply committed to the gaelicisation policy. Indeed, the proposal could have been adapted for the other colleges and had the government been seriously committed to gaelicisation, it would have given this idea some consideration.

Eventually, the grievances of the teachers were settled and opposition to the closure died down. The affair showed the shallowness of the government's commitment to the Irish language. In Coláiste Chaoimhín, it had a very successful school, judged by the standards of the times. As a college it was renowned for the enthusiasm of its staff and pupils for the language. This

---

44. *The Christian Brothers' Educational Record*, p. 299.
45. Memo to the Taoiseach against the closing of Coláiste Chaoimhín, Christian Brothers' Archives, Coláiste Chaoimhín Papers.

was acknowledged by an editorial in the *Evening Mail*, a newspaper not given to promoting the language policy:

> The college was established some 12 years ago, and in Gaelic circles its reputation stood high. It was staffed by teachers with an infectious enthusiasm for the language, and the solid practical work that was done there earned the admiration of all who had any contact with it and saw the results it achieved. Those who passed through its courses emerged as very competent Irish speakers – and such are rare enough in spite of the large doses of the language that have been served up to our youth during the past 15 years and what is, perhaps, more important to the cause so dear to the heart of the government, propagandists and apologists for the restoration of the ancient tongue, burning with conviction and sincerity.[46]

The closure of Coláiste Chaoimhín was ironic, as the college had accomplished more for the gaelicisation policy in the 12 years of its existence than anything else in the previous 20 years. It achieved exceptional results in public examinations. These included Leaving Certificate Examinations where students obtained first place in history, botany and general science in 1934, and in general science in 1935 and 1936. In 1938, students obtained first place in history, botany and general science, and seven students were awarded full marks in higher level Irish.[47] Outstanding results were also achieved at the Intermediate Certificate Examination. In addition the college made a notable contribution to Gaelic sporting endeavours, and many of its former students went on to distinguish themselves in this area. A number made outstanding contributions to education, and were noted contributors to the advancement of the Irish language. A further irony was that it was the college on which the least amount of money had been spent. The closure showed the somewhat hypocritical attitude of de Valera and Fianna Fáil, which only two years earlier had put before the public the 1937 Constitution, with its declaration in Article 8 that Irish was the national language – the first official language of the state.

---

46. *Evening Mail*, 8 August 1939.
47. *Irish Press*, 3 November 1938.

CHAPTER FOUR

Surviving with the help of Derrig:
1939–48

'The preparatory colleges have become white elephants'

The period 1939–48 was difficult for education in Ireland with a widening rift between the government and the INTO that was to culminate eventually in a prolonged strike by primary teachers in 1946. A significant contributory factor was the government's rejection of the findings of the INTO's *Report of the Committee of Inquiry into the use of Irish,* published in 1941. For much of this period, recruitment was at a low ebb. The series of measures taken by the Department to deal with the over-supply of teachers, which characterised the 1930s, resulted ultimately in the temporary cessation of recruitment by open competition to training colleges in 1938, and the temporary closure of St. Patrick's Training College in 1944.

The Emergency, as the Second World War was known in Ireland, was problematic for the preparatory system with a temporary cessation of recruitment during 1939 and 1940. Two colleges, Coláiste Éinde and Coláiste Moibhí, were taken over by the Department of Defence, and it was mainly due to determined efforts by Derrig that they eventually re-opened. For most of the 1940s, pupil enrolments in national schools declined with a consequent decrease in the number of teachers required (it was not until 1947 that enrolments began to increase). These factors, and the increase in the number of all-Irish secondary schools meant there was less need for the preparatory colleges.

Throughout this period, Fianna Fáil was in government and Derrig was Minister for Education from 1940–48. Money for government projects was in short supply and the disagreements between the Departments of Finance and Education over the preparatory system continued unabated. Buoyed up by its success in achieving the closure of Coláiste Chaoimhín, the Department of Finance planned to make further savings by amalgamating two of the girls' colleges.[1] While this would have been justified on the grounds of numbers and economic necessity, the Department of Finance was slow to pursue the proposal for fear of further upsetting the hierarchy. Relationships between the government and the bishops were already strained over the withdrawal of recognition from the De La Salle Order's Training College in Waterford (see chapter 3).

The Department of Education's fear of further offending the Catholic Church affected its recruitment policy. Members of religious orders continued to be accepted into training colleges, despite the fact that from 1938 on recruitment had been limited to students already in the preparatory colleges. The bishops were not the only difficulty to be considered when closing a preparatory college. There was also the outcome of the *McDonnell* case, which meant that the Department would have to pay compensation to redundant staff. In the early 1940s, the Department of Finance continuously sought to reduce costs and in the straitened economic conditions of the time, this was not unreasonable, particularly as the costs for the preparatory colleges were almost as high as those for the training colleges.[2]

COSTS OF PREPARATORY COLLEGES

The Department of Finance argued forcefully that considerable savings would be made if student teachers were recruited through open competition, instead of through the preparatory colleges. Such savings have to be seen in the context of the period, when over 50 per cent of primary teachers earned less than £4 a week.

Annual Costs of Preparatory Colleges 1939–1948

YEAR	ANNUAL COSTS	YEAR	ANNUAL COSTS
1939	£42,632-14-1	1944	£32,263-15-4
1940	£38,463-18-9	1945	£35,062-0-0
1941	£32,954-15-4	1946	£40,647-7-9
1942	£29,348-2-8	1947	£44,938-10-4
1943	£29,779-6-10	1948	£50,890-13-5

Source: *Reports of the Department of Education,* 1939–48

A further significant factor that favoured open competition was that it was much easier to regulate the numbers recruited, and to prevent the disastrous over-recruitment of the 1930s. However, the Department was determined

---

1. DF Papers, S25/4/34.
2. Jones, *The Preparatory Colleges,* p. 352.

25 The entrance to Coláiste Éinde, Salthill.

to keep the colleges open,[3] defending the system on the grounds that it provided vocational testing before entry to training. Considering the limited nature of teaching practice revealed in the *Report of the Committee of Inquiry into the Preparatory Colleges* in 1938,[4] this was a remarkable claim. The real reason for the Department championing the system was that ending it would be a severe setback for the language policy. Furthermore, it would allow the opposition to taunt the Fianna Fáil government about its lack of commitment to gaelicisation. In addition, the closure of a second college so soon after the closure of Coláiste Chaoimhín would be a harsh blow.

The question of which college to close was problematic. On the one hand, Coláiste Éinde's Galway location was more convenient for students from Donegal than Coláiste Íosagáin in remote Ballyvourney. The closure of Coláiste Éinde would be a blow to the Irish movement in the west and would arouse strong criticism in Galway. It would, however, be easier to use for alternative purposes. On the other hand, the De La Salle Order would not accept the closure of Coláiste Íosagáin, after only one year in operation, and the Department feared a public outcry over the high costs incurred in building the college. A further significant factor in any decision was the role of the hierarchy, in particular, the reaction of the bishop of Galway, manager of Coláiste Éinde.

3. DT Papers, S12307.
4. See Part I, chapter 3.

TEMPORARY CLOSURE OF COLLEGES CONSIDERED

The temporary closure of all the colleges was considered but this was resolutely opposed by Derrig. Instead he proposed providing extra scholarships for Fíor-Ghaeltacht students to fill the empty places, a proposal dismissed by the Department of Finance. Other proposals considered to prevent temporary closure included the speeding up of female recruitment for 1941 and 1942, and plans for refresher courses for national teachers. Detailed plans for courses for women at Coláiste Mhuire and for men at Coláiste Éinde were drawn up in 1941. However, these came to naught as de Valera refused to press the Department of Finance to make the necessary funding available.

Throughout this period, recruitment continued to be problematic as the Department was unable to forecast accurately the number of teachers required. Furthermore, because of the way schools were organised, the number of posts for male teachers was less than for females and recruitment had to reflect this. While a careful study of the annual birth-rate figures should have indicated the number of pupil enrolments likely four or five years later, the situation was complicated during the Emergency by the need to make allowances for emigration or even immigration.

The Department's efforts to resolve recruiting requirements became more problematic as it clashed with the Department of Finance over the issue. In 1940, the *Report of the Department of Education Committee on Future Requirements with regard to Recruitment for the Teaching Profession* recommended

26 Aerial photo of Coláiste Mhuire, Tourmakeady. *Courtesy Seán Ó Conghaile, chairperson of the Board of Management.*

that the five Catholic preparatory colleges be continued, as they would definitely be required from 1944–45 onwards. It further recommended that entrance examinations for the preparatory colleges should re-start in 1941 and that 75 women should be recruited to training colleges by open competition. These proposals were rejected by the Department of Finance which reiterated its preference for recruitment by open competition rather than through the preparatory system. In March 1941, it produced a memo showing that there were only 186 students in the five Catholic preparatory colleges, while domestic and teaching staff numbered 122.[5] This was a ratio of less than two students per staff member, and showed the justification for the Department of Finance's demands.

Throughout the struggle between the Departments of Finance and Education, Derrig was careful to ensure that de Valera was aware of developments and fully briefed in advance of cabinet meetings. This strategy was successful and eventually the Department of Finance accepted that it would not get its way. The fact that MacEntee, who was known for his confrontational style, had been succeeded as Minister for Finance by Seán T. Ó Ceallaigh[6] in 1939 may have influenced this decision.

Though Ireland was neutral, the Second World War had a considerable impact upon life in the Irish Free State. Two of the colleges, Coláiste

27 Coláiste Moibhí's premises in the Phoenix Park, formerly The Royal Hibernian Military School, now St Mary's Hospital.

---

5. DT Papers, S12307.
6. For biographical details of people named on this page see the Appendix.

Moibhí (see Part II) and C. Éinde, were particularly affected as their premises were taken over by the Department of Defence. The government's lack of commitment to the preparatory system and to the gaelicisation policy was clearly shown in the casual way it treated both colleges. There was, however, considerable difference in the way it approached the church authorities in the two colleges.

TAKE-OVER OF COLÁISTE ÉINDE

The Department's dealings with the Church of Ireland authorities were notable for the quiescent manner in which the minority accepted the government's decisions. (The takeover of Coláiste Moibhí is dealt with in Part II). The take-over of Coláiste Éinde, however, was not so easily accomplished due to the persistent refusal of the manager, Bishop Michael Browne, to accept the Department's plans. He insisted that a written agreement be given that the college would return to its Salthill premises at the end of the Emergency. Derrig also opposed plans to turn the college into a military hospital. He feared it was simply a ploy by the Department of Finance to close the college down, and in a memo for the government in 1942 he strongly defended the system:

> In 15 years of existence the preparatory colleges have become the pioneers and are looked on as the strongholds of Gaelic culture for the preliminary education of primary teachers in such a manner as to inspire in their future pupils the ideals necessary for the building of a nation. The intensively and generally Irish atmosphere outside and inside is everywhere recognised and because of these factors they have acquired a high propagandist value in national efforts. (They are) Models for secondary schools generally.[7]

In a further lengthy memo for the cabinet, Derrig claimed that the closure of Coláiste Chaoimhín, 'had a definite depressing effect on the whole Irish movement'.[8] He also warned that closure of another college would have 'very serious repercussions' on the gaelicisation policy. Though Coláiste Éinde had only 49 students in residence in a building with accommodation for 110 students and staff, he pleaded that the college catered especially for students from the Connacht and Tír Conaill Fíor-Ghaeltachtaí. Their transfer to Ballyvourney would create hardship and expense for both the parents and the state. He also estimated that staff compensation would cost £2,000, and predicted strong opposition from Bishop Browne.

To resolve the matter the cabinet set up a committee to examine the situation. *The Report of the Committee on the Provision of Hospitals in the West of Ireland* commended the suitability of Coláiste Éinde as a hospital and listed

---

7. *Ibid.,* S12807.
8. *Ibid.*

its excellent facilities. It also outlined efforts to find alternative accommodation for Coláiste Éinde, including examining Coláiste Mhuire at Tourmakeady. This, it decided, was unsuitable due to its poor location and small size, though it noted that like Coláiste Éinde, it was only 'half used'.

THE ROLE OF BISHOP BROWNE OF GALWAY

The take-over of Coláiste Éinde highlighted the role of Bishop Michael Browne as manager of the college. At first, Browne 'agreed to co-operate', though insisting Coláiste Éinde stay within his diocese. Subsequently, he laid down conditions for the take-over. They included protection of the teachers' rights and the return of the building at the end of the Emergency.[9] These demands caused consternation amongst senior civil servants, and led to high-level discussions between officials of the Departments of Finance, Education and the Taoiseach. They drafted a carefully worded letter, to be sent by de Valera to the bishop, giving the government's view that it could not bind itself and succeeding governments to his conditions. Meanwhile, the possibility of the college returning to the original location, Tigh Furbacha, where it had been from 1928 until 1931, was considered. It could accommodate 35 pupils and staff with facilities for daily Mass in a nearby church. This was important, as earlier, in 1928, the opening of Coláiste Éinde had been delayed when Browne's predecessor, Dr O'Doherty, had insisted that arrangements for the provision of a chapel or oratory be made before work started on the college buildings.

INVOLVING ARCHBISHOP McQUAID

The matter remained unresolved for another year. In April 1943, Browne agreed to the east wing of the college being taken over by the army. How this happened is a matter for speculation. But the arrangement was not very satisfactory for either party. The work of Coláiste Éinde was restricted, as only 40 students could be accommodated, while the army had insufficient accommodation for its patients and staff. Efforts to persuade Browne to allow the army to take over the whole building continued unsuccessfully until 2 August 1944, when the Department decided to involve the archbishop of Dublin, Dr John Charles McQuaid,[10] in the matter.

As manager of St Patrick's Training College, Drumcondra, McQuaid had been involved in negotiations concerning that college and its staff in relation to the period when it was not functioning as a training college. In August 1944, the Department wrote to McQuaid about the possibility of moving Coláiste Éinde to St Patrick's, which was empty due to the ban on recruitment.

---

9. Memo to the cabinet, 21 April 1942, DT Papers, S12653.
10. For biographical details see the Appendix.

28 Medical and Military Staff pictured outside Coláiste Éinde when in use as a Military Hospital. *Courtesy George Guest.*

In view of McQuaid's immediate agreement, Browne had no choice but to accept the Department's proposal. He insisted, however, that one room in the Galway building be retained by the college and that the name of the college be kept on the gate, saying:

> I would like to place it on record that I do not see much validity in the reason advanced by the Department of Defence over its use of the whole of the college. They have not proved any urgency arising from an increased number of patients.[11]

He also insisted that other buildings in his diocese, Lough Cutra Castle and Kilscornan Castle, be considered as possible locations for the college should the army's stay at Coláiste Éinde be longer than anticipated. This was accepted by the Department.

The episode illustrated the power of Browne as manager of the college and the deferential way in which the cabinet bowed to his will. Browne's insistence on conditions for the take-over was allowed to delay the provision of a military hospital for over two years. This was a matter which could have been of considerable national importance. When the project was first conceived in 1942, it could not have been predicted which way the global conflict would develop and the need for such a hospital could have become urgent. An example of the way in which Coláiste Éinde might have been needed had already occurred in September 1939, when the liner *Athenia* was sunk off the west coast of Ireland and hundreds of passengers were rescued by a small Norwegian vessel, the *Knut Nielsen*, and landed in Galway. More

11. Letter from Bishop Browne to Department of Education, 7 August 1944, Galway Diocesan Archives, Browne Papers.

than 100 uninjured passengers from Europe, Canada and the United States were accommodated in Coláiste Éinde.

CRITICISM OF GOVERNMENT POLICY

While the episode showed the cabinet's desire to avoid a confrontation with the bishop, the possibility that Browne's intransigence suited Derrig must not be overlooked. While much of Browne's determination to impose his conditions may have been due to his autocratic nature, he was also well aware that once the building was taken over, it was unlikely to become a preparatory college again. Indeed, few believed that the college would re-open in Galway; a view reflected in a critical editorial, *The Unwanted Colleges*, in a national newspaper in September 1944:

> The strange idea was conceived by the Department of Education 18 years ago that children of 12 (sic) years were capable of deciding that they had a vocation for teaching and that, if they so decided, the proper thing to do with them was to put them in a college all by themselves for four years, doing a secondary school course which they could have done at any existing secondary school. In accordance with this scheme seven preparatory colleges were provided and equipped at a cost to the taxpayer of more than £500,000.[12]

The editorial was scathing in its criticism of the entrance examination. It recalled that it was possible for a boy from the Gaeltacht 'with Irish acquired by accident' to secure a place in a college to the exclusion of a boy from an English-speaking district 'with Irish acquired by effort'. This could occur despite the latter having scored higher marks, not only in the aggregate of subjects, but even in the Irish language. Pointing out that the INTO had protested in vain against this system, it angrily denounced the Department's failure to assess recruitment requirements more accurately:

> While this strange experiment was being worked on these strange lines a still stranger thing was happening. Evidently simple mathematics is not their strong suit in the Department of Education. The Department's own returns had been showing that schools were becoming fewer and fewer and that the school-going population was declining at an alarming rate. But the Department continued to train a surplus of teachers who joined the ranks of the unemployed. Finally, the officials woke up and at once fell into a panic. They closed down the training colleges proper – this is the only civilised country in which training colleges were ever closed down – and they restricted the number of students to be admitted to the preparatory colleges.

This criticism was thoroughly deserved, though the editorial was careful not to lay the whole blame for the system on Derrig whom it said had to answer

---

12. *Irish Independent,* 1 September 1944.

'only for the sin of its continuance, not of its origin'. Referring to the numbers of students the editorial went on:

> Built and equipped to house some 650 students the seven (sic) preparatory colleges when the public last obtained any figures from the Department had only a third of that number. The preparatory colleges have become white elephants. The Board of Works, which spent so much public money in laying them out for students, will now exercise their skill in spending more money in turning at least one of the colleges into a hospital.[13]

Somehow the fact that Coláiste Chaoimhín had been closed in 1939 escaped the writer's notice. This did not lessen his vitriolic criticism of how public money had been consumed by the system. The editorial ended by reiterating the dubious claim of the Commission on Vocational Organisation,[14] that 'the work done in the colleges might possibly have been done in the existing secondary schools, a view which we ourselves expressed several years ago'. This was untrue because at the time the colleges were established, they were the only second-level residential 'A' schools. Furthermore, they pioneered teaching through Irish at both Intermediate and Leaving Certificate levels.

When the Emergency ended in 1945, to the surprise of everybody in Galway, Coláiste Éinde returned to Salthill, but its tenure continued to be somewhat insecure. The election of the First Inter-party Government in 1948 brought an intensified drive to eradicate TB, and the take-over of the college as a hospital was considered once more. But nothing came of it and the college was allowed to stay at its Salthill premises.

The treatment of Coláiste Éinde and Coláiste Moibhí showed the ambivalent attitude of the Fianna Fáil Government to the preparatory system and once again illustrated the casual way students and staff were treated. There was little regard for their needs or for the disruption of teaching which occurred when the colleges were taken over. Indeed, the colleges were fortunate that their premises were returned to them when the Emergency ended. Neither the Fianna Fáil Government, nor its successor, the First Inter-party Government, showed any great desire to keep their commitments to the colleges.

THE INTO INQUIRY INTO THE USE OF IRISH

The careful manner in which the hierarchy was treated contrasted with Derrig's attitude to the INTO. Furthermore, the minister's refusal to listen to the teachers' views on compulsory Irish led to increasingly strained relationships between the teachers and the Department, which were a major

---

13. *Ibid.*
14. The Commission on Vocational Organisation, chaired by Bishop Browne, was established by de Valera in 1937. Its report was presented in 1943.

feature of the 1940s. As early as 1930, teacher dissatisfaction with the language policy had begun to manifest itself at the annual congress of the INTO. Six years later it resulted in a resolution establishing a committee of inquiry into the use of Irish as a teaching medium. The strategy of the five-member committee, all experienced teachers with 'highly efficient' ratings, was to elicit information by sending questionnaires to over 9,000 members of the organisation. The questionnaire had seven different sections dealing with teachers' perceptions about teaching through Irish. These were headed:

    I. The Teacher and the School
   II. Infants
  III. Standards I, II, and III
  IV. Standards IV to VII
   V. The Religious Programme
  VI. General
 VII. Observations

In 1939, the committee produced an interim report, but it was almost six years after the committee had been established that the final *Report of the Committee of Inquiry into the use of Irish* was published. The report found that certain subjects of the curriculum, mathematics, history and geography, were affected detrimentally by teaching through Irish. Only two subjects, singing and needlework, remained unaffected. These findings were not unexpected, but the findings regarding infant teaching were devastating. The majority of teachers were of the opinion that teaching through Irish imposed a mental strain on young children:

> The constant use of Irish tends to kill enthusiasm and love, due to the inevitable monotonous nature of the work. It puts a strain on the child and dulls the normal receptiveness of his mind. It tends to make the 'All Irish' policy defeat its own ends.[15]

The section on infant teaching through Irish concluded with these damning remarks:

> Living as he is in an atmosphere of repression there is the further danger of his associating the language with what is unpleasant and distasteful. A positive dislike of the language may easily be developed and the ill effects of such an attitude cannot be too strongly stated.[16]

Also of considerable significance was Section V, where teachers were asked whether instruction in religion was given through Irish. The responses showed that in the vast majority of schools religious instruction was given in the language of the children's home. This was a further indication of the

---

15. *Report of Committee of Inquiry into the use of Irish*, p. 12.
16. *Ibid.*, p. 24.

lack of church support for the gaelicisation policy. Had the hierarchy given their whole-hearted commitment to the Irish language, all aspects of religious teaching would have been through Irish.

In a general observation on the gaelicisation policy, the report stressed with considerable realism that for compulsory Irish to be successful, support from both home and society at large was necessary:

> The school is failing in its purpose. It is divorced from home and society. Out of 168 hours in a week the child sleeps 70. Of the 98 remaining, 30 are spent in schools that is 1:3. We believe that the majority of parents are anxious for Irish to be known and understood by their children but according to replies a very considerable minority, if not antagonistic, are certainly apathetic. The attitude of parents does not seem to have been adverted to by those directing the Irish revival.[17]

The report called for a return to the vernacular as the medium of teaching subjects other than Irish, with more time for Irish conversation lessons. It also called for the standardisation of Irish spelling, the simplification of Irish grammar and the raising of the school leaving age to 15.

The Department, however, refused to listen to the teachers' views. Instead, Derrig criticised teachers for not using Irish for ordinary conversation between themselves and complained that the standard of work in senior classes was too narrow. This showed how far Derrig's attitude had hardened. As recently as 1934, he had expressed doubts about the wisdom of using only Irish in infant classes:

> I will be very glad if, from time to time, our inspectors and teachers could come together - or teachers on their own - to see whether the question of having only Irish in the infant school from the first day, or whether a little English should be allowed, until the child becomes accustomed to the new atmosphere.[18]

A year later he had warned that the state could not depend on the schools alone to revive the language. Indeed, in an earlier annual report in 1932–33, the Department had acknowledged that the policy was not succeeding.

Yet paradoxically, it was during this period that *Notes for Teachers* was published by the Department. Its stated aim was to make Irish speakers out of the children of the Galltacht, so that by the age of 14 they would be able 'to express themselves freely, fully and correctly, in the native language'. Derrig was also the minister who introduced the *Revised Programme of Primary Instruction* in 1934. It insisted that infants be taught entirely through Irish and strengthened the Irish programme for higher classes, while modifying requirements in other subjects.

In 1942, Derrig dismissed the findings of the *Report of the Committee of Inquiry into the use of Irish* as propaganda. Despite his disdainful attitude in

---

17. *Ibid.*, p. 60.
18. *Dáil Reports*, 11 April 1934.

public, however, the following year he presented a memo on the language policy to the cabinet.[19] In it he acknowledged that much of the time and effort put in to teaching Irish at school was ineffective, because pupils had no use for Irish once they left education. Nevertheless, he stubbornly refused to consider a review of the language policy.

LIFE IN THE COLLEGES DURING THE EMERGENCY

The Emergency created many administrative problems for the colleges, even for the new purpose-built college at Ballyvourney. The Munster boys' college opened there in September 1940 under the new name, Coláiste Íos-agáin. Entries in the diary of the religious community noted the effects of the Emergency. In January 1943 it recorded: 'The monthly oil supply is often late; no light till 19 January and no heating for nine days.' Another entry for the same month, noted that 'since 1941 damp has been developing in the floor, wall and roof, and as the supply of crude oil is meagre, lights have to be out at 8.30 pm nightly'.

Some colleges fared better than others for food. The three girls' colleges had farms, which supplied them with milk and vegetables, while the boys' colleges had vegetable gardens. Indeed, Coláiste Éinde had such a good supply that they were able to sell the surplus. Due to difficulties with transport, however, the principal had to request the Department for permission to hire a donkey and cart at a cost of £10 to get the vegetables to market.

The Emergency also affected students' lives but the Department showed little concern for their welfare. Regardless of transport problems caused by fuel shortages, it continued its practice of sending students to colleges with little consideration for either distance or convenience. In one case, a Cork

29 Coláiste Íosagáin.

19. Memo on the Position of the Irish Language, DT Papers, S13180.

student was sent to Coláiste Bhríde where she started sleepwalking. This was diagnosed by the college doctor as due to anxiety at being so far from her family. He recommended that she should be sent to a college nearer home.[20]

The students were not the only ones affected by the Emergency. When recruitment to the preparatory colleges was resumed in 1942, there were difficulties regarding staffing, particularly where part-time teachers with specialist qualifications, such as music, were required. From 1938, the Department had been trying to improve the musical education of students, and a special course of piano, theory, voice training, ear tests and singing, was introduced. In addition each college had a choir, and concerts were frequently organised. At the beginning of the 1940s, principals of colleges where there was a qualified member of staff were told to implement the new programme. Four colleges – Coláiste Mhuire, Coláiste Bhríde, Coláiste Íde and Coláiste Éinde – were able to, but special arrangements had to be made for Coláiste Moibhí and Coláiste Íosagáin. The problem at Coláiste Moibhí was soon resolved, but coming to an arrangement for Coláiste Íosagáin was not so easy because of its remote location.

In May 1944, the principals of Coláiste Íde, Coláiste Bhríde, Coláiste Íosagáin and Coláiste Mhuire met to discuss their staff requirements, as teachers who had left had not been replaced. A memo on the meeting illustrated their difficulties and the unsympathetic attitude of the Department of Finance.[21] In order to provide teaching in certain subjects, it had become necessary for some nuns to take on the post of matron in addition to a part-time teaching post. In Coláiste Bhríde, the matron taught for about 14 hours a week, while the matron in Coláiste Mhuire also taught music. Sr Paschal had been a 'professor' from 1934 to 1940, and when student numbers declined she became the matron. Subsequently, with the introduction of the new programme in music she was appointed music teacher while continuing to act as matron. A comment on the Department of Finance file noted: 'Matron's duties can't be very onerous, if she can do 13 hours per week music teaching'.

NUMBERS APPLYING FOR PLACES IN THE 1940s

Numbers applying to enter the preparatory colleges had begun to decline in the late 1930s. This was probably due to the high level of unemployment among primary teachers, due to over-recruitment in that period. Nevertheless, even before the cessation of recruitment to preparatory colleges in 1939, numbers were high with well over 1,000 students applying annually. The resumption of recruitment in 1941 saw a large increase in the number of girls applying for entry. A likely explanation for the increase was that many of those who had been unable to apply due to the cessation of recruitment in 1939 and 1940 applied in 1941. A similar explanation is likely for

---

20. DF Papers, S25/5/38.
21. *Ibid.*, S20/37/27.

Applications for Places in Preparatory Colleges 1936–46

	Total	Boys	Girls
1936	1,443	494	949
1937	1,199	376	823
1938	1,163	372	791
1939	Cessation of recruitment		
1940	to Catholic colleges		
1941	1,039		1,039★
1942	1,434	509	925
1943	1,464	472	992
1944	892	290	602
1945	871	281	590
1946	833	285	548

★ Recruitment of girls only allowed.

Source: *Reports of the Department of Education, 1936–46*

the increase in the number of boys applying in 1942. It would appear from these figures that the changes in the conditions for entry resulted in a considerable decrease in the numbers applying in 1944, though it is difficult to say which particular change or combination of changes was responsible. An increase in the number of scholarships awarded to Fíor-Ghaeltacht students may have had some influence on the matter. A more likely explanation is that the Department had become much less generous in its grants to students. In the early 1940s there was a considerable increase in the number of students paying full fees with a corresponding decrease in the number paying no fees.

Average Fees at Preparatory Colleges late 1930s and 1940s

	Average fee		
1937/38	£7–11s.–0d.	1947/48	£15–9s.–6d.
1938/39	£7–12s.–1d.	1948/49	£17–13s.–3d.

Source: *Department of Finance Papers, S25/15/34*

The registers of Coláiste Mhuire and Coláiste Íosagáin show that in both colleges the number of students paying full fees had risen to 30 per cent in 1943. This was almost double the number of students throughout the system, 15.7 per cent, who paid full fees in the 1930s.

THE PRIMARY TEACHERS' STRIKE

The end of the 1940s was dominated by the primary teachers' strike, which was to have profound effects on primary education for many years. Teacher discontent, which had been simmering for a long time, finally erupted in a strike in 1946. For many years primary teachers had been striving for increased salaries, better conditions and a say in policy-making. The teachers' grievances went back to 1923, when the Free State Government cut their salaries by 10 per cent. In 1934, a further nine per cent reduction was introduced in conjunction with a new pension scheme promulgated at the same time. These reductions were bitterly resented. Small increases in 1938 and in 1942 did little to ameliorate the situation as they were inadequate due to the higher cost of living. Meanwhile, teachers' anger increased as they watched civil servants and others of a similar professional status receiving larger increases.

The salary issue was not the only reason for the increasing tensions between the teachers and the Department. Derrig's prickly personality was another factor. According to T.J. O'Connell[22] of the INTO, he was inclined to take criticism 'directed to his administration as being personal to himself'; and at times, when relationships between the INTO and the Department were strained, he refused to attend the organisation's annual conference (Congress). Derrig's response to the INTO's *Inquiry into the Use of Irish* exacerbated relationships. A further factor was the Department's assertion that teachers were not doing enough to improve the standard of Irish in senior classes.[23] The INTO angrily denounced such claims:

> It is difficult to keep patience with this kind of criticism .... The Department would lose nothing in dignity if it made it clear, that the present language programme in schools is necessarily an experiment, since the problem it is intended to solve, is one for which no clear solution yet exists.[24]

In 1943 the Department added to the teachers' grievances by making the Primary School Certificate Examination compulsory for all pupils in sixth standard. This innovation was regarded as successful by the Department, as the examination was held in the majority of schools, and approximately 70 per cent of pupils passed. The examination was first introduced on an optional basis in 1929 on the advice of Fr Timothy Corcoran. During the 1930s, opposition to the examination developed among teachers, and in 1935 a resolution calling for its abolition was passed at Congress. As a result of the examination becoming compulsory, the emphasis in the schools changed from oral to written work. This was later acknowledged to have been a mistake by the Commission on the Restoration of the Irish Language.[25]

In October 1945, the INTO decided to take strike action. Two factors influenced this decision. Public opinion was with the teachers and they had the support of the hierarchy, particularly of Archbishop McQuaid. His role

22. For biographical details of people named on this page see the Appendix.
23. *Report of the Department of Education*, 1941/42, p. 16.
24. *Irish School Weekly*, XLV, 9 and 16 October 1943.
25. The Commission on the Restoration of the Irish Language, *Summary of the Final Report*, 1963, p. 67.

in the teachers' strike was crucial, because of his influence over the priests who were the school managers. Throughout the negotiations he kept in close touch with the INTO and Derrig. A confidential letter from Derrig to McQuaid in February 1946, gives some insights into the minister's stern attitude to the teachers:

> I told the teachers that the new salary scales cannot come into force until after the Emergency. I told the INTO that a strike will do no good and may do untold harm. Most of them admit this. But they are bent on challenging the government's authority. I have done all I can. If it becomes a question of asserting the government's authority I must make up my mind to face the new situation.[26]

Despite an attempt at mediation by McQuaid, the strike began on 20 March 1946 and lasted almost eight months. Only the schools in Dublin were closed. The publication of a letter from McQuaid at the beginning of the strike swayed waverers to join it and strengthened public support for the teachers. Their powerful ally wrote:

> Your organisation must have no doubt that the clerical managers of this city and religious superiors have full sympathy with the ideal of a salary in keeping with the dignity and responsibility of your profession as teachers .... You will as Catholics, at once understand that clerical managers and religious superiors, by reason of their religious status, may not adopt strike action. For the same reason they may not refuse to comply with the lawful commands of the civil authority in what concerns the keeping open, and operating of their schools. Neither may they penalise a teacher, now or later, for the mere fact that he or she has chosen to accept the direction of the central executive committee of the INTO.[27]

Despite McQuaid's support, however, the government refused to come to an agreement with the teachers, and the strike dragged on and became increasingly bitter. The public continued to support the teachers, a view that was reflected by the *Irish Times:*

> The strike is now nine weeks old. Deadlock is complete. The next step lies with the government. Mr. Derrig said he offered the teachers the highest scales which the country could afford and in effect that the strike could only be terminated by their unconditional surrender. This is rank folly.[28]

McQuaid made several attempts to persuade de Valera of the justice of the teachers' claim, but he was unsuccessful in bringing about negotiations for a settlement. With widespread public support for the teachers, the strike continued but the government refused to consider arbitration. Eventually, the

26. Letter from Derrig to McQuaid, 8 February 1946, Dublin Diocesan Archives, McQuaid Papers.
27. *Irish Times,* 20 March 1946.
28. *Ibid.,* 22 May 1946.

strike ended with the teachers' surrender on 31 October. Then, 'in deference to the wish expressed by the archbishop of Dublin, as the spiritual
authority for the education of the children of the diocese of Dublin', the
central executive committee of the INTO accepted an invitation from
McQuaid to direct the teachers to return to work. The end of the strike was
'without prejudice to their natural rights, or to their just and equitable
rights'.[29] This obsequious statement typified the attitude of teachers and of
the general public to the all-powerful role of McQuaid and the church in
education at that time. Furthermore, the absence of any reference to children or teachers of other denominations was typical of that period when the
monolithic Catholic Church dominated Irish society.

For the INTO, the strike was of major significance and the spirit of the
strikers became embedded in the organisation's psyche, with its memory
invoked frequently over the following three decades. Despite being forced
to give in, however, the organisation had made considerable gains. It had
achieved a higher profile, and brought the importance of education to the
attention of the public, who accepted that the teachers were entitled to reasonable pay increases. Protracted salary negotiations were in progress when
a general election was held early in 1948. A significant result of the strike
was that Fianna Fáil lost support amongst the public and many teachers
joined Clann na Poblachta, a newly-formed political party with a radical
social manifesto. This transfer of support was seen as a contributory factor in
the defeat of Fianna Fáil, and the formation of the First Inter-party Government in 1948.

RECRUITMENT IN THE LATE 1940s

The strike had little effect on recruitment and large numbers continued to
be recruited to the profession through the preparatory colleges and open
competition. In the late 1940s, the numbers seeking entry to the preparatory
colleges began to decline, while the figures for those entering training colleges by open competition increased. Three factors may have influenced this
trend. Fees at preparatory colleges were increased from £40 to £50 per
annum at this time. There was also a greater availability of second-level
education, particularly of 'A' schools, and therefore less need for the preparatory colleges. A third factor was the increase in salaries gained by the
teachers as part of the strike settlement in 1949. This gave an added impetus
to recruitment by open competition in the following years. However, only
a percentage of those who passed the entrance examination for the training
colleges obtained places.[30] Similarly, only a fraction of those who passed the
entrance examination to the preparatory colleges actually gained a place.

29. O'Connell, *100 years of progress: the story of the Irish National Teachers Organisation 1868–1968*,
    p. 231.
30. Jones, The Preparatory Colleges, p. 402.

As the Emergency ended, Ireland emerged from its isolation to a post-war Europe where change was widespread. Radical changes were taking place in society, with an impetus towards social and economic reform. Furthermore, in education second-level schooling came to be regarded as a right for all. School-leaving ages were extended, and the liberalisation of discipline, curricula and teaching methods began to transform education. There was a similar desire for change in the Irish Republic, which was accentuated by the ending of the Emergency, the approach of a new decade and by Fianna Fáil's long period in government.

It is possible that similar educational reforms might have been implemented in Ireland but for the general election in 1948. Some months before the election, a Departmental Committee on Educational Provision, established by Derrig in 1945, presented a comprehensive plan recommending far-reaching changes. These included raising the school-leaving age to 16, the provision of second-level education for all and a broadening of the curriculum in both primary and second-level schools. It also proposed that the state establish a new type of school, the senior school, to provide free education for all children from 12 to 15 or 16 years. As early as 1942, Derrig had drawn up a comprehensive school building programme to be undertaken during the post-war period. An outline of it had been sent to Archbishop McQuaid to ensure the hierarchy's support.[31]

THE INTO'S *PLAN FOR EDUCATION* 1947

The Department, however, was not the only body considering changes in the educational system. In March 1947, the INTO published *A Plan for Education,* a document containing wide-ranging proposals for reforming Irish education. Many of the proposals were radical for the times, particularly those for the recruitment and training of primary teachers. It described the prevailing methods of recruitment as 'leaving very much to be desired', especially the preparatory system, which it criticised severely.

Condemning the system for segregating candidate teachers at 14 years of age, it called for its abolition, proposing instead a common system of training for primary and secondary teachers. The Plan envisaged that students would be educated at university for the first three years, followed by a one-year training course, concentrating on teaching practice. This was a radical proposal for the times, though the INTO had been advocating university education for primary teachers since the 1920s. The organisation believed that such a system of recruitment would attract the best candidates to teaching and, consequently, fewer candidates would leave training or teaching for other careers.

The section dealing with the language revival emphasised that Irish should be taught in the primary school as 'a living language' and that written Irish

---

31. Dublin Diocesan Archives, McQuaid Papers.

should be postponed until the pupils had some practice in written English.[32] The publication of the Plan coincided with the end of Fianna Fail's period in office. Whether that party would have been more sympathetic to its position than the First Inter-party Government was, is a matter for conjecture. The Plan itself contained many exciting proposals for recruitment, which received little attention from either government.

Another group which continuously castigated Fianna Fáil over the gaelicisation policy was the Gaelic League, though for most of this period, 1939–48, this erstwhile powerful organisation was in decline. Advocates of the gaelicisation policy were not without influence, however, and in 1946 Comhdháil Náisiúnta na Gaeilge was established as a co-ordinating body for a number of Irish organisations, including the League. Comhdháil was not slow in instituting a more aggressive policy. A typical example of its robust approach was a demand that the government do more to save the language:

> Never was a language saved that was so close to death as Irish. Comhdháil Náisiúnta believes that Irish can be saved and that the public wants to save it. There is a need for a long-term policy. A fight to save the soul of Ireland.[33]

Typical of Comhdháil's militant approach to government was its belief that 'every organisation and institution, that gets public money or help from the state should be made to use Irish as much as possible'. It also called for greater emphasis on spoken Irish and for oral tests in all school and public examinations. Throughout the 1940s, however, opposition to the gaelicisation policy continued to increase. Typical of this was an editorial in *The Leader*, which declared:

> It is foolish to ignore the substantial opposition which arises in private conversation ... that the effort to save Irish is too late and therefore doomed to failure.[34]

FIANNA FÁIL AND THE GAELICISATION POLICY

How justified were groups like Comhdháil in attacking Fianna Fáil? When the party first came to power in 1932, much of the gaelicisation policy formulated by Blythe and the Cumann na nGaedheal Government had been in operation for almost 10 years. An assessment of its progress would have been opportune, but with the change of government this did not happen. It is a matter for speculation whether a Cumann na nGaedheal/Fine Gael Government, with a renewed mandate from the people, would have found it easier to review and modify the policy in 1932; and whether Blythe would have realised that the aims of the language policy were too ambitious and

---

32. Irish National Teachers' Organisation, *A plan for education*, p. 42.
33. Memo in Irish from Comhdháil Náisiúnta na Gaeilge, UCD Archives, Blythe Papers.
34. *The Leader*, 14 October 1944.

been pragmatic enough to modify it, is difficult to say. It was unfortunate that on assuming office Fianna Fáil did not institute a reappraisal of the policy and set more realistic goals. This was due to a number of factors. The restoration of the language and the re-unification of the island were the party's much vaunted twin aspirations, and as this was the party's first time in government, it was pre-occupied with assuming control of the affairs of the nation. In addition, the wounds of the civil war were still raw. Fianna Fáil was not going to give the opposition an opportunity to accuse it of being less than committed to the gaelicisation policy initiated by the Cumann na nGaedheal Government.

Fianna Fáil believed that it could do better and it began its first term in office by implementing the gaelicisation policy with renewed vigour. One of the more visionary projects associated with the gaelicisation policy occurred in 1935 when the Ráth Cairn Gaeltacht was established by relocating Irish-speaking families from Connemara to Co Meath. In education, Fianna Fáil introduced the *Revised Primary Programme* in 1934, while its increased emphasis on Irish in the public service made it impossible for those without fluent Irish to gain promotion.[35] By 1948, the number of civil servants fluent in Irish had increased to 20 per cent, though the number in the Department of Finance was as low as seven per cent, which helps to explain their dogged antipathy to the preparatory system. That same year a confidential *Report on the Use of Irish in the Civil Service* noted that the decline in the number of native speakers in the Gaeltacht was continuing, and that less than half of the Gaeltacht population were Irish speakers.[36] Indeed, these inquiries showed that attempts at gaelicising the civil service had failed in all but one respect. They had succeeded in giving the state an appearance of gaelicisation, which satisfied those who, suffering from the trauma of post-colonial mindset, hungered for a new cultural identity. In addition it fulfilled their need to emphasise how much the new state differed from the old regime.

Despite the failure of the policy revealed by various inquiries, the pretence was kept up that the country was bilingual. It was in keeping with this aspiration that the place accorded to the language in the first Constitution was upgraded by de Valera in the 1937 Constitution. This was de Valera's main contribution to the gaelicisation policy, though he could claim some other successes with regard to the language itself. Considerable progress was made in standardising the grammar, vocabulary and spelling of the language, resulting in the publication of *Litriú na Gaeilge: An Caighdeán Oifigiúl* in 1945.[37] There was also an increase in the number of books and periodicals in Irish produced annually.

A major difficulty for Fianna Fáil throughout this period was its relationship with the Catholic church. On a number of occasions the government

---

35. Confidential memo, The use of Irish in the civil service, UCD Archives, Blythe Papers.
36. *Ibid.*
37. Ó Riain, *Pleanáil Teanga in Éirinn 1919-1985*, p. 74.

found itself in disagreement with the hierarchy, and when this occurred the government gave way to the bishops. Indeed, as one commentator noted, 'reform proposals were abandoned once de Valera detected signs of episcopal opposition'.[38] One example of this, which was of considerable significance for the gaelicisation policy, was the provision of second-level schools in the Gaeltacht,[39] where upon the hierarchy expressing disapproval, the government abandoned the proposals. Had the government's proposals been implemented, the whole history of the preparatory system would have been different, for fewer Gaeltacht students would have entered the colleges. The provision of second-level schools in the Gaeltacht was an issue about which Derrig had shown genuine commitment, but the failure of de Valera to support him led to the collapse of the project. Other examples of Fianna Fáil giving in to the hierarchy which were significant for the preparatory colleges were the dispute over Waterford Training College and the take-over of Coláiste Éinde by the army in 1942, which was delayed for over a year by the bishop of Galway. Furthermore, the fear of offending individual bishops prevented the Department of Finance forcing the amalgamation of preparatory colleges in the early 1940s. These episodes clearly demonstrated that throughout its 16 years in government, Fianna Fáil bowed to the hierarchy's wishes even though, on occasions, it meant giving way on its cherished gaelicisation policy.

A further factor which may have contributed to de Valera's failure to pursue the gaelicisation policy with any great vigour was the lack of consensus in the cabinet. It included strong-willed individuals, such as Lemass[40] and MacEntee, neither of whom greatly favoured the language policy, while there were others, such as Frank Aiken, who in February 1946 made the extravagant prediction that the majority of people in the country would be speaking Irish in 20 years.

There has been much speculation as to why de Valera appointed Derrig as Minister for Education in 1932 instead of Frank Fahy, who had shown himself to be a capable shadow minister. It has been suggested that this was to ensure that de Valera was in a better position to influence policy in a department where there was much scope for church–state conflict.[41] Indeed, de Valera's failure to move Derrig when relationships with the INTO became strained is difficult to understand, and may have been due to tensions within the cabinet itself. It is also difficult to understand why de Valera did not make changes to the gaelicisation policy during his 16 years as Taoiseach, or during the period from September 1939 to June 1940, when he was also Minister for Education, as he was aware that attempts to gaelicise the state through the schools had failed. He did offer to set up a commission of Dáil deputies in 1941 to examine the language issue but nothing came of it.[42]

---

38. Ó Buachalla, *Education policy in twentieth-century Ireland*, p. 199.
39. See Part I, chapter 3.
40. For biographical details of people named on this page see the Appendix.
41. Ó Buachalla, p. 65.

As Fianna Fáil's period in government drew to a close, the increase in the birth-rate which commenced in 1942 began to affect primary schooling through increased enrolments and demands for more teachers. However, as statistical information of this kind took so long to work its way through the Department's bureaucratic system, it was the 1950s before the increases began to have serious effects on recruitment, with significant consequences for the preparatory colleges. Thus the system gained a respite which enabled it to continue into the next decade.

42. *Ibid.*, p. 351.

CHAPTER FIVE

A period of stagnation ending in swift demise: 1948–61

'The death sentence has been passed on the colleges'

For much of this period, 1948–57, life in Ireland differed little from the previous decade. The slow economic recovery of the post-war period continued, though the rate of growth was not sufficient to overcome the nation's two main problems, unemployment and emigration. Nevertheless, there were some exciting political changes. After 16 years of Fianna Fáil rule, the first Inter-party Government was elected in 1948. It lasted until 1951, when the débâcle over the mother and child health scheme[1] contributed to its collapse and the return of Fianna Fáil to power for a further three years. Despite the unseemly end to the first Inter-party Government, the electorate was willing to entrust the affairs of the nation to a second coalition government in 1954. This lasted until 1957, a year that was to be a turning point in Irish life with the return to power of a reinvigorated Fianna Fáil.

Two major changes soon followed. *The First Programme for Economic Expansion* was published in 1958 and a year later de Valera was succeeded as Taoiseach by Seán Lemass.[2] The country was now led by a number of younger ministers, eager to change things. It also meant that the portfolio of education was upgraded. New policies were formulated and more resources allocated to it, reflecting the politicians' realisation that the education system had a significant role to play in the economic and social development of the country.

---

1. Dr. Noel Browne, the Minister for Health, planned to introduce a free medical scheme for mothers and children. This was so strongly opposed by the medical profession and the hierarchy that the government withdrew its support from Browne, who resigned.
2. For biographical details of people named on this page see the Appendix.

Throughout the period 1948–57 there was little difference between the policies pursued by Richard Mulcahy, Minister for Education in the two Inter-party Governments, and his Fianna Fáil counterpart, Seán Moylan. During Mulcahy's first term as minister, recruitment became an important issue. Rising enrolments resulting from increases in the birth rate led to demands for more trained teachers, with disputes between the Departments of Education and Finance as to how this could be achieved. The Department of Finance's solution was the abolition of the marriage ban, while the Department of Education advocated the establishment of an additional training college. For much of this time, the preparatory system stagnated, as the former persisted in its efforts to end the system, while the latter continued to defend it, though the ease with which the Department of Education proposed converting Coláiste Éinde into a training college in 1951 was ominous.

In the early part of this period, the morale of primary teachers was low following the humiliating end to the 1946 strike, and the government's rejection of the INTO's innovative *Plan for Education* the following year. The election of the first Inter-party Government led to increased expectations that their protracted salary negotiations would be speedily completed. But it was the beginning of the 1950s before they achieved their salary objectives. These gains made primary teaching a highly regarded career, and thereafter there was no shortage of candidates seeking to enter the training colleges.

A major characteristic of Mulcahy as minister, however, was his slowness to make radical change in any area. In opposition, he had showed exciting signs of new thinking, and a Fine Gael educational policy document written by him in 1947 had proposed a number of far-reaching changes.[3] Furthermore, he had promised an inquiry into one of the most controversial issues in Irish education, the use of Irish as a teaching medium. He had also acknowledged the need for a council of education, an objective dear to the INTO.

MULCAHY DISAPPOINTS

Such views led to increased teacher expectations that Mulcahy, who had supported them in the strike, would be a reforming Minister for Education. His first period in this office, however, was a severe disappointment. Mulcahy disappointed teachers by his failure to fully implement the recommendations of the Roe Committee (Report of the Committee on National Teachers' Salaries 1949) regarding their salaries, and to keep his promises about the language policy. He did, however, set up a committee of primary inspectors to examine the issue. This resulted in some modification of the

3. Memo on Fine Gael Educational Policy, UCD Archives, Mulcahy Papers, P7/C/132.

language programme in 1948, with the introduction of the *Revised Pro-gramme for Infants*. It allowed the teaching of English as an optional subject for infants and first class for half an hour per day. He then left the matter to the proposed council of education, which he established in 1950.

While Mulcahy's failure to make radical changes was due to his innate conservatism, it must also be seen in the context of the late 1940s, when the Irish language was a subject which could arouse great depths of passion. It was to avoid controversy that Mulcahy passed the matter to the council of education. The requirement that Irish be essential for state examinations became a live issue from 1949. As the numbers doing the Intermediate and Leaving Certificate examinations grew, and greater numbers failed due to the Irish requirement, growing public disenchantment with the language policy led to increased calls for an inquiry into the teaching of Irish. Public disillusionment with compulsory Irish was also reflected in the *Report of the Commission on Youth Unemployment* in 1951 (this commission, chaired by Archbishop McQuaid, was set up by the de Valera government in 1943).

Despite the public's increasingly negative attitude to the gaelicisation policy, there were some imaginative initiatives during this period which affected the language and Irish culture. They included the founding of Comhaltas Ceolteoirí Éireann (to foster traditional music) in 1951, and of Gael-Linn (to produce newsreels and films in Irish and to promote business in the Gaeltacht) in 1953, and the establishment of the Department of the Gaeltacht in 1956. In addition, there was a remarkable growth in modern Irish literature, with works of international stature by Ó Cadhain,[4] whose most famous novel *Cré na Cille* (1949) was translated into several European languages, and by Ó Direáin and Ó Riordáin, two of the most important Irish language poets in the twentieth century. The Gaelic League also pros-pered and the number of branches grew from 100 to a peak of 198 in 1958.

The reform of teacher recruitment was another issue which Mulcahy passed to the council of education. Over the years his attitude to the prepa-ratory colleges had changed. In the 1920s, he had been an ardent supporter of the system, but by the 1940s he had joined the ranks of its critics. In 1944, he had this criticism of his predecessor, Derrig:

> The minister is continuing to look to the Irish-speaking districts for a large part of his primary school-teachers for the future, in spite of the fact that he knows that material has been criticised to some extent by both the educationists there, through whose hands they have passed, and by others connected with the pro-fessional side of education.[5]

Mulcahy's views were notable because, heretofore, criticism of the pre-paratory system had been confined to the INTO and politicians such as

---

4. For biographical details of people named on this page see the Appendix.
5. *Dáil Reports*, 13 June 1944.

T.J. O'Connell and T.R. Johnston.[6] By the 1940s it had become increasingly widespread. Mulcahy had also criticised Derrig for not conducting 'a major and systematic review' of the work of the training and preparatory colleges during their temporary closure. However, as minister he was slow to make changes to recruitment, excusing his inaction on the grounds that it could not be treated in isolation.

MULCAHY'S FAILURE TO REFORM RECRUITMENT

Mulcahy's failure to reform recruitment was to have serious consequences; for one of the main features of primary education during his period as minister was the growing shortage of trained primary teachers. This was mainly due to an increase in the birth rate which had begun in 1942. Other factors were the higher numbers of women teachers retiring voluntarily, the introduction of a more favourable pupil-teacher ratio, and the marriage ban, whereby female teachers had to resign their teaching posts on marriage. The need for more trained teachers increased tension between the Departments of Finance and Education. The former believed that the shortage of teachers could be overcome by ending the marriage ban, while the latter proposed the establishment of an additional training college.

The situation was further compounded by the failure of the Department to estimate accurately the number of pupils in schools. As early as 1947, a shortage of primary teachers was forecast, yet the Department failed to take decisive action to adapt recruitment accordingly. Instead of developing a strategy to deal with the situation, it depended on *ad hoc* measures. These included the recruitment of an additional 40 students per year to Carysfort Training College in 1947 and 1948,[7] while St Patrick's College, Drumcondra, was allowed to recruit an extra 20 students in 1951.

To cope with the increasing number of untrained teachers being employed in the schools, Mulcahy proposed turning Coláiste Éinde into a training college. Originally it had been planned as a training college for girls and it could easily be adapted to accommodate 160 students. Such a proposal showed that the Department's attitude to the preparatory system was changing. Previously it had always argued that two preparatory colleges were necessary for Gaeltacht boys, Coláiste Éinde for those from Donegal and Galway, and Coláiste Íosagáin for boys from Cork, Waterford and Kerry. The proposal to turn Coláiste Éinde into a training college was rejected in February 1951 by the Department of Finance, which proposed instead that the marriage ban be rescinded. The Department of Education, however, persisted in pressing for an additional training college, and continued to do so despite the unexpected change of party in government. The 1951 general election returned Fianna

---

6. For biographical details of people named on this page see the Appendix.
7. *Report of the Department of Education*, 1946/47, p. 2.

Fáil to power and Seán Moylan became Minister for Education. Despite these changes there were no adjustments in the Department's recruitment policy, or in the Department of Finance's response to the proposal. This was not surprising as MacEntee was once again Minister for Finance.

According to the Department of Finance, a new training college catering for 120–160 students would not be viable economically, even though there were only 165 students in St. Patrick's Training College, Drumcondra, in 1950, and 100 students in Mary Immaculate Training College, Limerick. It also dismissed the Department's effort to reduce large class sizes: 'Education wants to improve the pupil-teacher ratio to make it like the Six Counties. Out of the question. The British are paying for Northern Ireland'.[8]

The matter continued unresolved until October 1952 when the Department of Finance proposed that special courses in training colleges be given to university graduates to equip them as primary teachers. It also reiterated its demand for the marriage ban to be modified. Faced with such strongly-held opposing views, de Valera avoided a confrontation between Moylan and MacEntee by postponing a cabinet decision.

The fact that a Fianna Fáil minister was now proposing to turn a preparatory college into a training college does not seem to have caused de Valera any great anxiety. Indeed by 1952, even de Valera was confessing to reservations about reviving the language, and in a major review of the gaelicisation policy he spoke of the necessity to examine it dispassionately:

> It is time to take stock and to examine standards and methods dispassionately. For some years I have felt stocktaking necessary. But I hesitated, feared … it would be hailed by those who dislike the language as a defeat for the language cause and an occasion for a massed attack by its enemies.[9]

He still stressed the important role of the schools. However, he was less sure about how they should implement the gaelicisation policy:

> Purely written tests in examinations give a completely wrong bias to teaching. The early years are the best for language learning. There are two conflicting schools of thought. How can this fact be best used in our conditions? A compromise may be found.

On the question of recruitment, the new government was unwilling to broker a compromise between the Departments of Education and Finance. The increased enrolments and the subsequent shortage of teachers were of considerable significance for the preparatory system, for it was obvious that the quickest, cheapest and easiest method of recruitment was through open competition. Though Moylan had agreed to the proposal that Coláiste Éinde should become a training college, he adamantly refused to consider

---

8. DT Papers, S6369.
9. Memo on Irish Language Policy, DT Papers, S13180A.

any changes to the recruitment system. Meanwhile, the increased need for teachers saw the preparatory colleges full, though the numbers entering for the entrance examinations had declined considerably from the early days of the system. This was due to a number of factors. Second-level education had become more generally available. There was also an increased number of 'A' schools, where candidates intending to become primary teachers could obtain the required level of fluency in Irish. In addition the level of grants to preparatory students had dropped, and fees at the colleges had increased from £40 to £50 in 1948.

JUSTIFYING THE MARRIAGE BAN

The recruitment question continued to be an issue of importance for the government, and in February 1953 the Department of Education presented a memo to the cabinet supporting the retention of the marriage ban on a number of grounds:

> A married woman should be at home. Doing two jobs would be a strain. A substitute would have to be employed for two months' maternity leave. It would create unhealthy curiosity about pregnancy. Two incomes in one house would cause jealousy in the community. There are plenty of candidates for teaching. Civil servants have a marriage ban.[10]

This memo reveals the thinking of the period and is similar to the philosophy expressed in the 1937 Constitution. It also shows how prurient Irish society had become during the Emergency. Married women had been acceptable as teachers in the 1920s and early 1930s. However, the plea that a married woman should be at home, because doing two jobs would be a strain, was not credible in a society where many widows with children had no choice but to work outside the home to support their families.

As the two departments continued to disagree, the matter dragged on without resolution until the government eventually decided on a compromise in October 1953. The marriage ban would continue, but the minister could modify it in certain circumstances. The cabinet also sanctioned the employment of university graduates in national schools, and from 1953 teachers aged 65 could put off retirement from year to year, for up to a total of three years altogether.

When the issue next came before the cabinet a decision on a new training college was postponed. However, Moylan was instructed to arrange for the training of women university graduates as day students in existing training colleges. This decision was made without consulting the hierarchy, as noted anxiously by Moylan a week later:

---

10. DT Papers, S6369.

Can't discuss matter with the archbishop of Dublin unless I can tell him the new training college is being provided and that extern students are only an interim matter. The ecclesiastical authorities regard training under their control in residential training colleges as absolutely essential. In the case of national teachers it is of vital importance not to give the ecclesiastical authorities any reason to fear intention of departing from the traditional method of training teachers. Might get them to accept interim measure.[11]

This concern for the hierarchy's opinion led the cabinet to reverse its earlier decision, and to avert a confrontation with the church authorities it agreed at the end of 1953 that Coláiste Éinde should be turned into a training college for Catholic women teachers.

The Department's victory was short-lived. Early in January 1954, Moylan's secretary sent Archbishop McQuaid details of the proposal and requested an appointment for the minister to discuss the proposed training college in Galway. The letter was careful to say that the proposal was subject to the approval, in principle, of the ecclesiastical authorities:

Should such approval be forthcoming … the minister proposes to seek the approval, in principle, of his lordship, the bishop of Galway, who is manager of Coláiste Éinde, for the discontinuance of the preparatory college there and its replacement by a girls' training college and he would be glad to know whether such a course commends itself to his grace the archbishop of Dublin.[12]

Such a course, however, did not commend itself to the archbishop. As the shortage of trained teachers was greatest in Dublin, which had the highest numbers of school children, McQuaid preferred to have the additional new teachers trained in his diocese, where he could satisfy himself that they were being trained in accordance with his wishes. So the archbishop came up with an alternative proposal that extra students could be accommodated at Carysfort College.

Faced with this offer from the formidable McQuaid, Moylan agreed that by adding an extra storey for a dormitory to a new one-storey assembly hall under construction at Carysfort, accommodation could be provided for 100–120 extra students. The difficulty was financing the project. A memo from the Department of Finance summarised the problem:

Cost about £40,000. Community can't lend the college money. Could get a bank loan if repaid by state grants. Need agreement. Cheaper than Éinde. Cheaper to run. Could fall back on Éinde.[13]

Despite these difficulties, this costly extension received government approval within a week and Coláiste Éinde preparatory college gained a further

---

11. *Ibid.*
12. Dublin Diocesan Archives, McQuaid Papers.
13. DT Papers, S6369.

reprieve. Meanwhile, Moylan was left to explain the decision to Bishop Browne:

> The proposal for the training of additional women teachers has taken a turn, I had not anticipated, which would allow training of extra teachers without the necessity of providing another training college. With the making of some structural alterations and additions to Our Lady of Mercy College (Carysfort) accommodation can be provided for 100–120 students more than at present, and possibly, to admit 50–55 of them in September next.[14]

So through McQuaid's intervention, Carysfort College, a private institution, was enabled in 1954 to finance an extension costing £40,000, a considerable sum when the salary for female and single male teachers was finally agreed in December 1955 at £340 per annum rising by 20 increments to £640. Through providing extra residential accommodation in Dublin, the necessity for accepting graduate students as day students was avoided, and the church was able to retain its tight control over student intake and formation.

THE COUNCIL OF EDUCATION

One of Mulcahy's major achievements during his first term as minister was the establishment of a council of education in April 1950. This had been one of the INTO's demands from as far back as 1926, a demand which had been repeated in *A Plan for Education* in 1947. The council was instructed to examine the function and curriculum of the primary school. From the beginning, Mulcahy, who was a devout member of the Catholic Church, made it clear that no restrictions would be placed on the role of the churches in the management of schools.

Progress was slow and by the time the long-awaited *Report of the Council of Education on the Function and Curriculum of the Primary School* was published in 1954, Mulcahy was beginning his second term as Minister for Education. Those who were hoping for reform of the educational system were disappointed as it contained few fundamental changes. The main recommendations were that the curriculum should be extended by the addition of physical training, nature study and drawing, and that the Primary School Certificate Examination should be compulsory for class VI, the class in which primary education should be completed.

The conservative nature of the report was clearly demonstrated in its approach to the Irish language. While showing that it was aware of the paradoxes in the public's attitude to the language, the council readily accepted the *status quo* and was disappointingly short of new ideas. Indeed, the council's membership reflected the public attitudes, which probably accounted

---

14. Galway Diocesan Archives, Browne Papers.

for its own contradictory remarks on the subject. It had this to say of the position of the language in the constitution:

> Its title as the national language goes back over 30 years. To hold, however, that in a nation politically free a language can continue to be regarded as the national language while altogether ceasing to be used as a vernacular would seem to be a contradiction in terms.[15]

While in the next paragraph it stated: 'It is often argued and with some force that in our geographic and economic position the effort to revive Irish is unrealistic.' A little further on, the report gave the opposite view, claiming that Irish was the national language for the majority of our people, though it gave no evidence to support this contention:

> Few would deny that despite its recession in the last 100 years Irish still remains for at least the majority of our people the national language. The fact that another language is spoken by them requires that due regard be given to their needs in that language; it does not detract from the value and place of the traditional language.[16]

Later, it queried whether the teaching of two languages was detrimental, and while it acknowledged that no scientific research had been carried out in this area it concluded sanguinely:

> The majority of members conversant with post-primary education are of the opinion that the importance given to Irish in the primary school has not impaired the level of education of pupils entering post-primary school nor has it, on the whole, reduced the standard of the knowledge of English and other subjects.[17]

There is no sign that the council took into consideration that only a minority went on to post-primary school or that many others, who received only primary education had little choice but to emigrate to England or America as domestic servants or labourers. Here again the council's view contrasted with that of the *Report of the Commission on Youth Unemployment,*[18] which called for an examination of primary education and particularly of the teaching of Irish. The council report also ignored the findings of the INTO's *Inquiry into the use of Irish.*[19]

The council report was criticised for its deference to the *status quo* and its failure to view education in a wider social context. Particularly deplorable was its failure to call for greater participation in secondary education, or to include proposals for reforming a system where one-third of pupils left

---

15. *Report of the Council of Education*, par. 197.
16. *Ibid.*, para. 200.
17. *Ibid.*, para. 213.
18. Hyland and Milne, *Irish Educational Documents*, vol. II, p. 27.
19. See Part I, chapter 4.

school with only the Primary Certificate, while a similar number left without even that minimum qualification.[20] Nevertheless, Mulcahy was satisfied
with the council's findings and in November 1954 requested it to undertake
an examination of secondary education.

RISING COSTS OF PREPARATORY COLLEGES

The rising costs of the preparatory system during the 1950s led to persistent
arguments between the Departments of Finance and Education, regardless
of which government was in power. Demands for the closure of another
preparatory college by Gerard Sweetman[21], Minister for Finance in the second Inter-party Government, differed little from those of his Fianna Fáil
predecessor, MacEntee. Renowned for his conservative outlook, Sweetman
strongly opposed the social and liberal ideas developing in Fine Gael at that
time. Furthermore, he regarded the preparatory system as a highly expensive
method of producing teachers. In August 1954, he urged Mulcahy to reduce
costs by closing two of the six colleges.[22] Sweetman also wanted fees at training and preparatory colleges increased by 10 per cent. As fees for preparatory
colleges had been raised only once before, in 1948, this was not unreasonable, and in 1955 the Department agreed with surprising ease that they
should be increased to £55. The increase in fees, however, made little
impact on the rising annual expenditure from public funds on the preparatory colleges, which between 1950 and 1955 rose by 45 per cent.

Nowhere is there any evidence that the Department of Education considered such large expenditure alarming or that it had any plans for reducing
costs. Indeed, throughout the history of the colleges the Department's attitude to public expenditure was cavalier. Much of this may have been a reaction to the Department of Finance's emphasis on savings. Typical of that
department's approach in this period was a memo in 1957, querying the
necessity for the preparatory colleges, as Irish teaching was compulsory in all
schools and the system supplied only 25 per cent of students in the training
colleges.[23] It also included estimates of current expenditure on the colleges,
revealing considerable hidden costs, not included in the Department's
reports. These figures showed just how costly the preparatory system was as
a method of producing primary teachers, and that the Department of Finance
was justified in seeking a reduction in expenses.

The Department of Finance does not seem to have considered that
demands for more trained teachers and for an improved teacher/pupil ratio
were reasonable. It had little interest in the language policy or the Gaeltacht.
Nowhere was the contribution of the colleges to the language policy

---

20. Coolahan, *Irish Education: history and structure*, p. 45.
21. For biographical details see the Appendix.
22. UCD Archives, Mulcahy Papers, P7/C/154.
23. DT Papers, S22/15/34.

assessed or the cost of implementing the language policy in the civil service and in other state agencies discussed. Furthermore, the Department of Finance's ready acquiescence to the hierarchy's demands that graduates must spend a year in residential training colleges was in stark contrast to its attitude to the preparatory colleges:

> Our aim must be savings. Can't be directed to other non-productive demands. Country can't afford training of more teachers. Cheaper alternative methods of training must be implemented. Hierarchy opposed proposal of university graduates being accepted into national teaching service without having to pass through training colleges. Hierarchy insisted on one year's tuition at a training college as a national teacher.[24]

One of the main contributory factors to the high costs of the preparatory system was the way in which students were subsidised, though the numbers paying no fees had decreased considerably compared with those in the early days.[25] Furthermore, the agreement made by students before entering the system was a sensitive issue. From time to time, as a result of dissension between the Departments of Education and Finance, this question came before the cabinet. A memo from the Department outlined how the system worked:

> Parents and students accepted to preparatory colleges and training colleges have signed an agreement to complete the course and to serve for five years as national teachers. Failing this, they will repay such sums as the Minister for Education may demand. The maximum fees for both colleges is £500, if training college only, £230. No instance has occurred in the type of case in question in which the maximum amount fell to be refunded.[26]

There were also certain circumstances in which a refund would not be demanded. These included the death or permanent illness of a student; failure at examination despite a diligent effort; removal from college for causes not within the student's control, e.g. sub-normal mentality, uncouthness, lack of ability or capacity to learn; obtaining a university scholarship under one of the Department's schemes; failure to secure employment as a teacher; compulsory retirement of women on marriage; appointment as an inspector with the Department or to a post in a preparatory or training college.

REPAYMENT OF FEES AND CANDIDATES FOR THE RELIGIOUS LIFE

There was also the question as to whether those entering religious life should have to repay fees. A frequent occurrence, this was a sensitive issue

---

24. *Ibid.*
25. See Part I, chapter 3.
26. DT Papers, S14787.

involving the Catholic Church, a body all governments were wary of offending. When the issue arose in October 1951, the Departments of Education and Finance took their customary opposing views. A memo from the Department of Education emphasised that the minister, Seán Moylan, took a serious view of the position:

> Feels that in the circumstances of this country the call to a religious vocation must be recognised as having a special urgency, and not of its nature, to be compared in any way with a desire to exchange the teaching profession for another secular vocation. Between 16 to 23 desire to enter religion; the minimum, only in comfortable financial circumstances, acute problem of conscience; heavy burden on parents.[27]

Such pleading had little effect. Instead, the Department of Finance's response showed how highly subsidised students at both the preparatory and training colleges were:

> The State has provided secondary education and/or training facilities at reduced costs. Fees at preparatory colleges are only £50 per year. Training college grants are £67–10s to £115 a year and a student pays £40 a year for which he obtains full board and lodging with instruction. Those unable to pay £40, part or all of the fee is lent by the Department and must be repaid. If not teaching for five years, must repay grants to training college plus money lent. Reduction in amount for every year of service as a national teacher after the first two years.[28]

The Department of Finance also claimed that the agreement was freely entered into, the obligation to repay was 'of long standing', and religious orders gained by accepting candidates who were already trained teachers. It further asserted that the practice had been for each individual case to be considered on its merits, a practice the Minister for Finance wanted to continue. When the two views were presented to the cabinet in October 1951, the Department of Education's proposal was approved. This was hardly surprising as the government would not have wanted to risk upsetting the hierarchy so soon after the débâcle over the mother and child health scheme.

1957–61: FACING AN INCREASINGLY PRECARIOUS FUTURE

The rate of change in education accelerated in the period from 1957 to 61. Two changes of particular significance for recruitment were the introduction of an oral Irish examination as part of the Leaving Certificate Examination and a reform of entry regulations to training colleges. These changes were to greatly affect the preparatory system, and its future looked increasingly

---

27. *Ibid.*
28. *Ibid.*

precarious from 1957 on. Two years later, the decision was finally taken to end the system. Once taken, the government tried to divest itself of the colleges as quickly as possible with little effort to recoup the large amounts of public money spent on them.

During the late 1950s there were a number of features in Irish life which, combining together at that time, ensured the end of the preparatory system. The main factors were an improvement in the country's economic condition and increased opposition to the gaelicisation policy, while the greater availability of second-level education made the preparatory system unnecessary. The most significant factor, however, was the attitude of the hierarchy, which at its midsummer general meeting in June 1959 decided:

> The time has now come when all places in these colleges should be allocated on a competitive basis and the policy of reserving a number of places for natives of the Gaeltacht discontinued. The archbishop of Tuam and the bishop of Elphin were asked to make this proposal to the minister on behalf of the hierarchy.[29]

Throughout the history of the system, there was nothing to indicate that the bishops were unhappy with the way in which it operated. Indeed, the strong religious ethos of the colleges and the strict control exercised by the religious orders who ran them would have given the hierarchy few grounds for complaint. However, in 1956 an episode which resulted in the expulsion of a large number of students from Coláiste Éinde brought the system to the attention of the bishops. As the students concerned were from the Donegal Gaeltacht, it focused attention on the entrance examination which gave preference to Gaeltacht students.[30] The controversy aroused the wrath of the manager of the college, Bishop Browne of Galway. He decided that it was time for Coláiste Éinde to become a diocesan college, and his efforts to effect this brought about the end of the preparatory system.

The affair came to notice in the early months of 1956, when staff at the college became aware that pilfering of foodstuffs and other materials was going on. An investigation began which led to the discovery that a number of senior boys were leaving their dormitories at night and going to the maids' quarters, where they indulged in various forms of sexual activity. After lengthy interrogations lasting two days it was discovered that 14 boys were involved. An investigation by the Department followed. The resulting expulsions caused consternation and an angry deputation from Donegal met the Department secretary. The deputation alleged that there was poor discipline in Coláiste Éinde and that such behaviour had been going on for years.[31] Furthermore, they pointed out that the parents had given their children to the state in *loco parentis,* and they believed that the large number expelled demonstrated the lack of supervision. They stressed that the supply

---

29. Dublin Diocesan Archives, McQuaid Papers.
30. See Part 1, chapter 2.
31. Ó hEithir, *Over the bar,* p. 87.

of Donegal pupils to Coláiste Éinde could be jeopardised. They also insisted that the problem would not have occurred had the college been in Donegal, where the parents would have been more in touch. A similar incident happened in Coláiste Íosagáin in 1945.[32]

The episode revealed a sorry state of affairs in the college. The bishop's immediate reaction was to consider closing the college and this, along with a different system of selection, was among a number of possibilities he listed. It is not possible to say whether he discussed these recommendations with the minister. Past students, however, believed that the bishop threatened to close the college, something no minister would have wanted in such circumstances. Certainly, Mulcahy went out of his way to please Browne at this time, at one stage going so far as to lend him his ministerial car.[33] Browne's consideration of the need for a different system of selection was an indication that it was due to his efforts that the hierarchy passed its resolution of June 1959.

On 26 March 1956, Browne wrote to Mulcahy informing him of changes to be made regarding discipline in Coláiste Éinde and warning him that:

> The whole background and conduct of students during vacation should receive careful consideration … a very serious matter of schools in Donegal developing a proprietory interest in sending pupils for training irrespective of their suitability for teaching. That is a matter on which managers and bishops have a vital interest and already I know opinions are being formed as to the quality of teachers who have passed through the training colleges.[34]

The relationship between primary schools in Donegal and Coláiste Éinde was of concern not only to Browne but also to many in that county, including the bishop of Raphoe. He told Browne that there was 'a bad drop' in the culprits, who were from Gweedore. Some years earlier, boys from that area had been in trouble with the seminary authorities.

The episode at Coláiste Éinde was a key factor in the demise of the preparatory system, for Browne became convinced that the system should be ended and began to use his considerable influence to achieve that objective. Subsequent correspondence between the bishop and the departmental secretary indicates that in pursuing this aim Browne kept in close touch with the Department. Furthermore, the episode alarmed the hierarchy and awakened the bishops to the need for greater vigilance in accepting students into the training colleges. This resulted in their decision that preference should no longer be given to Gaeltacht students. Once they agreed on this point, the Department knew it would be possible to end the system.

---

32. Ó Muircheartaigh, *From Dún Síon to Croke Park*, p. 27.
33. Galway Diocesan Archives, Browne Papers.
34. *Ibid.*

MAJOR CHANGES IN IRISH SOCIETY

In the late 1950s, the failure of the gaelicisation policy became increasingly obvious. In 1956 a new approach was taken by the second Inter-party Government with the establishment of the Department of the Gaeltacht. This was a significant development, which resulted in the setting up of the semi-state body, Gaeltarra Éireann, to bring industries to Gaeltacht areas. This policy highlighted the ambivalence of the government towards the Gaeltacht and showed its lack of concern that increasing tourism and industrial development would hasten the demise of the language by encouraging the spread of English. The establishment of the Department of the Gaeltacht also brought increased pressures for the preparatory colleges, as people in the Gaeltacht began campaigning for them to accept more pupils from the locality in which they were situated.[35] Furthermore, as negative attitudes to the language became more pronounced, there was less need for the preparatory colleges whose main function was to produce students who were fluent in the Irish language.

The year after the episode at Coláiste Éinde, 1957, de Valera was returned to power. His final years as leader of Fianna Fáil were marked by two significant developments. In 1958, *The First Programme for Economic Expansion* was launched and the Commission on the Restoration of the Irish Language was established. Moreover, as the end of the decade approached, it was obvious that major changes were taking place in Irish society. These were reflected in the 1960 Broadcasting Act and the establishment of a national television service in 1961. Television was a major agent in hastening the pace of change. In addition, education gained a higher profile as greater resources became available, and parental expectations rose with a growing public awareness of its importance. The necessity for educational planning and the promotion of equality of opportunity and wider access to education became major elements of government policy. Such issues influenced the decision to initiate the *Investment in Education* study in 1962.

A further factor contributing to the demise of the preparatory system was growing evidence of public disquiet with compulsory Irish. This was reflected in the low priority given to programmes in Irish on Teilifís Éireann. There was also an increasing number of comments in the press expressing concern about falling educational standards, and in particular about the number of children leaving school illiterate. The following is a typical example:

> Facts are beyond controversy. These children face the world as semi-illiterate .... Can scarcely read or write. Arithmetic, geography, history and other elementary subjects are little more than names to them ... 50,000 Irish boys and girls who finish their education – God save the mark – at the age of 14 are destined for the emigrant ship.[36]

---

35. Roinn na Gaeltachta Papers, R22.
36. *Sunday Independent,* 29 December 1957.

Similar concern was expressed in a denunciation of the language policy in January 1958 by a leading academic, Fr E.F. O'Doherty, professor of psychology at UCD, who pointed out that all available research on bilingualism recommended that children should be taught their native language and other subjects through its medium:

> However, the words 'native language' or 'mother tongue' are conventionally used in this country by many people to refer to the ancestral language rather than to the language of the primary society into which the child is born.[37]

The public's concern was reflected in a motion in the Dáil in October 1959 calling for a referendum on the subject. Furthermore, the public's readiness to accept changes to the gaelicisation policy was demonstrated by Fine Gael's 1961 election manifesto which proposed the abolition of compulsory Irish. It further promised that Irish would no longer be necessary to pass the Leaving Certificate Examination or to obtain entrance to the professions, but would be treated in the same manner as other subjects. As a sop to language enthusiasts, the manifesto promised to provide assistance for language organisations such as the Gaelic League and Gael-Linn, and to increase the number of Gaeltacht scholarships. That a major political party felt able to make such proposals was an indication of how far public opinion had changed and marked another phase in the dismantling of the language policy.

CHANGES IN EDUCATIONAL POLICY

The appointment of Jack Lynch[38] as Minister for Education in 1957 hastened the demise of the preparatory system, as he was from a different generation to de Valera and other senior Fianna Fáil personnel. A major concern for Lynch was recruitment, as the shortage of trained teachers was acute. In an effort to increase the number of trained teachers and to reduce class size, he made three important changes. These were of particular significance for the preparatory system. In spring 1958, he announced the introduction of an oral Irish examination as part of the Leaving Certificate Examination from 1960 on. A little while later, it was announced that all candidates entering training colleges from 1959 on, would have to be successful at personal suitability interviews, as well as at oral tests in English and Irish, conducted by Department inspectors. Finally, he announced the rescinding of the marriage ban from 1 July 1958.

The introduction of an oral Irish examination resulted in a significant change of emphasis in the teaching of Irish. With one-sixth of the marks at the Leaving Certificate Examination allocated to oral Irish, candidates from ordinary secondary schools would have to reach a high standard of fluency

---

37. O'Doherty, E.F., 'Bilingual school policy,' in *Studies,* Autumn 1958, p. 268.
38. For biographical details of Lynch and Hillery see the Appendix.

in the language. To cater for that need, a new Gaeltacht industry soon developed. Irish colleges were established to provide summer courses, where students could learn the language by the 'total immersion' method. This was the death-knell of the preparatory colleges, for it meant that fluency at oral Irish would no longer be their prerogative. Furthermore, by the 1950s the insistence on student-teachers having some preliminary teaching experience before being accepted into training colleges was finally discarded. This had been a requirement of training systems since their earliest days and had been a significant feature of the monitorial and pupil-teacher systems. A further indication that the days of the preparatory colleges were numbered was the reform of recruitment procedures. The introduction of personal suitability interviews and oral tests in English and Irish meant that, for the first time in the history of the colleges, preparatory students would have to compete for places and would not automatically continue on to training college. This had become a cause of considerable resentment, as it had prevented many better qualified candidates from outside the preparatory colleges from entering the profession.

Lynch's decision to rescind the marriage ban was of considerable significance, because the Department had opposed such a move for many years. According to Lynch, the ban had led to the appointment of many untrained teachers to schools, particularly in remote areas, while approximately 105 trained teachers, with an average of 11 years' service, were affected by it each year.[39]

ENDING THE SYSTEM

Lynch, however, did not stay long in Education, and when de Valera eventually retired in June 1959, Dr Patrick Hillery became minister. As minister his innovations included the establishment of comprehensive schools, regional technical colleges and the Commission on Higher Education. With the departure of de Valera and others of his age and mentality from active politics,[40] the closure of the preparatory colleges was inevitable. Furthermore, for the first time in their history, the Minister for Education did not champion the cause of the colleges. The momentous decision to end the system was taken at a cabinet meeting on 13 November 1959 and, once taken, the government was quick to dispose of the properties. A memo from the Department to the government[41] recommending closure included an analysis of students currently in the training colleges. This showed to what extent the system was failing. While the number of male students from

---

39. Dáil Reports, 11 June 1958.
40. Three of de Valera's close associates died around this time, Fahy in 1953, Derrig in 1956, and Moylan in 1957, while another dedicated Gaeilgeoir, Mulcahy, retired from the leadership of Fine Gael in 1959.
41. Cabinet Minutes, 9 November 1959, DT Papers S12307.

Catholic preparatory colleges was 40 per cent, the number of female students was as low as 25 per cent, but of far greater significance were the figures for native speakers. Male students were 17 per cent of the total intake in the training colleges, while the number of female students from the Gaeltacht was less than 10 per cent. Overall the number of native speakers was 11.6 per cent.

The memo stressed that closure had been 'under consideration for some time'. This was probably a reference to the episode at Coláiste Éinde. It was an important factor in bringing about the demise of the system, though to avoid public controversy the government had waited until the matter had been forgotten before taking the closure decision. Considerable savings would also be made, not just by closing the colleges, but through the sale of their premises and the farms attached to Coláiste Íde, Coláiste Bhríde and Coláiste Mhuire. The memo further asserted that as secondary education through Irish was available in a large number of schools, the money saved would be better spent providing more scholarships for Gaeltacht students to second-level schools and universities. According to the memo, the main objections to the system were:

> Students chose their future careers at too early an age. The question of fees meant pressure of a most compelling nature on a student to proceed to a career for which he may have a positive distaste. Specialising began too early, resulting in segregation at 14, which was bad educationally.

In addition the memo noted that the age of selection had been condemned by the INTO in *A Plan for Education*.[42] This was an interesting reference, in view of the fact that at the time of its publication in 1947, its proposals had been rejected by the Department and the minister, Derrig.

Material presented to the cabinet included the following statement from the Rev. Dr Donal Cregan, president of St Patrick's Training College, Drumcondra, supporting the abolition of the system:

> Boys should be free for as long as possible to choose a career. The preparatory college system forces choice at 14, before he can have a proper appreciation of the implications of the decision. This results always in a group of students from the preparatory colleges with no sense of vocation, completely bored and uninterested in their work. The staff of the training college's opinion is based on many years' experience that neither in personal qualities nor in academic attainments are preparatory college students in general equal to open competition students.[43]

Cregan's view was later to be contradicted by the staff of Coláiste Éinde, who, in a communication opposing the closure, noted that four of the six

---

42. See Part I, chapter 4.
43. DT Papers, S12307.

gold medals for excellence in St Patrick's Training College in 1959 were obtained by past students of the Galway college.

The Departmental memo was significant for an important factor which went unmentioned: the decline in academic standards in the colleges, particularly a deterioration in performance at Leaving Certificate Examinations. Pupils no longer obtained the high results achieved in the early years of the system. A study of Leaving Certificate results at the preparatory colleges in the late 1950s[44] shows that just over one-third of students were unlikely to have obtained places in training colleges had they been in competition with other students. Furthermore, as every preparatory student would have easily obtained honours in Irish, these results show a marked decline in academic standards in the colleges. A further factor worth noting is the gender difference, particularly in the category of four or more honours, where there were twice as many girls as boys. Obviously aware of such results, the Department had begun to pursue a more rigorous policy with regard to preparatory students. An example of this was in Coláiste Íosagáin,[45] where students who were not studying satisfactorily were interviewed by an inspector. Two other students had not been allowed to continue their course at the college. In addition, as a result of the interview system for entry to training college, three students had not been called to training.

The timing of the closure decision, coming so soon after de Valera's retirement, is an indication that his support had been a factor in the preparatory colleges' continuation. A further significant factor in the closure decision was the attitude of the Catholic Church. The traditional practice of ensuring the bishops' approval before making a major decision, was carefully adhered to. A letter from Tarlach Ó Raifeartaigh,[46] secretary of the Department, to Bishop Browne shortly after the cabinet decision in November 1959, shows Browne's influence. Ó Raifeartaigh informed Browne that the minister was waiting

> to avail himself at an early date of some suitable occasion to announce the ending of the system, its replacement by an extended scholarship scheme and the intention to use the college buildings for purposes connected with the promotion of the Irish language, including, where possible, their use as secondary 'A' schools.[47]

Ó Raifeartaigh assured Browne that he had informed the minister that Browne would be 'favourably disposed' towards Coláiste Éinde being transferred to him for use as an 'A' school.

The government's decision to increase the number of scholarships for Gaeltacht students at second and third-level was important, for it immediately

---

44. Jones, The Preparatory Colleges, pp. 503–504.
45. Diary of Coláiste Íosagáin, 24 March 1958.
46. For biographical details see the Appendix.
47. Galway Diocesan Archives, Browne Papers.

reduced the strength of opposition to the closure. The minister promised to increase the number of secondary school scholarships to 80, to treble the number of university scholarships to 15 and to double the number of places in domestic science training colleges.

Referring to the disposal of the buildings, the Department's memo noted that they were worth one million pounds.[48] While compensation would have to be paid to the staff, the ending of the system would result in savings of £50,000 per annum. What finally sealed the fate of the preparatory system, however, was that the closure proposal came from the Minister for Education and was approved by the Minister for Finance. This was ironic. The closure decision must have been one of the few occasions in the history of the colleges when the two departments were in agreement. Indeed, a further touch of irony regarding the closure was the speed with which it was accomplished. The system, which had been dogged by bureaucratic delays throughout its history, ended in less than two years.

An indication that the matter was to be dealt with promptly came two days later, on 13 November 1959, when the decision to close the five Catholic colleges was approved in principle by the cabinet. The Minister for Education was given authority to investigate turning the colleges into 'A' schools and extending the scholarship scheme for Gaeltacht students to secondary schools and universities. A further prompt decision was made three weeks later on 7 December 1959, when the cabinet decided that an entrance examination to the preparatory colleges for 1960 would be held, and the minister was given permission to announce the decisions.

OPPOSITION TO THE CLOSURE DECISION

The minister delayed making a public announcement, and news of the impending decisions was first broken by the Irish language weekly newspaper, *Inniu*. On 4 March 1960, it carried rumours of a new scholarship scheme to replace the preparatory system. This resulted in considerable opposition to the closure. The following week, the writer, Breandán Ó hEithir, a past pupil of Coláiste Éinde, denounced the closure in a passionate letter. He wrote that 'the death sentence had been passed on the colleges', and queried if any evidence had been given in their defence. Ernest Blythe also condemned the closure in an article in the *Sunday Independent* on 13 March 1960. The following month, the magazine *Comhar* devoted much of its April edition to the issue, including a sharply critical leading article and contributions by the Gaelic League, Comhdháil Náisiúnta na Gaeilge and the INTO. An invitation to the Minister for Education to contribute was refused. In its contribution, the Gaelic League outlined the history of the system and, not unexpectedly, praised the academic standards and sporting

---

48. Cabinet minutes, 9 November 1959, DT Papers, S12307.

achievements of the colleges. It also recalled the contribution of past pupils to the language movement. It ended with a complaint that the League had not been consulted about the move.

A similar stance was taken by Comhdháil. It pleaded that the colleges should not be closed until there were more ordinary Irish-speaking boarding schools to replace them. It also wanted measures to ensure that the standard of Irish among primary teachers would not decline and requested a meeting with Dr Hillery to put its views to him. The INTO had never favoured the system. It outlined its original objections to the colleges, selection at too early an age and the method of selection, whereby students from certain areas of the country were favoured. It further complained about the narrowness of the students' formation, living and learning for four years within a college where all the students were intended for the same profession.

Comhar invited Blythe and past pupils from four of the colleges to write about their experiences. Blythe's piece is noteworthy, because he revealed that he had been unhappy with the way in which the system had developed. He believed that the curriculum should have been broadened to include modern languages, and the rules changed to allow students who did not want to become teachers to leave the system quickly and easily. Whether he

30 Leaving Certificate Class at Coláiste Moibhí 1961.
Back: Bláthnaid Ní Láiste, Fíora Rodhcroft, Cairilín Ní Ghabhann, Caitlín de Ruitéal;
Middle: Milréad Riach, Eithne Nic Arrais, Iris Ní Chothúin, Norma Veitch, Bhealraí Ní Ghabhann, Proinnséas Ní Shuantáin,
Front: Eithne Ní Shiaghail, Áine Hic, Mairéad Nic Uigín, Gleadas Ní Allúin, (príomh-oide), Siobhán Ní Choillithoir, Maedhbh Nic a tSiúil, Mairéad Fhuireastál. *CICE Archives*.

would have made such improvements had he continued in government is a matter for speculation. Not unexpectedly, the four former students wrote in favour of the colleges and emphasised the ease with which students from the Galltacht became fluent in the language.

Opposition from other Irish language bodies included a statement from the Gaelic League. It queried why a judgement on the system had not awaited the report of the Commission for the Restoration of Irish. In June 1960, the League's executive committee called on the minister to postpone his decision until it had been examined by the government in the light of whatever recommendations might be made by the Commission. A similar resolution from the Comhairle Connacht of Muintir na Gaeltachta was sent to the Taoiseach in December 1960. Further criticism came from the Irish language newspaper, *Amárach,* which deplored the closure of the colleges, particularly Coláiste Íde, where, the paper pointed out, outstanding results at the Leaving Certificate Examination had been obtained in 1960.

COLÁISTE MOIBHÍ TO STAY OPEN

The growing opposition forced Hillery to make the closure decision public. On 24 May 1960, he told the Dáil that while the preparatory colleges had been needed in the 1920s, recent reforms in recruitment meant they were no longer necessary. An exception, however, was Coláiste Moibhí, the college for Protestant students, which was to remain open as a preparatory college.[49] Once the government's proposals to continue the colleges as 'A' schools and to extend the scholarship scheme became known, most of the opposition petered out.

As soon as the closure decision was taken by the cabinet, the speed with which the Department reacted was remarkable. Arrangements for the transfer of the properties became a priority and the minister quickly made approaches to the managers of the five colleges. Agreement was received from each of the five bishops. It was not surprising that in June 1960 the matter received the following cursory mention in the hierarchy's minutes:

> As it was understood that those colleges would be handed over to the communities in charge of them to be conducted as secondary schools the bishops did not think that any action on their part was asked for.[50]

About the same time, the colleges received official notification of the closure decision. Four of the five bishops accepted the proposal to turn the college in his diocese into an 'A' school. The exception was the bishop of Raphoe, manager of Coláiste Bhríde, who pointed out that there was no

---

49. See Part II, chapter 10.
50. Dublin Diocesan Archives, McQuaid Papers.

scope for another 'A' school in the area, where secondary education was already well catered for. With only one college to dispose of, the Department suggested Coláiste Bhríde could become a residential primary school, similar to Ring College, Co. Waterford.

Rumours about the disposal of the properties soon spread and led to some unusual proposals: the Hon. F. Ross de Moleyns, a son of Lord Ventry, the previous owner of Coláiste Íde (who had sold the property to the Land Commission in 1922 for £7,000), wrote to Taoiseach Seán Lemass in September 1960 offering to turn the college, formerly known as Burnham House, into a centre for deep-sea angling and other sporting activities, while early in 1961 a newspaper reported that Bord Fáilte wanted to turn the college into a 200-room hotel. In Galway, there were rumours that Coláiste Éinde was to become a Butlin's Holiday Camp.

DISPOSAL OF COLÁISTE ÉINDE

The rumour about Coláiste Éinde was without foundation, as the Department and Bishop Browne had already reached an agreement about its future.[51] Furthermore, Browne's proposed retention of the teaching staff made the proposal attractive. It meant that expensive compensation would not have to be paid and that disputes in this area would be avoided. In addition, the transition from preparatory college to 'A' school would be less problematic. On 8 March 1961, Browne announced that the government had accepted his offer for the college and its lands. Also included was a nearby site on Threadneedle Road for a boys' primary school, which he persuaded the Department to include. Later, in May, he obtained recognition for a temporary national school on the site. This was a shrewd move on Browne's part to ensure the provision of future pupils for the new college. Indeed, the skilful manner in which Browne organised the changeover was noteworthy. By pleading that diocesan resources were limited due to the construction of a new cathedral, he persuaded the Department to come to special arrangements for capitation grants and teacher quotas for the new college. In September 1961, the college became an 'A' school with an enrolment of 113 pupils, including 69 former pupils. Browne was not slow in charging realistic fees, which were £100 per annum for boarders and £20 for day boys.

As soon as the closure decision had been approved by the cabinet, the Department had begun negotiations with the administrators of the colleges. However, it was not until May 1961 that Hillery told the Dáil that these negotiations were under way and that tenders would be invited for Coláiste Bhríde. This was a little disingenuous, as in February 1961 the

---

51. Galway Diocesan Archives, Browne Papers.

Minister had been instructed to dispose of the colleges on the following terms:

> Coláiste Éinde, estimated value £95,000: Bishop of Galway offered £40,000 in instalments of £2,000 per annum for the lands, buildings and all equipment.
>
> Coláiste Íosagáin, estimated value £50,000; Provincial of De La Salle Order offered £10,000 in annual instalments of £1,000 starting 1964/65.
>
> Coláiste Mhuire, estimated value £35,000; Mother Superior of the Mercy Order, Tuam, offered £10,000 in instalments starting in 1964.
>
> Coláiste Íde, estimated value £35,000; The Mercy Order, Tralee, offered £10,000 in annual instalments.[52]

Originally, the nuns offered only £9,000 for Coláiste Mhuire but this was not accepted and the minister was given special instructions regarding the sale of Coláiste Íde and Coláiste Mhuire:

> In addition to such sums as he may be able to obtain from the orders concerned, for the total effects of each college, but in the event of his failing to obtain any such additional sums he be authorised to accept £10,000 for the lands, premises and effects of each college.

A condition of sale was that each of the four colleges would be used as an 'A' school for not less than 20 years. This was stressed by the minister in a memo in February 1961, which showed the government's sensitivity to criticism over the closures:

> The Minister for Education regards it as of paramount importance that, where possible, they should be kept as class 'A' secondary schools. It is essential to his policy of encouragement of the use of Irish in schools that no action of the government should reduce the number of secondary schools in which Irish is the medium of instruction and general communication. It might be interpreted as showing a lack of interest in the revival of Irish and invite a charge that while exhorting others to forward the language by all ways possible the government is suppressing schools under its own direct control in which Irish is the language.[53]

As the bishop of Raphoe was not interested in acquiring Coláiste Bhríde, its disposal was problematic. However, before it was put to tender, the Capuchin Order offered £20,000 to obtain Falcarragh as a house of studies. This offer was recommended for acceptance by Hillery on the following grounds:

> In view of (a) the great Franciscan tradition in the matter of Irish scholarship (b) the beneficial effect the introduction of an order, such as the Capuchins, would

---

52. DT Papers, S12307C/61.
53. *Ibid.*

have on the Gaeltacht area and (c) Falcarragh is amply catered for with secondary 'A' schools the offer of the Capuchin order be accepted.[54]

It is likely that the offer would have been accepted, but for some anxiety in the cabinet about the low prices recommended by Hillery. Indeed, they were so low that Lemass was moved to refer the matter to the attorney-general for advice on whether 'the sale of state property in these five cases, at less than the estimated market value, could be regarded as an individual endowment of religion, and therefore a contravention of article 44.2.2 of the constitution'. The attorney-general's considered opinion, however, was that it could be 'regarded as an endowment of education, and not of religion, in cases other than Falcarragh'.[55]

With this advice in mind, the government decided not to accept the Capuchin offer for Coláiste Bhríde. Meanwhile, efforts to sell the college premises continued without success, and a memo to the government in May 1961 reported that Fr Vergilius had repeated his offer. Despite the fact that a higher offer had been received 'elsewhere' of which the Taoiseach had been informed, Fr Vergilius's offer was accepted. The secretive manner in which the properties were sold aroused concern, however, and in May 1961 the Federation of Catholic Lay Schools passed a resolution calling for a full investigation into the matter by the Comptroller and Auditor-general, and by the Dáil Committee for Public Accounts.[56]

A noteworthy feature of the sale of the properties was that the Department of Finance accepted such reduced offers for properties which had been estimated to be worth one million pounds when the closure decision was first cited in December 1959. The acceptance of these reduced offers was excused on the grounds that the conditions attached to the sale of the colleges reduced their value:

> The government should be aware that the possibility of selling at prices anywhere near the market value is further reduced by the disposal of properties to communities at present in occupation, or to alternative communities, nominated and appointed by the local bishop at a price which the community may be able and willing to pay.[57]

Indeed, the Department of Finance's acceptance of the Office of Public Works' later estimate of £250,000 as the market value of the properties was remarkable, as was its failure to query how the value of the properties decreased from the earlier estimate of one million pounds. Furthermore, the prices recommended by the Minister for Education for acceptance, and agreed by the cabinet in February 1961, amounted to a mere £80,000 in

54. *Ibid.*
55. Cabinet memo, 17 February 1961, DT Papers, S12307.
56. *Irish Independent,* 10 May 1961.
57. DT Papers S12307C/61.

instalments over 20 years, for four of the colleges. In addition, payment for Coláiste Íosagáin and Coláiste Mhuire would not start until 1964. Hillery's weak explanation for this vast difference was that they wanted the colleges to continue 'under altered arrangements', so they had to deal with the existing administrators of the colleges and to settle with them. 'Every endeavour was being made to have them continue as 'A' schools.'[58]

As the preparatory system came to an end, the final act in the dismantling of the gaelicisation policy was announced. Newly-qualified teachers would no longer be required to obtain the bilingual certificate which, since 1936, had been compulsory for students leaving training college. This had ensured that there was a high standard of fluency in the language in the training colleges. In 1961, the bilingual certificate was replaced by an oral examination, which teachers had to pass within five years of qualifying.

---

58. *Dáil Reports,* 16 May 1961.

CHAPTER SIX

The preparatory system – success or failure?

'Their influence on the nation's children was incalculable'

For almost four decades successive governments tried to gaelicise the nation through the education system. The 1959 decision to close the preparatory colleges indicated a significant change of direction, for the colleges had been a fundamental part of the state's education policy for over 30 years. The decision was also a clear indication that the government intended to lessen the emphasis on the Irish language in the schools. Though efforts at gaelicising the nation had failed, the emphasis on cultural nationalism in the first decades after independence had resulted in sufficient change in the country at large to ensure that the new state's character and identity differed considerably from pre-independence days.

Over 4,500 student-teachers were educated at the preparatory colleges. Much information regarding the colleges, for the thesis on which this book is based, was gathered by interviewing former students and teachers. Others filled in questionnaires. Though chosen on a fairly random basis, an effort was made to include students from each decade in each college. Many of them were looking back over 30, 40, 50, and in the case of the early students, 60 years. This chapter will examine the strengths and weaknesses of the system as seen in the light of their experiences, while remembering that their recollections may be somewhat coloured by time.

In assessing the contribution of the preparatory system to Irish education, certain key points must be considered, such as the aims of those who established it, the context in which it was set up, and the changing political and educational background in which it operated from 1926 to 1961. The system was established to assist the gaelicisation policy by providing the training colleges with a supply of Irish-speaking candidates, including a large number of students from the Gaeltacht. It was also to provide student-teachers with a much better education than had been given by the existing recruitment systems, namely, the monitorial system and the old pupil-teacher scheme, for during the 1920s, it had become obvious that all candidates entering training colleges needed to have passed the Leaving Certificate Examination.

Judged on these narrow criteria, the system was successful. From the beginning, it provided the training colleges with a supply of Irish-speaking candidates, though the inclusion of a large number of students from the Gaeltacht took longer to accomplish. In addition, preparatory students were better educated than those who were recruited through the older arrange-ments, and they had excellent results at both the Intermediate and Leaving Certificate Examinations. The system was also successful in providing suffi-cient numbers of candidates for training during a period of transition when the old forms of recruitment were coming to an end and the new pupil-teacher scheme and open competition were being developed. Furthermore, the early preparatory students played a significant role in the gaelicisation of the training colleges. Indeed, with their entry to training in 1931, the work of the training colleges was almost entirely through Irish and the Depart-ment could declare with satisfaction:

> Irish has become the everyday language of the four Roman Catholic training colleges. Both inside and outside the colleges it is noted that the students use Irish as a matter of course. Practically all the work in the training colleges is done through the medium of Irish.[1]

By 1933, the training colleges were producing primary teachers who were not just fluent in the language, but were able to teach Irish and to teach through Irish.

The success of the system has to be seen in the context of the times. A major aim of the newly-established Irish Free State was to achieve a cultural revolution by emphasising the Irish language, history and the distinctive Irish culture of the country, and the gaelicisation policy was one of the few radical initiatives undertaken by the Irish government in 1922. The prepa-ratory colleges were intended to play a significant part in the gaelicisation process. Unfortunately, the policy was drawn up during the War of Inde-pendence when military activities precluded lengthy debate, and the heady fervour of the times created unrealistic expectations. This resulted in ambi-tious and somewhat simplistic plans for the gaelicisation of the new state. Nevertheless, the language was to play a significant role in the new leaders' efforts to ensure that the new conditions reflected their ideology. Further-more, many of the leaders in the struggle for independence, such as Pearse, Blythe, Fitzgerald, Ó Caoimh, Lynch, 'Sceilg' and Beaslaoi,[2] were writers who naively believed their own propaganda. Their zeal in learning the lan-guage enabled them to become fluent in Irish. This made it difficult for them to comprehend the magnitude of the task facing the new Ireland.

---

1. *Report of the Department of Education*, 1930/31, p. 6.
2. For biographical details of people named on this page see the Appendix.

THE EFFECTS OF THE CIVIL WAR

The civil war and its aftermath also contributed significantly to the failure of the gaelicisation policy. Indeed, the deep divisions between the pro-Treaty and the anti-Treaty sides resulting from the brutality of the civil war led to the language policy becoming a 'sacred cow'. The fanaticism of some of the revivalists meant that any attempt to review or change the policy was avoided by others, who feared that their commitment to the new state would be questioned, and that they would be labelled 'pro-British'. The bitterness which developed from the civil war was all the greater because each side saw itself let down by former comrades, friends, and even by family members, a betrayal which was harder to endure than that by one's enemies. Furthermore, the savagery inflicted by both sides did considerable psychological damage to the cause of Irish nationalism and destroyed the idealism which had inspired many of those involved in the fight for freedom. Indeed, so deep were the divisions resulting from the civil war that rational debate about it was not possible until the 1980s.

Following so soon after the War of Independence, the civil war wreaked havoc on the country's finances. The precarious stability of the new state was weakened and, but for stern action by Cosgrave's government in dealing with the anti-Treaty forces, it might have disintegrated. For these reasons, the gaelicisation policy was no longer given the same priority as in the pre-1922 days. Efforts at reviving the language soon devolved on two bodies – the civil service and the education system – both of which were under the control of the government. Furthermore, the failure of members of successive governments to set an example by speaking the language doomed the revival and led to the policy being regarded with scepticism by the general public. Also notably absent from the new state's gaelicisation policy was any budgetary planning or provision for research into similar language programmes in other countries. For Fianna Fáil, there was the added difficulty of its own language enthusiasts, who included de Valera,[3] Derrig, Moylan, Seán T. Ó Ceallaigh and Aiken. While they were active in politics the gaelicisation policy was allowed to continue. For almost 40 years, successive governments left the strategy virtually untouched and relied almost entirely upon the civil service and the education system to carry the burden of gaelicising the nation.

The gaelicisation policy failed in both areas. By 1959, over one-third of the civil service had little or no Irish, while in the Gaeltacht almost half the public servants were incompetent in Irish.[4] The gaelicisation policy also damaged the education system by narrowing the curriculum with an over-concentration on one subject. After eight years of language teaching, few pupils could converse naturally in Irish and for those who could, there was

---

3. *Ibid.*
4. Ó Tuathaigh, G., 'Language, literature and culture in Ireland since the war', quoted in Lee, *Ireland, 1912–1985: politics and society*, p. 672.

little necessity to do so outside the classroom. Excluding the civil service and the education system, efforts at gaelicising the nation were more cosmetic than real.

One area where efforts to gaelicise education were successful was the preparatory system. Its high costs, however, soon led to tensions between the Departments of Finance and Education, and the history of the system was dogged by disputes between the two departments.

FAILURE TO REFORM THE CIVIL SERVICE IN 1922

Much of the Department of Finance's scepticism about the gaelicisation policy stemmed from the failure to reform the civil service at the foundation of the state. One of the first measures promulgated by the new government in 1922 was the insistence that schools had to teach Irish from St Patrick's Day on, and it immediately instituted a programme for teachers to learn the language. Yet nothing was done about the civil service, where the vast majority of personnel remained in the same positions which they had under the old British regime. Many of them had little regard for the gaelicisation policy. This was of particular importance in the Department of Finance which had control of budgetary spending for the other departments. This allowed it to reduce the preparatory course from five to four years,[5] thereby creating difficulties for the teaching of Latin and the introduction of a modern language. The Department of Finance was also responsible for the introduction of the ill-advised agreement whereby students had to promise to teach for five years in a national school or, on failing to do so, had to repay their fees. This led to unsuitable people becoming teachers.

Attempts by the Department of Finance to control rising costs failed due to poor planning in the Department of Education. This was clearly demonstrated in a number of major areas, such as the futile efforts to build a training college in Galway in the 1920s, the over-supply of trained teachers in the 1930s, and the shortage of qualified teachers in the late 1940s and 1950s. The early years of the preparatory system were dogged by the inability of the Department to forecast accurately the cost of establishing seven residential colleges, which eventually came to about three times the original estimate. There were also long delays in providing the colleges with permanent homes, due to endless bureaucracy and mismanagement.

Throughout this period, the hierarchy played a major part in all educational decisions, and its authority was unquestioned. This was a period in Irish history when it was generally accepted that schools, hospitals, orphanages and industrial schools should be controlled by the Catholic church and managed by religious orders. One of the first actions of the Irish Free State

---

5. See Part I, chapter 1.

government was the closure of the non-denominational Marlborough Street Training College,[6] a clear indication that the new state intended the church to have control of teacher training. Few decisions were taken without the hierarchy's prior agreement, for the failure to ensure the local bishop's approval could be costly.

The hierarchy was happy that the preparatory system continued as long as it did, because it gave the church a powerful influence in the formation of future teachers, by educating them at residential colleges with a strong religious ethos. It was not until the episode at Coláiste Éinde in 1956 that the hierarchy was alerted to the system's weaknesses. By this time, the government wanted to end the preparatory system and, through negotiations with Bishop Browne of Galway, became aware that the hierarchy would not oppose the decision. Furthermore, by offering the colleges at very low prices to the bishops in whose dioceses they were located, or to the religious orders which ran them, it defused opposition from that quarter.

THE COLLEGES' CONTRIBUTION TO THE REVIVAL OF IRISH

Despite the failure of successive governments to gaelicise the country, it can be claimed that the preparatory system greatly assisted efforts to revive the Irish language. When the colleges were established, the language was in a precarious state. The number of native speakers was in decline. The Gaeltacht continued to contract, and Irish was spoken mainly in remote areas of the country. The structure of the language was also somewhat problematic. Consisting of a number of dialects, it had no standardised spelling, grammar or terminology. Through the preparatory system large numbers of students from the Galltacht learned Irish easily. The system also proved that Irish could be used to teach the Leaving Certificate course and led the way for the provision of courses taught through Irish at third-level institutions, practices which many educationalists in the 1920s had asserted were not possible. Furthermore, many former preparatory students went on to become teachers at third-level institutions and in this way helped the language to develop so that it could be used to express the most abstract intellectual thoughts. By bringing students from different Gaeltacht areas to the same college, a certain standardisation of the grammar and vocabulary of the language took place. The writer, Breandán Ó hEithir, described his experience at Coláiste Éinde:

> Linguistically, it was like a vat into which almost all the dialects and regional accents were poured and out of which something close to a standard speech, based on the living language, emerged.[7]

---

6. *Ibid.*
7. Ó hEithir, *Over the bar,* p. 41.

Nevertheless, from its inception the preparatory system had fundamental weaknesses, such as entry at too early an age, the fee system, and segregation of students into a group where everyone was intended for the same profession. Certain other faults developed over time. These included the agreement to repay fees, the high costs of the system and the monopoly preparatory students had on places in training colleges, which prevented better qualified students from becoming teachers, particularly in later years. The length of the preparatory course also made it difficult to regulate the number of entrants to primary teaching in relation to the number of teachers required in any given year. Furthermore, it took six years to qualify as a teacher through the preparatory system whereas those entering through open competition took only two years. This was particularly problematic in the 1930s, when there was a surplus of trained teachers and in the 1950s when there was an acute shortage of teachers.

Other complaints included the failure to broaden the curriculum. Indeed, many students resented the failure to teach Latin to Leaving Certificate standard and the lack of a modern language. Furthermore, though most of the colleges were in the Gaeltacht, students seldom met Gaeltacht people. In addition the failure to reform the system, and the ill-judged changes made at Blythe's insistence to ensure the entry of Gaeltacht students to teaching, strengthened the opposition of the INTO to the system.

PAST STUDENTS' RECOLLECTIONS

As with any school experience, there were varieties of opinions amongst former students. A further difficulty in assessing their recollections was that there were seven colleges, and while they were very similar in many respects each was a separate entity. The majority of past pupils interviewed or questioned, however, recalled their period at a preparatory college as 'happy'. Typical of their comments were those of a student at Coláiste Mhuire in the late 1930s, who declared that she 'had loved teaching and taught happily for many years'. Many found the experience congenial, even stimulating, and described the preparatory colleges as 'fine for their times'. Most made lifelong friendships. There were others, however, who said that as they had no previous experience of being at a boarding school, they had nothing with which to compare their experience.

The replies of those who had had previous second-level education varied. A student at Coláiste Bhríde in the 1930s recalled her time there as preferable to two years at a convent in Letterkenny. A student at Coláiste Mhuire in the 1940s, however, recalled having less freedom there than in her previous school. Many of those who had been to other second-level schools were teachers' children, and their comments on the system were more perceptive. A former student, who described her first school as 'appalling' and who enjoyed her time at Coláiste Mhuire, recalled that 'the challenge for those of above average intelligence was inadequate'. This was a period when large numbers left school at 14 to start their working life. The more fortunate began apprenticeships at that age. Nevertheless, a criticism accepted by all those questioned, including those who felt that the system should not have been ended, was that the age of entry should have been older.

The claim by critics that segregating student teachers in preparatory colleges led to an unhealthy emphasis on one career, was accepted by some former students. Others stated that, 'There is little doubt that many not suited to teaching became teachers by default'. A student at Coláiste Chaoimhín in the 1930s recalled a heavy stress on teaching as their future career, and that any other 'calling was frowned upon'. However, this was not a difficulty in other cases and the emphasis seems to have varied from college to college. A former teacher at Coláiste Bhríde believed that segregation led to 'inbreeding' and that having all students aiming at becoming teachers made it 'a kind of closed shop'.

Even the staff of Coláiste Éinde who, as might be expected, opposed the ending of the system, showed an awareness of these weaknesses. In a memo to the Department they wrote:

> The system holds an immediate attraction for parents and teachers to send the more intelligent children for this entrance examination, and thus get them 'off their hands' once and for all, with a future guaranteed. When they enter the college, their outlook is narrowed and confined, and they are hampered in their freedom of choice; and although they may have no real taste for the teaching profession, they follow the line of least resistance, they proceed to training college, and become, in many cases, only indifferent teachers, etc.[8]

There was also a tendency for certain schools to enter a whole class for the annual entrance examination, while in other areas the tradition grew up for the best pupils to sit the exam. 'One entered for the examination, there wasn't a choice', was how one past student explained his reason for entry to a preparatory college, while another said: 'It was the teacher's idea to help me to get a steady, pensionable job.' Others replied that they wanted a secondary education and this was the only possibility, particularly for those who lived long distances from second-level schools. Indeed, some past students admitted that they disliked teaching: 'We were the *crème de la crème*. I was a good teacher but I hated teaching and I left when I got married. Later I went into business.'

Critics claimed that the preparatory system was used by students as a means of obtaining cheap second-level education, and there is a certain amount of truth in this. Several former students acknowledged that had it not been for the preparatory colleges they would not have received secondary education. According to one: 'It was the only education my family could

---

8. Memo on the closure of Coláiste Éinde from the staff of the college, Galway Diocesan Archives, Browne Papers.

afford,' while another said: 'I was offered a four-year scholarship (as a boarder) and my widowed mother who was finding it hard to make ends meet, thought it was a chance too good to miss.' A third gave this explanation: 'I entered because I got a scholarship, which I lost after the first term because of a means test.' Sometimes, however, the lack of means and the desire to become a teacher were not incompatible, and a number of former students claimed that they had wanted to become teachers, despite their family's limited finances. A former student at Coláiste Moibhí asserted: 'I entered because of a desire to be a teacher. There was no convenient secondary school nearby with fees suitable to the family's commitments.' A past student of Coláiste Bhríde said:

> It was wonderful for us poor people, from large families, who would not have had a chance to be educated. It was great for those like me, who loved teaching. Others I don't know.

There were of course many students who wanted to become teachers, and whose family incomes were not so limited. One of the first students in Coláiste Bhríde said: 'I loved Irish and still do. It [Coláiste Bhríde] was the surest path to entry to Carysfort [Training College] for anyone wishing to teach in a primary school.' An almost identical reason was given by a student who entered Coláiste Moibhí in the late 1950s.

In all the colleges there were a number of students from teaching families. Typical of them were twins, Sr. Columban and Sr. Kilian Horgan, two of the earliest students of Coláiste Íde. They wished to follow their parents, whom they described as 'dedicated and very successful national teachers'. One former student's father had been president of the INTO. Another, whose parents were both teachers, said her father wanted one of his seven children to follow him into teaching. It is clear from the comments of those from teaching families, that their parents held the colleges in high esteem. One such former student recalled that her father, a native speaker, believed that she would get the best possible education at Coláiste Mhuire. While a former student from Coláiste Moibhí in the 1950s said that her mother, who had been an open competition student, believed that 'preparatory students had an advantage over other students due to their proficiency in Irish'.

STRICT DISCIPLINE

One criticism of the colleges was that the students had little freedom and were all expected to conform to a rigid pattern. A student in Coláiste Mhuire in the 1940s said that they were never encouraged to speak out, or to mix with other schools or to go out. Discipline varied from college to college, as a student who experienced three colleges recalled:

> Coláiste Chaoimhín was just like an ordinary boarding school. We didn't do teaching practice. There was a lot of concentration on exams. In Coláiste Éinde things were not so strict. We were allowed out by ourselves in summer. I learned to swim in Salthill. It was much stricter in Coláiste Íosagáin.

The emphasis on discipline was more relaxed in Coláiste Moibhí, where according to a former student in the 1940s:

> Teachers treated you as if you were mature! After class and at week-ends we could change out of uniform. Visits to relatives or friends were allowed on Sundays after church. Phoenix Park was a safe place for cycling and we enjoyed a spin at week-ends, with very little traffic.[9]

This relaxed attitude continued throughout the 1950s when the college moved to Shankill, and students frequently visited the nearby town of Bray on afternoons when they were not engaged in sporting activities. In addition daily newspapers were provided in the students' dining-room.

While there was no corporal punishment in any of the colleges, the threat of expulsion '*Cuirfear abhaile thú*', a threat often carried out, was effective in ensuring obedience. Such conditions had their effect, and the system was successful in producing balanced people devoted to their religion, happy to accept the *status quo,* and ready to mould the next generation in the same way. Occasionally former students at a college during the same period had differing recollections of their experience. One former student at Coláiste Chaoimhín from 1934–38 recalled it as a 'spartan place, having the dark, gloomy appearance of a prison', while a class-mate recalled it as 'a beautiful building in a pleasant part of Glasnevin'. Both agreed that discipline was harsh, with one student adding: 'loneliness and unimaginative teaching contributed to my discomfort'. A third student of the same period had a different recollection: 'There was a friendly atmosphere, which helped me to settle down.'

The emphasis on discipline depended on the order running the college. Both Coláiste Íde and Coláiste Mhuire were run by the Mercy Order and a similar atmosphere prevailed in both. A former student described Coláiste Íde in the late 1950s as 'very convent-like, with silence in the corridors and toilets. Fear prevailed throughout – the fear of being caught and being reprimanded verbally.' While another former student of the same period described it as 'puritanical' and 'regimented' with the students treated like novices. Nevertheless, many students considered 'at one time or another' entering the order and one or two did every year. Life in Coláiste Mhuire was similar to that in Coláiste Íde. A student at Coláiste Mhuire in the mid-1940s described it as 'joyless and exam-orientated':

---

9. Foxton, E., 'Memories of Coláiste Moibhí 1945-49', *PSA Newsletter,* 1999, p. 7.

31 Sr. Fionnbarra, a former student at Coláiste Mhuire and Coláiste Íde, with former teachers at Coláiste Mhuire, Sr. Imelda, 1955–71, Mother Mary Sacred Heart, 1927–1946 and Sr. Paschal, 1934–70.

> It was a grind, day in and day out. An extraordinary military barracks-style regimentation prevailed. Life was run by the clock. Letters from home were opened and read. I got a letter from a medical student once and I was almost expelled.

Nevertheless, a student who was at the college in the late 1940s recalled being very happy at Coláiste Mhuire, though looking back she realised that the colleges were too enclosed, that they were out of step with modern trends in secondary education. Other less sensitive students regarded their time at a preparatory college as 'simply part of the growing-up process. Everyone went to boarding school'.

A LIBERAL EDUCATION

The colleges run by the Mercy Order, however, contrasted with Coláiste Bhríde, which was run by the Loreto Order, where a student with an urban background from the 1930s recalled appreciatively how the friendliness of the young staff helped her to settle down and adjust to the quietness of the country and the change of language. Coláiste Bhríde's past pupils described it as an 'excellent' school, which gave them a very liberal education with many extra-curricular activities. Indeed, from the beginning of the college, the Loreto Order insisted on the Department supplying them with musical instruments for a school orchestra and on having a sister in charge of music, though she was not on the official staff at first. The nuns also encouraged occasional visitors.

Teaching in Coláiste Bhríde differed from the other colleges. A student from the 1930s recalled Iníon Ní Inse (Henchy), an outstanding history teacher, who encouraged the students to give their opinions in class:

> We were always expected to get *'céad áit in Éirinn'* (first place in Ireland) and in our Intermediate Examination the youngest in the class got 110% i.e. maximum marks plus the bonus for doing the examination through Irish.

A former teacher described the pupils in the late 1940s and 1950s as so well motivated that one could relax and hold debates in class.

One criticism of the system was that the curriculum was too narrow for student teachers. The standard of teaching and the level at which certain subjects were taught varied from college to college. In the 1930s, botany, chemistry and physics were studied in Coláiste Mhuire, while higher mathematics for the Leaving Certificate were taught to the more able students. On the other hand, the standard of English teaching in Coláiste Chaoimhín was not high because of the large number of Gaeltacht students, although some students attributed it to the poor quality of the teacher, a native Irish speaker, who 'instilled in us an intense hatred of the subject'. A past student recalled:

> More than any other subject the teaching of English, even at the lower level, was abysmally lacking in any of the standards by which a modern language and its literature should have been treated. I am certain that the teacher contributed heavily to the failure.

Nevertheless, the teaching of English in Coláiste Éinde in the 1940s was of a high standard and the writer Breandán Ó hEithir was very disappointed with the dullness of the English course at UCG, for the quality of teaching in Coláiste Éinde had led him to expect something more exciting.[10] Yet according to another former student from 1947–51 the college was a boring place, with:

> No imagination in the teaching and where students were never stretched. The pick of the country was amongst the pupils but they only did the bare minimum. They never developed their potential.

The failure to teach Latin to examination level caused deep resentment among some of the students, who believed that it was a deliberate policy 'by somebody' to discourage primary teachers from going to university. For students with means, however, Latin was not a problem as those who wished

---

10. Ó hEithir, *Over the bar*, p. 41.

to proceed to third-level could afford grinds for matriculation. Also much regretted was the absence of a modern language. When the colleges were established, it was envisaged that French would be part of the curriculum, and it was taught in Coláiste Bhríde.

Nevertheless, there were some former students who defended the system on the grounds that the education provided was similar to that which was available in other schools of the period. A student who won a Fíor-Ghaeltacht scholarship to UCG believed her schooling at Coláiste Mhuire in the 1940s compared favourably with that of other second-level institutions, while a student at Coláiste Éinde in the 1950s described his education there as 'liberal and well-rounded'. The colleges were often criticised as being too examination-oriented and their excellent results were attributed to cramming. Outstanding examination results were frequently obtained, particularly during the early years. An example of this was a student at Coláiste Mhuire, who got first place in Ireland in the Leaving Certificate Examination in physiology and hygiene, in 1936. Later in the 1930s, another student at the college gained 10 honours at the Leaving Certificate Examination, including botany, chemistry and physics, as well as first place in the Laois county council scholarship examination. The following year, her sister obtained full marks in five subjects in the Leaving Certificate Examination. Especially notable were results obtained in 1938 by a class in Coláiste Chaoimhín.[11] Good results were not unusual, as the majority of students were bright, clever people, who had already demonstrated their ability by passing a very difficult entrance examination to obtain a place. Furthermore, to ensure that students focused on their studies, the threat that they would be sent home in disgrace if they failed their examinations, provided added motivation to study.

TEACHING PRACTICE

An important feature of the colleges was the emphasis on teaching practice which was one of the justifications for the continuation of the preparatory system. This varied from college to college, and opinions differed as to its value. None of the students at Coláiste Chaoimhín could recall doing any, while in other colleges it was often little more than a charade. A student in Coláiste na Mumhan in the early 1930s recalled his experience:

> For two, maybe three, weeks towards the end of third year we 'taught' one lesson once or twice a week in the Boys' National School in Mallow. We were not given any advice, instruction or direction except the subject we were to teach. I remember having a picture of a large sow, a pink and black one, lying on her side and her bonhams feeding or clambering over her. All I did was ask questions.

---

11. See Part I, chapter 3. See also *Irish Press*, 3 November 1938.

According to a student at Coláiste Mhuire in the 1940s, teaching practice was not quite so casual and each student had to prepare a lesson which she taught to her own class with the teacher as supervisor and critic. This was similar to the procedure at Coláiste Éinde in the 1930s, which was described by one student as 'of very little use, merely window dressing'. A similar opinion was expressed by a former student at Coláiste Bhríde in the 1930s. By the late 1950s, however, teaching practice was taken more seriously at the college, with an emphasis on good use of the blackboard and visual aids.

Each of the seven colleges made a distinctive contribution to the development of their students as individuals, and while each college had its own particular ethos, all were marked by certain features, such as an emphasis on the Irish language, nationalism, religion (with the exception of Coláiste Moibhí) and sport. An outstanding feature of all the colleges was that they gave most students a love of the Irish language which remained with them for life. Indeed, the colleges more than fulfilled the aspirations expressed for them by President Cosgrave[12] that they would be 'thoroughly Gaelic,' with the use of Irish not confined to the classroom, but permeating all activities. Furthermore, learning a language by the 'total immersion' method was very successful, as shown by this recollection from a student in Coláiste Chaoimhín in the 1930s:

> I was entirely happy in Coláiste Chaoimhín. Essentially, I felt that students were engaged in a kind of missionary endeavour because of the feeling that as well as preparing for the profession of teaching, we were dedicated to the advancement of the Irish language. A certain idealism was basic to our teaching and training. That never entirely deserted my way of thinking in later life.

In the early years of Coláiste Chaoimhín, it was not unusual for the boys to be heard speaking Irish in the local post office or on the trams or buses.[13] The colleges also fostered an interest in Irish culture through regular sessions devoted to Irish dancing, music and traditional singing.

While each college was a 'mini-Gaeltacht', some of the colleges were more nationalistic than others. The most nationalistic was probably Coláiste Chaoimhín where attendance at soccer or rugby matches was strictly forbidden and merited expulsion, though no-one was ever caught. Run by the Christian Brothers, a former student recalled that boys were reprimanded for wearing red or blue ties. The emphasis in Coláiste Bhríde and Coláiste Íde was mainly on Irish culture, though one of the early students of Coláiste Íde recalled that 'Pádraig Mac Piarais was idolised'. Other students from the same period at Coláiste Íde recalled famous writers visiting the college, such as Peig Sayers, 'Kruger' Kavanagh, Muiris Ó Súilleabháin, Seán A Chóta (Ó Caomhánaigh), and An File Ó Duinnsléibhe. A student of the same college in the 1950s recalled:

---

12. See Part I, chapter 2.
13. Ó Flaitile, 'Coláiste Chaoimhín,' *An Réiltín,* Fómhar, 1956, p. 6.

32 De La Salle Br. Bernardine Doyle, vice-principal Coláiste Íosagáin, 1947–59.

> Sr Borgia (the Principal) went out of her way to help us to feel proud of our heritage. There was a lot of emphasis on culture – plays and music – not so much on books. It was a healthy nationalism with no apologies for the British being in the North and no bending over backwards to please spoilt unionists. It was very healthy. There was no hatred of the English in England either.

A former teacher at Coláiste Íosagáin recalled his time there during the 1950s:

> They were the happiest years I spent anywhere. Conditions were near perfect. Not jingoistic but there was an ordinary enthusiasm for the language.

THE GAELTACHT LOCATION

Four of the colleges were established in the Gaeltacht so that students would meet native speakers in everyday settings. Nevertheless, there was little contact between the students and the native speakers. A teacher who taught at Coláiste Mhuire for over 30 years expressed the view that the colleges might have succeeded just as well in urban areas, as each was a self-contained 'mini-Gaeltacht'. The colleges were also to provide second-level education for Gaeltacht students and in this they were successful. All the colleges, except Coláiste Moibhí, had large numbers of Gaeltacht students, particularly Coláiste Íde, where students came mainly from the Cork and Kerry Gaeltacht. It was believed that by having a large number of Gaeltacht students, Galltacht students would find it easier to learn the language. But little effort was made to assist Gaeltacht students at English. A Gaeltacht student in Coláiste Íde in the late 1950s recalled being unhappy, as she found

English very difficult, and while she was very good at Irish there was a neg-ative image of the Gaeltacht among some of the staff. An unexpected result, which never occurred to those who founded the system, was that due to being in a totally Irish-speaking environment, some students were not as good at English as they might have been.

Some former students were quite disapproving of the preparatory system. A student at Coláiste Chaoimhín in the 1930s believed that the way in which Gaeltacht students were selected at entrance was unconstitutional. A student in the same class claimed that it resulted in the majority of student teachers coming from a few parishes in the west of Ireland. This perception was not borne out by the research, although it showed that often students did come from the same schools and parishes. In some places a tradition of sending students to preparatory colleges developed. The success of Coláiste Moibhí, however, where there were less than half a dozen Gaeltacht stu-dents throughout its history, showed that it was not necessary to have large numbers of Gaeltacht students for the colleges to be successful. Indeed, at times the two groups did not mix easily, though this varied from college to college. Often there was considerable resentment among Galltacht students at the presence of Gaeltacht students, 'who paid no fees, were dressed by the college, given travelling expenses and pocket money, while we were obliged to pay for everything, fees, travel etc'.

Differences in academic standards between the two groups were also problematic. The poor standard of English of Gaeltacht students caused some resentment, particularly as those who failed English at the Leaving Certificate Examination were allowed on to training college. While the treatment of Gaeltacht students varied from college to college, those at Coláiste Mhuire in the 1940s did not find it a particularly welcoming place. They felt that they were treated as second-class citizens, not by their peers, but by the nuns, who gave Gaeltacht students the impression that they should be eternally grateful for free education.

Many students resented the random way in which they were sent to a college far from home, even though there might have been one nearer. Particularly unfortunate were students from the Donegal Gaeltacht, who were sent in the early years to Coláiste na Mumhan, and following the débâ-cle at Coláiste Éinde in 1956 were sent to Coláiste Íosagáin. In addition the Department often started students in one college and then transferred them to another. Sometimes, there was a reasonable explanation for the move, but often it was just a ploy by the Department to adjust numbers which it had failed to get right in the first place. Furthermore, the sudden closure of Coláiste Chaoimhín clearly demonstrated the uncaring attitude of the Department towards the students, when 25 students were moved from that college to Coláiste Éinde for a year and subsequently moved to Coláiste Íosagáin to finish their course.[14]

---

14. See Part I, chapter 3.

THE TEACHERS

Much of the success of the colleges was due to the calibre of the teachers. The early teachers had a great enthusiasm for the language and taught it with missionary zeal. Amongst them were Mother Teresa Joseph O'Sullivan, a relative of the 1916 revolutionary, Austin Stack, who taught at Coláiste Bhríde; Aindrias Ó Muimhneacháin, who taught in Coláiste Chaoimhín, Micheál Ó Siochfhradha, who taught in Coláiste Chaoimhín and later in Coláiste Moibhí, and Síle Ní Shúilleabháin, later Dr Síle Dudley Edwards, who taught at Coláiste Íde. Many of the teachers were highly qualified and went on to become lecturers at third-level institutions. As in all educational establishments, there were other teachers who, despite a deep commitment to the language, could not be described in such glowing terms.

COULD THE COLLEGES HAVE CONTINUED?

Many former students thought that it was a mistake to end the system, which they believed could have survived if certain changes had been made. A student at Coláiste Mhuire in the 1940s felt that the automatic entry to training colleges which preparatory students enjoyed should have been abolished because:

> Some students didn't bother to work. They knew they had places in the training colleges. By and large, however, the quality coming out of the preparatory colleges was very high.

Amongst those who felt that the system could have continued 'in a modified form' were the staff at Coláiste Éinde, who drew up a memorandum opposing the closure of the college in 1959.[15] They believed that most 'serious-minded' boys and girls of 15 or 16 would know their preferred career, and it would be easy to make an assessment of their suitability for teaching. They proposed that 15 or 20 pupils, who had completed the Intermediate Certificate Examination with honours, should be selected each year and sponsored by the Department as candidates for teaching in an ordinary 'A' secondary school. This was similar to the way in which Coláiste Moibhí operated from 1969 onwards.

Many of the former students claimed that the standard of Irish in primary schools had declined due to the closure of the colleges. One former student commented that 'with the advent of Gaelscoileanna this matter is being rectified in a healthier way'. Others, however, believed that the closure was a contributory factor, but not the cause of the decline in the standard of Irish and that the influence of the media and foreign travel had greater effect.

---

15. Memo from the staff of Coláiste Éinde, Galway Diocesan Archives, Browne Papers.

OIFIG AN OIDEACHAIS NAISIUNTA,

BAILE ATHA CLIATH.

5th February, 1927.

COLAISTE IDE - BURNHAM HOUSE, DINGLE.

Madam,

I am to state for your information that the Minister for Education with the concurrence of His Lordship, the late Most Reverend Dr. O'Sullivan, Bishop of Kerry, has appointed the following as professors in Colaiste Ide:-

Caitlin M. Ni Bhuachalla, B.A.,N.U.I.
(First Class Honours and First place),Post-graduate scholar and winner of Donnellan Prize. (Secondary Teacher).
Loreto Hall,
St.Stephens Green,
Dublin.

Sile Ni Shuilleabhain, Trained Teacher. First place Easter Scholarship exam,1924. First place Training College Examinations 1925 and 1926.

Ballybunion Convent,
Co. Kerry.

Maire C. Ni Chathasaigh, B.A. (Hons.) N.U.I.
Secondary Teacher.

Marist Convent,
Tubbercurry.

I am, Madam,

Your obedient servant,

[Sgd] Labhras O Brolcha

Sister Columbanus,
Convent of Our Lady of Mercy,
St. John's,
Tralee.

33 Letter from Ó Brolcháin sanctioning the appointment of teachers at Coláiste Íde in 1927. *Courtesy The Mercy Order.*

Some, such as this former student from the Donegal Gaeltacht, took a more reflective view:

> It is convenient to say that the closure of the colleges led to a falling in the standard of the teaching of Irish .... It has always been my view that an ounce of goodwill is better than a ton of fluency. I am sorry to say I have come across students of my years who would never have received second or third-level education were it not for their being native speakers. The same people would reply in English when addressed in Irish. The non-Gaeltacht students of my class, I have always found anxious and willing 50 years afterwards to carry on dialogue in Irish.

Others criticised the gaelicisation policy and blamed inspectors for turning teachers against Irish by putting too much stress on its teaching. One commented, 'I often thought that it was typical of a young country to push the language rather than to nurture it, to make it fashionable even'. According to a former student of Coláiste Éinde who became an inspector, the reopening of the colleges was a frequent topic for discussion amongst his colleagues, as there had been 'a terrible deterioration in the standard of Irish in the schools'. Opinions, however, were divided among them, though it was accepted that the great advantage of the preparatory system was that there was 'no pain in learning Irish'.

Any assessment of the contribution of the preparatory system to Irish education must include consideration of the role played by former preparatory students in primary education and in education generally since the late 1920s. The vast majority became primary teachers and spent their whole careers teaching in schools throughout the country. Others moved to second-level schools, often specialising in teaching Irish. Many of those who were students in the final years of the colleges were still in the education system in 2000. As teachers, former preparatory students' work in the classroom influenced generations of students. In addition there were many former students who influenced education in other ways. Outstanding amongst them was Diaglán Ó Braonáin from Coláiste Éinde who became secretary of the Department. Others whose influence spread well beyond their own schools wrote textbooks or became members of the inspectorate. Past pupils from each of the boys' colleges became members of the inspectorate. At one stage, approximately one third of the inspectorate were former preparatory students. They included Séamas de Buitléar and Breandán Ó Croinín, who both played a major role in education in the 1960s, leading to the implementation of the Curriculum for Primary Schools in 1971.

NOTABLE PAST PUPILS

Other past pupils made their mark in third-level education, particularly those who were holders of Gaeltacht scholarships. A number of them did not enter teacher training but went on to university. Outstanding amongst them was the late Dr Colm Ó hEochaidh, a past pupil of Coláiste Íosagáin who became president of UCG and chaired the New Ireland Forum established by the government in 1983 to examine the Northern Ireland conflict. Also outstanding were past pupils of Coláiste Éinde, Uinsin Mac Cába, who became professor of Mechanical Engineering at UCD, and Seán Mac Fhloinn, who later became a science professor at Louisiana University. He was one of three experts chosen by Washington to send to Moscow for technical negotiations at one point during the Cold War.[16] Other past students who entered a wide range of professions included Seán de Bláca, who became a heart surgeon, and Micheál Ó Cearbhaill a nuclear physicist in the United States, both from Coláiste Íosagáin, while from Coláiste Éinde Dr Liam Ó Gormáin joined the Irish Management Institute, Diarmaid Mac Aodhagáin became personnel manager of Allied Irish Bank, and Seosamh Mac Cába was head of the Educational Building Society and later of the Industrial Development Authority.

Other former students became lecturers in training colleges. Most notable of these were Sr Regina Durkan, a former student of Coláiste Mhuire who became president of Carysfort Training College (and led the objections to the closure of the college when it was announced in 1986); Millicent Fitzsimons, a past pupil of Coláiste Moibhí, who was vice-principal of the Church of Ireland Training College from 1969–72; and the Horgan sisters, Sr Kilian and Sr Columban, former students of Coláiste Íde, who were lecturers in Carysfort Training College for many years.

Many former students influenced education through the INTO, where a number held high office. Former presidents included John Joe Connolly, Michael McGarry, Brendan Gilmore, Liam McCluskey and Micheál MacSuibhne, all from Coláiste Éinde, Tomás Ó hEoghanáin from Coláiste Íosagáin and Sally Sheils from Coláiste Moibhí.

The love of the Irish language, which the colleges nurtured in their students, resulted in many of the former students making a considerable contribution to the language movement. They included Donncha Ó Laoire, one of the first class in Coláiste Chaoimhín in 1927, who was secretary of Comhdháil Náisiúnta na Gaeilge; Micheál Mac Cárthaigh from Coláiste Chaoimhín who became president of the Gaelic League; and Micheál Ó Muircheartaigh, the distinguished commentator on Gaelic games, a past pupil of Coláiste Íosagáin, who was chairman of Bord na Gaeilge from 1992 to 1999.

Other language organisations where past students achieved high office included Gael-Linn where Liam Ó Muircheartaigh from Coláiste Éinde served for a period as president and to which Muiris Bodhlaeir, a past pupil of the three boys' colleges, also made a substantial contribution, and Cumann Gaelach na hEaglaise, where past pupils of Coláiste Moibhí played

---

16. Ó Ceallaigh, S., *Coláiste Éinde 1928–2003, Seachtó Cúig Bliain faoi Bhláth*, p. 3.

34 Sally Sheils, President of the INTO 1995/96, a past pupil of Coláiste Moibhí. *Courtesy Moya Nolan.*

a major role. Former students also contributed to the development of Gaelscoileanna. These included Sr Philomena Ní Mhocháin and Máirín Feirtéar from Coláiste Íde. Indeed, it was not an exaggeration to praise the contribution of former preparatory students to the language revival in these fulsome terms:

> From the very first day that they left the colleges they did their best for the language and the country and their commitment and dedication is no less today.[17]

Many former students, who had been imbued with a love of Gaelic games, did much to cultivate a fondness for these sports in their pupils and gave their free time after school to coach them. Many of these former students went on to hold high office in the Gaelic Athletic Association. They included Seán Ó Siocháin, Coláiste na Mumhan, who was director-general of the GAA, and Séamas Ó Riain from Coláiste Éinde, who held the office of president from 1967 to 1970.

A number of former students joined Raidió Éireann, and later Raidió na Gaeltachta and RTE, where their linguistic skills were useful. Amongst them were Pádraig Ó Mealóid from Coláiste Íosagáin; Pádraig Ó Gaora

17. Ó Flaitile, p. 6.

and Liam Mac Con Iomaire from Coláiste Éinde; Liam Bodhlaeir, a past pupil of the three boys' colleges and Póilín Ní Chiaráin from Coláiste Mhuire. Others who were gifted musicians also broadcast frequently: Breandán and Caoimhín Mac Cnáimhsí, Seán Ó hAodha and Peadar Ó hUallacháin from Coláiste Chaoimhín, and Aindrias Ó Gallchobhair from Coláiste Éinde. Other students from Coláiste Éinde who were involved in broadcasting included actor Eoghan Ó Súilleabháin and Micheál Ó Conghaile.

Some outstanding past students made a number of career changes. The multi-talented Liam Develly, a pupil at Coláiste Éinde from 1947 to 1951, taught for a while and later became well-known as a singer and compère. For a period he worked in RTE. Subsequently, he was called to the Bar and became a Circuit Court judge. Similarly, Fachtna Ó hAnnracháin, a pupil at Coláiste Chaoimhín from 1934 to 1938, started out as a teacher. Later, he took a law degree and for a time worked in the legal department of RTE. Subsequently, he moved to the Music Department where eventually he became head. Another multi-talented past pupil of Coláiste Chaoimhín, Breandán MacCnáimshí, taught for 15 years and enjoyed teaching. He too, was a frequent broadcaster with Raidió Éireann. Later, he obtained an MA degree in Celtic Studies and became a lecturer in St Patrick's College, Maynooth, where he was much involved in the production of a new lectionery in the vernacular for Mass. Subsequently, he worked as a translator in Leinster House and for the European Union in Brussels, where as chief jurist linguist, his work entailed examining laws for translation.

Each college produced its own crop of distinguished past pupils. A number who started as teachers later entered politics. They included past pupils of Coláiste Éinde, Donnchadh Ó Gallchobair and Pádraig Ó Tuathail, who held cabinet posts as Minister for the Gaeltacht. Others from the same college who entered politics included Clem Coughlan, who represented a Co. Donegal constituency, and his brother, Cathal Coughlan, who succeeded him in the Dáil. Some former students made a contribution to the arts. They included the writer Breandán Ó hEithir, Abbey actor Peadar Lambe, and Capt. Seán Ó Fiacháin who established the Mercier Press, all from Coláiste Éinde, and singer Seán Ó Sé and writer Diarmaid Ó Súilleabháin from Coláiste Íosagáin.

FEW DISTINGUISHED WOMEN

One of the notable features of the period spanned by the preparatory system is how the careers of the men contrasted with those of the women. A number of past students, however, both male and female, made a contribution to religious life. This was one of the few areas in which women were allowed to exercise leadership in those days when it was generally accepted that a married woman's place was in the home. In addition, many female teachers had to leave the profession because of the marriage ban which was

35 Sr. Baiste, a former pupil and the last principal of Coláiste Íde, under the management of the Order of Mercy.

in operation from 1936 until 1958. For the others, there were few promotion prospects except in small schools. In larger schools which were run by religious orders, the posts of principal and vice-principal would have been held by members of the order, and in schools staffed by lay teachers such posts were usually held by men.

Past pupils who rose to positions of importance in religious orders included Coláiste Íde past pupils, Sr Mairéad Ní Loinsigh, who became mother provincial of the Salesian Order; Sr Cora Feirtéar, who became mother general of the Mercy Order, and Sr Baiste, the last principal of Coláiste Íde while it was run by the Mercy Order. Furthermore, the ordination of women to the priesthood in the Anglican Communion has allowed former students of Coláiste Moibhí to be ordained in different parts of the world.[18] Men who entered the church included the Right Rev. Augustine O'Sullivan from Coláiste na Mumhan, who became Abbot of Glenstal Abbey, and Fr Parthalán Mac Phaidín, Fr A. Ó Gallchobhair, Fr Pádraig Ó hÉalaidhe, and Fr Seán Ó Cannain CSSR Rome, who were all past pupils of Coláiste Éinde, while the Rev. Fred Phillips, a Church of Ireland rector, was a past pupil of Coláiste Moibhí.

---

18. See Part II, chapter 10.

The contrast between the number of male past pupils and the very few female past pupils who rose to positions of eminence in the Department is noteworthy. Exceptions were Áine Ní Chonaill from Coláiste Íde and Millicent Fitzsimons from Coláiste Moibhí, who became infant organisers. There were, however, a small number of outstanding women who rose to positions of influence outside education. These included Ita Meehan, a former pupil of Coláiste Mhuire, who became deputy secretary of the Department of Posts and Telegraphs and a director of Telecom Éireann and the Bank of Ireland; Frances Condell from Coláiste Moibhí who was Mayor of Limerick in the 1960s, and Maura Roche, from Coláiste Mhuire, who became a district court judge. The distinguished High Court Judge, Mary Laffoy, is also a former pupil of Coláiste Mhuire. Amongst those who entered Coláiste Íde during its final years as a preparatory college were broadcasters Seosaimhín Ní Bheaglaoich and Dairíne Ní Chinnéide.

That so many former preparatory students subsequently had outstanding careers is noteworthy, particularly as many of them did not come from privileged backgrounds. While it may appear that a large number of preparatory students did not continue on to primary teaching, or did not stay long in the profession, overall this group was only a small proportion of the number of students who passed through the preparatory colleges, which totalled over 4,500.

The closing of the preparatory colleges marked the end of an era in teacher recruitment and in education generally. Despite the failure to reform the system and to correct its inherent weaknesses, it was a successful educational experiment. From its establishment in the late 1920s, it quickly produced well-educated students, able to complete the training college course successfully, at a time when the inadequacy of existing recruiting methods was becoming more apparent. It also provided opportunities for Gaeltacht students to obtain second-level education. But its greatest success was that it produced teachers who were fluent in Irish, competent to teach through Irish and able to contribute to the new state's gaelicisation policy. The majority of them, in whom a love of the Irish language and a desire to pass it on to succeeding generations had been fostered in the preparatory colleges, spent their whole careers in primary teaching. As such, their influence on the nation's children was incalculable. That they were dependable people, in whom respect for their religion, a love of their country and a desire to inculcate these characteristics in succeeding generations were ingrained, was in many ways of immense value, particularly at a time when these characteristics were highly regarded. For an educational system to have primary teachers imbued with such personal attributes was some achievement. With such results the preparatory system was indeed a successful educational experiment.

Coláiste Moibhí
a case study

Coláiste Moibhí: the school that saved a community 1927–95

CHAPTER SEVEN

Getting the college off the ground

The first principal: Irish language enthusiast
GEORGE RUTH 1927–28

Part II examines the life and work of a preparatory college. The choice of college for the study was influenced by the availability of resource material. Coláiste Moibhí was chosen because it was one of the few colleges where the full contents of the register were available. Other source material included information supplied by former students through questionnaires and interviews. In addition the author was a student at the college from 1959 to 1961.[1] A typical preparatory college was marked by certain characteristics, the most dominant being the focus on the Irish language. The majority of preparatory colleges were situated in the Gaeltacht in a remote part of the country. Each college was a 'mini-Gaeltacht' with the work in the classroom and all extra-curricular activities undertaken through Irish. The intake of pupils, too, was distinctive with many of them from the Gaeltacht. Also noteworthy was the ethos of the colleges where nationalism, religion, and sport predominated.

On 25 April 1927, the first students entered Coláiste Moibhí's Glasnevin premises in Dublin. Coláiste Moibhí was similar to the other colleges in many respects. Like them, its outstanding characteristic was the emphasis on the Irish language, with all classes and extra-curricular activities undertaken through Irish. It differed from the other colleges, however, in significant ways, the most obvious being that it was for Protestant students. Staffed by lay teachers, religion was not emphasised to any great degree. It was also co-educational, which was unusual in those days. There were few native speakers amongst its students. It was not in the Gaeltacht but, like Coláiste Chaoimhín, was located in Dublin. The smallest of the colleges, it was to have 540 students during its existence as a preparatory college and, unlike

---

1. Coláiste Moibhí was the subject of her unpublished MLitt thesis, 'Recruitment and Formation into the Church of Ireland Training College,' Dublin University, 1989.

the other colleges, it was not closed in 1961. It was needed to provide facilities for Protestant students to learn Irish before entering the Church of Ireland Training College in Dublin.

Throughout its existence, Coláiste Moibhí was the only 'A' school under Protestant management. It played no small part in helping the Protestant minority to come to terms with the new Ireland. Indeed, its contribution to the development of the religious minority's acceptance of the new state was out of all proportion to its size. By providing Irish-speaking students for the Church of Ireland Training College, it enabled one of the most important Protestant institutions in the new state to survive. It also ensured the survival of the Church of Ireland's separate network of primary schools. Had they disappeared, the survival of the Protestant community in the 26 counties would have been in jeopardy, for the church was dependent on its primary schools to build up a strong sense of Protestant identity and to pass on its teaching to each new generation in an overwhelmingly Catholic environment.

There are few papers regarding the college still in existence. A major source of information is the college register. Similar to those in the other colleges, it is the only register to contain the Department's original instructions for principals. It still bears the warning that the Department had a similar register and that the two books had to agree totally. The register contained each student's name, date of birth, name and address of parent or guardian, the student's year of entry to the entrance examination and examination number, date of entry to the college and of leaving, plus the reason for leaving. Four columns for fees, one for each year of the course, were included as well as the student's Intermediate and Leaving Certificate Examination results.

EARLY NEGOTIATIONS

Originally, it was proposed that the Dublin preparatory college would be for all denominations. This would have been welcomed by the Church of Ireland if it were to be organised on 'wholly undenominational lines'.[2] In October 1925 a deputation composed of the archbishop of Dublin, Dr John Gregg, the bishop of Cashel, and the principal of the Church of Ireland Training College, the Rev. Dr Henry Kingsmill Moore,[3] met the Minister for Education. When it became clear that a non-denominational college was not possible, Gregg refused to have anything to do with it. MacNeill then proposed a separate preparatory college for Protestant students. Throughout Coláiste Moibhí's 68-year existence, the preparatory college and the Church of Ireland Training College (CITC) were to be closely interlinked.

---

2. Kingsmill Moore, *Reminiscences and reflections,* p. 293.
3. For biographical details of Gregg and Moore see the Appendix.

As with the other preparatory colleges, the Department was keen to get Coláiste Moibhí established as quickly as possible. In May 1926 Kingsmill Moore was informed that the new college would open in the following September and was asked to co-operate in 'mustering pupils'. However, few Protestant students entered the examination for the preparatory colleges in April 1926, and permission had to be obtained from the Department of Finance to hold a supplemental examination for them.[4]

At first, efforts were made to establish the college at Claremont House, Glasnevin. Originally the seat of the eighteenth-century Irish postmaster general, Lord Claremont, the house was taken over by Dr Charles Orpen in 1819. It became the Claremont Institution for the Deaf and Dumb. With the opening of the Catholic institutions for the deaf in Cabra, the numbers at Claremont decreased. Following partition, numbers declined further, and in 1928 fell as low as seven.[5] During 1926 a plan to adapt the building for a preparatory college at an estimated cost of £10,000 was considered but did not come to fruition. Instead Coláiste Moibhí began in April 1927 in two different buildings, Glasnevin House, on St Mobhi's (sic) Road, and in Marlborough House at the tram terminus. During the first term, both boys and girls were accommodated in separate dormitories in Marlborough House, with classes in Glasnevin House. In November 1927 the boys were transferred to Glasnevin House, though they continued to have their meals in Marlborough House.

Glasnevin House, a large well-appointed two-storey building with a basement, was built by Sir John Rogerson, a shipping magnate whose memory is perpetuated in the name of one of Dublin's quays. In 1807 it became the home of the Lindsay family, the area's principal landlords in the nineteenth and early twentieth centuries, after whom Lindsay Road is named. Subsequently, the house was sold to the Holy Faith nuns. Marlborough House had a more chequered career. Between 1834 and 1922, female students of Marlborough Street Training College resided there. From 1927 to 1933 it was home to Coláiste Moibhí and then to Coláiste Éinde. Later, it became a juvenile detention centre and continued as such until the 1970s, when it was demolished and the Meteorological Centre was built on the site.

The preparatory college took its name from its location on St Mobhi's Road, Glasnevin, and was called St Moibhi's College by English speakers. The area had long been associated with the early sixth-century saint whose feast day is 12 October, and to whom the local Church of Ireland parish church is dedicated. Mobhi 'Ciaránach' (meaning flatfaced), a monk from the monastery of Clonard, founded a monastic school on the banks of the Glas Naedhan, the Naedhe stream, a tributary of the river Tolka. His students included Colmcille of Iona, Ciarán of Clonmacnoise, Canice of Finglas and Comhgall of Bangor.[6]

4. DF Papers, S20/9/25.
5. Pollard, Rachel, *The Avenue: the History of the Claremont Institution 1816–1978*, p. 24.
6. O'Doherty and Mahon, *St Mobhi's Church Glasnevin: A short history and guide*, p. 11.

36 Glasnevin House. Home to Coláiste Moibhí 1927–33.

Coláiste Moibhí's management was similar to that of the other colleges, with the bishop in whose diocese the college was located, appointed manager. Archbishop Gregg agreed to this, while making it known that he did not agree with the gaelicisation policy. Gregg, whose grandfather, Right Rev. Dr John Gregg, Bishop of Cork, Cloyne and Ross, was an Irish speaker, took the pragmatic view that the policy was in existence and Protestants should accept it. According to his biographer:

> He did not pretend to agree with the government's policy, but he could not regard the existence of Irish as an excuse to prevent them (Protestants) from taking their places in the civil service. The more difficulty that it presented was a challenge to them to say that whatever difficulties there were, they were not going to be beaten by them.[7]

Gregg had a further cause to welcome the establishment of Coláiste Moibhí, coming as it did at a time when the Church of Ireland Training College was experiencing difficulties in training sufficient qualified candidates.[8] These difficulties, and the effects of partition, had reduced a flourishing national institution to a small college serving only the declining Protestant minority in the Irish Free State. Furthermore, the drop in numbers resulted in a loss

7. Seaver, *John Allen Fitzgerald Gregg, Archbishop*, p. 119.
8. Parkes, *Kildare Place*, p. 149.

of income, as training colleges were funded according to the number of students enrolled. To add to its difficulties, the training college was required to transform itself into an Irish-speaking institution.

In the 1920s, there were approximately 800 primary schools under Church of Ireland management in the state. It was estimated that 50 newly qualified teachers per year were necessary to meet the needs of the schools. CITC's role in supplying teachers with strong church loyalties was vital, for the Protestant churches regarded their separate system of education as of extreme importance in ensuring their distinctive presence in an overwhelming and increasingly Catholic state. Their main fear regarding mixed education was that it would lead to mixed marriages, which because of the harsh *Ne Temere* decree[9] meant cultural annihilation for the minority. The new state's gaelicisation policy was a further difficulty for the minority, many of whom were vigorously opposed to it.

PROTESTANT ATTITUDES TO THE IRISH LANGUAGE

The Irish language aroused a variety of reactions amongst Protestants. There had always been Protestants who had a deep interest in the language, mainly because of its antiquarian value. Furthermore, much of the work done for the preservation and restoration of Gaelic culture in the nineteenth century was carried out by Irish Protestants, such as George Petrie, Charles Graves and Henry Brooke. Others saw the language as a useful means of proselytism. The use of Irish for proselytising did not last long, partly because financial support from England for organisations such as the Irish Church Missions dwindled. But it led to the establishment in 1838 of a chair in Irish at Trinity College Dublin, largely at the behest of the Society for the Promotion of the Education of the Native Irish through the Medium of their own Language.

There was also a third group, who studied the language in search of a national identity. One of the most significant people in this group was Samuel Ferguson, a president of the Royal Irish Academy and the leading Irish poet in English in the nineteenth century. Ferguson was described by W.B. Yeats as the founder of Anglo-Irish literature. He looked to the Red Branch cycle of Gaelic myths and Cúchulainn for his inspiration, as did Standish O'Grady and Douglas Hyde, both sons of the rectory. The language was also important to Thomas Davis and his campaign. Other Protestants who were inspired by a love of the language included the Rev. Maxwell Close. He helped to maintain the Society for the Preservation of the Irish Language, and later became the patron of the Gaelic Union, the forerunner of the Gaelic League. There was also the Rev. Euseby Cleaver, who paid for Irish

9. This insisted that all children of an inter-church marriage were brought up as Catholics.

classes in Gaeltacht schools in the 1870s. He also sponsored a prayer book in Irish written by a Catholic priest. The Protestant who made the most important contribution to the language movement was Douglas Hyde, one of the founders of the Gaelic League. Unfortunately, its foundation coincided with the growth of Irish nationalism and the propagation of the view by writers such as D.P. Moran and Daniel Corkery that the Irish nation was *de facto* a Catholic nation. Despite this, the professors of Irish at the National University, Queen's University, Belfast, and at Trinity College in the early twentieth century were all Protestants.

There were also those Protestants who regarded Irish as a peasant language. Chief among them was Provost J.P. Mahaffy of TCD who declared that 'all the Irish language textbooks used in schools are either silly or indecent'. His action in banning Pearse from addressing a meeting in TCD has become legendary.[10] Unfortunately, such episodes helped to form a general perception of Irish Protestants as being against the Irish language. In fact, the Church of Ireland was not without its own Irish language zealots. Among them were Seán O'Casey, James Deacon, George Irvine and Ernest Blythe, who formed a committee to agitate for services in Irish.[11] Blythe and O'Casey were instrumental in starting a series of Irish services in St Kevin's Church, South Circular Road, Dublin. These included a service to mark the opening of the Oireachtas in August 1907. Previous to this, the Rev. J.E.H. Murphy, professor of Irish at TCD, held an Irish service annually on St Patrick's Day[12] but the four, who were ardent members of the Gaelic League, wanted more frequent services in Irish.

Efforts at establishing regular Irish services led eventually to the founding of Cumann Gaelach na hEaglaise, also known as the Irish Guild of the Church, in January 1914. Its objects were to promote the use of the Irish language in church services, to collect suitable hymns and devotional literature from early Irish sources, and to encourage the use of Irish art and music in the Church of Ireland. The guild received support from many well-known people, including Dr Kathleen Lynn, Lennox Robinson, Jack Yeats, Roger Casement, Douglas Hyde, Lord Monteagle, the lord chief justice, and a number of bishops and clergy. But some of the members were extremely nationalist in their views and many of the more moderate members left.

THE GAELIC CHURCHMAN

The guild organised Irish classes and had its own magazine, *The Gaelic Churchman,* which was edited and financed from 1919 until her death in 1925, by Miss Nelly O'Brien, a wealthy member of the Inchiquin family and a granddaughter of William Smith O'Brien. A staunch republican, she was a

10. Dudley Edwards, *Patrick Pearse: the triumph of failure*, p. 39.
1. Letter from Blythe to Lil Duncan, Papers of Cumann Gaelach na hEaglaise, RCB Library.
2. *Gaelic Churchman*, April 1919, p. 14.

An t-Eaglaiseac Gaedealac
The Gaelic Churchman.

VOL. III. No. 5. OCTOBER, 1921 PRICE SIXPENCE

CONTENTS.

PRICE, SIXPENCE. Annual Subscription, 6s.; post free, 7s.

Printed for The Irish Guild of the Church, by an Gaeḋeal-Cóṁluct Taiġ um Clóḋóiṗeáċt, ṗoillṗeoiṗeáċt aġuṗ Cṗáċċáil, Teo, and published by the proprietors at 39 Harcourt Street, Dublin.

37 *The Gaelic Churchman*, vol. III, no. 5, *Courtesy Dáithí Ó Maolchoille, Cumann Gaelach na hEaglaise.*

member of the executive committee of the Gaelic League and a founder of Craobh na gCúig gCúigí, nicknamed 'The branch of the five Protestants', because of its number of Protestant members. She founded the O'Curry Irish College at Carrigaholt and was involved in the establishment of St Brendan's, a multi-denominational all-Irish school in Dun Laoghaire. *The Gaelic Churchman* often contained trenchant criticism of the Church of Ireland:

> The church must remember its role as church of the garrison is over. It is no longer the servant, or dependant, of the state. It must now become the servant of the people.[13]

On other occasions the clergy were exhorted to remember that they were 'servants of God and not agents of the British Empire', while the whole church was derided for being identified with one side only in the struggle for independence.

The magazine's contents included Irish lessons and translations of hymns and prayers. In addition it promoted the guild's views on church matters, advocating a separate Irish missionary society, the advancement of women in the Church of Ireland, and that Holy Communion should be the church's principal service. The guild's political activities included the organisation of a petition against conscription, the sending of a deputation to the archbishop of Dublin seeking his intervention for a reprieve for Kevin Barry in 1920, and the holding of a reception for de Valera in 1921. During the 1921 Peace Conference, the guild made continuous intercession for its success at St Ann's Church in Dublin. In 1922, it called for 'proper facilities for religious worship' for Protestant political prisoners.

Needless to say, the guild welcomed the new state's emphasis on Irish, but there were others among the Protestant community who saw the language policy as an attack on their faith and as an effort to convert them to Catholicism. All kinds of Protestants spoke out against compulsory Irish and, despite personal threats and hate mail, some of them kept up an unceasing campaign against it.[14] Amongst them was the Rev. Dr A.A. Luce, a fellow of TCD, who denounced compulsory Irish as 'political window-dressing' and who argued that it was 'a wrong to the religion of Protestants' because all the cultural associations within the Irish language were Catholic. Those who thought like this saw compulsory Irish as a form of disguised discrimination to prevent Protestants gaining posts in the public service.[15] This attitude was vigorously condemned in *The Gaelic Churchman*:

> The criminal folly of converting what should be essentially an educational and national question into a sectarian controversy is so obvious that we can only

---

13. *Ibid.*, November 1919, p. 3.
14. *Irish Times,* 1 November 1926 and 8 November 1926.
15. Jones, 'The attitudes of the Church of Ireland Board of Education to Textbooks in national schools, 1922–1967,' *Irish Educational Studies*, 1992, pp. 72–80.

marvel at the stupidity of so many earnest and otherwise good men. When a fellow of Dublin University bases his Protestantism on his ignorance of the Irish language and prostitutes his pen in such disservice of his church, little wonder if we are looked on by those outside as aliens in our own land.[16]

There were also others, amongst them the heads of Protestant secondary schools, who were against the gaelicisation policy on educational grounds. Typical of them was Canon A.E. Hughes, a leading Dublin clergyman, later bishop of Kilmore, who claimed that 'masses of an early generation of Free State citizens will be illiterate due to compulsory Irish'.[17] Other Protestant figures, such as the provost of TCD and the bishop of Tuam, took a more pragmatic attitude, similar to that of Gregg. In November 1926 the bishop of Cork, while claiming that the policy was doing irreparable wrong to a large number of children, declared that 'as long as Irish is the law of the land we are bound to fall in with it'. This view was not always popular and was frequently attacked in *The Irish Times,* then regarded as a Protestant newspaper. Typical of its attitude was a leading article in 1929 which declared:

> Compulsory Irish is not only a denial of intellectual freedom but a material menace to the Church of Ireland's youth. Yet, on this vital matter the church's leaders ... are dumb.[18]

The language aroused such controversy among Protestants that it was not surprising that as soon as the gaelicisation policy was announced in 1922, many Protestant primary teachers left for the North where Irish was not compulsory. Their loss, together with the failure to attract candidates with sufficient education to pass CITC's examinations, meant a shortage of teachers for Protestant primary schools. Because of these difficulties, the two Church of Ireland primates, the archbishops of Armagh and Dublin, wrote a letter to all their clergy to encourage recruitment to Coláiste Moibhí and to the revised pupil-teacher scheme. They described the situation with regard to recruitment:

> [It is] both dangerous and promising – dangerous because of the great difficulties experienced in keeping the training college supplied with students and the con- sequent difficulties of securing teachers ... promising ... because of the two special schemes which, if used, should put an end to both difficulties.[19]

Though Coláiste Moibhí was for Protestant students, entry to the college was similar to that of the other colleges – by successfully sitting the prepa- ratory college entrance examination. However, the high standard of the examination, particularly in Irish, made it difficult for Protestant candidates

16. *Gaelic Churchman,* January 1927.
17. *Irish Times,* 18 November 1926.
18. *Ibid.,* 23 November 1929.
19. Report of the board of education, JGS, 1927, p. 192.

to obtain places. So, to help the Protestant community, whose leaders had shown a certain goodwill towards the system, the Department reduced the standard for Protestant candidates and declared a certain number to be 'eligible exceptionally' each year.[20] The entrance results were published annually, and those marked with an asterisk indicated Protestant students who were permitted to enter Coláiste Moibhí although they had not reached the high requirements of the examination. Not all Coláiste Moibhí's students needed such help. Results for the years 1928–32, show that 27 per cent of candidates passed, while the rest were declared 'eligible exceptionally'.

THE EARLY STUDENTS

As with the other colleges, the Department was eager to get Coláiste Moibhí established. The first class of 20 students, six boys and 14 girls, two of whom were Presbyterian, which enrolled in April 1927, was the largest class ever to enter the college and had the biggest number of boys of any class in the college's history. According to the register, two boys were from Donegal, two from Dublin and one each from Longford and Wicklow, while the girls were from Carlow, Cork, Galway, Leitrim, Mayo, Roscommon and Sligo, with two from Wicklow and five from Dublin. The average age of the first class was 15 years and nine months. Two students did not complete the course; one failed the Intermediate Certificate Examination and the other was expelled. The rest all qualified as teachers. Three boys, George Kee, Michael Gyves and Fred Phillips, and three girls, Edith Harrison, Amy Hempenstall and Mary Taylor, went on to graduate from TCD.

Amy Phillips, (née Hempenstall) was one of the first students in Coláiste Moibhí. From Greystones, Co Wicklow, she entered CITC in 1931 and qualified as a teacher in 1933. Known by the nickname 'Toby', she taught in a number of small schools before marrying her former preparatory college classmate, Fred Phillips. From Dublin's South Circular Road, his father had worked in the Ordnance Survey Office but he died when Fred was young. Like Amy, Fred qualified as a primary teacher and taught in Kildare Place School and in St Stephen's School, Mount Street. Later he became a part-time broadcaster with Raidió Éireann. In 1947 he graduated from TCD and some time later decided to give up teaching and to enter the church. In 1952 he was ordained for a curacy in Dublin, before becoming rector of Ballinaclash, Co Wicklow. Following his untimely death in a motor accident in 1958, Amy returned to teaching and taught in Alexandra School for a number of years before retirement. A creative, imaginative person, she served the Church of Ireland in many ways, particularly through her work in religious education, the Sunday School Society, and Cumann Gaelach na hEaglaise. She gave these reasons for entering Coláiste Moibhí:

---

20. Parkes, p. 166.

I never wanted to teach in a secondary school. I wanted to have my own little country school. So I had to go through the training college. I was too old by a month for the scholarship to Celbridge (Collegiate School) by the time I had been taken from my private school in order to learn Irish. So the only option was the newly set up prep. school, Coláiste Moibhí.

Dora Smeaton (née Alexander) was another student in the first class at Coláiste Moibhí. From Co Leitrim, her soldier father was killed in the First World War. At Coláiste Moibhí she met Liam Smeaton, from a Scottish family residing in Rathdowney, Co. Laois. Liam and Dora were married in 1938. Dora taught in a number of schools including Windgates, Co. Wicklow; Templemore, Co Tipperary; St Catherine's, Donore Avenue, Dublin; and St John's School, Clondalkin. Like Amy, Dora Smeaton gave lifelong service to the Church of Ireland. The elder of her two sons, Brian, became a clergyman. She gave these reasons for entering the preparatory college:

I attended a Catholic convent – there was no Protestant school near. The young master who taught me was straight from training and excellent at Irish. He saw the ad. in *The (Irish) Times* and with my mother's hearty consent entered me for the advertised exam. for Coláiste Moibhí. I had to go to Clones from Leitrim to sit the exam. There was a whole crowd of boys and girls sitting for the exam from grammar schools but I was the only one called.[21]

Also in the first class was George Fitch who became principal of Kildare Place School in the 1960s.

In January 1928 the second class of 12, three boys and nine girls, entered. Four of them did not continue to CITC; one failed the Intermediate Examination, two were expelled, while the fourth, Kathleen Sullivan, died. Amongst this class was Minta Millar, a teacher's daughter. She entered CITC in 1931 and on completion of her course in 1933 became an Irish teacher in Alexandra College. During her time there she took a keen interest in the college's Irish Society, which she helped to found. In 1940, she gave up teaching when she married William Condell, vice-principal of Coláiste Moibhí. Also in the class was William J. Blennerhassett, who was for many years principal of St Michael's School, Limerick. He served as a consultant for the Church of Ireland board of education religious education curriculum, *Primary School RE,* in 1990.

In October 1928 the third class of five boys and eleven girls entered Coláiste Moibhí. Of this class, four did not continue; three failed the Intermediate Examination and the fourth was expelled. The rest qualified as teachers. Five went on to graduate from TCD. They included Harry Hannagen, Richard Rowntree, Alister Alcorn, Francis Coleman and Violet Howe who was also a respondent, i.e. gained over 70 per cent in her final TCD examinations.

---

21. Letter from Dora Smeaton.

38 Coláiste Moibhí 1928.

Back: Seóirse Mac Aoidh, Proinnsias Ó Colmáin, Seán Ó hEideáin, Liam Blennerhassett, Éamonn Baóiréad, Liam Smeaton, Feardorcha Mac Philib, Daithí Mac Aoidh, Alasdar Alcorn, Roibeárd Mac Adhaimh, Annraoi Ó h-Annagáin, Mícheal Ó Geibheannaigh, Seóirse Fitch, Risteárd Ó Caorthannáin,

Third Row: Eibhlín Ramsaigh, Máire Eibhlín Ní Ghabhann, Eibhlís Ní Pheatáin, Bláthnad Ní Shiomnaigh, Máire Bevan, Maedhbh Ní Airmheadhaigh, Maedhbh Blennerhassett, Eibhlís de Bhailis, Sinéad Ní Chinnseamainn, Gobnait Nic Rossa, Salcuach Nic Uilis, Aoife Ní Liseáin, Oilbhe Buchanan, Eithne Ní Earchadha, Máire Ní Tháillúir, Bláthnad Ní Mhuilleóir, Minta Ní Mhuilleóir,

Second Row: Róis Ní Dheaghain, Máighréad Ní Chonchubhair, Maedhbh Ní Dhonnchadha (ollamh) Máire Bean Uí Mhurchadha, (ollamh); Liam Condell, (leas phríomh ollamh) S. Ó Cadhla (príomh ollamh) Aodhnait Nic Aindriú, (bean-a-tighe) Eibhlín de Phiondargas, (ollamh), Dóra Nic Alasdair, Caitlín Ní h-Uaisle, Caitlín Crúc,

Front Row: Peggí de Brigg, Eibhlís Ní Ruaidh, Eibhlís de Brún, Salcuach Nic Aodha, Máire Ní Gréine, Daithí Ó Cadhla, Salcuach Nic Eochaidh, Fainnche Ní Mhurchadha, Áine Nic Uilis, Sorcha Hempenstall, Maedhbh Ní Chonaill. *CICE Archives.*

In October 1929 the fourth class of 16 students entered Coláiste Moibhí and all 16 entered CITC. They included Millicent Fitzsimons from Kilgarvan, Co Kerry, who had a distinguished career in education, including 14 years as an infant organiser with the Department, and three years teaching in a teacher training college in Nigeria. From 1967 to 75, she was vice-principal of CITC. While teaching in Derralossary NS, Co. Wicklow, she was much involved in pilot projects for the 1971 Primary School Curriculum, for which she wrote Irish textbooks. She died in 1985. The Past Students' Association presented a book in her memory to Church of Ireland College of Education library, and in 1986 her family presented a bible and silver plate for use in the college chapel. Her great-nieces, Emma and Anna Reynolds, were students in Coláiste Moibhí in more recent times.

Also in this class were George Griffin, from Co. Kerry, the first of a number of siblings to enter the college whose parents were both teachers, and Sam Adamson, for many years principal of St Andrew's National School, Lucan. There he taught with his wife, Zephra Mullen, who entered the college in 1930. Three members of the 1929 class went on to graduate from TCD, Irene Thompson and Eileen Hamilton, while George Griffin was a respondent.

In September 1930 the fifth class of three boys and six girls entered Coláiste Moibhí. They included Zephra Mullen and Rose Roberts, formerly Hamilton, née Wheatly, who taught for many years in North Strand Infants School. Also in the class were Richard Kirk, who graduated in 1943, and Francis Donaldson, who taught in North Strand but gave up teaching to enter the meteorological service. For many years he served as a lay reader in Ardfert Diocese.

In the early years the students came mainly from VII-VIII standards in national schools all over the country. A high proportion had urban addresses, something which soon changed. The average age on entry was 15 years with a number as old as 16. Despite the students' weakness at Irish on entry, results at state examinations were excellent, as the Department acknowledged in its annual report for 1930–31. Just how much was achieved by the teachers is shown by this student's recollection of his arrival in January 1928:

> The atmosphere was very strange and unusual at first – quite a shock actually. It hit one immediately on arrival – being greeted in Irish and unable to respond! By degrees, the system imposed itself on us and we learned to cope with varying degrees of success. I can't recall any outright hostility among the students, but it was definitely a different world from which we came. It was obviously an Irish/Gaelic ethos, but not oppressively so. We weren't brainwashed – but it would not be my choice now. There was an easy atmosphere of harmony and friendship in the place. We lived in a compliant age and there was general acceptability of the regime.

Living conditions at Glasnevin were reasonable for the late 1920s, though washing facilities consisted of a wash-stand with a basin and a jug of cold water. Bathroom facilities were meagre though perhaps standard for the time, and boys had to take a bath in pairs in Glasnevin House. Out-of-class facilities were minimal. One of the earliest students recalled the conditions:

> The classrooms were in Glasnevin House. There was but one dormitory for boys in Marlborough House, but in Glasnevin there were two, as numbers increased somewhat. When Seóirse de Rút (the first principal) left, the male students were transferred up the road to Glasnevin House. Though not 'Grade A' the dormitories were reasonably comfortable. Mass produced food was reasonably good in quality, if unattractively served. Staff invariably ate at a separate table. There was no tuck shop – so no extras.

As with all the colleges, the Department's plan was to get Coláiste Moibhí started as quickly as possible, and later to provide it with first-rate facilities. The subjects taught were Irish, English, mathematics, history, geography, drawing and singing. Latin was included later. In the early days there were no facilities for PE classes. In 1928 classes were provided by an outside part-time instructor in the dining-hall of Marlborough House. At first, hockey was played in winter on an undersized pitch at Glasnevin House and later a full-sized pitch was rented nearby. A little tennis was played in summer. There was a library but opinions varied about its value. One student remembered with delight discovering *The Imitation of Christ* and the thrill of reading *Cúirt an Mheán Óiche* for the first time:

> I enjoyed the reading sessions on Sunday evenings when we were allowed to choose a book from the library … and a good library it was …. A whole new world was opened to me. I still remember the thrill of hearing *Cúirt an Mheán Óiche* for the first time. The perfection and rhythm and polish of it! The beauty of word and image! A whole new world of poetry and music and literature of which we had known nothing.

However, another recalled that suitable reading material was limited and that there were few reference books.

In October 1928 Archbishop Byrne, manager of nearby Coláiste Chaoimhín, reluctantly agreed that male students from Coláiste Moibhí would be taught experimental science and botany by Tomás Ó Lúbaigh in the science laboratory at Coláiste Chaoimhín. This was on the strict understanding that 'the externs were not to mix with students of Coláiste Chaoimhín', a condition that was kept to the letter.[22] Br Hurley, the principal of Coláiste Chaoimhín, arranged the classes for Coláiste Moibhí from 5.00 pm to 7.00 pm

---

22. Dublin Diocesan Archives, Byrne Papers.

when the Coláiste Chaoimhín students were in study. The visiting students were strictly supervised. This temporary arrangement lasted several years and Byrne reluctantly renewed it each year, expressing the hope that it would be the last time. In 1931, Ó Brolcháin informed Byrne that work would soon start on the refurbishing of the former Royal Hibernian Military School to accommodate Coláiste Moibhí. Byrne quietly acquiesced, though not out of any ecumenical motive. The archbishop was negotiating with the Department that on Coláiste Moibhí's departure, Glasnevin House would be transferred to Canon Dudley, manager of the Catholic Glasnevin Model School, to replace the current school buildings. Things did not work out as planned, however, as work on the Hibernian School was delayed and it was 1934 before Coláiste Moibhí moved to the Phoenix Park. Once more the Department's inability to keep to planned timetables and the casual *ad hoc* way it dealt with the colleges was clearly demonstrated. Indeed, it was remarkable that the preparatory colleges kept going despite their accommodation difficulties, and this was no small tribute to the teachers who, out of love for the language, endured many hardships.

While Coláiste Moibhí was in Glasnevin, it was easily accessible, and many famous and interesting people, including Douglas Hyde, and the writer, 'An Seabhac', Pádraig Ó Siochfhradha,[23] visited the college. One of the early students recalled their visits:

> Two distinguished scholars of Irish visited the college during my stay there, to address the students and stimulate an interest in Irish literature. Dr Douglas Hyde from UCD spoke to us about the language and recited some of his own poetry. Little did we realise then that he would be the first President of Ireland. 'An Seabhac' also visited us and introduced us to his own work, *Jimín*. He also accompanied us on an historical tour in an open charabanc.

As with all the preparatory colleges it was not easy to find teachers, and appointing staff to Coláiste Moibhí was problematic. Not only had they to be fluent Irish speakers, able to teach through Irish to Leaving Certificate standard, but they had to be Protestant as well, which made it difficult to find suitable candidates. The first principal, George Annesley Ruth (Seóirse de Rút), was seconded from the civil service. Because of the Department's haste to get the college underway, and the difficulty in getting a suitable person as principal, it was quite happy to accept Gregg's suggestion that Ruth be appointed temporarily, even though he had no teaching experience. It was also difficult to find a matron, and Ruth's wife, May, became the college's first matron because she could speak Irish. Department officials considered it 'an unsuitable arrangement to have husband and wife as principal and matron'.

---

23. For biographical details of Hyde and Ó Siochfhradha see the Appendix.

Keogh Bros. Ltd., Dublin.

39 George Ruth (Seóirse de Rút) first principal of Coláiste Moibhí. *Courtesy Risteárd Giltrap.*

40 May Ruth. *Courtesy Risteárd Giltrap.*

GEORGE RUTH: THE FIRST PRINCIPAL

Born in 1883, Ruth was a member of Craobh na gCúig gCúigí of the Gaelic League. A junior executive officer at the General Register Office, he was seconded first to the Boundary Commission and afterwards to the statistical branch of the Department of Industry and Commerce. As he had a degree in Irish, Latin, English and Irish history from the National University of Ireland, it was agreed that he should be transferred on loan to Coláiste Moibhí as temporary principal to get the college started. The question of a permanent appointment was to be considered later. Under his direction, Coláiste Moibhí got off the ground, with a friendly and homely atmosphere pervading the place. After a short time, however, it was realised that for the college to be successful, a principal with teaching experience was needed.

An Irish language enthusiast, Ruth, with other members of his family, had been involved in founding Cumann Gaelach na hEaglaise in 1914. He was honorary secretary until 1934, when he moved from Dublin to live in Co.

Kerry. Ruth was a regular contributor to *The Gaelic Churchman,* and Celtic spirituality and the need for the Church of Ireland to return to its early roots were frequent themes of his writings. In 1924 Ruth married Mary May Leeson Marshall from Callinafercy House, Milltown, Co Kerry.[24] Born in 1891 she was the only daughter of Mabel Godfrey and Markham Leeson Marshall, an Oxford graduate and barrister-at-law, who later became deputy lieutenant for Kerry and a captain in the Royal Munster Fusiliers. Her mother, the eldest daughter of Sir John Godfrey of Kilcoleman Abbey, Milltown, Co Kerry, died when May was a baby and so she was brought up by her grandmother, Lady Mary Cordelia Godfrey. Lady Godfrey played a major role in the community in which she lived and often brought her granddaughter to visit different parts of Co. Kerry, including the Blasket Islands and Valentia. There, May was exposed to the Irish language, a language also spoken by her nurse and various servants at Kilcoleman Abbey. In 1905, May was sent to boarding school in England, which she detested. Five years later, she 'came out' during the Dublin season. During the First World War she served as a volunteer nursing aide, and subsequently became one of the first women in Ireland to qualify as a physiotherapist. Her wedding service to George Ruth in Milltown Church was conducted in Irish. On his retirement from the civil service in Dublin the couple lived at Callinafercy, Milltown. Following Ruth's death, May lived on there with her widowed aunt, the Dowager Lady Godfrey. May Ruth lived to a great age and died in St Luke's Home, Cork, in August 1988. Her obsequies were conducted in Irish by Canon G.A. Salter, chaplain to St Luke's. Following her death, Máire Ní Ghuithín from the Blasket Islands praised the Ruths for their commitment to the Irish language which they both spoke fluently. She recalled how when the college began it had three maids and a cook from Galway. Later Eibhlín Ní Ghuithín and Eibhlín and Saora Williams from Dingle worked with her. When they were going home for Christmas Mrs Ruth gave them cakes decorated with icing and ribbons:

> Bhí an bheirt acu ana-Ghaodhlach agus Gaodhluinn bhlasta acu. Bhí cócaire and triúr chailíní ón nGaillimh ag obair ann ar dtúis. Ina dhiaidh sin is cuimhin liom Eibhlín Ní Ghuithín ón Oiléan Thiar agus beirt eile, Eibhlín and Saora Williams ó Chathair Deargáin i bparóiste na Cille ag obair ann. Agus sinn ag dul abhaile don Nollag thugadh Bean de Rút cístí deasa dúinn le ríbíní agus 'icing' orthu.[25]

A keen musician, Ruth was presented with a rare old Egan harp as a wedding present by the guild's members. He was also an accomplished bell-ringer and a member of the guild of ringers of St Patrick's Cathedral. A plaque in the cathedral's ringing room commemorates a record peal made in 1911 by a number of ringers including Ruth. In his later years, Ruth

24. I am indebted to John Knightly for details of May Ruth's life.
25. Walter McGrath, Cork Holly Bough, 1988, p. 21. I am indebted to John Knightly for drawing my attention to this.

41 The Ruths' wedding in 1924. *Courtesy John Knightly and Valerie Bary.*

represented Ardfert Diocese at the Church of Ireland general synod, the church's chief law-making body, where he often defended the government's language policy. From 1934 to 1947 he was also a diocesan representative on the church's board of education. He died suddenly one morning in February 1947 on his way to Dublin. Both the Ruths were pioneers with a great devotion to the Church of Ireland. It was largely due to George Ruth that the Church of Ireland conference of 1932 took place, while May Ruth had the distinction of being the first woman to be elected to the general synod in 1952.

THE EARLY TEACHERS

Other members of the early teaching staff included Eileen Penrose, who came from Coláiste na Rinne. She was remembered as being very small in stature, gentle and friendly by nature. According to a student of that period: 'She related rather well to the students and was very encouraging to those who found the going difficult.' Miss Penrose was not in good health, and in 1930 had to take six months' leave for treatment in Switzerland. On her return she was ill again in March 1931. Miss Penrose eventually left the college when she got married. History and geography were taught by Seán MacEachain, who spoke an Ulster dialect of Irish. A Protestant, he was reputed to have taken part in the 'Troubles'. A frail man in poor health, he died prematurely from tuberculosis on 24 March 1930. One of the early students recalled him:

> He spoke thoroughly fluent Irish. Sincere and dedicated, he taught history and geography, as it was then rather unattractively taught. I would think that the

response from his students wasn't total. Unfortunately, he died prematurely and before he had time to make a significant impact on the development of the college.

Other early staff also included Máire Bean Uí Mhurchadha, a Catholic teacher, who taught English well, but because of her religion her appointment was only temporary. Indeed Gregg accepted it with reluctance, and though the post was advertised each year, no suitable Protestant could be found. Relaxed and easygoing, she had an engaging presence. She knew many of the modern poets and writers of the time personally, and the students enjoyed her classes. MacEachain was succeeded temporarily by Micheál Ó Siochfhradha, an Irish scholar of some repute, who was seconded from the inspectorate to Coláiste Moibhí for a short while. A native speaker from Dingle, and a brother of the writer 'An Seabhac', he was an excellent and popular teacher who, it appears, developed a wonderful rapport with the students. When a substitute could not be found during Miss Penrose's illness he seems to have taken on her work as well.

The provision of an Irish-speaking chaplain to Coláiste Moibhí was problematic, due to the scarcity of Irish-speaking clergy.[26] In the early days, the local curate, the Rev. James Ruby, took some religion classes in English. Ó Brolcháin, however, showed the same readiness to provide funding for religious instruction for minority denominations as he had for his own, though the attitude of the Church of Ireland to the religious formation of students was much less rigorous than that of the majority church. Compared with the other preparatory colleges, where a religious atmosphere pervaded, the attitude to religion was quite different in Coláiste Moibhí. Sunday was also treated differently. In accordance with the prevailing ethos of the times, students attended the nearest church of their denomination and the remainder of the day was treated as a day of rest with a period for reading in the evening. A student of the period recalled:

> I think our superiors were understanding people on the whole, who encouraged us to be responsible, if not too independent. The working day was rather long with a half-day off on Saturday only. Sunday was rather boring, with games strictly disallowed.

Despite the difficulties in getting teachers for Coláiste Moibhí, a student from the first class recalled those early days in idyllic terms:

> There was a wonderful relationship between teachers and pupils. They spent much of their free time with us. We were introduced to good music and taught to play Bridge – in Irish of course – and there was a good library. As we were a small group we were taken on visits and many famous people came to see how the school was working. We were always treated as adults and learning was made attractive to us.

---

26. DF Papers, S25/15/34.

Nevertheless the work of the principal can not have been easy as the question of staffing was problematic in the early years. This was compounded by the Department's lack of urgency in decision-making. In February 1927, before the college opened, the Department decided that teaching staff would be limited to a principal and two full-time 'professors,' one female and one male. A vice-principal would be appointed when numbers expanded. It was not long before it was obvious that more teachers would be necessary. This was acknowledged by the chief inspector during the college's second term.[27] However, no new appointments were made, even though a second class was admitted in January 1928. Unhappy with the situation, Gregg and Ruth met with the Department in May to impress upon officials the need for more staff for the following September. It was agreed that a vice-principal, and four teachers in addition to the principal, should be employed. This decision, however, was subject to the approval of the Department of Finance. It was loath to sanction the arrangement, claiming that the college already had more staff and less students than the other preparatory colleges. To cut down on costs, it suggested appointing a female vice-principal but the Department of Education argued that the person appointed should be a man as he would take over as principal eventually. It pointed to Coláiste Moibhí's special difficulties. The college was coeducational and operated from two sets of premises, ten minutes walk from each other.

FINDING IRISH-SPEAKING DOMESTIC STAFF

Ruth also had problems regarding domestic staff to contend with. The Department's rule that all staff, including domestic and ancillary, had to be Irish speakers created extra difficulties. The Department's failure to appoint sufficient domestic staff was a further aggravation. When the college started in April 1927, the Department sanctioned the appointment of Mrs Ruth as matron, with a cook and two maids to assist her. These arrangements soon proved inadequate and a crisis developed in this area. Early in May 1927, Ruth wrote to the Department urgently seeking another maid, as the cook and the two maids were working from 6.00 am to 10.00 pm while the matron was doing the maid's work and had only one afternoon off.[28] Three days later, Mrs Ruth herself wrote in desperation, seeking extra domestic help as the cook and the two maids had decided to leave. This alarmed the Department and on 17 May another maid was appointed, and in the middle of June, a porter, Richard Mc Fadden, a bachelor and fluent Irish speaker, who had served in the Irish army. Though the number of students was small, there were many demands on Mrs Ruth, including an outbreak of German measles in February 1928. That same month she was off work due to an accident and a temporary matron had to be hired.

These were some of the difficulties which George Ruth had to overcome as principal during the first year of Coláiste Moibhí. Ruth has not been

---

27. *Ibid.*
28. *Ibid.*, S20/9/27.

given sufficient credit for his role in establishing the college, and has been overshadowed by his better known successor, John Kyle. Such, however, was the commitment of George and May Ruth to the Irish language that they were willing to leave their comfortable home and their pleasant life to take on the challenge of establishing an Irish-speaking boarding school, despite the fact that neither of them had any teaching experience. Nevertheless, this unusual couple was successful in getting Coláiste Moibhí off the ground and in establishing a happy atmosphere in the college, as one of the first students recalled:

> There was a wonderful relationship between teachers and pupils. We were all aware of the concern and affection which teachers had for us and which lasted long after we had left. We were like a family and I well remember the last day of the first term when we were almost reluctant to go home.

The same student went on:

> I'll always be grateful for my time at Coláiste Moibhí. From an educational point of view I have not seen better. Many educational methods only being discovered now, were used by our teachers. For example, learning geography began by learning how to map the roads round the college, using tapes etc. and finding out how to use a theodolite. We were introduced to good music. We listened to records and discussed them. So we had music appreciation before the subject became popular in schools. We had a lot of freedom and a lot of fun and we being the pioneers were allowed to make the rules for the school. Only the rules demanded by us were established and we began to understand the necessity for rules in a community. In spite of working entirely through Irish, we did very well in public exams and later, when I travelled round the country I always found Coláiste Moibhí students in posts of responsibility, chairing meetings, officers in organisations etc.

She had this to say about Ruth's efforts as a teacher:

> He was most energetic in promoting the language, but he had little knowledge of young people of the sort he had to deal with and little teacher training. Nevertheless, I remember him with respect; he did his best in a difficult situation.

Another student recalled his time at the college with the Ruths:

> George Ruth was a kindly, humane, cultured and fatherly man with a deep and sincere love of the Irish language. Under his direction Coláiste Moibhí got off the ground with a friendly and homely atmosphere pervading the place. His wife, May, was equally involved on the domestic side and both were very popular with the students. I can't really say to what extent he succeeded in motivating his staff to achieve maximum results, but I think he isn't given enough credit for bringing about a smooth transition from the former system of education to the new all-Irish orientated approach. He was a good man.

CHAPTER EIGHT

Making the college 'a marked success'

The second principal: school inspector
JOHN KYLE 1928–34

In September 1928, John Andrew Kyle (Seán Ó Cadhla) became the second principal of Coláiste Moibhí when the temporary arrangement with the Ruths came to an end. From Co. Antrim, Kyle was educated at Foyle College and studied classics at TCD. He was elected a scholar in 1913 and graduated with honours in 1915. He also had a degree from Oxford University. A northerner from a unionist background, he had become interested in the Irish language and its revival. He was seconded from his post as an inspector with the Department to help with establishing the college. In later years, he was a governor of CITC, a member of the Church of Ireland board of education and chief inspector in the Department. To Kyle is given the credit for Coláiste Moibhí's early success, and as principal he oversaw the move to the college's new premises in the Phoenix Park in 1934.

Kyle imposed a strict regime with an emphasis on academic success. Students were fined half a crown if heard speaking English. Three students were expelled for fairly minor offences. One of the early students recalled Kyle:

> He was a wonderful head in every way – friendly, approachable and a good disciplinarian without being too strict. Staff and students admired him tremendously and everyone got on splendidly with him.

Another student gave this view:

> Seán Ó Cadhla was a very cultured man, an excellent teacher, as, of course, he was the head inspector (sic) of primary schools and a good disciplinarian, never unjust. Always understanding in the matter of midnight feasts and the like. He always left one with the feeling that this fault wouldn't happen again

A more balanced description was given by this former student:

> J.A. Kyle was a department inspector, who was brought in to intensify the policy
> as regards the restoration of Irish and to generally raise the standard, with a strong
> desire to improve academic achievement, to the exclusion of a more liberal
> approach. Discipline was tightened (there were expulsions), and sanctions (fines)
> were introduced for speaking English. A man of commanding presence, he was
> very efficient, thorough and hardworking, and expected his students to be like-
> wise. He taught Irish to a junior class, and did it extremely well, but I couldn't
> see him inculcating the same love for the language as his predecessor (only an
> opinion of mine). He certainly made his mark and was duly promoted to the
> highest post in the inspectorate.

In dealing with the difficulties of establishing such a unique school, Kyle
showed tact and wisdom, as his reply to a request from Cumann Gaelach na
hEaglaise that the students attend Irish services shows: 'He would encourage, but could not command, his students to attend'.[1]

THE APPOINTMENT OF WILLIAM CONDELL
AS VICE-PRINCIPAL

With the Ruths' departure from Coláiste Moibhí at the end of the 1927/28
school year the Department sanctioned a number of new teaching appointments. In August 1928, William T.E. Condell (Liam Ó Conaill) was appointed
vice-principal by Gregg. Condell, who graduated from TCD in 1927, had
been teaching at Kilkenny College for seven years and for five years had been
in sole charge of Irish teaching there. His Irish, however, was not very fluent.
A Department memo in February 1928 noted that he could only hold a simple
conversation.[2] Following an interview with officials, it was suggested that
he should go to the western Gaeltacht for intensive study of the spoken
language during July. Ó Brolcháin arranged to have Condell's appointment
sanctioned from 1 July, as Condell, who was not in an incremental post,
would have no holiday pay from Kilkenny College. Ó Brolcháin was keen to
appoint Condell as 'there was a complete dearth of Protestant teachers with
Irish qualifications'.

   The manner in which Condell was treated was typical of Ó Brolcháin's
generosity. For the next 40 years Condell was to teach mathematics at
Coláiste Moibhí. In later years he also taught pass level art. A cultured individual, he made great efforts to widen his pupils' interests in literature and
in classical music. Keen on vocal music, he sang for many years with the
Culwick Choral Society and Dublin University Choral Society. In 1940 he
married Minta Millar, who had been a student at Coláiste Moibhí.

---

1. Minutes of Cumann Gaelach na hEaglaise, 10 November, 1933.
2. DE Papers 19137 Box 409 27/2/28.

Throughout his career at Coláiste Moibhí, Condell or 'Connie' as he was later called by his pupils, struggled to impart mathematical knowledge to his students. One of them described his classes:

> Teaching the abstract without sufficient fluency on the part of the teacher, with an inadequate supply of textbooks, and being forced to cover the Intermediate Certificate course in two instead of three years, made the accomplishing of good results at Leaving Certificate problematic. Textbooks were also entirely inadequate and substandard. (*Céimseata* by MacNioclás was the only geometry text).

A student from the early years had this to say about Liam Condell:

> A cultured individual, he was rather reserved at first and it took him some time to develop an easy relationship with the students generally. He had an apartment, a cubicle 10' by 10' of his own on the landing between two dormitories in Glasnevin House, where he acted as a rather benevolent house master. Being a brilliant mathematician himself he could, I think, be a little intolerant of those less well endowed and occasional flashes of temper occurred, but generally speaking in the circumstances his self-control was praiseworthy – he was by no means a martinet.

The same student recalled Condell's enthusiasm for sport:

> He enjoyed playing rugby football and was an enthusiastic and prominent member of Monkstown 1st XV, so his weekends were spent in the carefree company of that fraternity and he enjoyed the post-match convivialities to the full! He enjoyed a special relationship with his prefects which was mutually advantageous, especially when he sometimes overslept and had to be rudely summoned to class without the sustaining comfort of his bacon and eggs! On the whole a rather likeable person. He sometimes played as 'sub.' on the school hockey team – and most enthusiastically too. He a 14 stone burly prop forward, looked a little incongruous among 10 skinny novices!

Also appointed in 1928 was Miss Florence Maeve Dennison (Maedhbh Ní Dhonnchadha), who taught English to Leaving Certificate level and some Irish at junior level. Nicknamed 'Bunty' by the students, she was an earnest and conscientious teacher, who trained as a primary teacher at CITC from 1918 to 1920. She taught for a number of years in Mountshannon National School, Co. Clare. In 1927 she obtained the Árd-Teastas in Irish. Her main interest outside of Coláiste Moibhí was drama, and she was a keen theatregoer who loved to spend her summer holidays at Stratford-on-Avon. She spent much of her free time going for walks and was fond of knitting. While presiding over the students at study she knitted continuously as she read from a book open on a large book stand. An early student had this to say about her:

> She was one of the quieter members of the staff, who did not impose herself unduly on us and for which we were very grateful. She seemed a remote sort of

person remaining apart from the mainstream of college events and not integrat-
ing very happily with the students or their interests. Her reserve was, I think,
naturally reciprocated but I daresay she fulfilled her role to the satisfaction of the
Department. She didn't appear to be in any way religious or church orientated.

Another important appointment made at this time was that of a new
matron, Enid Anderson (Aodhnait Nic Aindriú), who succeeded Mrs Ruth
in September 1928. Nicknamed 'Biddy' by the students, she was a rather shy
individual with a somewhat brusque manner. An excellent caterer, as her fluency in Irish developed she became the domestic science teacher. Later she
took charge of physical education classes. In the early years, she also acted as
swimming instructor. An October 1928 memo[3] shows the great difficulties
which Coláiste Moibhí had in providing domestic science classes in the early
years. Miss Anderson, who trained at Kilmacud College, had obtained a
teacher's diploma in domestic economy in 1923, and had taught for several
years before coming to the preparatory college in 1928. Though highly qualified, she was not sufficiently fluent in Irish to take domestic science classes. So
one of the other teachers, who had done a domestic science course, explained
the lessons while Miss Anderson did the demonstrations. The classes took
place in the evenings, and Miss Anderson received six shillings per hour extra.

As always, such extras were queried by the Department of Finance,
which claimed that the matron already had heavy responsibilities and feared
that abnormal duties 'of a disciplinary nature may fall to her lot in this college
owing to its mixed composition'.[4] The Department of Education disagreed,
pointing out that no domestic science had been taught in the college due to
a lack of facilities, and now the two-year programme had to be covered in
12 months. The results of the 1929 Intermediate Certificate Examination
showed that the teaching method was not unsuccessful with six honours,
12 passes and only two fails. The post was advertised again the following
year, but this time there was only one candidate, who was considered
unsuitable. This left the Department in a quandary as Miss Anderson was
about to leave for another post as matron in a secondary boarding school in
Dublin, with a much higher salary and longer holidays, and where Irish
would not be required. A dedicated teacher, she had, at her own expense,
through private study and by spending her vacations in the Gaeltacht,
improved her Irish. In Ó Brolcháin's opinion, she was 'a real find', whose
loss to Coláiste Moibhí would be 'irreparable'. There was 'no reasonable
possibility of replacing her'.

He proposed that she be paid £160 per annum to act as matron and to teach
domestic science. The Department of Finance responded by suggesting a
reduction in another teacher's salary and, in addition, that Ó Brolcháin should
bargain with Miss Anderson over her pay. Fortunately for all concerned, she
agreed to accept £150 per annum and a temporary appointment until Coláiste

---

3. DF Papers, S20/9/27.
4. *Ibid*.

Moibhí moved to its new premises. A student from the early years recalled Miss Anderson:

> She could portray a rough and ready candour but, at the same time, she was effi-cient and caring when the need arose. She had a fairly direct approach and made her presence felt when the situation required it. Her office was directly over the principal's in Marlborough House where she always seemed to treat 'callers' sympathetically. She took her responsibilities seriously and was well liked.

The appointment of an Irish-speaking chaplain to the college was of consid-erable importance and the matter was the subject of correspondence between Gregg and the Department in September 1928. The work was to include teaching religious instruction, visiting at intervals and 'supervising the reli-gious and moral life of the students'. The Department proposed that the chaplain should be paid £50 per annum for these duties. In addition it would contribute seven shillings and sixpence per person to the church attended by the students on Sundays. This led to long correspondence between the Departments of Finance and Education, with the former querying how the 'old regime' had funded Protestant chaplains to training colleges. In response, the Department pointed out that when CITC was first established a chaplain had been appointed, but subsequently this appointment had ceased, as reli-gious instruction classes were given by clergy on the staff. However, 'pew rent' of £30 per annum was paid to the church attended by the students. In the case of Marlborough Street Training College, Methodist, Presbyterian and Church of Ireland chaplains had been appointed under the British regime and each was paid a capitation fee of one pound. 'Pew rent' was not paid and ministers from nearby churches acted as chaplains. The college also had a full-time Catholic chaplain, who said Mass daily.

In the light of these precedents, the Department proposed in January 1929 that a pound per week, for each week the college was in session, should be paid to the chaplain, plus a donation to the church. An official in the Department of Finance noted dryly:

> Apart from the Gilbertian way in which Education shows solicitude for the moral and religious welfare of the students we cannot object to the provision of a chaplain.[5]

By May 1929 the matter appeared settled, but two months later, Archbishop Gregg wrote to inform the Department that he wished to appoint the Rev. R.A. Byrn, the local rector, as chaplain. He was to be paid £10 per annum for general religious and moral supervision. As he had no Irish, the Rev. Paul Quigley (An tOirmh. Pól Ó Coigligh), a native speaker from Co Galway, would give twice weekly religious instruction classes in Irish, at £40 per year. Ordained in 1909, Quigley was Rector of Carbury, Co. Kildare,

---

5. *Ibid.*, S25/10/34.

from 1921 to 1929 when he was appointed rector of Lusk, Co Dublin, a post he held until 1945. A member of Craobh na gCúig gCúigí of the Gaelic League, Quigley was an Irish scholar who published *The Standard Grammar of Modern Irish* in 1924, and, with Ruth, translated much of the Church of Ireland's liturgy into Irish.

As students from different Protestant denominations attended Coláiste Moibhí, provision had also to be made for Presbyterian students, who attended Abbey Presbyterian Church, Rutland Square (now Parnell Square), and this increased the costs. Eventually, it was agreed to pay £40 per annum to Quigley as well as 7s. 6d. per student to St Mobhi's Church, Glasnevin, and to Abbey Presbyterian Church. Later in 1934, the Presbyterian Church requested that a Presbyterian chaplain be appointed. With Gregg's approval, it was agreed that he should provide one half-hour class per week for which he would receive £10 per annum. In 1938, a similar request made by the Methodist Church was granted on the same terms.

Expenditure on religion at Coláiste Moibhí 1927–28 & 1928–29

	Subscription to St. Mobhi's Church Glasnevin	
1927/28:	26 students @ 7/6 per student	£9 – 15s.- 0d.
1928/29:	41 students @ 7/6 per student	£15 – 7s. 6d.
	Subscription to Abbey Presbyterian Church	
1927/28:	4 students @7/6 per student	£1 – 10s. - 0d.
1928/29:	5 students @7/6 per student	£1 – 17s. - 6d.
	Chaplain's payment	£40 – 0s. - 0d.
Total		**£68 – 10s.- 0d.**

Source: *The National Archives, Department of Finance Papers, S25/10/34*

The Department was content to agree to Gregg's proposal, but the Department of Finance was quick to point out that a full-time Catholic chaplain cost only £130 per annum, and that he 'gave more service'. A Department of Finance official commented:

> I thought we had this question settled but the archbishop (C of I) has proved himself stiffer in negotiations than was expected. Taking all things into consideration, we can hardly resist the terms for which he holds out. We were prepared take advantage of the failure of the churches to apply for payment.[6]

Opinions among the early students varied as to the effectiveness of the teaching of religion. One student recalled:

> Religious instruction strangely didn't seem a priority. We read the Bible – full stop – no discussion or explanation, no questions! A Rev. P. Quigley belatedly took charge of R.I.

---

6. *Ibid.*

Another student had a different recollection:

> RE like (in) all other (Protestant) secondary schools of the period was badly done by. The Rev. Paul Quigley taught us and took the Sunday services in St Patrick's Cathedral. There was dogmatic moral teaching, as everywhere else, but little scholarship. But one thing we had which other schools didn't have, was an appreciation of the Church of Ireland liturgy, a pride in our ecclesiastical past and a realisation of the beauty of the liturgy in the Irish language, for which it seems to be particularly suited.

The post as history and geography teacher was filled eventually by Oscar Willis (Oscar Diarmuid MacCárthaigh Mac Uilis). Nicknamed 'Joe' by the students, he was the most colourful member of staff. Born in Killarney in 1904, he was the son of an artist father, Richard H.A. Willis, and sculptor mother, Jean Maria Twiss. His father died when Oscar was two. A past pupil of St Andrew's College, he studied modern languages at TCD, graduating with a first-class honours degree and gold medal in 1925. At Trinity, he was a founder member of the Gaelic Society and honorary secretary of the College Choral Society. He qualified as a barrister but never practised. He worked for a time in the civil service before going to teach at Coláiste Moibhí. Seldom heard to speak English, he was anti-English in his outlook. An accomplished linguist, Willis spoke Irish, English and French as a child at home. His interest in languages continued throughout his life. Fond of travelling, he liked to learn the language of a country before visiting it. In later years he was reputed to know several languages, including Portuguese and Swahili. His method of learning a new language was to write the vocabulary in a small notebook which he pored over while presiding at meals in the student dining-room. Somewhat eccentric, in his early years he was noted for shaving his hair, while in his later years following a visit to Africa, he wore a fez. Always dressed in homespun tweeds, he taught the students to weave *criosanna* (belts) and liked to knit string vests during study time. He taught Irish dancing and played the fiddle for the weekly dancing sessions. A kind and generous person, he often invited students to his home in Dalkey where he delighted in showing off a currach he had made as a young man. Throughout his life Willis belonged to a number of Irish language societies, including An Comhdháil Cheilteach and Craobh na hÉireann. On his death his friends established a competition for the harp in his memory at Oireachtas na Gaeilge. An early student described Oscar Willis as 'enigmatic':

> One could write a book or nothing about Oscar depending on one's philosophy or outlook! He came to Coláiste Moibhí as Seán MacEachain's successor, steeped in Irish history and nationalism. I don't know if it rubbed off! Certainly not permanently. He was fiercely pro-Irish and at the same time he was stridently anti-everything British! You wouldn't find him speaking English under any circumstances – even the English version of foreign name places was taboo! In spite of his prejudices he imparted information in an orderly and systematic,

though rigid, fashion but his teaching of Irish history had to have a definite bias. Apart from his teaching, he didn't involve himself very much in other school activities and I can't recall if he had any interest in games or hobbies. He was mostly a loner I think. He spent his spare time knitting. He enjoyed visiting the Kerry Gaeltacht where I, subsequently, once met him in kilts and, in my presence, he displayed a rich fluency in French when confronted by a non-Irish speaking tourist.

The final long-term member of staff at Coláiste Moibhí was Hazel Campbell (Héasail Nic Ailín). From a Co. Derry teaching family, she trained at CITC from 1924–26. There she was awarded a silver medal for teaching. She taught in Malin, Co. Donegal, before being appointed to Coláiste Moibhí. Nicknamed 'Smutty' by the students because of her dark eyebrows, she was an imaginative and stimulating teacher. She taught Latin and junior English and Irish. Unlike the other staff, she was not strongly nationalistic in her outlook and did not always share their views. In 1960, she took early retirement and went to live in Spain. She died in England in February 1988.

These teachers, Liam Condell, Oscar Willis, Enid Anderson and Maeve Dennison, were to stay at the college until the late 1960s. One of the early students commented:

> In spite of their relative inexperience in this unique departure in education it could be said that generally they performed conscientiously according to their lights and coped as sincerely as they could in a setting without precedent.

In September 1934 Miss Anderson became a full-time 'professor' and her sister, Betty (Eilís Nic Aindriú), was appointed matron. The matron had considerable work to do, as it was not unusual for large numbers of students to become ill.

THE COLLEGE DOCTOR

As with the other colleges there was continuous haggling over salaries and costs. In June 1930 questions arose about the salary to be paid to the college's medical officer. From the beginning of Coláiste Moibhí, Dr Dorothy Price of Fitzwilliam Place, a Protestant doctor who could speak Irish, was appointed. Born in 1890, Elinor Dorothy Price (née Stopford) was a niece of Alice Stopford Green, the nationalist historian and writer. She studied medicine at TCD. Despite her unionist upbringing, she became a supporter of Sinn Féin and a member of Cumann na mBan. She took the anti-Treaty side in the civil war. After her graduation in 1921, she spent part of 1921 and 1922 as a dispensary doctor in Co. Cork where she often treated wounded members of the IRA. Of a somewhat idiosyncratic disposition, she smoked a pipe, wore riding breeches and used an eyeglass.[7] In 1924 she married district justice Liam Price. While working at St Ultan's Hospital she developed an interest in childhood tuberculosis, in which she became a foremost authority. In 1937 she introduced the BCG vaccine to Ireland and five years later published a book on the subject, entitled *Tuberculosis in Childhood*. She died in 1954.

Though Dr Price was a well-known supporter of the republican movement, Blythe questioned how much Irish she knew and why the post at Coláiste Moibhí should be confined to Protestant doctors.[8] This was probably because she was not a Cumann na nGaedhael supporter. Eventually, a salary of £70 per year was agreed. Dr Price seems to have had quite an amount of work to do, for there were frequent outbreaks of serious illness in the early years of the college. Occasionally, students were sick for the major examinations. In the class which entered in January 1928, Minta Miller was sick at the Leaving Certificate Examination. This class had already lost Kathleen Sullivan, who died in first year. In the October 1928 class, Margaret O'Connor was sick at the Intermediate Certificate Examination. Later she was awarded an entrance scholarship by TCD. In the October 1929 class, Patricia Clarke was sick for the Intermediate Certificate Examination, while Millicent Fitzsimons was sick for the Leaving Certificate. Usually, when students were ill for examinations the Department allowed them to continue on to training if they had a good academic record.

Dr Price often had to deal with epidemics, which in those pre-penicillin times could have a severe impact. In January 1929 there was an outbreak of flu which eventually became so bad that the matron and 26 students were ill at one time. In the following December there was an outbreak of diphtheria. The year after, there was another outbreak of illness which necessitated a nurse being hired to help. In March 1931 there was a further outbreak of flu and this time 18 students, Miss Penrose and the matron, Enid Anderson, caught it. Department memos record that 11 students and a 'professor' were ill in March 1935 while 25 students, a 'professor' and two maids were ill the following month. In 1936 there was a major outbreak of measles.

EXAMINATION RESULTS

Despite all the difficulties in starting the college and finding teaching staff, the examination results were of a high standard. This was particularly noteworthy considering that the shortened course had allowed the students less time to study for the examinations, which were undertaken in Irish. Those who did the Intermediate Certificate Examination in 1929 had entered the college in April 1927, which gave a term for the college to become established and only

EXAMINATION RESULTS 1927–1930

Date of Entry to C. Moibhí	No. entered	Year of Intermediate Exam	pass	hons	fail	Year of Leaving Certificate Exam	No. Entered	pass	hons	fail
April 1927	19	1929	10	5	4	1930	10	3	7	0
April 1927						1931	7	1	6	0
Jan. 1928	11	1929	4	4	3	1931	8	2	5	1★
Oct. 1928	14	1930	5	5	4★	1932	12	–	12	0
Oct. 1929	15	1931	5	8	2★	1933	14	4	10	0
Sept. 1930	9	1932	5	4	–	1934	11	1	10	0

★ *includes students sick at examination.*

two years to complete their Intermediate studies. Ten of these students went on to do the Leaving Certificate Examination in 1930. The remainder did the Leaving Certificate Examination in 1931 along with those who had entered the college in January 1928. One boy, Edward Barrett, who entered the college in January 1928, did the Intermediate Certificate Examination in 1929 and the Leaving Certificate the following year, gaining honours at both examinations.

Results at the Leaving Certificate Examination were excellent, better than at many Protestant secondary schools, and compared well with those of other preparatory colleges. According to a former student: 'No special coaching was given. We were the cream. We wanted to work and we did, and we were well taught.' Another student said:

> We had good results in the exams because of the atmosphere of the college. Good working conditions. Of course, there were so few of us that we got a great deal of personal attention.

As many of the students were over 15 at entry, they were probably quite mature in their attitude to work. Some had been to other secondary schools. Others, as their fees indicate, were from lower socio-economic backgrounds, which probably meant that they took advantage of the opportunities the college afforded them. All 28 boys who did the Leaving Certificate Examination between 1930 and 1938 entered CITC and completed their courses satisfactorily. Two were awarded entrance scholarships by TCD and 18 went on to graduate, four being respondents. But due to a shortage of posts for men in primary schools in the 1930s, some took positions in secondary schools. Bill Kleinstuber became vice-principal of St Patrick's Cathedral Grammar School, while Victor Wheatly taught in Clones High School, Mountjoy School, Mount Temple School and at one time was headmaster of the Hibernian Marine School. A talented amateur actor, he gave a lifetime of service to the Church of Ireland, and at the time of his death in February 2003 he was honorary secretary of the select vestry of All Saints' Parish, Raheny.

Approximately 14 per cent of male students left teaching after some years, but those who stayed in primary education continued as respected principals until retirement. Amongst those who left teaching were Edward Barrett, who established a successful motor business; Cecil Hyde, who taught in Avoca School, Blackrock, for 10 years before setting up a craft business; Frank Donaldson and Fred Phillips. Those who stayed in primary teaching included Harry Hannagen, principal of Glasnevin; George Griffin, principal of Greystones; Richard Rowntree, principal of Kill O' the Grange; George Fitch, principal of Kildare Place; William Blennerhassett, principal of St Michael's School, Limerick; and Sam Adamson, principal of St Andrew's School, Lucan.

Robert Morley, who was a pupil at the college from 1932–36, became principal of St Michael's School, Limerick. He died in 1946.

The girls' examination results were not as good as the boys and a number of girls failed the Intermediate Certificate Examination in the early years. The Leaving Certificate results for these years, however, were excellent with only three students failing out of 143 (28 boys and 115 girls), and Coláiste Moibhí's results compared well with those of the other preparatory colleges. The Department was pleased with the college's success: 'The result (1930) was especially remarkable having regard to the fact that these students' knowledge of Irish was very limited on their admission to the college.'

The system which the Department operated in the colleges, whereby failure to pass the final examination in each year meant dismissal, must have ensured that the students worked hard and that students likely to fail were weeded out early on. The chief reason for students leaving Coláiste Moibhí seems to have been illness, though some were not allowed to continue because of poor results. During 1927–37 a number of girls left, or had to repeat a year, because of poor health. This was mentioned 10 times in the college register. Most of the girls stayed in primary teaching, although some had to retire due to the marriage ban. A small number in each year went on to graduate from TCD, a number of whom were respondents. They included Margaret Mitchell, Dorothy Griffin and Gladys Allen, all 1933–37, and Sarah Armour and Dorothy Farnham, both 1934–38.

FRANCES CONDELL: MAYOR OF LIMERICK

One of the college's most outstanding past pupils, Frances Condell (née Eades), was from this period. In 1962 she was the first Protestant to be elected Mayor of Limerick since the foundation of the state. A class-mate had this recollection of her:

> Frances "Fanny" Eades married Robert Condell, a Limerick business manager in June 1937. She had been a student in Coláiste Moibhí from 1931–35 when she entered CITC. She withdrew from training in March 1936, and served as a teacher only intermittently due to the marriage ban then in force. Instead, she involved herself enthusiastically in business, social and political activities in her native city and was duly elected to Limerick Corporation in the early 1960s. She was subsequently unanimously elected as the first female Mayor of Limerick, a post she filled with dignity and distinction. She enjoyed the privilege of welcoming President J.F. Kennedy to Limerick and he was so impressed by her speech of welcome that he declared it to have been the best address he had heard during his visit to Ireland.

In 1964 Dublin University conferred an honorary degree on Mrs Condell. There is also a street named after her in her native Limerick.

42 Frances Condell, Mayor of Limerick with President John F. Kennedy and Taoiseach Seán Lemass during the President's visit to Limerick in 1963. *Limerick Leader*, 30 June 1963.

THE PHOENIX PARK: 1934–40

Eventually, work on the college's new premises was completed, and Coláiste Moibhí moved to the Phoenix Park in January 1934, where it occupied the west wing of the former Royal Hibernian Military School, today St Mary's Hospital. Designed by Francis Johnston as a home for the orphans of soldiers, the school had been given a royal charter in 1769. With the change of government the school closed. At one stage, the Department had proposed that the Church of Ireland Training College should move from Kildare Street to another part of RHMS, but the board of governors had turned the idea down.[9] There had also been a proposal in 1927 to move the Domestic Economy School at Kilmacud to RHMS when the lease expired on its Dundrum premises. At the same time the possibility of Coláiste Moibhí opening at RHMS had been suggested by the Department, but instead the Army School of Music moved there.

On 8 May 1934, Éamon de Valera officially opened Coláiste Moibhí's new premises at RHMS. This was significant because heretofore Coláiste Chaoimhín was the only college to enjoy such an official ceremony,[10]

---

9. Jones, Recruitment and Formation, p. 157.
10. See Part I, chapter 2.

43 Archbishop John Gregg with Éamon de Valera at the Official Opening of Coláiste Moibhí. *CICE Archives*.

though both Coláiste Chaoimhín and Coláiste Íde had opened on the same day, 1 March 1927. There is no mention of official openings of the other colleges in either the national or local papers. Why was there an official opening for Coláiste Moibhí? It is likely that the government wanted to use the occasion as a propaganda exercise to demonstrate its generosity to the Protestant minority, particularly as that minority had been quite vocal in opposing compulsory Irish. Archbishop Gregg, as manager of the college, presided at the ceremony which was attended by Thomas Derrig, the Minister for Education; Mr M. Franklin, the chief inspector; and Br Ward, president of Coláiste Chaoimhín.

In welcoming the guests, Gregg thanked the government

> cordially and heartily for agreeing with the greatest goodwill that there should be a Protestant preparatory college and preparation for the Church of Ireland Training College. We could have not have expected anything more in courtesy and goodwill than we have received from the government of the Irish Free State.

Gregg's speech was significant because he referred to opposition from the minority to compulsory Irish:

> The question of compulsory Irish was an anxious and difficult one. His personal opinion had always been that whatever their personal views, when the matter was a government regulation it should be done without hesitation and with the best heart they could put into it. There was nothing more undesirable than that people should make a grievance out of such a matter of educational routine. He had no sense of grievance. They might have their private opinions, but his feeling was that where it had been made part of the curriculum it should be done with goodwill. He was glad to see so many young people taking up the study of Gaelic. If the young people did not study Irish they could not hope to secure posts under a system in which Gaelic played an important part in the country in which they lived.[11]

Gregg also made a significant reference to the need for students entering training colleges to have second-level education. Up to the end of the 1920s, it had been quite common for students to come from primary schools where they had been working as monitors or as pupil-teachers under the old scheme.

It was not surprising that Gregg was so fulsome in his gratitude, for the refurbishment of the former RHMS had cost £44,381–8s–3d, a considerable sum of money. Facilities included a fully equipped science laboratory, two hard tennis courts and a sports field, facilities which few other schools had:

> It is necessary to see the great beautiful rooms, the swimming bath with its terrace and dressing rooms, the gymnasium elaborately equipped and where

---

11. *Irish Times* 9 May 1934.

44 (a) Rev. James Breakey, Pádraic ó Brolcháin, Éamon de Valera, Archbishop John Gregg, John Kyle, and Thomas Derrig at the Official Opening of Coláiste Moibhí. *Irish Times* 9 May 1934.

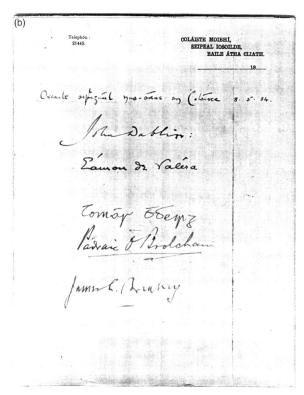

44 (b)   Signatures of dignitaries attending the Official Opening of Coláiste Moibhí *CICE Archives.*

badminton can be played, the stage on which Gaelic plays are performed, the horticultural plots, the hard courts for tennis and the two hockey pitches, to realise the variety of the students' life. The study hall, the highly modernised classrooms, the large wide cubicles with hot and cold water laid on, the dining-room, the kitchens not surpassed in any college of these islands; while most of our people are unaware that such comfort and elegance exist in any educational establishment.[12]

No expense had been spared. A new road had also been provided so that the college would have its own separate entrance, and £135 had been spent by the Board of Works to plant trees and fruit bushes in the 1.5 acre garden. The ever-vigilant officials in the Department of Finance, however, queried some of the costs, particularly £2,000 for new furniture. The Department defended the expenditure on the grounds that the furniture in Glasnevin was over 20 years old, of inferior quality, came from the training colleges, and was unsuitable in size for the new preparatory college. In addition the provision of extra accommodation meant that the number of students could be increased from 45 girls and 11 boys, to 55 girls and 20 boys.

An editorial in *The Irish Times* praising Coláiste Moibhí reported that since 1929, 86 per cent of entrants had passed the Intermediate Examination, 46 per cent with honours, while 98 per cent of entrants passed the Leaving Certificate Examination, 79 per cent with honours. It concluded, 'From every point of view the college has proved to be a marked success'.[13]

As Kyle's period of secondment from the Department came to an end he could look back on his six years at Coláiste Moibhí with considerable pride. The college was well and truly established in fine new buildings in the Phoenix Park, with a permanent and committed teaching staff, producing students with successful academic results, fluent in Irish and well able to hold their own in the Church of Ireland Training College.

---

12. *Ibid.*, 14 February, 1938.
13. *Ibid.*, 9 May 1934.

CHAPTER NINE

Dogged by upheavals

The third principal: Gaelic scholar
LIL DUNCAN 1934–51

Shortly after the establishment of the college in the Phoenix Park, Kyle's period as principal came an end and he was succeeded by Lil Duncan (Lil Nic Dhonnchadha) in September 1934. The search for a Protestant teacher with Irish had led to her appointment in January 1933. She had earlier been approached to join the staff when the college opened.[1] This offer she had refused as she feared that she might be dismissed by the Cumann na nGaedheal Government for refusing to take the Oath of Allegiance. Lil Duncan was particularly acceptable to Gregg, and she agreed to come to Coláiste Moibhí on condition that her salary would be the same as at Alexandra School, where she had been teaching for the previous ten years.

Born in Belfast in 1891, Lil Duncan's father was a civil servant. The family lived in a number of places, including Holywood, Co. Down, and Coleraine, Co. Derry, before moving to Dublin in 1907. Lil's mother, Georgina Ffolliott L'Amie, who had trained as a teacher, was from Wexford Huguenot stock.[2] Lil was educated at Alexandra College and read Celtic studies, modern languages and literature at Trinity College, where she became a scholar. In 1914 she was one of the first 10 women to graduate from TCD, receiving a first-class honours degree in Celtic studies and a gold medal. She taught at Mercer's School, Castleknock, before becoming an Irish teacher at Alexandra.

Known to the students as 'Zip', because on her first day at the college she wore a knitted jumper with a zip fastener, Lil had a great love of Irish. Her reserved manner, however, did not make her an ideal teacher. For much of her life she was a member of the Gaelic League and held many offices in that organisation. An ardent nationalist, she was a staunch supporter of de Valera.

---

1. Ó Glaisne, *Coláiste Moibhí,* p. 60.
2. Ó Glaisne, *De Bhunadh Protastúnach,* p. 292.

45 Lil Nic Dhonnchadha, principal of Coláiste Moibhí, 1934–1951. *Courtesy Risteárd Giltrap.*

In 1955 she was chosen as president of Oireachtas na Gaeilge. She was a founder member of the Cumann Gaelach na hEaglaise, though she only became deeply involved in that organisation in 1936. A regular attender at services in Irish, she continued to attend even when she was almost unable to walk. Her 90th birthday was celebrated with a party in Dáil Éireann. She died in March 1984, aged 92. She was responsible for much of the work in translating parts of the 1965 Irish language version of the Church of Ireland prayer book. The 1961 Irish language hymn book contains some original work and translations by her. She was a member of the board of Christ Church Cathedral for many years, and the cathedral and Cumann Gaelach na hEaglaise were beneficiaries in her will. Lil served on several public bodies, including Raidió Éireann's Advisory Council and the Cultural Relations Committee of Ireland. She also wrote for a number of periodicals, including *Ériú, Feasta, An tUltach, Focus* and the scholarly *Revue Celtique*. During her retirement she returned in the late 1950s to TCD as a temporary lecturer in Irish. A colleague of the period, Dr Mae Risk, recalled that she was well able to take her place in the common room.

Opinions differ about Miss Duncan as a teacher. A former student recalled:

> Lil Duncan was a very unusual lady. One had to applaud her for her tremendous courage, the best kind of courage, moral courage. She was a great scholar, impatient of lesser students and she had a great and absorbing love of the Irish language and Irish culture. She had a cold manner, and did not easily communicate with the young, but underneath that manner she was a very affectionate person and a loyal friend.

For others, Miss Duncan's outstanding characteristic was her nationalism. A student recalled that she was a cold person and fanatically nationalistic. Another recalled that she never went to church on Remembrance Sunday, while a third student of the period commented that Oscar Willis and Lil Duncan were 'very anti-English. They'd put you off Irish'.

Domestic staff in the Phoenix Park included six maids, a cook and a woman cleaner who came in two days weekly. As in the other colleges, they had to be Irish speakers. A Co. Donegal woman, Bríd Butler, who worked as a maid there, recalled her experience:

> The first thing they taught me was how to answer a switchboard phone. Each of the 'professors' had their own phones. My duty was to answer the hall door, and help in the *seomra bia* and look after the students if they should get sick in the classroom. We all spoke Irish …. You know what was said to me, that if I were found talking English during my duty in the college I'd be reprimanded. The Protestant students at the college were learning Irish. They would run to you and say: '*Caidé an Ghaeilge a chuirfidh tú ar sin? Caidé chuirfidh ar seo?*' They'd have enough Irish to get there and then they'd perfect it once there.[3]

---

3. Butler, Bríd, 'Áras an Uachtaráin re-visited', *Dearcadh* 2001/2002, The Ardara View.

HYDE AS PRESIDENT

Bríd Butler saw a different side to Miss Duncan. She had these recollections of working at Coláiste Moibhí and of often meeting Douglas Hyde at the college when he called to see the principal:

> I have never come across two who loved Irish so much as Dr Douglas Hyde and Lil Nic Dhonnchadha – two Protestants. They were real Wolfe Toners. Lil would have a class 2–3 times a week, for maybe an hour or two hours. If someone came in while she was in the classroom, I would bring them into the parlour, make tea, chat to them and keep them company. I got to know Douglas Hyde. He started to come to the college and I got to know him through Lil Nic Dhonnchadha .... He always wore plus fours and a big báinín jacket, hand knitted socks, and brown shoes. To me he was a man of about 6 foot.

She recalled Hyde's appointment as president of Ireland:

> It came about that he was to be made president of Ireland. All the hullabaloo! Lil was delighted. We were over and back to Áras an Uachtaráin, getting things ready. Then the day came; he was unanimously chosen as president of Ireland.

Before his inauguration Hyde had invited Bríd to join his staff at the Áras. She agreed to think about it:

> I had a chat with Lil. She said: 'If you think you can better yourself by going to Áras an Uachtaráin, I won't keep you.' I said, 'I couldn't leave you. But, I have a few sisters at home, and if you think they'd fit in I'd like them to come.'

Two of her sisters joined the staff at the Áras. Her sister, Maura, became the president's personal maid.

Another person who knew Lil Duncan well was Dr Donald Caird,[4] Church of Ireland archbishop of Dublin from 1985–1996. He gave this description of her in a lecture in 1989:

> Lil was a friend of Hyde's for over 40 years. She was strong-minded and very learned. She knew French, Irish, German and Russian. She was not a very good teacher. Her first love was for the language.

A RESOUNDING SUCCESS

For the first five years of Lil Duncan's time as principal, life was uneventful and the college was a resounding success. In the 10 years of its existence it had succeeded in producing sufficient numbers of Protestant students for CITC who were fluent in Irish, competent to teach through Irish, and also

---

4. For biographical details see the Appendix.

46 A class in Coláiste Moibhí in the Phoenix Park 14 February 1938. *Courtesy The Irish Times.*

of sufficient academic ability to pass the training college and TCD examinations. Furthermore, the college possessed first-rate facilities in the park. Indeed, so successful were the college's first 10 years that *The Irish Times,* which had no great fondness for the gaelicisation policy, carried a long article in February 1938 lauding Coláiste Moibhí as 'a successful experiment' and fêting the students as 'Reconcilers of the Present and the Past.' Destined 'for the most part' to spend their lives in rural areas, the writer claimed that the future of Protestantism in the new state would depend on them:

> As such (they) are called on to play an unusual part … a part of heroic responsibility and inspired courage. They defend and uphold the faith of their forefathers in a new spirit. All ideas of this faith becoming a dominating force are gone … abandoned for ever. But Protestantism, no longer seeking ascendancy, will loyally contribute to the welfare of the country that shelters it. It accepts the hope that its existence may be useful, if not necessary, to the new order of things. The continuance of its existence at all, rests mainly with those who keep its lonely flame kindled in country districts.

Acknowledging the importance of the primary school as the place in Ireland where most people received their early education, the writer went on:

> What they learn there colours all their moral and mental outlook. If the Church of Ireland, and other Protestant churches are to survive at all, it will be because

the primary schools of their denominations have willed it to be so. It will rest with the pupils of these schools to accept or reject the full privileges of citizens; to remain within the state, useful and honoured; or to allow themselves and their religion to be gradually crowded out, not by numbers or any kind of sectarian ascendancy, but by their own laziness and inertia.

Referring to Protestants and the Irish language, the writer praised 'the new system of education which includes a knowledge of Irish' and declared his belief that bilingualism would increase mental efficiency and intellectual alertness. He continued:

> The Protestant population of this island is supposed to be specially unwilling to learn Irish. If this is the truth it would be interesting to know the reason. For the Protestant population of any country long vaunted a freedom from all prejudice in education. Since the superiority of a bilingual nation is now universally admitted, we should expect to find the Protestant classes and masses to the forefront of the movement. But the truth is that the Protestant conscience is not yet fully awakened to its duty – its duty, not to the powers that be, but to its own responsibility.

The article included a fulsome description of the college's magnificent facilities and declared:

> The Government of Éire has done all in its power to help the minority and to give them the opportunity of sending out teachers as fully equipped in all its requirements as the largest and most famous Catholic college can supply.

It concluded by asking whether the students realised the significance of their future role as Protestant primary teachers:

> These happy clever looking girls in their pretty uniforms and their fine carriage look at us straightly and independently. Do they know how much depends on them? At least they are enjoying life at present. They soon become fluent in Irish, the language used in college life, and can presently say as one of them expressed it, 'All we need to say and more'.

Students of that period included Katherine Smyth, née Mitchell. She spent her whole career in primary teaching, including a long period in Taney Parish National School in Dublin. There she and her husband, Robert (Bobby) Smyth, saw the school develop into the largest primary school under Church of Ireland management in the Republic. Their daughter, Hazel Riordan, who was a student in Coláiste Moibhí from 1958–1960, retired in 2003, having been an infant teacher for many years in Taney, where she also developed the school orchestra. Another former student from this period was Dorothy Griffin. One of a number of siblings from a teaching family, she taught for many years and was principal of Zion National School from 1974 until the 1980s when she took early retirement due to ill-health. Also at Coláiste Moibhí at this time was Anne Peters (née Dukelow). From Durrus, Co. Cork, she was a student at Coláiste Moibhí from 1939 to 1943. Anne's mother had been a primary teacher but died in 1936. Anne herself went on to graduate in 1947 and to marry Frank Peters, who was a student at the college from 1933 to 1937. In 1943 he graduated with a BA degree (respondent) from Trinity College and later obtained the higher diploma in education. Frank taught as an assistant teacher in Kildare Place Boys' School for seven years before leaving in 1948 to teach in Wesley College. Later, he became head of the Irish department at The High School in Dublin. Most of the former students had only happy recollections of their time in the Phoenix Park. A student who had been at another post–primary school recalled:

> All my family were teachers. I wanted to be one too. I entered the preparatory college. It was lovely in the park. The food was very good and the surroundings beautiful. We had a good hockey team and lots of tennis. Lovely cubicles. I remember only happy times.

Nevertheless, she was critical of the curriculum:

> I thought we were a bit restricted and at the time I couldn't see much point in doing all subjects through Irish. I was glad I had three years in Dundalk Grammar School.

While the period of Coláiste Moibhí's sojourn in the Phoenix Park was mostly idyllic, it was not unaffected by the over-supply of teachers which was a major aspect of recruitment in the 1930s. The surplus of teachers had a considerable effect on CITC and male students fared particularly badly. A student who had received assistance from the Candidate Teachers' Training Fund described his efforts at repaying the assistance in 1933: 'Can only send £5. Only got three weeks' work as a substitute. Would be glad to do any work of any description which you might hear of'.[5]

The shortage of teaching posts left teachers with little choice. They often had to act as 'unpaid curates'. In addition to their teaching duties, they were expected to play the organ, run the choir and teach in Sunday school. Life in a parish could be difficult for a young teacher with a demanding manager:

> He was highly indignant because I refused to come back for Christmas Day .... I expected school difficulties but not social difficulties. I am responsible for school, choir, organ and numerous other things.[6]

---

5. Hodges Papers, CICE Archives.
6. *Ibid.*

As the shortage of teaching posts meant that students who were able to play the organ were the first to be employed, music lessons, funded by the governors of CITC, were provided at Coláiste Moibhí from 1940. By this time, all students at CITC were trained in church music and organ or harmonium playing.

CONTINUED DISSATISFACTION WITH THE GAELICISATION POLICY

Many members of the Church of Ireland continued to be unhappy with the gaelicisation policy and often expressed their dissatisfaction at meetings of the general synod, the church's law-making body. In 1939 a resolution was passed requesting the Minister for Education to inquire into the effects of the teaching of Irish and of teaching through Irish. Despite this dissatisfaction, the 1939 general synod continued to support Cumann Gaelach na hEaglaise with an annual subsidy of £100 for services in Irish. Furthermore, the same general synod was told that revised proofs of part of the Book of Common Prayer in Irish had been handed over to the publishers. This showed how far the church had come in accepting the 'new Ireland'.

When it was obvious that Derrig was not likely to hold an inquiry into the teaching of Irish, the Church of Ireland board of education decided to follow the example of the INTO and to organize its own inquiry. This was not well received in some quarters and led to criticism of Protestants in general:

> As a body, long-continued pride of place, backed up by a foreign power and possessed of loaves and fishes which that power put in their hands at the expense of the native Irish, has given them a certain traditional mentality which finds difficulty in adjusting itself to change of power and patronage. They seem to have still the minds of those who made Poyning's law or the framers of the penal code....[7]

The results of the Church of Ireland inquiry were similar to those of the INTO inquiry, published in 1942.[8] The main finding of the Church of Ireland inquiry was that:

> Except in schools where the teachers and pupils alike are of super-normal capacity the development of the pupils has been retarded by intensive teaching of Irish and more particularly by teaching through Irish.[9]

It also found:

> That the use of Irish outside the school has not increased, and, in certain cases, where 10 years ago Irish was frequently heard there is now no use made of the language outside the school.[10]

---

7. Mgr Cummings PP, Dean of Elphin, *Irish Times*, 22 May 1939.
8. See Part I, chapter four.
9. Report of the board of education, JGS,1942, p. 210.
10. *Ibid.*, p. 232.

To avoid learning Irish, many Protestant children in border areas went to schools in Northern Ireland. An estimated 500 children crossed the border daily.[11] Those families with means sent their children to private schools where Irish was not a problem. Derrig was determined to end this practice and the Department brought a test case against parents of children attending a private school in Co. Wexford. When this was unsuccessful, Derrig brought in a new school attendance bill, giving the minister the right to certify schools as to their suitability. It also gave him the right to refuse a certificate to a child attending an uncertified school inside or outside the state. The bill was passed by the Oireachtas but because of its constitutional implications, President Douglas Hyde referred it to the Supreme Court. There it was found to be repugnant to the constitution and the whole matter was dropped.[12]

There is a tendency to believe that Protestants were treated generously in the Free State. But was this really so? There were several major issues on which they sought help from the Department. These included the *Revised Programme of Primary Instruction* where Derrig was loath to allow them any concessions. Indeed, in response to a deputation from the Protestant National Teachers' Union, which in 1935 sought some lessening of the programme's insistence on teaching infants through Irish only, he declared:

> The Revised Programme was an attempt to put into operation the (gaelicisation) policy in respect of infants; that the position with reference to the language in this country was unique, and without precedent in the history of education in other countries and that with general co-operation much could be accomplished.

He also asked:

> Did the minority require special treatment? The majority had accepted the conditions and special treatment for the minority would require special legislation.[13]

The Protestant teachers' concerns were supported by the Protestant school managers. A deputation from the Dublin School Managers' Association (DSMA) met the Minister for Education in 1936. Eventually, an arrangement was made between the Department and the Church of Ireland board of education that when the revised programme was not carried out in full because of the manager's opposition, the blame would not fall on the teacher. The Department would take the matter up with the manager.[14]

Another issue about which the minority sought help from the Department was with regard to textbooks. As early as 1922 the DSMA complained that many textbooks contained 'certain doctrines of the Christian religion

---

11. Seanad Reports, 21 January 1943.
12. Akenson, *A mirror to Kathleen's face*, p. 128.
13. Minutes of the PNTU, 29 March 1935.
14. Report of the board of education, 1937, JGS, p. 223.

which were not believed or accepted by Protestants'. In the 1920s, the Department's attitude to the minority was conciliatory. Later, it was to harden considerably and the content of textbooks continued to be a cause of concern for the minority for another three decades.[15] Other areas where the Department was sympathetic to the needs of the minority were the provision of school transport for Protestant children in isolated areas, and school enrolment numbers.[16] The Department also made concessions to help CITC with recruitment.

THE EMERGENCY YEARS

From 1939 on, Lil Duncan's period as principal of Coláiste Moibhí was to be severely tested as the college's location changed so often – from the Phoenix Park to Kildare Street in 1941, followed by five years in Merrion Street, a return to the Phoenix Park in 1946 for two short years before moving to Shankill. This was a difficult period for the preparatory colleges. Coláiste Chaoimhín was closed in 1939, Coláiste na Mumhan moved to Ballingeary in July 1940 where it reopened as Coláiste Íosagáin. Coláiste Éinde was taken over by the Department of Defence. Recruitment was also severely restricted in an effort to absorb the large number of unemployed teachers. While the 1930s were dominated by over-recruitment, the following decade was characterised by a shortage of teachers. For Coláiste Moibhí, the difficulties began with the onset of the Second World War, or the Emergency as it was known in Ireland.

Doreen Flanagan (née Bray) was a student at the college from 1937 to 1941. Following a period as principal of Donnybrook National School in Dublin and a part-time lecturer in needlework at CITC, she emigrated to England. There, she had a very varied career teaching at different levels, including borstal girls aged 17 to 21. She recalled her experiences at Coláiste Moibhí:

> The Second World War started in September 1939 when I was in Rang B (third year). My first memory of the Emergency was the provision of thin blackout curtains for the huge windows of the dormitory. We had to sew little brass rings on them to attach them to the walls. Ration books had to be handed to '*bean a tí*' [the matron] each term. I can only recall that we were entitled to half an ounce of tea and eight ounces of butter per week. There was no imported fresh or dried fruit in those days.[17]

Discipline was a further challenge for Duncan, particularly when part of the block in which the college was located was taken over by the army as a hospital:

---

15. Jones, 'The attitudes of the Church of Ireland Board of Education to textbooks in National Schools, 1922–1967' in *Irish Educational Studies* 1992.
16. Jones, Recruitment and Formation, pp. 132–139.
17. Doreen Flanagan, 'Recollections of The Emergency' in *PSA Newsletter, 1998*, p. 18.

Some girls thought the proximity of such macho men was a bonus. One day, some of them climbed up a tree where the soldiers pounded the beat on guard duty underneath. They proceeded to drop fir cones on the lads and were noticed by the *Príomh-Ollamh* whose window overlooked them. Their punishment was to write an essay '*Oireann modhúlacht do chailíní*' roughly translated 'Girls should be modest'. One day, as we were playing hockey the soldiers were doing arms drill. In the interval we proceeded to copy them with hockey sticks. We were good at presenting arms.[18]

Duncan was not without a sense of humour. Another student recalled an occasion when a young sentry, watching the principal go to her car, shouted at her, 'Hi Blondie', which produced a half smile on her face.

TEACHING PRACTICE

It was during this period that efforts at assessing preparatory students as future primary teachers were first put into practice with the requirement that students teach one lesson to their classmates annually. According to Doreen Flanagan:

> I believe the first 'lesson each term (sic) taught to our own class' was started when we were in Rang C (second year). I remember teaching the 'trade winds' in geography one year and the poem, 'That's the Way for Billy and Me' in Rang A (fourth year). I had a boyfriend called Bill (now my husband) and got a right ribbing from my friends.

COLÁISTE MOIBHÍ IN KILDARE PLACE 1941

The early 1940s were very problematic for the college. At the end of 1940, Coláiste Moibhí's fine premises in the Phoenix Park were taken over by the army as a military hospital. From 27 January to 31 August 1941, the college was accommodated in the Church of Ireland Training College in Kildare Place. This created tensions between both colleges, which were exacerbated by shortages of fuel for heating and cooking, and difficulties over food supplies. Contingency plans for evacuation had to be made and air-raid drill practised. In Kildare Place, Coláiste Moibhí was quite separate from the training college students, and classes were held in a neighbouring government department, while art lessons took place at the College of Art. Gym classes were held in the basement, which was underground. Known to students as 'the dungeon', it served as an air raid shelter when there were alerts. Tennis was played at Fitzwilliam Place that summer, and students studied for their examinations in St Stephen's Green. As a result of efforts to improve the standard of music in preparatory colleges in the early 1940s,

---

18. *Ibid.*

James Stanilaus O'Brien joined the staff for weekly music lessons. A gifted musician, 'Stan' had a B Mus degree from UCD and taught for many years in the primary school attached to St Patrick's Training College. Keenly interested in German culture, he was president of the Irish German Society in the 1960s.

Doreen Flanagan had vivid memories of Coláiste Moibhí's period in Kildare Place:

> We were called 'lodgers' or 'paying guests'. I was prefect in one of the rooms in 'Cock Loft' – freezing in winter, too hot in summer. The CI(TC) servants adjoined us and used to put 'Kit Kats' for us under the door. The night the land-mine fell near Amiens St. station, our beds wandered around the floor.[19]

She also recalled another memorable wartime occurrence:

> One morning a British fighter chased a German bomber. We were reading *The Irish Times* at a window and Frances Good fainted. The streets were very dark due to the blackout and there were soldiers at Leinster House.

In addition to the problems due to the Emergency conditions, there were difficulties over payments to CITC. Initially, the Department agreed to pay one pound per week for board and residence for each student and five pounds for each teacher, but it refused to pay for a student or teacher who became absent through illness. Upon CITC's insistence, it agreed to pay ten shillings per student. There were also considerable difficulties for the five staff members, who had been provided with board and residence in the

The Buildings of the Church of Ireland Training College, showing the Statue of Archbishop Plunket.

47 Kildare Place in 1937. *CICE Archives.*

---

19. Letter from Doreen Flanagan.

Phoenix Park, and who had to vacate CITC's premises during the holidays. Indeed, accommodation was so restricted that Lil Duncan had only a bedroom and an office. She was forced to rent a flat in Harcourt Street so that she had somewhere to keep her books and possessions. A Department memo records Lil's comments that the period in Kildare Place was 'very uncomfortable and had affected her health'.[20]

CANON EVELYN CHARLES HODGES

The college's stay in Kildare Place must have created tension for Duncan, as her relationship with the principal of CITC, Canon Evelyn Charles Hodges, cannot have been easy due to his outspoken criticism of the gaelicisation policy. Born in 1887, Hodges was the son of a country clergyman. Educated at Mountjoy School, Dublin, he studied mental and moral science at TCD, where he was an outstanding student. He graduated in 1910 with a first-class honours degree and was awarded a gold medal for the excellence of his examination results. The following year he was ordained, and after two curacies in Dublin he was appointed organising secretary of Dublin, Glendalough and Kildare diocesan board of education and diocesan inspector of schools in 1917. While in that post he obtained the higher diploma in education in 1920, and three years later the BD degree from TCD. In 1924 he became rector of Rathmines and four years later he succeeded Canon Kingsmill Moore as principal of CITC.

Of a gregarious cheerful nature, Hodges wanted to liven up the Church of Ireland which he considered rather dead. Highly-strung with an abundance of nervous energy, he was an able organiser and a gifted preacher who was remembered for his oratory long after his death in 1980. Fond of controversy, he wrote many articles and letters to newspapers. Hodges tried to modernise the training college, because he believed that this was necessary if students from secondary schools were to be attracted to primary teaching. In making changes, however, he created much resentment. He was also well aware that for students entering the training college to be successful, they would have to have passed the Leaving Certificate Examination. But he never faced the fact that due to the weakness of Irish teaching at Protestant secondary schools, sufficient candidates who had passed the Leaving Certificate Examination could not be obtained from that source. Had it not been for Coláiste Moibhí, the separate system of Protestant national schools could not have survived. From the outset Hodges disliked the preparatory college and seldom praised the contribution of its former students to transforming CITC into an Irish-speaking institution.

Acutely aware of the need for this transformation, Hodges made efforts to learn Irish and succeeded to the extent that he was able to take prayers.

---

20. DF Papers, S25/15/34.

48 Canon E.C. Hodges, principal of the Church of Ireland Training College, 1928–1942, *PSA News 1984*.

He also encouraged the use of Irish for ordinary conversation at recreation and other activities. Hodges's interest in Irish was strengthened by the Department's ruling that from 1933 on, a certificate of proficiency in written and oral Irish was necessary for appointment to a permanent position in a primary school. As many of the students at CITC were not from the preparatory college, their Irish was weak. Hodges persuaded the board of governors to pay for students to visit the Gaeltacht in 1933 and 1934. Despite his policy of encouraging the use of Irish at CITC, he often publicly attacked teaching through Irish. In 1937 he wrote in *The Irish Times*:

> The whole of education is being attacked by a microbe of unreality .... Any attempt to teach through a language not the language of the home is bringing an element of unreality into education and harmful.[21]

Moreover, following the publication of the results of the Church of Ireland inquiry into the teaching of Irish in 1942, speaking as the church's spokesperson on education, Hodges declared:

> It may be said that the language is worth the price, that it is prospering and more and more people are speaking it. There is not a word of truth in that – quite the contrary.[22]

Hodges was unfortunate in being principal of CITC at a time when the emphasis on the Irish language was at its greatest. He was unfortunate also that he was principal of one of the Church of Ireland's most important institutions at a time when the church itself was going through a period of continuous decline and fewer teachers were needed. His failure to adjust the

---

21. *Irish Times* 18 November 1937.
22. *Ibid.*, 7 May 1942.

St. Moibhí's
Preparatory
College,
Chapelizod,
Co Dublin.

*General View of the
Buildings.*

TEACHERS
IN
TRAINING.

Church of
Ireland
Training
College.

*Within the
Entrance at
Kildare Place.*

Circular Letter to the Clergymen, the Teachers, and the
Parents of the Church of Ireland, issued with the approval
of His Grace the Archbishop of Dublin, Manager of both
Colleges.

December, 1937.

49 *Teachers in Training,* leaflet to encourage entrance to Coláiste Moibhí. *CICE Archives.*

number of students recruited to the number of teaching posts available was a grave mistake. Though over-recruitment was a feature of the national scene, it had specific effects on CITC. In 1935 he forecast that not more than 40 women would be in CITC in 1939. The actual number was 19. In March 1937, in a memo which showed that 62 teachers were without permanent posts, he predicted that it would take three years to absorb the surplus teachers. On his advice, the numbers in training were reduced. Yet the following November, he informed the board of governors of CITC that the surplus must have been absorbed, as it had been impossible to fill several temporary vacancies. The same month the Department restricted admission to the training colleges to preparatory college students only. This agitated Hodges who produced a leaflet, *Teachers in Training,* which was widely distributed. It promoted entry to Coláiste Moibhí and promised bonuses of £5 for teachers who successfully prepared the first 10 candidates for Coláiste Moibhí from 1938 on.

A CRISIS IN RECRUITMENT

In February 1938 the crisis regarding recruitment came to a head at a crucial meeting, chaired by Gregg and attended by CITC's governors, members of the Church of Ireland board of education, the church's principal education committee, and a representative of each diocesan board of education in the Free State. At this meeting Hodges pressed for an immediate application to the Department for admission to CITC of a limited number of candidates by open competition. He also asked that no 'exceptional' recruitment for Coláiste Moibhí[23] be allowed, though he must have been aware that if this policy were put into effect the preparatory college would have few pupils and would have to close.

At the meeting, the headmaster of Mountjoy School, William Anderson, proposed that pupils be admitted to Coláiste Moibhí after the Intermediate Certificate Examination for a two-year course to the Leaving Certificate Examination. The requests for after-Intermediate entry to Coláiste Moibhí and for a limited number of entrants by open competition to CITC were both refused by the Department. It did, however, allow one candidate to be admitted 'exceptionally' to CITC in 1939. In a further concession, it allowed recruitment to Coláiste Moibhí to continue, although recruitment to the other preparatory colleges was suspended from 1939 to 1941. Why the request for after-Intermediate entry was refused is difficult to understand, as the Report of the Committee of Inquiry into the Preparatory Colleges in 1938 had recommended that 10 per cent of places in each college should be awarded to students who had successfully completed the Intermediate Certificate Examination.[24] Furthermore, such students were, occasionally, admitted

---

23. See Part II, chapter 7.
24. See Part I, chapter 3.

to Coláiste na Mumhan and Coláiste Íosagáin for a three-year course which included repeating the examination through Irish after one year.

From 1938-42 the number of students at CITC became so small that the college's future was in jeopardy, and there was severe pressure on Hodges, who became ill as a result. The transfer of Coláiste Moibhí to Kildare Place worsened matters, confirming Hodges' worst prejudices about the preparatory college, and in December 1941, he complained that its students were 'lacking in general education and culture':

> They are taught under somewhat unusual conditions through a language other than their home language, which is not in accordance with general education principles, as approved by the Church of Ireland authorities.[25]

Indeed, his view of preparatory students was shown clearly in a letter to the Department where he described them as 'not the best type of teachers for national schools':

> They were likely to enter preparatory colleges for economic reasons of the parents rather than for any vocation which they may have themselves for the profession.[26]

Hodges's criticism of Coláiste Moibhí students was unfair. While it is possible that some parents may have used Coláiste Moibhí as a means of gaining free or cheap secondary education, many of those who qualified for remission of fees were not only good teachers, but gave a life-time of service to the Church of Ireland. For most of the early years, the fees at preparatory colleges were £40. Unlike the other colleges, there were always some students in every class at Coláiste Moibhí who paid full fees.

Hodges also complained that the Coláiste Moibhí students were segregated from other young people with different career intentions. Here it must be remembered that for most of this period, until 1938, it was the only coeducational preparatory college. While it was the same size as many Protestant secondary schools, it had much better facilities in the Phoenix Park than most of them had. Furthermore, there was little emphasis on students becoming teachers, as a student recalled:

> In the four years at Coláiste Moibhí we weren't aware we were student-teachers. We were just treated as people and the change from Coláiste Moibhí to Kildare Place was quite surprising for many of us. In Kildare Place we felt the burden of our responsibility and had to behave with the dignity expected from candidate teachers.[27]

---

25. Minutes of CITC, 10 December 1941.
26. *Ibid.,* 16 June 1938.
27. Memo from student.

The complaint that the Coláiste Moibhí students were lacking in culture was probably true of some but was likely to have been true also of some open competition students. Primary teachers of this period often came from rural backgrounds with a very different local culture to that desired by Hodges. At Coláiste Moibhí, the staff tried to broaden the pupils' outlook, and students often visited art galleries or exhibitions recommended by Mr Condell, who also tried to widen their musical interests. Mr Willis too tried to interest them in music and taught them to play several instruments, including the harp, and Coláiste Moibhí had its own 'orchestra' at this time. A student of this period had this recollection of those times:

> 'Professor' Willis had 'an orchestra' and taught us to play several instruments, some of which he brought from his own collection at home for our use. He gave us lessons on the harp and we used the music as background for plays we were putting on. I seem to remember only pleasant things. There must have been some times (that were) not so happy but those can't have been frequent. I enjoyed all my student days, exams and games alike.

Another student of the same period recalled:

> Liam Condell encouraged us to take an interest in the arts and we went to exhibitions of Mainie Jellett, Nano Reid, Maurice McGonigle et al as well as calling in regularly to the National Gallery and the museum nearby.[28]

Hodges also complained about the age of entry and while he was correct in his view that pupils entered the preparatory colleges at too early an age, figures for Coláiste Moibhí show that the average age of students entering between 1927 and 1939 was 15. Hodges's complaint that Coláiste Moibhí students were not taught through their home language showed his prejudicial view of the preparatory college. He opposed the government's policy on teaching through Irish and often attacked it publicly. Although much of his criticism was justified, learning through Irish at secondary school was very different to being taught through Irish as an infant. There are only two occasions recorded in reports of Hodges praising Coláiste Moibhí. In 1931 he described the college's Leaving Certificate Examination results as 'particularly gratifying' and, in 1943, on leaving CITC, he acknowledged the preparatory college students' ability at Irish:

> It is true that much of the skill in Irish was due to St Moibhí's preparatory college from which most of the students in later years have been admitted.[29]

A further reason for Hodges's dislike of Coláiste Moibhí was the attitude of the teachers to religion. He tried to inspire his students with a love of, and

---

28. Peters, *PSA Newsletter 1996*, p. 1.
29. Hodges, E.C., 'A review of the Church of Ireland Training College, 1927–43', *CITC Report 1942–43.*

50 22 Upper Merrion Street, home to Coláiste Moibhí 1941–46. Now the Merrion Hotel.

loyalty to, the Church of Ireland and to foster qualities of character and self-reliance. These qualities he believed were necessary for Protestant teachers living in isolation in remote areas. He also believed that if students were imbued with a high ideal regarding their life's work, they would be enabled to persevere against discouragement and discontent. In an attempt to foster their spiritual life he laid great emphasis on daily worship in CITC's chapel. He believed that by participating in the liturgy and music, students would come to appreciate the church's worship and be able to share in the life of the parish in which they taught. This, he felt, would also help them to see the importance of their role in the church's life.

At Coláiste Moibhí, Lil Duncan and her staff placed little emphasis on the religious side of education. All students were expected to attend their prescribed places of worship on Sunday mornings, but they were free to go where they liked on Sunday evenings. Many of them tried different places of worship and were encouraged to do so. A student of the period recalled:

> Students went to their prescribed church in the morning and then anywhere else. I went to Methodist services in the evenings and to spiritualist meetings. The staff had a very open attitude to religion and encouraged their students to think for themselves.

Lil Duncan was a devout member of the Church of Ireland but not all her staff were so inclined, as Hodges would have discovered when Coláiste Moibhí was resident in Kildare Place.

22 UPPER MERRION STREET 1941–46

The Department would have been happy for Coláiste Moibhí to have stayed in Kildare Place for the duration of the Emergency, but it is unlikely that either Hodges or Duncan would have wanted to continue the arrangement for very long. On 1 September 1941 Coláiste Moibhí moved to the former Orthopaedic Hospital at 22 Upper Merrion Street. Directly opposite Government Buildings, with three storeys and a large basement, it was one of four large Georgian town houses built by Lord Monck for wealthy merchants and nobility in the 1760s. No. 22, where he lived, was known as Monck House. No. 24, Mornington House, was the birthplace of Arthur Wellesley, Duke of Wellington. For most of the twentieth century, the houses were used as state offices. In 1995, work on restoring the houses began and today they make up The Merrion, a luxurious hotel. No. 22 was to house the college until 1946. A student recalled life there:

> The small back garden was pleasant if you wanted to read or study, but on most afternoons we could go for a walk in Stephen's Green or window shop in Grafton Street. On reflection, the freedom to go shopping and to wander around

the city was a great privilege. A stop at the Swiss Chalet on the way back to buy one of the luscious cream horns was an occasional treat. On half-days, instead of the usual walk, off went one or two groups to play hockey. Some walked while others cycled .... As we played our matches our opponents were often baffled as instructions, encouragements and rebukes, were all *trí Gaeilge.*[30]

The same student recalled the atmosphere in Merrion Street as 'strict, disciplined, caring, suitable for young people of that era who were accustomed to this within the family'.

Florence Armstrong was a student at the college from 1942 to 1947. She repeated a year due to illness. Along with three classmates, Ida Blennerhassett, Frances Sloane and Violet Wilson, she won an entrance scholarship to TCD in 1947. All four went on to graduate from the university. Florence spent her whole career in teaching, including four years in Nigeria as head of a second-level Federal Government College. As principal of St Patrick's National School, Dalkey, she developed a reputation for the high quality of her teaching. One of the first to recognise the importance of involving parents in school management, and to believe that children of different faiths and of none should share the same classroom, she became principal of the first multi-denominational school, Dalkey School Project National School in 1978, a post she held for 13 years. Following retirement, she spent some time teaching in Tanzania with the Church Mission Society and later worked as an educational consultant in Zambia. She recalled life during the Emergency:

> Like all institutions food was rationed. It was crowded in Merrion Street with limited facilities. The main recreation was walking. The staff had our welfare at heart but often overlooked the importance of our maturing. At that time, Coláiste Moibhí fulfilled a need for country students who otherwise would not have had an opportunity to reach second and third-level education.

As the Emergency continued, the cramped conditions and food rationing had their effects. Food was in short supply and lacked variety – the diet consisted mainly of potato pudding, pulses and black bread. Fever broke out and several students were taken to hospital. Two of the 1941 class, Sheila Fry and Anne Rogers, died from tuberculosis. Another student of the period had this to say about her time in Merrion Street:

> Fever broke out and several of the students were in Cork Street (fever hospital) and our afternoons were spent in 'crocodiles,' 20 or so in a 'croc' walking the streets and not allowed into shops. The food was very poor, potato pudding, pulses, black bread. We did most of our 'swotting' for the Leaving and Trinity Entrance in Stephen's Green.

---

30. Maud Jamieson, *PSA Newsletter* 1995, p. 1.

There was also an outbreak of religious fervour and students held prayer meetings where speaking in tongues was common. Coming to examination time, there was a strange outbreak of hysteria which was dealt with firmly by Miss Duncan. This was probably a reaction to the war. Blackouts were continuous and '*Múch an solas*' ('put out the light') the frequent cry. Examination pressure was constant, with Coláiste Moibhí students sitting TCD's entrance examinations as well as the Leaving Certificate. Many of the students rose at 5.30 am to study.

The college's situation in Merrion Street contrasted greatly with that of the Phoenix Park, and conditions were made more difficult by the Emergency, something which affected the whole country. In Merrion Street, the college had severe difficulties functioning, as the house was old and difficult to run. Domestic staffing levels were inadequate. A report from Miss M. Vaughan, *Ard-Thimthire Tighis,* in 1944 noted that the principal and the matron had to do a lot of extra work and recommended that a messenger boy and a boiler man be employed.[31] Accommodation was limited and only the principal, the matron and one teacher could reside there. Indeed, the principal's accommodation was so restricted that Lil Duncan had to continue to maintain a flat away from the college, whereas in the Phoenix Park her spacious apartment included two sitting rooms, a study, four bedrooms and a maid's room. As it was anticipated that the college's stay in Merrion Street would be of short duration, she had been content to pay the rent for the flat, but as time went on she requested the Department to pay the £65 per annum rent.

THE REV. T.F. BLENNERHASSETT

It was during this period that the Rev. Thomas Francis Blennerhasset was appointed catechist in succession to the Rev. Paul Quigley. This was how he explained his appointment:

> I was asked by Archbishop Barton and Miss Duncan to take on the post in 1943. I had forgotten most of my Irish so I went to the Gaeltacht to refresh it.[32]

He was to continue in the post until the college closed in 1995. Born in Co. Waterford in 1915, and educated at The King's Hospital and Trinity College Dublin, he graduated with a first-class honours degree in mental and moral science in 1937. He was ordained two years later and served two curacies in Dublin. In 1947, he was appointed rector of Balbriggan where he stayed until 1958 when he was appointed rector of Howth, a post he held until his retirement from the full-time ministry in 1990. Fond of travel, he was renowned for leading pilgrimages to the Holy Land and other places of biblical interest. In 1976 he was made a canon of Christ Church Cathedral, Dublin. He and

---

31. DF Papers, S25/15/34.
32. Interview with Canon Blennerhassett.

Lil Duncan were firm friends, and in accordance with her wishes he conducted her funeral service in 1984. Entirely in Irish, the funeral took place
in Howth with only two relatives, a cousin and the cousin's son, in attendance. News of her death was not published until a week later. Blennerhassett
was well versed in the conduct of services in Irish, as he often officiated at
the regular services of Cumann Gaelach na hEaglaise. A genial character,
'Blenner', as he was called by the students, was popular with both students
and staff. In teaching religious education, he followed his own course and
liked to encourage students to raise issues for discussion:

> His method was profound in its simplicity. He would take a well-known passage
> of scripture, either from the teaching of Jesus or one of his apostles. It would be
> read from the current New Testament in Irish and then it would be used as the
> basis for a discussion on the relevance of the Christian faith to current affairs.
> Frank allowed the discussion to wander as widely as his pupils wished, so long as
> they showed they were alert and using their brains. In an age when much of
> 'education' consisted of learning prepared texts by rote, his pupils found in his
> classes a freedom which stimulated them all.[33]

This contrasted greatly with the methods pursued by religion teachers in the
other preparatory colleges. In March 1993, the board of governors of CICE
marked 'Blenner's' 50 years' service to Coláiste Moibhí with a dinner hosted
by Archbishop Donald Caird. Amongst those who paid tribute to his work
were representatives of each of the six decades he taught.

51 Former student Lynn Maloney makes a presentation to Canon T.F. Blennerhassett to
mark his 50 years as RE teacher at Coláiste Moibhí. Centre is Risteárd Giltrap, principal of
the college.

---

33. Stokes, Canon A.E, *PSA Newsletter,* 1999, pp. 41 and 42.

While in Merrion Street, the college accepted male students again, and in 1942 a class of 12 students, 10 girls and two boys entered. The latter had been recruited at the insistence of the Presbyterian church which had become alarmed at the shortage of male teachers. A student recalled:

> These young Monaghan men were the first male students to be admitted for some years, as the college had stopped recruiting boys in the 1930s. They were safely housed in the YMCA in Rathmines from which they commuted daily.

Demands for male teachers were few, as they were not allowed to teach infants or junior children or to work in a one-teacher school. Between 1943 and 1952, five male students were accepted into Coláiste Moibhí, and one man entered CITC by open competition in 1943. The board of CITC was loath to admit men, as most Protestant schools were one-teacher units. This meant that there were few posts for male teachers. In addition there was no accommodation for them, as much of the Kildare Place premises had been rented out to provide an income for the college. This, however, did not deter the Rev. Dr James Irwin, a Presbyterian minister, who negotiated these entries with the Department. A personal friend of de Valera, he was a member of the executive of Fianna Fáil from 1945 until his death in 1954.[34]

SCHEME FOR SECONDARY TEACHERS TO LEARN IRISH

An ardent nationalist, Irwin was keen to encourage young Protestants to become teachers of Irish at secondary schools, and devised a scheme whereby prospective secondary teachers would learn Irish at Coláiste Moibhí. In 1948, *The Irish Times* reported:

> As Protestant schools have found it difficult to get Protestants qualified to teach Irish or other subjects through Irish, a scheme has been devised by the Department of Education at the suggestion of the Rev. Dr J.A.H. Irwin of Lucan by which prospective secondary teachers may be educated at Coláiste Moibhí, the Protestant preparatory college.[35]

Nothing came of this scheme, though it is briefly mentioned in the General Synod Report of the Board of Education.

RECRUITMENT IN THE 1940s

From the late 1940s, a shortage of trained primary teachers developed. The Protestant community was particularly affected, as it was dependent on

---

34. For biographical details see the Appendix. I am indebted to the Presbyterian Historical Society for details about Irwin.
35. *Irish Times*, 9 January 1948.

CITC to supply its needs. Indeed, the failure of Hodges and the Department to match student numbers to teacher vacancies was to be problematic for the minority's schools. The Emergency was a difficult period for CITC when its numbers declined considerably.

This decline was due mainly to two factors, the inadequate teaching of Irish at Protestant secondary schools and the ban on recruitment by open competition to CITC. This meant that during the early 1940s, all candidates entering CITC came from Coláiste Moibhí. This limitation, and the small numbers in CITC, agitated Hodges. In 1941, efforts were renewed to persuade the Department to change recruitment rules for CITC. A deputation was sent to Derrig in January 1942 requesting the restoration of entry by open competition for a guaranteed number of students with a pass in Leaving Certificate Irish on certain conditions. It also repeated the request for the introduction of after-Intermediate entry to Coláiste Moibhí.

This time, Derrig agreed to allow a minimum of three women per year for three years to be admitted to CITC with not less than 60 per cent in pass Irish at Leaving Certificate, on condition that they obtained honours in Irish at TCD at the end of their first year of training. He also agreed to admit to Coláiste Moibhí approximately nine candidates for the four-year course, and a minimum of three girls per year to enter after the Intermediate Certificate Examination on certain conditions. They were to be between 15 and 17 years of age on 1 August of the year of the examination and to have passed the Intermediate Certificate Examination with honours, obtaining honours in Irish and a pass in English, history, geography and mathematics. They also had to pass oral tests in English and Irish and a singing test. In 1943, the first after-Intermediate student, Olive Frazer, entered Coláiste Moibhí. A total of 61 students were to use this means of entry to teaching between 1943 and 1961.

Hodges believed that once recruitment by open competition restarted, the cream of Protestant secondary schools would enter the training college, and he put great efforts into publicising the need for teachers. Between 1943 and 1952, 104 students applied to enter CITC by open competition but only 69 were successful. During the same period, 221 students applied to enter Coláiste Moibhí, of whom 102 were successful.[36] These numbers show that there was no shortage of Protestant candidates for primary teaching. The problem was reaching the standard for entry to the training college, particularly at Irish. For those attending Protestant secondary schools, the standard of Irish teaching was inadequate. For many others unable to afford secondary schooling, the only hope was a place in Coláiste Moibhí. In the 1920s, many Protestant candidates had entered CITC from convent and Christian Brother schools but in the 1930s and 1940s this source dried up.

---

36. Jones, *Recruitment and Formation*, p. 247.

THE RETURN TO THE PARK

With the ending of the Emergency, Coláiste Moibhí looked forward to returning to its former premises in the Phoenix Park, having been five years in Merrion Street. The question of its return, however, was to cause much political controversy. Early in 1946, the college's location was discussed by the cabinet in a wrangle between four government departments. A number of local politicians made representations to Seán MacEntee, the Minister for Local Government and Public Health, that the Phoenix Park premises should continue as a hospital. They pointed out that the 380-bed hospital was bigger than any of the existing voluntary hospitals in the city. Furthermore, its use as a sanatorium for tuberculosis patients could help clear the long lists of patients waiting for treatment of this highly infectious disease. MacEntee urged the Department to maintain the hospital until a proposed sanatorium at Santry was ready in two or three years. In a memo to the government, he forecast an increase in demands for treatment of tuberculosis cases, as the introduction of mass radiography was revealing a large number of hitherto unsuspected active areas of the disease.

This presented a dilemma for the government, as the number of students in Coláiste Moibhí was small compared to the hundreds who could be treated for TB. But the college had to leave Merrion Street, as the premises were urgently needed by the Department of Lands. So the Department of Defence agreed 'under pressure' to vacate the Phoenix Park premises. Derrig, the Minister for Education, used Coláiste Moibhí's significance for the minority community to support his argument for the college's return to the park:

> Coláiste Moibhí caters for Protestant students only and I attach considerable importance to the success of this college. You know as well as I do that a large proportion of the Protestants in this country do not favour our national aspirations, culturally or politically, and I regret to say that the teaching of the Irish language in Protestant schools leaves much to be desired.[37]

He went on to underline the significance of Coláiste Moibhí's role in inculcating a nationalistic outlook among Protestant teachers:

> Coláiste Moibhí in addition to making them competent Irish speakers endeavours to give its students a thoroughly Irish outlook so that later when they are teachers these schools may attract the Protestant youth to the Irish viewpoint. Any check on Coláiste Moibhí would be a source of intense satisfaction to the reactionary Protestant element. It might be held against us that because the college is for the benefit of the religious minority we are indifferent to its welfare and make patent our indifference by uprooting the college whenever it suits our convenience to do so, without regard to the adverse effect of these transfers on the efficiency of the college.

---

37. DT Papers S13905.

He added that upheavals and removals had retarded the progress of the college. It had been housed in three locations before its premises in the park were taken over. It then moved to Upper Merrion Street where the 'grossly unsuitable' conditions had affected the health of both students and staff, and led to vigorous protests by the college's medical officer against the maintenance of Coláiste Moibhí there. Derrig stressed that he could not put off re-opening the college in the park, even if necessary repairs would have to wait until the holidays.

This memo gives an insight into how Derrig regarded the role of Coláiste Moibhí. It also gives his view of the teaching of Irish in Protestant schools and of those Protestants who criticised the language policy. Plainly, Derrig saw the preparatory colleges not just as being in the vanguard of promoting the Irish language; he also had expectations that teachers from the colleges would be used to propagandise the nationalist viewpoint. This admission is of importance because Coláiste Moibhí received little special treatment, despite its significance.

Derrig's view eventually prevailed. On 11 September 1946, Coláiste Moibhí returned to its former home in the Phoenix Park. Emily Foxton (née Smithson) recalled her time there in the annual PSA Newsletter, (the past students of CICE newsletter) in 1999:

> My memories of Rang C (second year) and Rang B (third year) spent in the Phoenix Park are pleasant ones. The emphasis was on hard work but the atmosphere was friendly and conducive to learning. Teachers treated you as if you were mature! After class and at week-ends we could change out of uniform. Visits to relatives or friends were allowed on Sundays after church. Phoenix Park was a safe place for cycling and we enjoyed a spin at week-ends, with very little traffic. There was not much emphasis on sport but hockey was played in all weathers!

She also recalled teaching practice:

> It was in Rang B that I taught my first lesson to fellow classmates. We were allowed to choose a subject so I taught a geography lesson about India with emphasis on tea-growing. It gave me an opportunity to draw on the blackboard. I have never forgotten the orange pekoe leaf. The lesson was followed by constructive criticism and discussion.

SHANGANAGH CASTLE SHANKILL: 1948–1968

The college's stay in the park was to be of short duration, and in September 1948 it moved to Shanganagh Castle in Shankill, Co. Dublin. Built about 1797[38] by General Sir George Cockburn, it was less than a mile from

---

38. Hone, Craig and Fewer, *The New Neighbourhood of Dublin*, p. 206.

52 Shanganagh Castle, home to Coláiste Moibhí 1948–1968.

53 An Grianán.

Shankill on the Bray Road. Set in extensive grounds containing the ruins of the old church of Kiltuck and bounded on the east by the sea, the house was later extended and castellated by the architect G. Morrison. Cockburn stocked his mansion with a collection of Italian marbles and paintings, and he had a fine library. Upon his death, Shanganagh passed into the ownership of Mrs Rowan Hamilton, who died there in 1920 in her 100th year. Mrs Hamilton's grandson was Harold Nicholson, the UK diplomat, author and publisher, famed for *The Harold Nicholson Diaries 1930–39*. His wife was the writer Vita Sackville-West, creator of Sissinghurst gardens at Sissinghurst Castle in Kent. Nicholson recalls Shanganagh Castle in his diaries. For a time before Coláiste Moibhí moved there, the castle was used as an hotel and it still had a large ballroom with a beautiful maple floor. The castle's chequered career continued after it was vacated by Coláiste Moibhí in 1968, and it became a detention centre for young offenders, a role it continued until 2003.

As the premises at Shankill were too small to accommodate Coláiste Moibhí, temporary sleeping quarters, known as An Grianán, were built. Later, a new wing was added to the old castle with four new dormitories providing sleeping accommodation for 20 students in each of the two large ones and for six students in each of two smaller ones. Each student had her own cubicle complete with wash-hand basin, while bathroom facilities were first-rate. The grounds also had two hard tennis courts and a hockey pitch. A student who entered the college on its first day in Shanganagh recalled:

> It was my first day also. 'Zip' was principal until Christmas 1951. I liked her. She was kind to me when my grandmother died. She was tall and dignified, a real lady. She taught Irish to Rang A. She was very reserved and quite distant. The students were in awe of her. Yet they went to Condell to petition her to stay on till the end of their time in Rang A. The teachers were very friendly to the students. 'Bunty' took us to Shakespearian plays. Condell and 'Joe' often took students to their homes.

Nance McLindon (née Leeson) from Co. Wicklow was in the same class. A dedicated Gaeilgeoir she taught in Coláiste Moibhí at one time and was a strong supporter of Cumann Gaelach na hEaglaise. Her husband, Rev. Donald McLindon, rector of Enniscorthy, was drowned in a boating accident in 1970. Their daughter, Sheelagh, was a student at Coláiste Moibhí from 1984–87.

THE LATE 1940s

Relationships between the Department and the Church of Ireland became strained during the late 1940s, mainly due to the language policy. Separate inquiries, conducted by the INTO and the Church of Ireland board of education, showed teacher dissatisfaction with the gaelicisation policy, but the Fianna Fáil government refused to consider these findings. The formation of the first Inter-party Government in 1948 brought expectations that the policy would be modified. One group which particularly welcomed the formation of the new government was the Protestant minority. For them, the period 1922–45 was a definite era of decline, when the number of children at Protestant primary schools decreased annually from approximately 20,000 in the mid-1920s to approximately 10,500 in the mid-1940s. A shift in the size pattern of Protestant schools also took place, and by the mid-1940s they were mainly one-teacher units. The first Inter-party Government modified the language policy with the introduction of the New Revised Programme for Infants. This allowed English teaching as an optional subject for infants and first class for half an hour daily. But it disappointed those in the Church of Ireland who had hoped for greater changes.

Though Hodges had been appointed bishop of Limerick in 1943, he still acted as spokesperson on education for the Church of Ireland. Teaching through Irish and recruitment continued to be major issues. In November 1948 Hodges met with Mulcahy, the Minister for Education, to discuss these issues, particularly the difficulties of teaching through Irish in one-teacher schools.[39] According to a confidential note by Mulcahy on the interview, Hodges told him they had been expecting a 'mitigation of emphasis on Irish' from the new government; however, a complaint had been received from a teacher that an inspector had been seeking an extension of teaching through Irish in his school.

Following the interview, the Church of Ireland board of education carried out a survey among Protestant teachers on teaching through Irish and on the possibility of extending this to higher classes in the primary school.[40] Observations regarding Irish teaching in one-teacher schools were also requested. Replies were received from 150 teachers, and the findings were sent to Mulcahy. The board found that there was 'no hostility to Irish as such' and that teachers 'loyally administered the policy of the Department'. It went on:

> Not to use the home language of the children, be it Irish or English, is a psychological outrage upon the most helpless and inarticulate section of the community …. If a foreign atmosphere is introduced in school there is confusion and slumbering resentment in the minds of children.[41]

The board pleaded to be allowed to use English as a denominational privilege as:

> English is the language of the Bible and prayer book and church services for the vast majority of our children, any deterioration in the standard of English hurts us from a religious point of view.

A confidential memo drawn up by the Department in response to the board's submission showed how far relations between the Department and the minority had deteriorated. The survey was described as:

> Just a device to give a semblance of disinterestedness to a stand that has been there all the time. Anyone familiar with the attitude of the Protestant element to Irish could have no doubt as to the kind of answer the said committee hoped to get from teachers.[42]

It added that the remarks about

> no hostility to Irish were due to Hodges's guilty conscience. No one in this instance at any rate alleged such hostility. There is no need to deny it. Hodges

---

39. 'Dr Hodges' Memo – Comments Thereon,' UCD Archives, Mulcahy Papers, P7/C/152.
40. Report of the board of education, JGS 1950, pp. 186–189.
41. 'Dr Hodges' Memo – Comments Thereon,' UCD Archives, Mulcahy Papers, P7/C/152.
42. *Ibid.*

knows in his heart hostility is there. We in the Department know it is there. Any attempt to deny it is either bluff or dishonesty.

It also asserted that the majority of Protestant teachers were poorly equipped for teaching Irish, were not 'at any great pains to improve their competency' and achieved 'poor' results. It continued:

> The only interest Protestants had in Irish, until compulsory, was to use it as a proselytizing agency in the remote areas to which the Irish-speaking population had retreated. Achill, Connemara and Dunquin can tell of Protestant interest in Irish.

The memo attributed the shortage of Protestant candidates to the unattractiveness of teaching in one-teacher schools:

> The inspectors are unanimous that the level of intelligence is low due to inter-marriage. Saw some of them myself and can bear this out. I cannot imagine a more distasteful assignment than to teach in some of the Protestant schools I saw.

Protestants were unaware of such views in the Department and, the following year, the honorary secretary of the Protestant School Managers' Association, Canon W.N. Harvey, wrote to Mulcahy on behalf of the managers. He repeated their objections to teaching through Irish and requested that less time be spent on the subject. When this did not happen the government was trenchantly attacked by a number of Protestant clergy. Harvey went so far as saying:

> We have heard much in newspapers about the police state in Northern Ireland but we should remember that there is a good deal of the autocratic in compulsory Irish in our own state.[43]

DEPARTMENTAL INQUIRY INTO IRISH TEACHING IN PROTESTANT SCHOOLS

Stung by these much publicised remarks, Mulcahy ordered a departmental inquiry into the teaching of Irish in Protestant primary and secondary schools. A confidential Department memo on Protestant secondary schools drawn up in 1950,[44] showed that out of 47 schools only 24 prepared pupils for the Leaving Certificate, and that out of a total enrolment of 3,584 pupils, only 79 took Irish at Leaving Certificate level. An analysis of the results showed that 51 per cent of boys failed compared with 14.7 per cent of girls. Six girls obtained honours at Irish in the Leaving Certificate examination.

---

43. *Irish Times,* 11 May 1950.
44. 'Position of Irish in Protestant Secondary Schools,' 9 June 1950, UCD Archives, Mulcahy Papers, P7/C/152.

The memo is notable for its failure to note that many pupils received only one or two years of secondary education. It did acknowledge, however, that a number of schools had a tradition of teaching Irish to a high standard. These included Alexandra College, The Diocesan School for Girls (an Intermediate school only) and Celbridge Collegiate School, which was noted for the high number of students who entered CITC. The poor Irish results showed the need for Coláiste Moibhí, as Irish was of such importance in recruitment to CITC.

The Department attributed the high failure rate to the attitude of the head teacher:

> The general practice of heads is to attack Irish in public on every occasion – prize day etc. Pupils cannot be expected to exert themselves at a subject when they know it is unwanted and earnest Protestant teachers of Irish have frequently complained to me of the harmful effects of such attacks on efforts in class. If the head is friendly to Irish the language will thrive as well as any other subject. He will see to it that pupils are well grounded in the fundamentals of the language and that teachers have a competent knowledge of Irish.

The following year, the Department drew up an internal report into the teaching of Irish in Protestant primary schools. This disagreed in places with the earlier confidential memo of 1950.[45] Regarding qualifications, it said that Protestant primary teachers held similar qualifications to other teachers and were generally competent in Irish. Most of them had passed through Coláiste Moibhí and CITC and had obtained the bilingual certificate. It also reported that 'many young teachers – and many older ones too – are animated by a good spirit in teaching Irish'. This report showed some openness on the question of teaching infants through Irish describing it as 'very debatable'. Nevertheless, despite this openness, the Department's report showed a biased stereotypical view of the Protestant community:

> It must be remembered that the Protestant population, though relatively small, is extremely powerful financially and able to provide for its own young people irrespective of Irish, not only in this country but also overseas.

While it was true that some Protestants were 'powerful financially', there were large numbers who were not, and the Protestant community was not able to provide secondary education for its young people. It is clear from both the memo and the report that the Department was ignorant of its own statistics. These showed, that while there was an acute shortage of recruits for CITC throughout the 1940s, there were plenty of less well-off Protestants seeking to enter Coláiste Moibhí with its subsidised fees. Had the Church of Ireland been able to provide secondary education for those candidates who

---

45. 'Irish in Primary Schools under Protestant Management,' *Ibid.*

were unable to gain admission to the preparatory college, there would have been no recruitment problems for CITC.

By 1949, the shortage of Protestant primary teachers was acute, and as a large number of Catholic teachers were teaching in Protestant primary schools, the Church of Ireland House of Bishops issued a pastoral letter on recruitment. This led to an increase in applications for CITC in the 1950s. A further factor may have been the increased status gained by primary teachers following the Roe Tribunal Awards.[46] It was also a new decade and the pupils of the 1950s were further removed from the 1922 era, with consequent reduction in hostility to the Irish language. Another significant factor was the increased number of Protestant students who entered CITC from Catholic schools.

The new decade also brought changes for Coláiste Moibhí. At the end of 1951 Lil Duncan retired. During her 17 eventful years as principal the college had moved four times. It had gone from its beautiful surroundings in the Phoenix Park in 1941 to the narrow confines of the Church of Ireland Training College in Kildare Street. Following that it had endured cramped accommodation in Merrion Street for five years before returning to the Phoenix Park. Two years later it had gained a new abode at Shanganagh Castle in Shankill. Through all the upheavals Lil had kept the college going, never deviating from the high ideals which were her inspiration.

---

46. See Part I, chapter 5.

54 Gleadas Ní Allúin, principal of Coláiste Moibhí, 1952–1984. *Courtesy Oireachtas na Gaeilge*.

CHAPTER TEN

Living with uncertainty

The fourth principal: former student
GLADYS ALLEN 1952–84

The 1950s brought a major change at Coláiste Moibhí. At the end of 1951 Lil Duncan retired as principal and was succeeded by Gladys Allen (Gleadas Ní Allúin), a former student of the college. From a farming background, her father died when she was young. Gladys Allen grew up in Co. Wicklow and attended Donoughmore National School, Donard, where her mother was her teacher. It was from her that Gladys acquired her love of the Irish language, which she never lost. Her secondary education included two years at Preston School, Navan, followed by four years at Coláiste Moibhí from 1933 to 1937. She entered CITC in 1937 where she won medals for good teaching and for the best scripture lesson. Four years later she graduated with a BA degree from TCD and subsequently became one of the first former students of Coláiste Moibhí to obtain the diploma in biblical studies at TCD. Her teaching career began in 1939 as a temporary teacher in a small school in Ballinlough, Co. Roscommon. Shortly afterwards, she was appointed to a post at Dundalk Grammar School. There she was in charge of the junior school which she reorganised along the lines of a primary school. In 1942 she became principal of Powerscourt School, Enniskerry, Co. Wicklow.

A strong personality, she imbued her students with a love of the Irish language. Possessed of a good sense of humour, she was an excellent teacher. Known affectionately as 'Polly', her students recalled her with fondness. As principal of Coláiste Moibhí, she coped well with what could have been a difficult situation, as her staff were so much older and she had once been their pupil. A very private person, she had a keen interest in sport and often umpired the students' hockey matches. She loved gardening and took great delight in looking after the rose-beds at the front of Shanganagh Castle.

As it was difficult to get domestic staff, Miss Allen's sister, Enid, became matron of the college in the 1950s. The Department suggested that she should learn Irish. She oversaw the transfer of students from An Grianán to the new dormitories. In August 1957, she left the college following her marriage to Donald Doherty earlier that year. Miss Allen's mother also lived with her in Shankill. Miss Allen was to spend 32 years at the college and to oversee its final move from Shankill to Rathmines in 1968. There, in addition to being principal of Coláiste Moibhí, she was vice-principal of CICE from 1975 to 1984. In 1979, she was president of Oireachtas na Gaeilge. Following retirement in 1984 she lived in Bray, Co. Wicklow, until her untimely death on 3 December 1986. Her funeral service took place two days later in Holy Trinity Church, Rathmines, where the address was given by the archbishop of Dublin, the Most Rev. Donald Caird.[1] A well-known Gaeilgeoir and an old friend of Miss Allen's, he was chaplain to Coláiste Moibhí from 1960 to 1969 when he was rector of Rathmichael Parish.

A memorial to Miss Allen, presented by the Past Students' Association of CICE, hangs in the college chapel in Rathmines. An explanatory note beside a commemorative wall hanging, designed by Elisabeth McArthur, lecturer in arts and crafts at CICE, states:

> The batik includes imagery of some of the things Miss Allen held dear ... Moone Cross, her garden flowers and little cat, the Wicklow hills and the Táin. The light represents the light she shed, and the thorn tree the troubles she overcame on her way through life.

A student who was at the college during both Lil Duncan's time as principal and the change-over to Miss Allen remembered:

> I never felt more indifferent to a teacher than I did to her (Lil). I felt she really should not have been in charge of young adults. She did not seem to have any rapport with them. Miss Allen seemed like a breath of fresh air – young with lots of energy.

Another student had this to say of Miss Allen:

> She was a wonderful teacher who could make the most uninteresting material come alive. She had a great sense of humour. In an age when praise and encouragement were rarely given she was quick to affirm and commend her students. She had a tremendous love of the Irish language which she imparted to her students. Her enthusiasm for it was such that her students could not but be attracted to the language.

THE 1950s

During the 1950s, as enrolments at primary schools continued to rise, a further shortage of primary teachers developed. The number of vacancies in

---

1. For biographical details see the Appendix.

Protestant schools increased, mainly due to the marriage ban, though the stabilising of Protestant enrolments was a further factor. Eventually, the government was forced to rescind the marriage ban in 1958. Despite the rise in numbers attempting to enter CITC by open competition, the need for Coláiste Moibhí continued to be as great as ever.

As with the other preparatory colleges, there was a tradition in certain areas of sending students to Coláiste Moibhí. One such area was Malin, Co Donegal, where Miss Campbell had been a young teacher. During this period Evelyn Fulton (1951–53) and Ethel Stewart (1953–57) came from Malin as did four Colhoun sisters, Norma (1950–54), Wendy (1954–58), Iris, (1957–61) and Doris (1960–64). All four qualified as primary teachers and taught in schools in the Republic. Wendy, Iris and Doris went on to graduate from TCD. Both Iris and Doris were lifelong teachers. Doris (Clements) taught for many years in St George's School, Tubbercurry, until its closure in 2002. In 1995, she became one of a number of former students to be ordained in the Church of Ireland. In 2005, she became a canon of Killala Cathedral. Also ordained were Rev. Fred Phillips (1927–30), Rev. Shirley Kingston (née Larke) (1957–59), Rev. Joyce Rankin (1958–63), and Rev. Avril Bennett (1978–80). Others were ordained in different parts of the Anglican Communion, the Rev. Gladys Olsen (née Dalton) (1948–52) in the church in Canada, and Canon Dr Myrtle Langley (1953–57) in the Church of England. Another distinguished past pupil from this period was Wyn Bryan (1951–53). A past pupil of Celbridge Collegiate School, she taught in St Andrew's National School, Rialto, in Dublin, for many years. A TCD graduate, she became a lecturer in Mary Immaculate College of Education, Limerick.

A student of the period spoke of her reasons for entering Coláiste Moibhí:

> I wanted to be a teacher. There was no other secondary school suitable for me. Entering at 13 + was not too early for me because I had decided at a much earlier age that I wanted to teach. For many others, however, it was much too early. My first impressions of the college were of the lovely building and gardens. The teachers seemed very old. I was terrified. Some of them had a genuine interest in the students' well-being. Miss Allen, in particular, was a caring person as well as being a most efficient teacher and administrator.

The Taylor sisters were also students at the college at this time: Gertrude (1950–54), Mary (1953–55) and Joan (1955-59). All three went on to graduate and at one time were respectively headmistresses of Masonic Girls' School, Celbridge Collegiate School and Mercers School. Other outstanding students of the 1950s were Hilda Kavanagh, Beryl Tilson and Hazel Crawford. Hilda Kavanagh (née Clinton) (1954–57) was from Co. Mayo. She later specialised in teaching children with disabilities and spent many years as principal of a special needs school in Castlebar. A graduate of TCD and UCG, she also undertook further studies at Geneva, Ontario and Leicester. In 1994, she was Calor Gas Housewife of the Year. Beryl Tilson

55 The Rev. Gladys Olsen, a former student of Coláiste Moibhí.

(née McConkey) (1953–57) from Co. Monaghan was principal of Taney NS for many years. During her time, a large extension was added to the school building. A graduate of TCD, she took a keen interest in religious education. She was a contributor to the religious education programme, *Primary School RE,* published in 1990, and a member of the religious education curriculum committee which produced *Follow Me* in 2001. Hazel Crawford (née Jolley) (1956–60) started teaching in 1962 in Rathmichael NS, Shankill, Co. Dublin. Under her leadership, the school grew considerably and became particularly known for the European dimension to its curriculum. In 1977, Mrs Crawford became a participant in the first European Network for primary schools, and since then the school has undertaken a number of educational initiatives, including piloting French teaching at primary level and exchange visits with a school in Lyons with which it is twinned.

During the late 1950s, hockey came to assume a major role in the life of the students. Coláiste Moibhí joined the Leinster Schools' Hockey League in

1956–57 and won the Intermediate Schools Cup in 1958 and 1960. Much of the organisation of matches and practice was done by the girls themselves, particularly by the hockey captain, with some assistance from Miss Allen and Mr Condell who often umpired home matches. Coaching was provided by students from Ling Physical Education College. Coláiste Moibhí had a number of outstanding hockey players at this time. Among them were Mavis Walker from Co. Donegal, who was selected to play for Leinster, and Katherine Howe from Co. Cork, who played on both cup-winning teams. The coach in 1960 was Elaine Bradshaw, who later became a renowned international golfer.

Other extra-curricular activities included visits to the Abbey Theatre for the pantomime in Irish and to Christ Church Cathedral to participate in the annual citizenship service. Students also enjoyed Sunday evening youth services at nearby Crinken Church and the after-service hospitality of the rector, the Rev. E. M. Neill, father of Archbishop John Neill. Groups of students were also taken by Mr Condell to musical events such as a performance in Trinity College of Bach's Mass in B Minor by Dublin University Choral Society of which he was a member. Mr Condell also organised musical evenings at the college when he introduced students to classical music. Occasionally, well-known musicians, such as Dr Hazel Morris and F.W. 'Billy' Dungan, performed at the college. Other activities which absorbed much free time included the annual Irish dancing competition, when students were divided into groups and had to compose their own set dance, and the annual display of articles made in the home economics class. Occasionally, students took part in radio programmes, such as *Ar Fuaid na Tíre* on Raidió Éireann or in religious services in Irish on Raidió na Gaeltachta.

A TIMELY INTERVENTION

For most of Gladys Allen's tenure as principal life at Coláiste Moibhí was relatively calm compared to the upheavals faced by her predecessor, Lil Duncan. Yet behind the outward appearance of tranquillity, there were times when the college's future was under threat. Indeed, it is likely that Coláiste Moibhi would have been closed along with the other colleges in 1961 but for a timely intervention by Gladys Allen.[2] Through her involvement in discussions on Páipéar Bán na Gaeilge she became aware of rumours that the college might be closed. Convinced that the college had a significant and worthwhile future and supported by eminent Gaeilgeoirí, such as An tAthair (later Cardinal) Tomás Ó Fiaich, Canon Cosslett Ó Cuinn, Aindreas Ó Muimhneacháin, Seán Óg Ó Tuama, and Ruairí Brugha, she appealed to the Department not to close the college. She was reassured to learn from officials in the Department that they agreed with her. The unique role of Coláiste Moibhí in providing Irish-speaking recruits to CITC was recognised by the

2. Revington, C.E.F., 'Developments within the Church of Ireland Training College in the 1950s and 1960s.' Unpublished MEd paper, TCD, 1979, p. 39.

56 The team which won the Intermediate Schools' Hockey Cup in 1960.
Back: Oilbhe Ní Choille, Siobhán Ní Bhuidhre, Héasail Jolley, Fíora Roycroft, Dóirín Ní Shionnáin, Sibéal Raghait;
Front: Bhealraí Ní Ghabhann, Maedhbh Nic a tSiúil, Caitríona Nic Eochaidh, Rae Bhairéid, Norma Veitch. *CICE Archives.*

Minister for Education, Dr Hillery. It was decided that Coláiste Moibhí alone would continue as a preparatory college. According to the minister this was because he 'was not satisfied that Protestant secondary schools could supply CITC with sufficient suitable candidates'.[3] So once more Coláiste Moibhí differed from the other preparatory colleges. It was not closed in 1961 but continued as a preparatory college until 1968.

During this period, Charlotte Brown (née Huston), the first of a large teaching family from Mohill, Co Leitrim, entered the college. Other members of the family to become teachers were Geraldine, who was a student at Coláiste Moibhí from 1965–69, and Niall, Noel, Emmet and Hazel. After a period teaching in Zion NS, Noel became an inspector. Also at the college during the 1960s was Máire Roycroft (1963–67). From Ballydehob, Co Cork, an area which supplied many students to the college, currently she is principal of St Luke's NS, Douglas. An active member of the INTO, she received an INTO Bursary Fund Award in 1994 to study the professional development of the primary principal, for which she received an MEd degree. A member and former chairperson of the Irish Primary Principals Network, she also served on the NCCA Irish Curriculum Committee. In 1996 she was seconded to work with the NCCA. Ruby Morrow (1964–68) was also a student during this period.

---

3. Dáil Reports 24 June 1960.

She qualified as an educational psychologist and became an inspector with the Department. Currently, she is a lecturer in special education at CICE. Also in the 1964 class was Hazel Allen (née Hay) from Co. Donegal, the current principal of Kildare Place School. Occasionally there were students who did not become teachers. Among them was Bibi Baskin from Co. Donegal, who later became well known as a television personality.

ANOTHER CRISIS REGARDING THE COLLEGE'S FUTURE

After a number of years passed in relative tranquillity in Shankill, the future again appeared uncertain as there were rumours that the Department was about to close Coláiste Moibhí on the grounds that it was costly to maintain and rather 'a loose end in civil service terms.'[4] There is reason to believe that this might have happened but for another intervention by Miss Allen. A crisis over the college's future arose while she was attending a summer conference:

> Availing of the opportunity presented by the conference she proceeded to ensure that any attempt to close the last remaining preparatory college would be vigorously opposed. Others at the conference shared her views and an impressive delegation was assembled which made immediate representations to the Minister.[5]

Following their representations, a solution was found by departmental secretary Seán Mac Gearailt. The Department agreed to have Coláiste Moibhí

57 The Church of Ireland College of Education, Rathmines, Dublin, home to Coláiste Moibhí, 1968–1995.

---

4. Revington, p. 40.
5. '*Profile – Miss Allen,*' in PSA News 1984. See also Parkes, *Kildare Place,* p. 182.

moved to the new training college under construction in Rathmines. There an extra floor was added to the residence block, and a suite of classrooms built in the grounds to accommodate it. The two colleges shared the new campus which was located in the grounds of Rathmines Castle, the former home of the Jobling-Purser family. The castle was demolished but the outhouses and magnificent trees were kept. Shortly before Coláiste Moibhí's move to Rathmines, three of the college's long-serving staff retired and a party was held in Shankill on I June 1968 when warm tributes were paid to W.T.E. Condell, Enid Anderson and Maeve Dennison. Former students from different decades and many different parts of the country travelled long distances to be present. Sadly Oscar Willis did not live to enjoy retirement. Early in 1969, while still teaching at Coláiste Moibhí, he was taken ill and died a few days later.

RATHMINES CASTLE

At Rathmines, the college became known as the juniorate of the Church of Ireland College of Education (all training colleges became known as colleges of education in 1974). Entry was restricted to after-intermediate students for a two-year senior cycle leading to the Leaving Certificate examination. Amongst those on the teaching staff were Bríd Coyne, Phyllis Miller, Margaret Mack, Seán O'Dwyer, Maura Cousins, Canon A.E. Stokes, and the long-serving Rev. Frank Blennerhassett. Coláiste Moibhí students shared many of the activities of the CICE students, including daily worship in the college chapel and meals in the dining room. Much of the college's life and activities was conducted in Irish, but it was no longer compulsory for students to proceed to the college of education and to become primary teachers, though the majority of them did. While the small numbers in the classes allowed each student to receive considerable personal attention, they also militated against participation in team sports and activities requiring large groups. In addition some of the students missed the challenge and stimulation of larger classes and they were not wholly enamoured by the prospect of spending five years on the same campus.

During the 1970s male students were again admitted. Between 1970 and 1980 an average of 11 pupils, both boys and girls, entered the college annually. They included the Morton brothers, Nixon, vice-principal of Taney NS, and Edward, vice-principal of Kildare Place School, and James Malseed, who later became a member of NCCA social and environmental curriculum committee. Other outstanding students of the period included Irene Barber, one-time principal of Sandford NS and a member of the NCCA Irish Committee, and Carol Revington, who was for many years principal of Zion NS and is currently principal of Delgany NS. She has given tremendous service to the Church of Ireland on education committees, including the board of education. Both entered in 1970. Also there was Sally Sheils (née Davis) (1969–72), who entered from Alexandra College. She succeeded her father as principal of Sandford NS and in 1984 became principal of the North Dublin National School Project. A dedicated member of the INTO, from 1976 to 1984 she was an INTO delegate to the Dublin Council of Trade Unions of which she was vice-president from 1981 to 1984. In 1989 she was elected to the central executive committee of the INTO. Six years later, she became one of the youngest teachers, and one of the few females, to become president of the INTO in its long history.

FACING AN UNCERTAIN FUTURE WITH MISS ALLEN'S RETIREMENT

As Miss Allen's retirement approached, the future of Coláiste Moibhí was again uncertain. Aware that finding a new principal could be problematic, the board of governors of CICE undertook a review of the work of the two colleges. In November 1981 a memo was drawn up by the principal of CICE, Dr Kenneth Milne,[6] highlighting the shortcomings of Coláiste Moibhí as a secondary school, particularly the small number of pupils, the limited curriculum and the high dependency on part-time staff. It also highlighted the expectation of gains for CICE should the smaller college be discontinued.[7] These included the appointment of an additional lecturer to CICE to cope with the college's need to keep abreast of expanding curricular demands, particularly in audio-visual training. A further consideration was the provision of extra residential accommodation at a time when CICE third-year students, accustomed to 'living out', were finding it increasingly difficult to obtain suitable accommodation. Following consideration of the memo, the board of governors passed the following resolution unanimously:

1. Subject to a suitable alternative scheme for the maintenance of adequate recruitment to the college having been agreed with the Department, Coláiste Moibhí should be discontinued on Miss Allen's retirement.
2. The Department be asked to sanction the appointment, on Miss Allen's retirement, of an assistant lecturer to teach environmental studies and to have responsibility for audio-visual aids training in the college.

Subsequently, a scholarship scheme was devised whereby aspiring CICE candidates of modest means would be accommodated in existing Protestant secondary schools. This proposal was one of a number discussed by a deputation from CICE which met with senior officials of the Department in February 1982. The deputation emphasised the importance of CICE to the Protestant community and the need to ensure its standards were commensurate with standards in similar institutions. It also requested the appointment of an extra

---

6. For biographical details see the Appendix.
7. Minutes of Board of Governors of CICE, December 1981.

lecturer. In response the officials urged the deputation to request Miss Allen to postpone retirement for a year so that greater consideration could be given to the future of Coláiste Moibhí. With regard to Coláiste Moibhí's limited curriculum and its dependency on part-time staff, the Department proposed that these matters could be resolved by involving CICE staff in teaching in the college. The scholarship scheme was dismissed on the grounds of the inadequacy of Irish teaching at Protestant secondary schools. A decision on student accommodation was deferred to a later date.

Subsequent discussions[8] were unable to change the Department's decisions regarding the closure proposal, and the two colleges continued to be accommodated in the same premises as previously. Despite the board of governors' dissatisfaction with the Department's responses, the appointment of a new principal and of one full-time staff member was sanctioned in March 1983. Thus Coláiste Moibhí survived efforts by the Church of Ireland to close it down and continued into the 1990s. As a result of the Department's decision to involve a greater number of CICE staff in teaching in Coláiste Moibhí, classes were taken by Elisabeth McArthur in art, Kathleen Desmond in drama, Winifred Hughes in singing, while Elaine Browne taught instrumental music. From 1984–87, Michael Burrows, presently Bishop of Cashel & Ossory, acted as housemaster. A number of new teachers joined the staff, including Mary Hawkins and Fionóla Ni Chonghaile.

As Miss Allen retired she could look back over more than 30 years as principal. There had been long periods of relative stability both in Shankill and Rathmines. Yet behind the calm appearance of serenity there had been times of great stress particularly when the future of the college seemed under threat. During those three decades the college's role had changed a number of times. When she assumed the principalship in 1952 Coláiste Moibhí had been part of the preparatory system. Nine years later it had become the sole remaining preparatory college in the state. Then in 1968 it was transformed into the juniorate of the Church of Ireland Training College (later the Church of Ireland College of Education). Never daunted, Miss Allen was fearless in confronting those who would question the need for Coláiste Moibhí, and her dedication to education through Irish was nowhere more clearly demonstrated than when she postponed retirement for a year so that the college's future could be assured.

---

8. *Ibid.*

CHAPTER ELEVEN

The Final Years

The fifth principal: dedicated Gaeilgeoir
RISTEÁRD GILTRAP 1984–95

On Miss Allen's retirement in 1984, James Richard Taylor (Risteárd) Giltrap was appointed principal. Like Miss Allen, he was a native of Co. Wicklow who grew up at Glasheen, near Blessington, not far from where she had lived as a child. From a farming background, Giltrap was educated at The King's Hospital and studied English and Irish at Trinity College, Dublin. In 1955 he won the Thaddeus O'Mahoney Prize, awarded to the student with the highest marks in Irish in first year. In 1958 he graduated with a BA degree. He taught at Hibernian Marine School, Clontarf, while studying for the higher diploma in education, which he was awarded by the university the following year. That same year he became an Irish teacher in Wesley College, where eventually he was appointed head of the Irish department. While teaching he completed studies for An Teastas i dTeagasc na Gaeilge and An Ceardteastas Gaeilge, awarded by the Department of Education. His post-graduate studies included the two-year course for An Teastas i Litríocht na Gaeilge, organised by Prof. Tomás Ó Fiaich, (later Cardinal) at St Patrick's College, Maynooth.

Throughout his teaching career Giltrap was always cognisant of changes in the teaching of Irish and was deeply involved in the marking of Irish at the Leaving Certificate Examination, both as an examiner and as an advising examiner. Keenly interested in the history of the Irish language, his book, *An Ghaeilge in Eaglais na hÉireann,* for which he was awarded a prize at Comórtas an Oireachtais, was published in 1990. From 1995 until his retirement in 1999 he was an assistant lecturer in Irish at CICE. An active member of Cumann Gaelach na hEaglaise, he encouraged his students to participate in its services.

During his time as principal, Giltrap introduced new subjects to the curriculum including French, German, biology and computer studies. Visits to

58 Risteárd Giltrap, Principal Coláiste Moibhí, 1984–95.

the Dunquin Gaeltacht became regular features of college life. There, educational activities were organised by Micheál Ó Dúshláine, principal of Scoil Dhúnchaoin. In keeping with the college's focus on Irish, Giltrap established An Tobar, a monthly debating society where topical issues were formally debated. Occasionally other schools were invited to participate or well-known people were guest speakers. In May 1987 a perpetual trophy commemorating Lil Duncan, donated by Cumann Gaelach na hEaglaise to the society, was won by Linda Treacy for her outstanding contribution to the debating society. Other societies were An Cumann Gregg, organised by Harold Hislop, and later by Ivor Hayes, to engage with cultural and historical issues, while An Cumann Béarla catered for dramatic activities. For a number of years Harold Hislop was a housemaster at the college while teaching at Whitechurch NS where he later became principal. In 1990 he was awarded a PhD degree by TCD. In 1996 he was seconded to the NCCA and two years later, following a short period as secretary of the Church of Ireland board of education, he became a member of the inspectorate. Joyce Senior, who was a student during the college's final phase at Rathmines was also awarded a doctorate for her study on children with epilepsy.

In the early 1990s the future of Coláiste Moibhí was again under review. This time it was the Department which wanted closure. According to writer Risteárd Ó Glaisne,[1] rumours of the threat to the college spread amongst Irish language organisations and enthusiasts. But unable to obtain definite information, they were led to believe that the matter would be best dealt with in private, and that a public outcry might endanger the college's position. So negotiations between the Department and the church authorities continued with little publicity, eventually resulting in an announcement by Archbishop Donald Caird in October 1994[2] that the college would close the following June. As part of the closure negotiations, an enrichment

---

1. Ó Glaisne, *Coláiste Moibhí*, p. 193.
2. *Irish Times,* 12 October 1994.

59 Coláiste Moibhí debating team, winners of the Leinster final Gael-Linn debating Competition, 1992.
Front: Emma de Phóil, Colm Breathnach (múinteoir) Norma Ní Stíobhaird,
Back: Treasa Ní Bhustaird, Priscilla Nic an Iomaire, Julie Ní Mhofait. *CICE Archives.*

programme would be put in place in CICE to ensure that a high standard of Irish was maintained. This would include the appointment of an extra lecturer to oversee the enrichment programme. The closure was a personal source of sadness for Dr Caird, who was well known for his commitment to the Irish language.

Great sadness was also expressed by the Past Students' Association of CICE. In a press statement issued on 13 October 1994 by Dr Harold Hislop, president, and Eileen Jackson, vice-president of the Past Students' Association of CICE, it expressed concern that the standard of Irish in Protestant primary schools might be 'adversely affected by this development'. It deplored the lack of open discussion about the college in 'the wider Church of Ireland community', and called upon the Minister for Education 'to instigate a thorough review of the proposal, bearing in mind, not simply financial considerations, but also the wider social, educational and cultural role of Coláiste Moibhí.'

The closure decision, however, had the full support of the Minister for Education, Niamh Bhreathnach. She told the Dáil[3] that the college's 'continuation could not be justified on either financial or educational grounds'. She also revealed that the proposal for closure had first come from the Church of Ireland authorities in 1981. This proved the death-knell for the college. Despite its remarkable success in achieving high marks at Irish in the Leaving Certificate Examination, the only 'A' school under Protestant management finally closed in June 1995.

A Thanksgiving Service to mark Coláiste Moibhí's closure was held in the chapel at CICE on 23 June 1995. The Dublin and Glendalough Diocesan Magazine, *Church Review,* reported that those present at the service, conducted entirely in Irish, included the secretary of the Department, Dr Don Thornhill, inspectors Seán Hunt and Micheál Ó Fiannachta; Conradh na Gaeilge president Gearóid Ó Cearalláin, and past president Proinsias MacAonghusa. Also present were Daithí Ó Maolchoille from Cumann Gaelach na hEaglaise, and Deputy Trevor Sargent of the Green Party. Students from the early years of Coláiste Moibhí who were present included Dora Smeaton and Amy Phillips (1927), Richard Rowntree (1928), Patricia Aitkins (1929), Rose Roberts (1930), and her brother, Victor Wheatly (1934). Seven of the eight pupils of the college's final class were also present, Louise and Ruth Moffett, Deirdre Waters, Clodagh Chapman, Gwyn Ó Murchú, Georgina Nicholls and Ruth Gentleman.

In his address, Dr Caird, who joined Cumann Gaelach na hEaglaise in 1943, recalled how, as a pupil of Wesley College, he first encountered Coláiste Moibhí students at an Irish service in St Patrick's Cathedral in the early 1940s. He gave this explanation for the closure:

Thosnaigh an Roinn Oideachais ag cur brú ar Bhord Bainistíochta an Choláiste é a dhúnadh, toisc a chostaisí a bhí sé é a choiméad ar siúl. Bhí an costas de réir

---

3. *Dáil Reports*, 4 July 1995.

oiread an duine ag éirí an t-am ar fad go dtí go raibh sé ró-ard don Roinn é a dhíol. Sheas an Bhord i gcoinne dúnadh an Choláiste go dána chomh fada agus ab fhéidir leo é, ach tháinig an t-am ab éigean géilleadh dá thoil, mar bhí greim na Roinne ar an gciste agus bhí brí a cúise ag éirí níos soiléire an t-am ar fad.

The Department of Education began to press the board of management of the college to close it because it was too costly to keep it going. The cost per student was rising all the time until it was too high for the Department to pay. The board resisted the closure for as long as it could but eventually it had to yield because the Department's grip on the purse strings was tightening and the sense of its case was becoming clearer as time went on.

Past students from each of Coláiste Moibhí's former locations led prayers and reflections about their time at the college. The *Church Review* reported:

> Through all the memories there were common themes: the lasting friendships; the emphasis on freedom; the personal enrichment gained through learning Irish; all summed up in three words: *cairdeas, craic and cultúr.*

For the Protestant minority, the closure meant the end of a school which made one of the most significant contributions to Protestant education in the state. Without the preparatory college CITC could not have survived, and without Protestant teachers the minority's separate system of education would have ceased. Had this happened the minority culture could not have survived. By producing teachers with an easy fluency in Irish, Coláiste Moibhí helped to overcome the psychological barrier in this area for Protestants, and enabled the minority to become integrated in the new state.

Most of the college's students stayed in primary teaching, though a small number who went on to graduate, changed to teaching in second-level schools. Indeed, according to research conducted by Risteárd Giltrap in 1992, 75 per cent of all teachers trained at CITC and CICE since the foundation of the state came from Coláiste Moibhí. Furthermore, former preparatory college students were usually among the prize-winners in the training college. The vast majority of these students gave a lifetime of service to their pupils and to the Church of Ireland, and were leaders in all kinds of community activities.

The development of Coláiste Moibhí in its later years demonstrated how the preparatory colleges could have been adapted to suit the changed circumstances of the country in the latter half of the twentieth century. The college's success was based on the 'total immersion' method of language learning. This was a costly process in the case of Coláiste Moibhí, as it catered only for pupils from the Protestant community. With greater numbers, less expensive methods of funding similar schools might have been devised. But the success of any educational institution is dependent on obtaining dedicated teachers. Gifted people such as George Ruth, John Kyle, Lil Duncan, Gladys Allen, Risteárd Giltrap and their colleagues are essential, for without their devotion and idealism Coláiste Moibhí could not have survived.

An Uimhir Chláracháin	Bliain an Scrúdúcháin Iontrála	AINM	Dáta Beirthe	Uimhir san Scrúdúchán Iontrála	
133	1926	nic Seáin, Máire a.	3/8/10	2024	George Johnston Nora Naylor
134	„	ní Rógáin, Síle	24/4/11	2566	James Rogan
135.	„	ní Cnaimsíge, Cáitlín	10/9/10	2621	Bridget Bone
136	„	ní Gallcobair, Mairgréad	7/10/11	2631	Mrs Kate Gal
137	„	nic Giolla Ceapa, Mairg̃ a.	14/4/11	2634	James Kerr, R. Kerr a Reils
138	„	nic Parsín, Úine	5/10/10	2636	Mrs Bol ? Charles Mc
139	„	nic Giolla Eáin, Úine X	10/2/12	2640	Sophia Mc
140	„	ní Connaig, Úine R.I.P.	6/10/10	2646	Seán Ua Oi.
141	„	ní Suilleabáin, Eibhlín	6/10/10	2659	Timothy O'Su
142	„	ní Míoscáin, Gráinne	9/9/11	2702	Denis Mees
143	„	ní Donnbáin, Siobán	2/10/11	2761	Annie Don
144	„	nic Cába, Ríca	4/7/11	2791	Thomas Mc
145	„	ní Ragallaig, Nóra	1/4/11	2836	Joseph O'Re
146	„	ní Droigneáin, Mairgréad R.I.P.	4/10/11	2976	Micheal O
147	„	ní Lochlainn, Máire R.I.P.	15/5/11	3516	Mrs M. Loi Michael Lo
148	„	ní Seanáin, Eibhlís C.	22/10/10	3523	Thomas L.

60 The first page of the roll-book of Coláiste Bhríde. *Courtesy Cumann Staire is Seanchais Chloich Cheann Fhaola.*

PART III

Postscript
Irish today a living language

Since the decision to end the preparatory system, there has been an unprecedented number of changes in Irish education, reflecting the growth in political and public awareness of the importance of education. One of the areas of greatest change has been in the teaching of Irish. The closure of the preparatory colleges heralded a downgrading of the dominant role of the language in education generally, and particularly in the training colleges, where teaching ceased to be entirely through Irish. Despite these changes, however, the language continues to be a core subject in the primary school curriculum.

This position is reflected in recruitment, where the requirements for entry to teacher training include grade C or higher at honours level Irish in the Leaving Certificate Examination, for which a reasonable standard of fluency in the language is necessary. Furthermore, research in the area of language teaching has shown that the best way to learn a language is by the 'total immersion' method.[1] It was to this that the preparatory system owed its success, as each preparatory college was a 'mini-Gaeltacht'. Provision is still made today for student-teachers to learn Irish by this method, though such learning is undertaken in more realistic conditions. As part of their course, they spend some time in the Gaeltacht. While this is the best way to learn the Irish language, the amount of time spent by student-teachers in the Gaeltacht cannot compare with a four-year course in a preparatory college.

Since the preparatory system ended, it is generally accepted that the standard of Irish on entry to training colleges has declined,[2] though considerable gains have been made in other areas. Students entering training are more rounded people, having undertaken a five or six-year Leaving Certificate course, and with the expansion of the curriculum at second-level they are

---

1. Mairéad Ní Mhurchú, 'Canadian Immersion Education and its relevance to Gaelscoileanna', *Oideas* 43, Samraidh, 1995, p. 62.
2. Coolahan, *Irish Education: history and structure*, p. 225.

far better educated. Furthermore, they have chosen of their own accord to enter training and have made their choice at a more mature age though, due to the way in which the points system operates, primary teaching may not have been their first choice.

The teaching profession has seen considerable change, and the status of the primary teacher has been much enhanced. Nowadays, primary teachers undertake a three-year course and graduate with a university degree. In addition, increased resources have transformed the primary school, where conditions have been considerably improved by reductions in the pupil-teacher ratio. Increased promotion prospects and improved salaries have made primary teaching a much sought-after career and there is no shortage of candidates seeking to enter training. Unlike the past, when the majority of primary teachers could have been expected to teach for approximately 40 years until retirement, there are greater career prospects for qualified primary teachers. Now, it is possible to move to other areas of education, such as remedial, special or adult education, which were unheard of in the early years of the state.

At the beginning of the third millennium, efforts to preserve and revive the Irish language had been in progress for over 100 years. The language movement has gone through many different stages since the foundation of the Gaelic League in 1893 and, at times, the condition of the language has been so weak that pessimists have pronounced its death. Such pronouncements have been premature, however, and though the population of the Gaeltacht had shrunk to approximately 21,000[3] in 2000, an estimated 50,000 adults outside the Gaeltacht speak Irish daily. In addition, Irish is taught in all primary and second-level schools throughout the state, and there are few people in the country, apart from recent immigrants, who do not have some knowledge of the language. There is also a major difference in the way the language is taught today; the introduction of oral examinations at the Leaving Certificate Examination in 1958 led to the development of summer courses for students in the Gaeltacht. Based on the 'total immersion' method of language learning, they are greatly enjoyed by participants, some of whom gain an abiding interest in the language. This new emphasis on speaking the language has helped it to survive.

The development of Irish language radio and television stations, such as TG4, Raidió na Gaeltachta and Raidió na Life, has enhanced the language's prestige and the fact that it is now possible to communicate in Irish using the most modern technology shows its capacity to adapt and survive. There has also been considerable progress at official level. The Official Languages Act became law in 2003. It provides a statutory framework for the delivery of services through the Irish language. The first Irish Language Commissioner, Seán Ó Cuirreáin, was appointed in February 2004. The following year, the standing of the language was further enhanced following a unanimous decision

---

3. Uiseann Mac Dubhghaill, 'Uair na cinniúna don Ghaeltacht', *Cuisle,* Feabhra 1999, p. 10.

AN GHAELTACHT

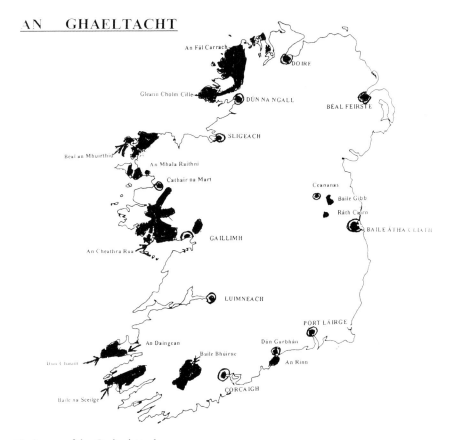

An Fál Carrach

DOIRE

Gleann Cholm Cille

DÚN NA NGALL

BÉAL FEIRSTE

SLIGEACH

Béal an Mhuirthid

An Mhala Raithní

Cathair na Mart

Ceanannas

Baile Gibb

Ráth Cairn

BAILE ÁTHA CLIATH

GAILLIMH

An Cheathrú Rua

LUIMNEACH

PORT LÁIRGE

An Daingean

Dún Garbhán

Baile Bhúirne

An Rinn

Dún Chaoin

CORCAIGH

Baile na Scéilge

61 A map of the Gaeltacht today.

by European Union foreign ministers that Irish will become the 21st official working language of the European Union on 1 January 2007. The improvement in the country's economy and increased foreign travel have effected a change in the public's attitude and strengthened awareness of the value of the language. In addition, the growth in the use of Welsh, Scots Gaelic and other Celtic languages, has brought about a new interest in Irish, as has an increased interest amongst the public in Northern Ireland. Furthermore, the need to find a national identity in an increasingly globalised world has made many look at the language afresh. Further evidence of increased interest is reflected throughout the education system, particularly in the dramatic growth throughout the whole island of Naíonraí (all-Irish pre-schools), Gaelscoileanna (all-Irish primary schools), and all-Irish post primary schools. In addition third-level institutions are providing an increased number of courses through Irish. Typical of these is Dublin City University, from which the first batch of students graduated in 1998 with B Sc degrees in finance, computing, enterprise and European languages, after a four-year course taught through Irish. There have been calls for an all-Irish university. Without the contribution of the preparatory colleges in the early years of the state, the language would be in a much weaker condition and arguably unable to respond to the upsurge of interest which has been a characteristic of the last decade of the twentieth century.

Though the colleges ceased to function as preparatory colleges in 1961, some of them are still in use for educational purposes of different kinds. These include Coláiste Mhuire, which continued as an all-Irish girls' boarding school run by the Mercy Order until 1990, when it was sold to the local community. Since then it has continued as a co-educational 'A' school with a lay principal. Similarly, Coláiste Íde is still an all-Irish girls' boarding school, though with the departure of the Mercy Order from the college in 1995, a parents' group has had to struggle hard to keep it open. Coláiste Éinde also continued as an all-Irish boys' school until 1970, though an 'all subjects through Irish' stream continued until 1984. In 1992, the school became co-educational with its first lay principal in 1993. As it celebrated its 75th anniversary in 2003, Ms Siobhán Quinn completed her first year as the first female principal.

The other colleges had more chequered careers and two of them, Coláiste Íosagáin and Coláiste Bhríde, are no longer educational institutions, though plans to use Coláiste Íosagáin as part of a third-level institution are under consideration. On ceasing to be a preparatory college, Coláiste Íosagáin continued as a boys' secondary school until 1988. The building then lay largely unused until the end of the 1990s when Udarás na Gaeltachta took possession of it. Proposals for its future use being considered include developing it in conjunction with UCC and the Department of Education.

When the Loreto Order left Coláiste Bhríde in 1961, it became a secondary boarding school for boys, Holy Cross College. This, however, closed in 1985 and a local voluntary co-operative, Comharchumann Estáit Bhaile Uí Chonaill Teo., was founded. With assistance from Udarás na Gaeltachta and the Regional Development Fund, it bought the house and lands. Unfortunately plans to refurbish the house and to restore the garden have not been successful. The sixth college, Coláiste Chaoimhín, which closed in 1939, was taken over by the Department of Defence for administrative purposes and is still used in this way though it retains the name Coláiste Chaoimhín. The final college, Coláiste Moibhí, closed in 1995. Its classrooms at the Church of Ireland College of Education at Rathmines in Dublin are currently used to train teachers in Special Education.

The imposing buildings, the former homes of the colleges, stand as a memorial to the preparatory system, which from 1926 until its demise in 1961, played an important role in the recruitment of primary teachers. But of far greater importance to the life of the Irish nation was the role played by their students in the promotion and sustaining of the Irish language in the early decades of the new state. That the language is in such a vibrant state is in no small measure due to them.

APPENDIX
Select biographies

Short biographies of people mentioned in the text

Frank Aiken (1898–1983), revolutionary and politician. He took part in the War of Independence and the civil war. He was chief of staff of the IRA until 1925. His political career began in 1927 when he was first elected to the Dáil and lasted until his retirement in 1973. He held several cabinet posts including Tánaiste from 1959 to 1969. A dedicated Gaeilgeoir, Irish was the language of his home.

Piaras Beaslaoi (1897–1965), Gaelic scholar and writer. A member of the Gaelic League, he took part in the Easter Rising. A journalist, he was editor of *An t-Óglach*. In 1918, he was elected MP for East Kerry. He took the Treaty side in the civil war and later served in the Free State army. In 1924 he left politics.

Ernest Blythe or **Earnán de Blaghd** (1889–1975), revolutionary and politician. From Northern Ireland, the son of a Church of Ireland father and Presbyterian mother, he was educated at the local primary school. In 1904, he joined the civil service in Dublin. Later he became a journalist. In 1913, he moved to Co. Kerry to learn Irish. He was a member of the Gaelic League, Sinn Féin and the Irish Republican Brotherhood. An organiser for the IRB, he was imprisoned several times and thereby prevented from taking part in the 1916 Rising. He was Minister for Trade and Commerce in both the First and Second Dáil from 1919 to 1922. He held a number of Cabinet posts in the Cumann na nGaedheal Governments, including Minister for Local Government, 1922–23, and Minister for Finance, 1923–32, Vice-President of the Executive Council and Minister for Posts and Telegraphs, 1927–1932. In 1933 he lost his Dáil seat and served in the Senate from 1934 to 1936, when he left politics. He had a long association with the Abbey Theatre where he encouraged the production of plays in Irish. From 1946–55 he was President of Comhdháil Náisiúnta na Gaeilge. In 1957 he published his two-volume autobiography, *Trasna na Bóinne*. In the sixties he was a member of the RTE Authority and of the Commission for the Restoration of the Irish Language.

Michael Browne (1896–1980), bishop of Galway. Born in Westport, Co Mayo, he was educated at St Jarlath's College, Tuam, and St Patrick's College, Maynooth, where subsequently he was professor of theology from 1921 to 1937. Known as a Fianna Fáil sympathise, he supported de Valera during the crucial mid-twenties when Fianna Fáil was coming into being. Despite his turbulent temperament he was appointed bishop of Galway in 1937 and was chairman of the Commission on Vocational Organisation set up by de Valera in 1939. During his period as bishop many new churches and schools were built, the most remarkable of these being Galway Cathedral which opened in 1966. His outspoken comments on public issues involved him in frequent controversy which he seemed to relish.

Noel Browne (1915–1997), radical reformer and politician. Born in Waterford, he qualified as a doctor in 1940. He was deeply committed to the eradication of tuberculosis which was widespread in Ireland at that time. Both his parents and two siblings died from the disease, and he himself was diagnosed with it as a student. A member of Clann na Poblachta, he was appointed Minister for Health on his first day in the Dáil in February 1948. As minister he carried out a successful campaign against TB. In 1950 he proposed introducing a free medical scheme for mothers and children. This was so strongly opposed by the medical profession and the hierarchy that the government withdrew its support from Browne, who resigned. Subsequently, he published the correspondence between himself and the bishops and the matter became a *cause célèbre*. He continued in politics as a member of different parties until retirement in 1982.

Cathal Brugha or **Charles Burgess** (1874–1922), soldier and revolutionary. A native of Dublin, he took part in the 1916 Rising. In 1918 he was elected a Sinn Féin MP for Waterford. He presided over the First Dáil in 1919 and was Minister for Defence from 1919 to 1922. Strongly anti-Treaty, he was killed in the civil war in July 1922.

Edward Byrne (1872–1940), Catholic Archbishop of Dublin. Born in Dublin, he was ordained in 1895 and served as curate in a number of Dublin parishes. From 1901 to 1904, he was vice-rector of the Irish College, Rome. Subsequently, he spent 16 years as curate at the Pro-Cathedral before being appointed an auxiliary bishop of Dublin. From 1921 to 1940 he was archbishop.

Donald Caird (1925–), Gaeilgeoir and Church of Ireland Archbishop of Dublin. A native of Dublin, he was educated at Wesley College and TCD where he was an outstanding student. He was ordained deacon in 1950 (priest in 1951) and served in different positions before becoming dean of

Ossory in 1969. The following year he was elected bishop of Limerick, Ardfert and Aghadoe. Six years later he was translated to Meath and Kildare as bishop. In 1985 he was elected archbishop of Dublin, a post he held until his retirement from the full-time ministry in 1996. Well known for his commitment to the Irish language he joined Cumann Gaelach na hEaglaise (The Irish Guild of the Church) in 1943.

Michael Collins (1890–1922), revolutionary and politician. He was born and educated in Cork. While working in the Post Office in London he joined the Gaelic League and the IRB. He took part in the 1916 Rising and in its aftermath was arrested and interned in Frongoch camp in North Wales. Later he became the leader of the IRB. During the War of Independence as director of intelligence he organised many clandestine operations against the British authorities. For these activities he gained renown as a folk-hero. His political career began in 1918 when he was elected MP for South Cork. In the First Dáil he was Minister for Finance. While de Valera was in America he became the *de facto* leader of the movement for independence. He was a member of the Irish delegation which negotiated the Anglo-Irish Treaty in 1921. The Treaty was accepted by the Dáil but rejected by a sizeable minority led by de Valera. This was to lead to the civil war. With the establishment of the Irish Free State, Collins became commander-in-chief of the Irish Free State Army and led the Government side in the civil war. He was killed in an ambush in Cork in August 1922.

Éamonn Coogan (1896–1948), deputy commissioner, Garda Síochána. From Castlecomer, Co. Kilkenny, he joined the Irish Volunteers in 1914. He was a civil servant in the Department of Local Government under W.T. Cosgrave when he was appointed assistant commissioner, Garda Síochána in 1922. Strongly committed to the ideal of an unarmed police force, he was one of the leaders of the organisation during the critical early years of the new state. On leaving the police he entered politics and was elected TD for Carlow-Kilkenny in 1944.

Timothy Corcoran (1872–1943), Jesuit priest and educationalist. Educated at Clongowes Wood College, where he was an outstanding student, he entered the Irish Jesuit Novitiate in 1890, and taught classics and history at his old school from 1894 to 1901. He studied philosophy at Louvain from 1901 to 1904. In 1903 he graduated from the Royal University of Ireland with a first-class honours degree in history, and was awarded the Royal University medal for Latin and English verse. Three years later, he obtained the higher diploma in education and was presented with a special gold medal for outstanding results. He studied theology at Milltown Park from 1906 to 1909, when he was appointed professor of education at UCD. In 1911, he received a LittD degree.

William T. Cosgrave (1880–1965), revolutionary and politician. Born in Dublin and educated at James's Street CBS, he was first elected a member of Dublin City Council in 1909. He joined the Volunteers in 1913 and took part in the 1916 Rising for which he was sentenced to death. The sentence was commuted and he was interned in Wales for a period. He won a by-election for Sinn Féin in 1917 and was Minister for Local Government in the First Dáil in 1919. A strong supporter of the Treaty, he became acting chairman of the Provisional Government following the death of Collins. Two months later he became President of the Executive Council. During the difficult early days of the new state he put great emphasis on the maintenance of law and order, and it was largely due to his courage and leadership that the fledging state survived. In 1932, following the defeat of his government, he showed great statesmanship when he handed over the leadership of the country to a Fianna Fáil Government and led his party into opposition. The following year he founded Fine Gael and was leader of the opposition until he retired from politics in 1944.

John A. Costello (1891–1976), lawyer, politician and taoiseach. He was born in Dublin and educated at O'Connell School and UCD. He was called to the Bar in 1914. His political career began in 1933, when he was elected to the Dáil. In 1948 he was asked to become taoiseach of an inter-party government as it was felt that he was the only person who could unite a number of diverse political groups. This government lasted until 1951. From 1954 to 1957 he led the second Inter-party Government.

Thomas Derrig or **Tomás Deirg** (1887–1956), revolutionary and politician. A commerce graduate of UCG and former headmaster of Ballina Technical School, his impeccable republican credentials included deportation and internment following the 1916 Rising, several terms of imprisonment and a period on hunger-strike in 1923. His political career began with his election as Sinn Féin MP for Mayo in 1918. A founder member of Fianna Fáil, his cabinet posts included Education, Posts and Telegraphs, and Lands.

Éamon de Valera (1882–1975), revolutionary, politician and statesman. He was born in New York, and grew up in Buree, Co. Limerick. He was educated at Blackrock College and UCD, where he studied mathematics. Later he became a teacher. He joined the Gaelic League in 1910 and the Irish Volunteers in 1913. He was commandant of the garrison at Boland's Mills during the 1916 Rising. After the Rising he was sentenced to death but was reprieved. As the senior surviving figure from the Rising, he became the leader of the republican cause. In 1917, he was elected president of Sinn Féin.

That same year he was elected MP for Clare. Following the War of Independence he was involved in negotiating a settlement with England, but refused to be part of a delegation which went to London for talks with the

British Government in 1921. His subsequent refusal to accept the Treaty, which was approved by the Dáil, led to the civil war. In 1926 he founded Fianna Fáil, which soon became the largest political party in the country. In 1932, the party was elected to government for the first time. From then until his retirement from party politics in 1959, he played a major role in Irish public life. He was elected the third President of Ireland in 1959, a post he held for two terms until 1973.

Frank Fahy (1880–1953), teacher and politician. From Co. Galway, he was educated at Mungret College, Limerick and UCG where he obtained a BA degree and the Higher Diploma in Education. He taught in the Christian Brothers' School in Tralee and later in Castleknock College. In 1927 he qualified as a barrister. His political career began in 1918 when he was elected Sinn Féin MP for Galway. In the First Dáil he was assistant to 'Sceilg,' the Minister for Irish. He took part in the First National Programme Conference in 1922. From 1927 to 1932 he was shadow Minister for Education. When de Valera formed his first government in 1932, Fahy was appointed Ceann Comhairle, a post he held until his death.

Desmond Fitzgerald (1888–1947), revolutionary and politician. Born into an Irish family living in London, where he learned Irish at Gaelic League classes. Later he moved to the Kerry Gaeltacht where he joined the IRB and organised the Irish Volunteers. He was imprisoned for sedition in 1915. Both he and his wife, Mabel McConnell, an Ulster Presbyterian, fought in the GPO during the 1916 Rising. Subsequently, he was interned in England. His political career began in 1918 when he was elected as a Sinn Féin MP. He was director of publicity during the War of Independence. A supporter of the Treaty, he was Minister for External Affairs from 1922 to 1927 and Minister for Defence from 1927 to 1932. He continued as a TD for a further five years and was a senator from 1938 to 1943. A scholarly man, he co-founded the Irish Academy of Letters in 1923.

John Allen Fitzgerald Gregg (1873–1961), Church of Ireland Archbishop of Dublin 1920–1939. Born in England, though his family was Irish, he was educated at Cambridge University and TCD. He was ordained in 1896 and served in parishes in Ballymena and Cork. From 1911 to 1915 he was Archbishop King's professor of divinity in TCD. In 1915 he was elected bishop of Ossory, Ferns and Leighlin. Five years later he became archbishop of Dublin. Gregg is generally acknowledged to have given courageous and wise leadership during a period of political turmoil. From 1939 to 1959 he was archbishop of Armagh.

Arthur Griffith (1871–1922), revolutionary and politician. A native of Dublin, he was educated at Strand Street CBS. On leaving school, he worked as a printer and journalist. Subsequently, he joined the Gaelic

League and the IRB. Following a period in South Africa in 1898 he returned to Ireland where he edited a series of newspapers including the *United Irishman*, and *Sinn Féin*. In 1905 he founded Sinn Féin. Its aims were to achieve a 'dual monarchy' between Britain and Ireland based on the Austro-Hungarian model and the establishment of a national assembly in Dublin. Through his writings he advocated passive resistance to British rule in Ireland. Though he took no part in the 1916 Rising, he was imprisoned as an agitator. In 1917 he was elected MP for East Cavan. He led the Irish delegation that negotiated the Treaty in 1921 and was President of Dáil Éireann until his sudden death in August 1922.

Michael Hayes or **Micheál Ó hAodha** (1889–1976), politician and academic. A native of Dublin, he was educated at Synge Street CBS and UCD, where he later became a lecturer in French. He took part in the 1916 Rising but escaped capture. In 1920, he was arrested and interned. The following year he was elected to the Dáil and appointed Minister for Education in 1922. He voted for the Treaty and subsequently became Ceann Comhairle in the first Free State Dáil, a post he held until 1932. He failed to be re-elected to the Dáil in 1933 but later was elected to the Senate, where he was a member until 1965. He was appointed professor of Irish at UCD in 1951.

Patrick Hillery (1923–), doctor and politician. He was a member of the Dáil from 1951–73. His cabinet posts included Education, Industry and Commerce, Labour, and Foreign Affairs. He was the country's first EU commissioner from 1973 to 1976, when he became President of Ireland, a post he held until 1990.

Dónall Lucius Hurley (1883–1972), Gaeilgeoir and Christian Brother. Born near Bandon, Co. Cork, he was from a family with a strong nationalist tradition. As a Christian Brother, he taught for 25 years in schools in different parts of the country, including Drogheda, Ennis and Clonmel, before being appointed the first principal of Coláiste Chaoimhín in 1927. Well known for his dedication to the language revival, he spent six years at the college. Subsequently, he held posts in a number of places including Dundalk and Our Lady's Mount, Cork, where he worked from 1952 to 1969.

Douglas Hyde or **Dúbhglas de h-Íde** (1860–1949), scholar, writer and first President of Ireland. He was born at Frenchpark, Co. Roscommon. Son of a Church of Ireland clergyman, he was educated at home and at Trinity College where he was an outstanding student. Originally, he intended to follow his father into the ministry but changed his mind. In 1888, he was conferred with an LLD degree. He taught in New Brunswick for a year before returning to Roscommon. There he devoted himself to literary pursuits and the revival of Irish. His first collection of folk-tales, *Beside the Fire,* was published in 1889 and *Love Songs of Connacht* in 1893, the year in which the Gaelic League was founded with Hyde as president.

In its early years he played a dominant role and the League was successful in raising the profile of the language and making it a vital force in the movement for national revival. His 1892 lecture on 'The Necessity for De-Anglicising the Irish Nation' marked a watershed in Irish history. In 1909 he was appointed professor of Modern Irish in UCD, a post he held until retirement in 1932. Unhappy with the League's involvement in the separatist movement, he resigned the presidency in 1915. Subsequently, he concentrated on his academic pursuits. When the office of President of Ireland was created, he was unanimously chosen by all parties and held office as president until 1945.

James Alexander Hamilton Irwin (1876–1954), Presbyterian minister and Irish nationalist. From Co Derry, he was educated at Magee College where he obtained a BA degree in 1900. Later he received an MA degree from the Royal University of Ireland, a BD degree from the Presbyterian Faculty of Ireland and a PhD degree from UCD. Following his ordination in 1903 he was minister at Killead, Co. Antrim, until 1926 when he moved to Scotland. He returned to Ireland in 1935 and ministered at Lucan and Naas. He was Moderator of the Synod of Dublin in 1942. In an effort to show that there was no sectarianism among Irish nationalists he travelled to America to support de Valera in 1920 and accompanied him on a speaking tour in the US. The two became personal friends. Irwin was a member of the Executive of Fianna Fáil from 1945 to 1954. In 1950 he received an honorary DLitt from the National University of Ireland.

Thomas Ryder Johnston (1872–1963), trade unionist and politician. A native of Liverpool, as a young man he was greatly influenced by James Larkin, and in 1913 he moved to Dublin to work with James Connolly and Larkin in the Irish Trade Union movement. From 1914 to 1918 he was president of the Irish Trade Union Congress. He was first elected to the Dáil in 1922 and was leader of Labour deputies in the Dáil until 1927. He lost his seat at the second election that year. Though no longer in the Dáil, he remained politically active until 1961.

Seán Lemass (1899–1971), revolutionary, politician and taoiseach. A native of Dublin, he left school at 15 to join the Volunteers. His republican career included participation in the 1916 Rising and the War of Independence, during which he was interned. He fought on the anti-Treaty side in the civil war during which he was captured and imprisoned. Gradually he moved away from militant republicanism and developed a reputation as a politician for his organising ability and pragmatic approach to economic planning. A founder member of Fianna Fáil, he held cabinet posts in all Fianna Fáil administrations until 1959 when he became taoiseach, a post he held for seven years. As taoiseach he emphasized economic development, efficient administration, and an open approach to Northern Ireland, exchanging visits with his Northern Ireland counterpart, Captain Terence O'Neill.

Arthur Aston Luce (1881–1977), philosopher and clergyman. A clergyman's son, he was ordained in 1907. A man of outstanding academic ability, he was awarded a DD degree in 1920 and an LittD in 1943. His academic posts at TCD included professor of Moral Philosophy from 1934 to 1949, vice-provost from 1946 to 1952, and Berkeley Professor of Metaphysics from 1953 to 1977. He was a Canon of St Patrick's Cathedral from 1930 to 1973.

Fionán Lynch (1889–1966), revolutionary, politician and judge. A native of Co. Kerry, he took part in the 1916 Rising and was imprisoned in Mountjoy Jail, where he went on hunger-strike in 1917. On his release he served two further terms of imprisonment in 1918 and 1919. He was an assistant secretary to Erskine Childers on the Treaty delegation. He became one of two Ministers for Education in the Provisional Government in 1922 and Minister for Fisheries from 1922 to 1923. Later he left politics to become a barrister and subsequently became a judge.

John (Jack) Lynch (1917–99), politician and taoiseach. A native of Cork, he qualified as a barrister while working as a civil servant in Dublin. An outstanding athlete, he was a member of the Dáil from 1948–81. His ministerial posts included Education, 1957–59; Industry and Commerce, 1959–65; and Finance, 1965–66. He was taoiseach from 1966 to 1973 and from 1977 to 1979. For much of his time as taoiseach the Fianna Fáil party was divided between support for Lynch and for his arch-rival, Charles Haughey, who along with Neil Blayney, was dismissed from the government by Lynch in 1970 on suspicion of gun-running.

Kathleen Lynn (1874–1955), doctor and revolutionary. Daughter of a country clergyman, she was one of the first women to take a medical degree in Ireland in 1899. Deeply committed to the Women's Suffrage Movement, her revolutionary activities included participation in the 1916 Rising as a member of the Irish Citizen Army, deportation and imprisonment. In 1919 she was elected to the first Dáil and voted against the Treaty. Subsequently, she took no further part in politics, but devoted herself to St Ultan's Infants' Hospital, which she co-founded in 1919.

Seán MacEntee (1898–1984), revolutionary and politician. Born in Belfast, where he qualified as an electrical engineer, he joined the Irish Volunteers and took part in the 1916 Rising, for which he was sentenced to death. This was commuted to life in prison. He was released the following year in the general amnesty. In 1918 he was elected as an MP. He fought in the War of Independence and on the anti-Treaty side in the civil war, for which he was imprisoned by the Free State Government. He failed to get elected in the 1923 elections but was successful in 1927. A founder member of Fianna Fáil, he became Minister for Finance in 1932 and held that portfolio a number of times. His other cabinet posts included Local Government, Industry and Commerce, and Health (twice). He was Tánaiste from 1959 to 1965.

Eoin MacNeill (1867–1945), scholar and revolutionary. A founding member of the Gaelic League in 1893, he was professor of Early and Medieval Irish History at UCD from 1908 to 1941. A member of Sinn Féin, he was chairman of the council that formed the Irish Volunteers in 1913, subsequently becoming chief-of-staff. He countermanded the order for the Easter Rising, which was planned without his knowledge by a secret Military Council within the Irish Republican Brotherhood. Despite this, he was sentenced to life in prison in the aftermath of the Rising, but was released the following year. First elected to parliament in 1918, he was Minister for Finance in the First Dáil in 1919. He took the Treaty side in 1922 and served as the Free State's first Minister for Education from 1922 to 1925. For much of that time, he was absent from the Department due to his work with the Boundary Commission, for which he was much criticised. This led to his resignation from the cabinet. In 1927 he lost his seat and left politics.

John Charles McQuaid (1895–1973), Catholic archbishop of Dublin. A doctor's son from Co. Cavan, he was educated at Blackrock College, Clongowes Wood, UCD and the Gregorian University, Rome. At the age of 18 he entered the Holy Ghost Order, and on his ordination in 1924 was appointed dean of studies at Blackrock College. Seven years later he became president of the college and the same year was elected chairman of the Catholic Headmasters' Association. In 1940 he was appointed archbishop of Dublin, a post he was to hold for over three decades. As archbishop he was an able administrator with an interest in social matters. A strong believer in church control, he sought to extend its power to third-level education and from 1944 annually repeated the ban, first pronounced by the hierarchy in 1929, forbidding Catholics attending Trinity College Dublin without the permission of their bishops. In 1951 his leadership of the hierarchy's opposition to the Government's Mother and Child Health Scheme underlined the power of the Catholic Church in the state, a power that was further illustrated by the subsequent fall of the First Inter-party Government. But his long period as archbishop found him out of tune with changes in society in the 1960s, when his style of leadership, with its strict control over his clergy, his autocratic rule of his diocese and his conservative attitude to other Christians, became increasingly outdated following the Second Vatican Council. In 1972 he retired from the episcopate and died the following year.

Kenneth Milne (1932–), historian, writer and educationalist. Educated at Mountjoy School, he graduated from TCD in 1955 with a degree in History and Political Science. Following a period teaching at The High School, Dublin, he was appointed secretary of the Church of Ireland Board of Education in 1963. In 1977 he became principal of the Church of Ireland College of Education, a post he held until 1985 when he became Church of Ireland director of religious education, Republic of Ireland. Following his retirement in 1990 he concentrated on his writings, which include *The Irish Charter Schools*, (Dublin: 1996), *The Church of Ireland: A History* (Dublin: 4th edn, 2003) and *Christ Church Cathedral Dublin: A History,* (Dublin: 2000), which he edited. A member of many influential committees, he is currently historiographer of the Church of Ireland.

Henry Kingsmill Moore (1853–1943), Church of Ireland priest and educationalist. Son of a clergyman he was educated at Balliol College, Oxford, where he graduated in 1877. Two years later he was ordained a deacon (priest in 1980) and served in Cork, Cloyne and Ross Dioceses until 1884, when he became principal of the Church of Ireland Training College in Kildare Street, Dublin, a post he was to hold for 43 years. In 1918 he was made a Canon of St Patrick's Cathedral. The Church of Ireland's foremost authority on education, he played a leading role in many educational negotiations over a long period. Following the establishment of the Irish Free State he established good relationships with government officials. In 1937 he published his memoirs, *Reflections and Reminscences* (London: 1930).

Seán Moylan (1898–1957), revolutionary and politician. From Co Cork, a self-educated building contractor, he took part in the War of Independence and the civil war. A close friend of de Valera, he first became a minister after the 1943 election when he was appointed Minister for Lands. His interest in education stemmed from his family background – both his parents and a brother were teachers. His efforts to bring an end to the primary teachers' strike earned him the respect of teachers, who welcomed his appointment as Minister for Education in 1951, a post he held until 1954. In the 1957 election he lost his Dáil seat but was appointed to the Senate and became Minister for Agriculture. He died suddenly in November 1957, only hours after resigning from the cabinet.

Richard Mulcahy (1886–1971), revolutionary, soldier and politician. A native of Waterford, while working as a clerk in the Post Office he joined the Gaelic League and later the Irish Volunteers and the IRB. He took part in the 1916 Rising for which he was imprisoned at Frongach in Wales. As chief-of-staff of the IRA, he played a leading role in the War of Independence. He took the Treaty side in 1921 and became commander-in-chief of the new State's army after the death of Collins in 1922. He was first elected to parliament as an MP in 1918 and subsequently was elected a TD in all Dáil elections, apart from 1937 and 1943, until he retired from politics in 1961. In the thirties he played a leading role in the Army Comrades Association, known as the Blueshirts, an organisation with fascist tendencies, founded to defend Cumann na nGaedheal meetings from IRA attacks. A founder member of Fine Gael and its leader from 1944 to 1959, he helped to form the First Inter-party Government in 1948. To his credit he agreed to allow John A. Costello to become taoiseach, when memories of his role in the civil war made him unacceptable to the other parties. He was Minster for Education from 1948 to 1951 and from 1954 to 1957.

George Nicholls or **Seóirse Mac Niocaill** (1881–1968), school inspector and revolutionary. From Galway, he was a member of the Gaelic league, Sinn Féin and the IRB. He was deported to England for his part in the 1916 Rising. In 1918 he was elected MP for Galway. He voted for the Treaty in 1922. He took part in the Second Programme Conference and was involved in establishing An Gúm, the Department section responsible for publishing Irish writing.

Liam Ó Briain (1888–1974), scholar and revolutionary. A lecturer at UCD, he was interned in Frongoch for his part in the 1916 Rising. He failed to get elected as a Sinn Féin candidate in South Armagh in the 1918 elections. He took the Treaty side in 1922 and, having been defeated in the elections to Seanad Éireann in 1925, he left politics. A noted Gaeilgeoir, from 1917 to 1959 he was professor of Romance Languages at UCG.

León Ó Broin (1902–1990), public servant and writer. A member of Sinn Féin, he was imprisoned during 1920–21 and then served as a non-combatant officer in the Free State Army. In 1923, he became the first administrative officer appointed to the new civil service. He served mainly in the Department of Finance and ended his career as secretary of the Department of Posts and Telegraphs. He wrote *Dublin Castle and the 1916 Rising* (1966) and edited *In Great Haste: the letters of Michael Collins and Kitty Kiernan* (1983).

Pádraic Ó Brolcháin (1876–1934), civil servant. From Carndonagh, Co Donegal, he came to Dublin as a young man and entered the civil service as a member of the staff of the Commissioners of National Education. A close friend of Griffith, following a period with the National Health Insurance Commission, he was appointed chief executive officer of National Education by Fionán Lynch, the then Minister for Education. A member of the Gaelic League from its foundation, he was a committed Gaeilgeoir who believed that his mission in life was to gaelicise the Free State's schools, and to achieve this objective he worked unceasingly until his sudden death in 1934. Irish was the language of his home.

Máirtín Ó Cadhain (1906–70), revolutionary, writer and teacher. From Spiddal, Co Galway, he qualified as a primary teacher but was dismissed from his post for IRA activities. Following a period of internment, he worked as a translator in Dáil Éireann and subsequently as a lecturer in modern Irish at TCD, becoming professor of Irish in 1969. Considered the most outstanding writer in Irish of his generation, his most famous novel, *Cré na Cille* (1949) has been translated into several European languages.

Pádraig Ó Caoimh (1897–1964), revolutionary. A teacher, he joined the Volunteers in 1916 and was imprisoned in England from 1920 to 1922. He fought on the Republican side during the civil war. In 1929, he became general secretary of the GAA. Páirc Uí Chaoimh is called after him.

Seán T. Ó Ceallaigh (1882–1966), revolutionary, politician and second President of Ireland. He took part in the 1916 Rising and was later interned. A close associate of de Valera, he strongly opposed the Treaty. A founder of Fianna Fáil, he was Minister for Local Government and Public Health (1932–39) and Minister for Finance 1939–45, when he was elected president.

Thomas J. O'Connell (1882–1969), teacher, trade unionist and politician. A native of Co. Mayo, he was educated at the local national school and St. Patrick's College, Drumcondra. He taught for fifteen years as a primary teacher before becoming general secretary of the INTO in 1916. He played a leading role in Irish education for over four decades and took part in many significant decision-making bodies, including the First and Second National Programme Conferences. He was deeply involved in the primary teachers' strike in 1946.

His political career began in 1922 with his election to the Dáil as a TD for Co. Galway, which he represented for five years. Subsequently, he was TD for South Mayo from 1927 to 1932, and was also leader of the Labour Party. From 1932 until 1944, he was a member of the Senate. For over thirty years he wrote a column in the *Irish School Weekly*, the official journal of the INTO. In 1968, he published *100 Years of progress: The Story of the Irish National Teachers' Organisation 1868–1969* as part of the organisation's centenary celebrations.

Máirtín Ó Direáin (1910–1988), poet. A native of the Aran islands, he was a poet of considerable stature. His most noted works are *Coinnle Geala* (1942), *Dánta Aniar* (1943), and *Ó Mórna agus Dánta Eile* (1957).

Éamonn Feithín O'Doherty (1918–1998), psychologist, philosopher and scholar. A graduate of Cambridge University he was ordained a Catholic priest in 1943. From 1949 to 1981 he was professor of logic and psychology at UCD.

Breandán Ó hEithir (1930–1990), writer and broadcaster. He grew up on the Aran Islands where his parents were primary teachers. He was a pupil at Coláiste Éinde from 1944 to 1948. He won a scholarship to UCG where he studied English, history and philosophy. His writings include *Lig Sinn i gCathú*, (translated as *Lead Us into Temptation*), *A Begrudger's Guide to Irish Politics, Sionnach ar mo dhuán* and *An Nollaig Thiar*. His autobiography, *Over the Bar*, was published in 1984.

Eugene O'Growney (1863–99), scholar and writer. From Ballyfallon, Co. Meath, his interest in the Irish language was aroused while at secondary school. This led him to perfect his knowledge of the language. Ordained a Catholic priest in 1889, two year later he became editor of the *Gaelic Journal* and professor of Irish in St Patrick's College, Maynooth. A founding member of the Gaelic League in 1893, he is chiefly remembered for *Simple Lessons in Irish*, first published in the *Gaelic Journal* and *Weekly Freeman,* and subsequently in book form in 1894.

Patrick S. O'Hegarty (1875–1955), civil servant and writer. Born in Cork, he was a member of the Supreme Council of the IRB. He swore Collins into that organisation in London. Later he became close to Griffith and adopted his non-violent outlook. As a non-combatant, he attempted to bring an end to hostilities during the civil war. From 1922 to 1944 he was secretary of the Department of Posts and Telegraphs. His writings include *The History of Ireland under the Union* (1922) and *The Victory of Sinn Féin* (1924).

John J. O'Kelly or **Seán Ó Ceallaigh** (1872–1957), revolutionary and propagandist. He was born on Valentia Island, facing Sceilg Mhicil. From that developed his nick-name 'Sceilg'. A journalist by profession, he was editor of the *Irish Catholic* for many years. In 1917 he was deported for making seditious remarks about the Roscommon by-election. In 1919 he was elected MP for Louth.

A leading Gaeilgeoir and a member of the Gaelic League, his appointment as Minister for Irish in the First Dáil in 1919 was due to his position as president of the League, which was then a very influential organisation. Much of his time as minister was spent 'on the run' or in prison. From August 1921 to January 1922 he was the first Minister for Education. During the civil war he did much fund-raising for the anti-Treaty side in the United States.

Joseph O'Neill or **Seosamh Ó Néill** (1878–1952), writer, scholar and civil servant. Born in Tuam, Co. Galway, he grew up on the Aran Islands, where his father was stationed with the RIC. He was educated at St. Jarlath's College, Tuam, and Queen's College, Galway. He also studied in Manchester and Freiburg. In 1908 he joined the Department of Education as an inspector and served in both the Primary and Intermediate Branches. From 1923 to 1944 he was secretary of the Department. He wrote a number of historical novels.

Tarlach Ó Raifeartaigh (1905–84), secretary of the Department of Education, 1955–1968. He also served on a number of educational bodies, including the Higher Education Authority and the Committee for Higher Education and Research of the Council of Europe.

Seán Ó Riordáin (1917–1963), poet. A native of the Ballyvourney Gaeltacht, he gained recognition as a unique and controversial poet in the fifties. His works include *Eireaball Spideoige* (1952), *Brosna* (1964), *Líonta Liombó* (1971) and *Tar éis mo Bháis* (1978).

Pádraig Ó Siochfhradha, 'An Seabhac' (1883–1964), writer and teacher. From Dingle, Co Kerry, he had a lifelong commitment to the Irish language. As a young man he was an organizer and teacher for the Gaelic League. A member of the Irish Volunteers, he was imprisoned three times for his activities. When the new state was established he joined the civil service, where for a period he worked for An Gúm. In 1932 he became a director of the Educational Company of Ireland. He was a member of the Senate from 1946 to 1954. Under the pen-name An Seabhac (the hawk), his many publications include *Jímín Mháire Thaidgh* and *An Baile Seo 'Gainne.*

John Marcus O'Sullivan (1881–1948), academic and politician. A native of Co. Kerry and a graduate of UCD, with a doctorate from Heidelberg University, he was appointed professor of history at UCD in 1909. Elected to the Dáil in 1923, he was Minister for Education from 1926 to 1932. Known for his European outlook, he represented Ireland abroad many times, particularly at the League of Nations. The main achievements during his period as minister included the holding of the Second National Programme Conference (1926), the establishment of the Commission on Technical Education (1926/27), the foundation of the preparatory colleges (1926), the passing of the School Attendance Act (1926) and the Vocational Education Act (1930), and the introduction of the Primary School Certificate (1929). Known for his genial personality, he was a man of great ability, yet he never learned to speak Irish.

Patrick Pearse or **Pádraig Mac Piarais** (1879–1916), revolutionary leader, writer and educationalist. Son of an English father and Irish mother, he was educated at the Christian Brothers' School, Westland Row, and UCD. Subsequently, he qualified as a barrister but practiced briefly. In 1897 he joined the Gaelic League which he served with a passionate devotion. In 1903 he became editor of the League's paper *An Claidheamh Soluis*.

A renowned critic of the education system, he had considerable experience as a teacher, having taught classes run by the League and later in Alexandra College, Westland Row CBS and UCD. In 1908 he opened his first school, Scoil Éanna, at Cullenswood House, Ranelagh. Two years later he moved to more spacious premises at The Hermitage, Rathfarnham. In 1913 he co-founded the Irish Volunteers and subsequently joined the IRB. He was executed for his part in the 1916 Rising.

Gerard Sweetman (1908–70), politician. Educated at Downside and TCD, he failed to get elected to the Dáil in 1932 and again in 1943, after which he was elected to the Senate. He was eventually elected to the Dáil in 1948 and was successful in all subsequent elections until his untimely death in a car crash in 1970. Prominent as an organizational figure in Fine Gael, he was chief whip in the First Inter-party Government and Minister for Finance from 1954–57 in the Second Inter-party Government.

George Thomson or **Seóirse MacTomáis** (1903–1987), scholar and Gaeilgeoir. From an Irish family, he grew up in England. As a young man he made regular visits to the Blasket Islands and Dunquin Gaeltacht to study the Irish language. In 1927 he became a Fellow of King's College, Cambridge, and four year later he was appointed a lecturer in UCG where he taught Greek through Irish. He was professor of Greek at Birmingham University from 1937 to 1970. Considered one of the most outstanding classical scholars of the twentieth century, he translated many classical works into Irish and did much work for An Gúm, the publishing section of the Department of Education. With Moya Llewelyn Davies he edited and translated Muiris Ó Suilleabháin's *Fiche Blian ag Fás* into English.

62 Coláiste Moibhí 1993. The final complete session of the college. Ina suí ó chlé: Gloria Mollison, Harold Hislop, Kerry Heuston, Íobhar Ó hAodha, Bn. de Brún, Bn. Uí Chonchradha, Risteárd Giltrap, Bn. Cousins, Bn. Uí Chadhain, Gwen Nic Liam, Ebhlín de Faoite, Michelle de Stainléigh. An dara sraith ó chlé: Zara de Liosla, Georgina Nic Niocail, Clóda Nic Róibín, Andrea Nic Stiofáin, Labhaois Ní Mhofáit, Hilairí Ní Chathail, Cearúilín Ní Mhórdha, Rút Gentleman, Sinéad Ní Chléirigh, Seiríl Nic Stiofáin, Siobhán Ní hIc, Diane Ní Mhacsuel, Méabh Swindell, Julie Ní Mhofáit. An tríú sraith ó chlé: Tomás MacGiolla Bháin, Melanie Ní Ghréacháin, Fraoch Ní Bhailcín, Linda Ní hÓráin, Labhaois NicGafraidh; Gwyn Ó Mhurchú, Seán Teskey, Wendy Wheeler, Rút Ní Mhofáit, Pricilla Petrie, Darinda NicPháidin, Léan Ní Mhuineacháin, Séarlait de Bhailís. *Courtesy Risteárd Giltrap.*

63 The last class of Coláiste Moibhí. The final year 1994–95. Ina suí ó chlé: Bean de Brún, Bean Uí Dheasmoinn, Bríd Ní Fhaoile, Bean Uí Chadhain, An Canónach de Blennerhassett, Risteárd Giltrap, Bean Uí Chonchradha, Valerie Long, Bean Uí Phiogóid, Laura Farrell. An dara sraith: Lynn Ní Mhaoldomhnaigh, Rút Ní Mhofáit, Seoighe de Brún, Labhaois Ní Mhofáit, Gwyn Ó Murchú, Deirdre Ní Thuairisc, Clodagh Chapman, Georgina Nic Niocail, Rút Gentleman, Norma Ní Stíobhairt. *CICE Archives.*

64 At the Thanksgiving Service to mark the closure of Coláiste Moibhí were the principal, Risteárd Giltrap, with Amy Phillips, Dora Smeaton and Dolly Hamilton Roberts, three of the early students at the college.

65 At the Thanksgiving Service for Coláiste Moibhí were Victor Wheatly, Máire Roycroft, Sydney Blain, Principal of the Church of Ireland College of Education, and Doreen Flanagan.

66 At the Thanksgiving Service for Coláiste Moibhí were Canon Frank Blennerhassett with Hazel Riordan and her mother, Catherine Smyth, both former students.

67 The principal of Coláiste Moibhí, Risteárd Giltrap, greeting Trevor Sargent, TD, of the Green Party.

68 Coláiste Moibhí student Dorinda Patterson receiving a fáinne from Archbishop Donald Caird.

69 Amy Phillips, one of the first class of Coláiste Moibhí, with Archbishop Donald Caird at the launch of a new hymn book in Irish in 1994.

70 Coláiste Moibhí students Ruth Gentleman and Georgina Nicholls greeting Bishop James Kavanagh at the annual Service in Irish for the Week of Prayer for Christian Unity in Christ Church Cathedral in 1994.

71 Linda Treacy receiving the Lil Duncan Award for her contribution to the Debating Society at Coláiste Moibhí from Archbishop Donald Caird.

72 Hazel Crawford, Principal of Rathmichael Parish National School, with Canon Fred Appelbe at the Official Opening of an extension to the school in 1998.

SELECT BIBLIOGRAPHY

I MANUSCRIPT SOURCES

A. The National Archives

Department of the Taoiseach Papers

MS S14787	Repayment of fees at preparatory colleges
S123074/61	Disposal of Coláiste Bhríde
S12307	Sale of preparatory colleges
S10577	Temporary closure of preparatory colleges 1941
S6369	Need for new training college in Galway 1954
S10999	Dáil questions re preparatory colleges 1943
S11339	Closure of de La Salle Training College Waterford 1939
S11258	Newspaper cuttings on Irish language
S2512	Higher primary schools in the Gaeltacht
S1730	Training of teachers 1922
S4460	Teachers' training
S13905	Coláiste Moibhí to be a sanatorium
S12807	Use of Coláiste Éinde as a military hospital
S11239	Blythe on Irish newspapers and films
S4828	White Paper on establishment of the preparatory colleges
S855	Irish Provisional Government 1922
S1575	Higher primary schools for the Gaeltacht
S13180A	Irish language policy 1943, 1949 and 1950s
S13180B	Commission on Revival of Irish 1958
S6369	Coláiste Éinde to be training college
S12307	1941 Refresher courses for teachers

Department of Finance Papers

S20/10/25	Summer Courses for national teachers 1925
S20/9/25	Beginning of the preparatory colleges
S7/18/25	Music in the preparatory colleges

S18/7/26	Appointment of principals, 'professors' etc
S22/1/26	Library books
S60/21/28	Excess expenditure
S60/22/28	Expenditure on Coláiste Moibhí
S20/4/28	Establishment of training college for national teachers at Galway
S25/11/28	Lease on Rockhill, Letterkenny
S25/8/28	Music at preparatory colleges
S25/5/28	The Munster College
S25/4/31	Special assistance for Fíor-Ghaeltacht students
S25/1/32	Use of preparatory colleges for Eucharistic Congress
S25/11/34	Staffing arrangements for Coláiste Chaoimhín
S22/4/34	Purchase of Furbough House
S25/4/37	Department Committee of Inquiry into the preparatory colleges 1937
S25/5/38	Music at Coláiste Moibhí and Coláiste Chaoimhín
S22/5/44	Take-over of Coláiste Éinde

Department of Education Papers

ED Central Registry

Box 44	History of Marlborough Hall and House
Box 457 20930	Parents against the teaching of Irish
Box 458 20983	Inspection of preparatory colleges
Box 409 19137	Appointments at Coláiste Moibhí
Box 423 19701	Memo on the Gaeltacht
Box 370 17634	Talbot House
Box 417 19418	Review of Inspectors' Reports
Box 138 8830	History of Irish language teaching end of the nineteenth and beginning of the twentieth century

Roinn na Gaeltachta Papers

D89	Scéimeanna Scoláireachtaí Meánscoile sa Ghaeltacht 1957–61
D45	An Ghaeilge scoláireachtaí samhraidh
R22	Coláiste Mhuire
R29	Scéim an Deontais £5 1958–59

B. UCD Archives

Blythe Papers

MS P24/15	Letter from Minister for Irish
MS P24/37	Blythe on the early preparatory colleges
MS P24/207	Map of Gaeltacht areas

MS P24/302	Special measures to help Fíor-Ghaeltacht students
MS P24/442	Assistance for Fíor-Gaeltacht students
MS P24/443	Plans to provide help for the Fíor-Ghaeltacht
MS P24/444	Correspondence with Joseph O'Neill secretary of the Department of Education
MS P24/445	Gaeltacht boys and the army
MS P24/303	Fíor-Ghaeltacht scholarships
MS P24/304	Correspondence re the preparatory colleges 1931
MS P24/927	Irish in the civil service 1934
MS P24/928	Irish in the civil service 1951

Mulcahy Papers

MS P7/C/50	1934 Revised Programme
MS P7/C/70	Scheme for preparatory colleges
MS P7/C/71	The Gaelicising of Ireland
MS P7/C/152	Material concerning Irish in Protestant schools
MS P/24/943	Circular re scholarships for the Fíor-Ghaeltacht 1959
MS P/24/979	Memo on Irish teaching from Comhdháil Náisiúnta na Gaeilge 1947
MS P/24/995	Memo from Blythe on the Irish language 1949

MacNeill Papers

MS LAI/H/134	Teacher Training
MS LAI/H/137	Grant-Aid for Preparatory School
MS LAI/H/141	Inspection staffs and Irish
MS LAI/E/25-7	Summer Courses for teachers
MS LAI/E/25	Irish Teaching in primary and secondary schools
MS LAI/F/277	Irish in schools

McGilligan Papers

C. Dublin Diocesan Archives
   McQuaid Papers
   Byrne Papers

D. Galway Diocesan Archives
   Browne Papers
   Coláiste Éinde Papers

E. Kerry Diocesan Archives
   Coláiste Íde Papers

F. Christian Brothers' Archives
Coláiste Chaoimhín Papers

G. Mercy Order Archives
Register of Coláiste Mhuire

H. De La Salle Brothers' Archives
Annals of Coláiste na Mumhan/Coláiste Íosagáin

I. In private possession
Register of Coláiste na Mumhan/Coláiste Íosagáin

J. Cumann Staire is Seanchais Chloich Cheann Fhaola
Register of Coláiste Bhríde and other papers

K. Church of Ireland College of Education Archives
Registers of Coláiste Moibhí and other papers
Hodges Papers
Kingsmill Moore Papers

L. Representative Church Body Library
Papers and minutes books of Cumann Gaelach na hEaglaise

M. By special permission
Minutes of the Board of Governors of CITC and CICE
Minute book of the Dublin School Managers' Association,
1922–1987
Minute book of the Protestant National Teachers' Union 1928-1949

II UNPUBLISHED THESES AND PAPERS

Doyle, K.R., 'The Irish Language as a curricular element in Irish primary education in the period 1831–1935,' M.Ed. thesis, University of Dublin, 1982

Jones, V.A., 'Recruitment and formation of students into the Church of Ireland Training College, 1922–1961,' M.Litt. thesis, University of Dublin, 1989

Jones, V.A., 'The Preparatory Colleges, 1926–1961: an experiment in Irish education', Ph.D. thesis, University of Dublin, 1999

Lynch, Deborah, 'The Preparatory Colleges, 1926–1960', M.Ed. thesis, University College, Galway, 1994

Ó Coileán, Antoine, 'Bunoideachais Dátheangach Lasmuigh den Ghaeltacht, Leirmheas Stairiúil, 1922–1984 agus oideas don todchaí', M.Ed. thesis, University of Dublin, 1985

Ó Murchú, Helen, 'Staidéar ar Dhátheangas imeasc Daltaí Bunscoile', M.Ed. thesis, University of Dublin, 1975

Perdue, E.C.T., 'The Rationale and development of the Church of Ireland primary school', M.Ed thesis, University of Dublin, 1976

Revington, C.E.F., 'Developments within the Church of Ireland Training College in the 1950s and 1960s', unpublished M.Ed. Paper, TCD, 1979.

III Printed Sources

A. Official Publications

Dáil Reports

Seanad Reports

National Programme Conference, *National Programme of Primary Conference* (Dublin: Browne and Nolan, 1922)

National Programme Conference, *Report and Programme* (Dublin: Stationery Office, 1926)

Coimisiún na Gaeltachta, *Report* (Dublin: Stationery Office, 1926)

Department of Education, *Revised Programme of Primary Instruction* (Dublin: Stationery Office, 1934)

Department of Education, *Rules for National Schools* (Dublin: Stationery Office, 1955)

Report of the Council of Education on the Function of the Primary School and on the curriculum to be pursued in the Primary School from the infant age up to twelve years of age (Dublin: Stationery Office, 1954)

Report of the Council of Education on the curriculum of the secondary school (Dublin: Stationery Office, 1966)

OECD Survey Team, *Investment in education* (Dublin: Stationery Office, 1966)

Bunreacht na hÉireann, (Constitution of Ireland) (Dublin: Government Publications Office, 1980)

Department of Education, *Questions set at the Examination for Entrance to Preparatory Colleges, 1926–60* (Dublin: Stationery Office)

B. Annual Reports

Annual Reports of the Department of Education 1922–1996

Journals of the General Synod of the Church of Ireland 1914–1996

Annual Reports of the Church of Ireland Training College, 1920–1960

C. Newspapers and Magazines

An Claidheamh Solais

An Dréimire

Anois

An Réiltín

Church of Ireland Gazette
Church Review
Comhar
Cuisle
Derry Journal
Evening Mail
Feasta
Gaelic Journal
Inniu
Irish Independent
Irish Monthly
Irish Press
Irish School Weekly
Irish Times
Misneach
Oideas
PSA News/Newsletter
Studies
Sunday Independent
The Gaelic Churchman
The Kerryman

IV Books, Pamphlets and Articles Relating To:

Irish Education

Akenson, D. H., *The Irish education experience* (London: Routledge, Kegan Paul, 1970); *A mirror to Kathleen's face: education in independent Ireland, 1922–60* (Montreal and London: McGill-Queen's University Press, 1975)

Atkinson, N., *Irish education: a history of educational institutions* (Dublin: Allen Figgis, 1967)

Aughmuty J.J., *Irish education: an historical survey* (Dublin: Hodges Figgis, 1937)

Coláiste Éinde PPA, *Coláiste Éinde 1928–1978* (Indreabhán: Clódóiri Lorgan, 1978)

Coolahan, J., *Irish education: history and structure* (Dublin: Institute of Public Administration, 1981)

Corcoran, T., 'The native speaker as teacher,' in *The Irish Monthly*, April 1923

Dowling, P.J., *A history of Irish education: a study of conflicting loyalties* (Cork: Mercier Press, 1972)

Dunn, S. and Morgan, V., *Recruits to teaching in Ireland, North–South* (Coleraine: The New University of Ulster, 1978)

Fenton, Séamus, *It all happened*: *reminiscences of Séamus* Fenton (Dublin: M.H. Gill and Son Ltd., 1949)

Irish National Teachers' Organisation, *A plan for education* (Dublin: INTO, 1947); *Report of Committee of Inquiry into the Use of Irish as a Teaching medium to Children whose Home Language is English* (Dublin: INTO, 1941)

Hyland A. and Milne K., ed. *Irish educational documents* Vol. I (Dublin: CICE, 1987); *Irish educational documents* Vol. II (Dublin: CICE, 1992)

Kelly, Adrian M., 'The Gaelic League and the Introduction of Compulsory Irish into the Free State Education System', in *Oideas* 41, 1993; *Compulsory Irish: the language and education in Ireland 1870s–1970s* (Dublin: Irish Academic Press, 2002)

McElligott, T. J., *Education in Ireland,* (Dublin: Institute of Public Administration, 1966); *This teaching life* (Dublin: Lilliput Press, 1986)

Moore, H. Kingsmill, *Reminscences and reflections from some sixty years of life in Ireland* (Dundalk: Dundalgan Press, 1938)

Ó Buachalla, S., *Education policy in twentieth century Ireland* (Dublin: Wolfhound Press, 1988)

Ó Ceallaigh, Séamus, ed. *Coláiste Éinde 1928–2003: 75 Bliain faoi Bhláth* (Galway: Coláiste Éinde, 2003)

O'Connell, T. J., *100 Years of Progress: The story of the Irish National Teachers Organisation 1868–1968* (Dublin: INTO, 1969)

O'Connor, A. V., and Parkes, S. M., *Gladly learn and gladly teach: a history of Alexandra College* (Dublin: Blackwater Press, 1984)

Ó Glaisne, Risteárd, *Coláiste Moibhí* (Baile Átha Cliath: Coiscéim, 2002)

Parkes, Susan M., *Kildare Place: the history of the Church of Ireland Training College, 1811–1969* (Dublin: CICE, 1984)

Pollard, Rachel, *The Avenue: the history of the Claremont Institution (1816–1978)* (Dublin: Pollard, 2001)

Titley, Brian E, *Church, state and the control of schooling in Ireland 1900–1944* (Dublin: Gill and Macmillan, 1984)

Irish Language

Corkery, D., *The fortunes of the Irish language* (Cork: Mercier Press, 1968, original ed., 1954); *The hidden Ireland. A study of Gaelic Munster in the eighteenth century* (Dublin: Gill and Son, 1967, original ed., 1924)

de Blaghd, Earnán, *Trasna na Bóinne* (Baile Átha Cliath: Sairséal agus Dill, 1957)

Gaelic League Pamphlets no. 12. *The Irish language and Irish Interme-diate education* (Dublin: Gaelic League, 1901)

Jones, Valerie, 'Government policy, the Church of Ireland and the teaching of Irish 1940–1950', in Pádraig Hogan (ed.) *Irish Educational Studies*, vol. x (Maynooth: Educational Studies Association of Ireland, 1991); 'The attitudes of the Church of Ireland Board of Education to textbooks in national schools, 1922–1967,' in *Irish Educational Studies*, vol. II (Maynooth: Educational Studies Association of Ireland, 1992)

MacNamara, J., *Bilingualism and primary education: a study of Irish experience* (Edinburgh: Edinburgh University Press, 1966)

MacNeill, Eoin, 'A plea and a plan', in *The Gaelic Journal,* March 1893

Nic Craith, Mairéad, 'The Irish Language in a comparative context', in *Oideas* 42, Samhradh 1994

Ó Croinín, Breandán, 'An Ghaeilge sa choras oideachais', in *Oideas*, Fómhar, 1988

O'Doherty, E.F., 'Bilingual school policy', in *Studies*, Autumn, 1958

Ó Domhnaill, Micheál, *Iolscoil na Mumhan: Coláiste na Rinne Geárr-stair* (Cork: Cló na Laoi Teo, 1987)

O'Donoghue, Tom, 'Educational innovation in the Donegal Gaeltacht: the case of the bilingual programme of instruction 1904–1922', in *Oideas,* Samhradh, 1994; 'Teacher-based curriculum development: the case of the bilingual programme of instruction, 1904–1922', in *Oideas*, Fómhar, 1988

Ó hEochadha, Séumas, agus Mac Craith, Nioclás, *Scéalta Mhicil Uí Mhuirgheasa* (Rinn Ó gCuanach: Coláiste na Rinne, 1997)

Ó Glaisne, R., *Cosslett Ó Cuinn* (Baile Átha Cliath: Coiscéim, 1996); *De bhunadh Protastúnach: rian Chonradh na Gaeilge* (Baile Átha Cliath: Carbad, 2000)

Ó Riain, S., *Pleanáil Teanga in Éirinn 1919–1985* (Baile Átha Cliath: Bord na Gaeilge, 1994)

Ó Tuama, Seán, (ed.) *The Gaelic League idea: the Thomas Davis lectures* (Cork: Mercier Press, 1972)

Pearse, P., 'The murder machine' in *Political writings and speeches* (Dublin: Talbot Press, 1966)

Pyle, Hilary, *Cesca's Diary 1913–1916: Where art and nationalism meet,* (Dublin: The Woodfield Press, 2005)

Irish History and Politics

Beckett, J.C., The *making of modern Ireland* (London: Faber and Faber, 1976)

Boylan, H., *A dictionary of Irish biography* (Dublin: Gill and Macmillan, 1998)

Brown, T., *Ireland: a social and cultural history, 1922–79* (Glasgow: Fontana, 1982)

Browne, N., *Against the tide* (Dublin: Gill and Macmillan, 1985)

Chubb, B., *The Constitution and constitutional change in Ireland* (Dublin: Institute of Public Administration, 1978)

Clarke, K., *Revolutionary woman: Kathleen Clarke 1878–1972, an autobiography* (Dublin: The O'Brien Press, 1991)

Collins, S., *The Cosgrave Legacy* (Dublin: Blackwater Press, 1996)

Coogan, Tim Pat, *Ireland since the Rising* (London: Pall Mall Press, 1980)

Cooney, John, *John Charles McQuaid, Ruler of Catholic Ireland* (Dublin: O'Brien Press, 1999)

Dwyer, T. Ryle, *De Valera: the man and the myths* (Dublin: Poolbeg Press, 1991)

Edwards, Ruth Dudley, *Patrick Pearse: the triumph of failure* (London and Boston: Faber and Faber, 1979)

Farrell, Brian, *Chairman or Chief: the role of Taoiseach in Irish Government* (Dublin: Gill and Macmillan, 1971); *Seán Lemass*, (Dublin: Gill and Macmillan, 1983)

Ferriter, Diarmaid, *The Transformation of Ireland 1900–2000* (London: Profile Books, 2004)

Fitzgerald, G., *Towards a new Ireland* (Dublin: Torc Books edition, 1973); *All in a life: an autobiography* (Dublin: Gill and Macmillan, 1992)

Foster, R., *Modern Ireland 1600–1972* (London: Penguin, 1988)

Garvin, Thomas, *The evolution of Irish nationalist politics* (Dublin: Gill and Macmillan, 1972)

Gillespie, Raymond, and Neely, W.G., eds., *The laity and the Church of Ireland 1000–2000: all sorts and conditions* (Dublin: Four Courts Press, 2002)

Hart, Peter, *The IRA at War 1916–1923* (Oxford: Oxford University Press, 2003)

Horgan, John, *Seán Lemass: the enigmatic patriot* (Dublin: Gill and Macmillan, 1997)

Hone, Joseph, Craig, Maurice and Fewer, Michael, *The new neighbourhood of Dublin* (Dublin: A & A Farmar, 2002)

Keogh, D., *Twentieth century Ireland: nation and state* (Dublin: Gill and Macmillan, 1994)

Lee, J.J., (ed.) *Ireland 1945–70* (Dublin: Gill and Macmillan, 1979); *Ireland 1912–1985: Politics and society* (Cambridge: Cambridge University Press, 1989)

Lyons, F.S.L., *Ireland since the famine* (London: Collins/Fontana, 1971); *Culture and anarchy in Ireland, 1890–1939* (Oxford: Oxford University Press, 1982)

MacDonagh, O., *States of mind: a study of the Anglo-Irish Conflict* (London: Allen and Unwin, 1985)

McRedmond Louis, (ed.) *Modern Irish lives: Dictionary of twentieth century biography* (Dublin: Gill & Macmillan, 1996)

Milne, Kenneth, 'Brave new world' in Stephen R. White (ed.), *A time to build: essays for to-morrow's church* (Dublin: APCK, 1999)

Mitchell, A., *Revolutionary government in Ireland: Dáil Éireann 1919–1922* (Dublin: Gill and Macmillan, 1995)

Moody, T.W. and Martin, F.X., (eds) *A new history of Ireland* (Oxford and New York: Oxford University Press, 1982)

Moore, H. Kingsmill, *Reminscences and reflections from some sixty years of life in Ireland* (London: Longmans Green, 1930)

Murphy, J.A., *Ireland in the twentieth century* (Dublin: Gill and Macmillan, 1975)

Mulcahy Risteárd, *Richard Mulcahy 1886–1971: A family memoir*, (Dublin: Aurelian Press, 1999)

Ó Broin, L., *Just like yesterday: an autobiography* (Dublin: Gill and Macmillan, 1985)

O'Carroll, J.P. and John A. Murphy, *De Valera and his times* (Cork: Cork University Press, 1983)

O'Doherty, T. and Mahon, L., *St. Mobhi's Church Glasnevin: a short history & guide* (Dublin: St. Mobhi's Parish, 1989)

Ó hEithir, Breandán *Over the bar* (Dublin: Poolbeg, 1984)

O'Farrell, Padraic, *Who's Who in the Irish War of Independence and Civil War 1916–1923* (Dublin: The Lilliput Press, 1997)

O'Higgins, T.F., *A double life* (Dublin: Town House, 1996)

O'Mahony, S., *Frongach: university of revolution* (Dublin: FDR Teo, 1987)

Ó Muircheartaigh, M., *From Dún Síon to Croke Park* (Dublin: Penguin Ireland, 2004)

Valiulis, Maryann Gialanella, *Portrait of a revolutionary* (Dublin: Irish Academic Press, 1992); *General Richard Mulcahy and the founding of the Irish Free State* (Dublin: Irish Academic Press, 1999)

Ryle Dwyer, T., *De Valera: the man & the myths* (Dublin: Poolbeg Press, 1980)

White, Terence de Vere, *Kevin O'Higgins* (Dublin: Anvil Books, 1986)

Younger, Carlton, *Arthur Griffith* (Dublin: Gill and Macmillan, 1986)

Church and State in Ireland

Acheson, Alan, *A History of the Church of Ireland 1691–2001* (Dublin: Columba Press and APCK, 2002)

Clarke, D.M., *Church and State* (Cork: Cork University Press, 1984)

Conway, W., *Catholic schools* (Dublin: Veritas, 1970)

Cooney, J., *The crozier and the Dáil church and state, 1922–86* (Dublin and Cork: Mercier, 1986)

Feeney, John, *John Charles McQuaid: the man and the mask* (Dublin and Cork: Mercier Press, 1974)

Keogh, Dermot, *The Vatican, the bishops and Irish politics, 1919–39* (Cambridge, London and New York: Cambridge University Press, 1986)

Mescal, J., *Religion in the Irish system of education* (London and Dublin: Gill and Macmillan, 1971)

McQuaid, J.C., *Catholic education, its function and scope* (Dublin: Catholic Truth Society, 1942)

Miller, D.W., *Church, state and nation in Ireland 1898–1921* (Dublin: Gill and Macmillan, 1971)

Murphy, Colin and Adair, Lynne, eds, *Untold Stories: Protestants in the Republic of Ireland* (Dublin: The Liffey Press, 2002)

Seaver, G., *John Allen Fitzgerald Gregg, Archbishop* (Dublin: Allen Figgis, 1963)

Titley, B.E., *Church, State and the control of schooling* (Dublin: Gill and Macmillan, 1984)

Whyte, J.H., *Church and state in modern Ireland, 1923–1970* (Dublin: Gill and Macmillan, 1970)

INDEX

Page numbers in italics refer to illustrations or captions